The Cultural Politics of English
as an International Language

LANGUAGE IN SOCIAL LIFE SERIES

Series Editor: Professor Christopher N. Candlin

The Cultural Politics of English as an International Language

Alastair Pennycook

LONGMAN

LONDON AND NEW YORK

Pearson Education Limited,
Edinburgh Gate,
Harlow, Essex CM20 2JE, England
and Associated Companies throughout the world.

*Published in the United States of America
by Pearson Education Inc., New York*

First Published 1994
Fourth impression 1999

ISBN 0 582 234735 CSD
ISBN 0 582 234727 PPR

British Library Cataloguing-in-Publication Data
A catalogue record for this book is
available from the British Library

Library of Congress Cataloging-in-Publication Data
Pennycook, Alastair, 1957–
     The cultural politics of English as an international language /
Alastair Pennycook.
        p.   cm. — (Language in social life series)
     Includes bibliographical references and index.
     ISBN 0–582–23473–5 (cased). — ISBN 0–582–23472–7 (pbk.)
     1. English language—Political aspects—English-speaking
countries. 2. English language—Political aspects—Foreign
countries. 3. Language and culture—English–speaking countries.
4. Communication, International. 5. Intercultural communication.
I. Title.   II. Series.
PE2751.P46   1994
420—dc20   93–45823
                                                                          CIP

Typeset by 8V in 10/12 pt Palatino
Printed in Malaysia (PP)

Contents

Author's acknowledgements

This book has grown over several years out of many contexts, too many indeed for me to acknowledge them all. First, it has developed from my doctoral thesis and I owe profound thanks to my supervisor, Roger Simon, who helped me to find ways of articulating and organizing the myriad of mixed thoughts that I brought to him. Jim Cummins and David Cooke, the other members of my committee, were also most helpful and supportive and, with Roger, played a crucial role in encouraging me to pursue my diverse and often contentious interests. Other people who were involved in various stages of my thesis also deserve acknowledgement: Ruth Hayhoe and Robert Phillipson. In the process of research and writing, I have been greatly helped by a large number of library staff, so my thanks to those often-unacknowleged workers between the books in Toronto, London, Singapore and Kuala Lumpur. Many people were also generous with their time and ideas, amongst whom, Asmah Haji Omar, Chua Beng Huat, Nesamalar Citravelu, Heah Lee Hsia, Hing Ai Yun, Nisai Kaewsanchai, Frances Lee, Catherine Lim, Ian Martin, Bhaskaran Nayar, Nirmala Puru Shotam and Makhan Tickoo. And thanks to those silent others who shared ideas and conversations and whose names I never knew or whose names they preferred not to be made public. As this book has entered its later stages of writing, Chris Candlin, the General Editor of the series, deserves special thanks for his encouragement and editoral advice.

This book has also grown out of the context of the many conversations, discussions, arguments and debates with people engaged in critical pedagogy and critical work in ESL at OISE; these include Lynn Earls, Tara Goldstein, Craig Jakobsen, Kubota Ryuko, Bob Morgan, Brian Morgan, Donna Patrick, Bonny Peirce, Perry Shearwood, Alice Pitt, Anita Sheth, Kathryn Tiede, Tony

Xerri and Handel Wright. My apologies for the vehemence of some of our arguments, for momentarily forcing this diverse group of people into one list, and for missing others out.

In addition, my work has been greatly suported from a distance by my parents, who have for too long had to suffer my insatiable desire to figure out the world. And finally, Arleen Schenke's ideas, imagination, tolerance, help and caring have played such a vast role in this book and my life that I cannot possibly do them justice here.

Publisher's acknowledgements

We are grateful to the following for permission to reproduce copyright material:

The author, John Agard c/o Caroline Sheldon Literary Agency for the poem 'Listen Mr Oxford Don' from *Mangoes & Bullets* published by Pluto Press, 1985; Mrs Ee Tiang Hong for an extract from the poem 'Statement' in *Tranquerah* by the late Ee Tiang Hong; the author, Shirley Geok-lin Lim for an extract from her poem 'Lament' in *No Man's Grove* (1985); the author, Edwin Thumboo for part of his poem 'May 1954' in *Ulysses by the Merlion* (1979).

We have been unable to trace the copyright holders of the song 'Third World Child' by Johnny Clegg and Savuka, and would appreciate any information which would enable us to do so.

Publisher's acknowledgements

ONE

The world in English

The very concept of an international, or world, language was an invention of Western imperialism.

(Ndebele, 1987, pp. 3–4)

To interpret People's English as a dialect of international English would do the movement a gross injustice; People's English is not only a language, it is a struggle to appropriate English in the interests of democracy in South Africa.

(Peirce, 1990, p. 108)

To speak means to be in a position to use a certain syntax, to grasp the morphology of this or that language, but it means above all to assume a culture, to support the weight of a civilization.

(Fanon, 1967, pp. 17–18)

INTRODUCTION: FROM KURT WALDHEIM TO JOHNNY CLEGG

Drifting on its lonely trajectory in search of other life-inhabited galaxies, the Voyager spacecraft carries recorded messages of greetings in fifty-five of the world's languages. But the principal message of greeting is delivered by the then UN Secretary-General, Kurt Waldheim, his Austrian-accented voice bidding anyone who may hear a welcome in the global, the universal, language: English: 'As the Secretary General of the United Nations . . . I send greetings on behalf of the people of our planet.'[1] The language chosen to speak on behalf of the five billion inhabitants of the globe is English. Meanwhile, back on the surface of the earth, from a small radio in a township shack in Soweto, come tumbling the words of a song by Johnny Clegg and Savuka:

1

> Bits of songs and broken drums
> are all he could recall
> so he spoke to me
> in a bastard tongue
> carried on the silence of the guns
>
> It's been a long long time
> since they first came
> and marched thru the village
> they taught me to forget my past
> and live the future in their image
>
> *Chorus* They said I should learn to speak
> a little bit of english
> don't be scared of a suit and tie
> learn to walk in the dreams of the foreigner
> – I am a third world child
> (*Third World Child*, Johnny Clegg and Savuka)[2]

These two brief snatches of English, from the UN Secretary-General and a South African singer, frame some of the questions I want to pursue in this book. How can I start to explore the implications of this spread of English in both its global (or even universal) expansion and its local contexts? In what ways can we both understand this prodigious spread – 'I send greetings on behalf of the people of our planet' – and at the same time take seriously the implications of 'learn to walk in the dreams of the foreigner'? What are the connections here between the Voyager spacecraft, the UN, a suit and tie, the dreams of the foreigner, forgetting the past, a third world child, and the English language? And how can we start to find ways of taking such connections seriously?

These and other questions have been pursuing me – and I them – for a number of years, especially as my life has come to intersect with many of these complexities more and more. As a teacher of English in Germany, Japan, Canada, China and now Hong Kong, as a traveller in Europe and Asia, as a resident of Quebec for two years, I have constantly sought ways of trying to understand the position of English in the world. As someone who watches the shifts and changes in the world with interest and as someone who is often deeply disturbed and angered by what I see around me – the deaths of children, the poverty and starvation, the pointless consumption and thoughtless pollution, the discriminations against people because of their colour, their language, their gender, their sexual orientation, their culture, their class – I find questions around local and global inequalities and injustices constantly return. And, over the years, I have become increasingly sure that these are connected, that it is essential for me, politically and morally, to work out the relationships between my work as an English teacher and what I see around me in the world.

Many questions come from small fleeting moments. Watching television as placards in English are waved to support Chinese students demonstrating for political change, Estonians demanding independence, Iraqis inveighing against the United States. What is the power and the effect of the English-speaking world and its media that placards are often most effective in English? How does that affect the demonstration and the protest? What were the complex relationships between the English-speaking media and the Chinese students' demonstrations and deaths in 1989? Or between these media and the 'Gulf War'? What role does CNN, for example, play in the construction and dissemination of world news? Why did Benazir Bhutto opt to allow CNN to broadcast in Pakistan, and why did Malaysia allow CNN for only half an hour each evening, interrupted by the evening call to prayer, only to change its policy recently and allow unedited broadcasting of CNN and the BBC World Service? One of the most poignant and painful examples of the connections between English and global media is given by Edward Behr (1978, p. 136), recalling an incident as Belgians were being evacuated from the newly independent Zaire: 'Into the middle of this crowd strode an unmistakably British TV reporter, leading his cameraman and sundry technicians like a platoon commander through hostile territory. At intervals he paused and shouted, in a stentorian but genteel BBC voice, "Anyone here been raped and speaks English?" '[3] This question, linking male violence, war and what the world hears about it, is not just an aberration of one conflict. According to Grant (1993), after the stories of the rape of Bosnian women started to emerge, Zagreb 'was teeming with foreign journalists, scouring refugee camps with a revival of that familiar wartime phrase: "Anyone here been raped and speaks English?" ' (p. 1, Section D).

As we watch the difficult dismantling process of the former Soviet Union and other Eastern European states, English seems to re-emerge constantly as these new states seek a new future. Discussing the significance of the newly emergent Central Asian states (Kazakhstan, Uzbekistan, Tadzhikstan, Turkmenistan, Azerbaijan and Kyrgyzstan), for example, Haroon Siddiqui points to the connections being developed between these states and other Muslim nations to the south, notably Pakistan, which is 'promoting joint ventures in tourism, banking, cement, textiles, and English language teaching' (Haroon Siddiqui, 1992). What are the implications here, as these nations redefine their ethnic, linguistic and religious identities, of the export of English language teaching from Pakistan? And what kind of English is this that is mixed up in trade relations in Central Asia? What intrigues me here is not so much how this 'variety' of English differs from other forms of English as a linguistic system, but rather to what uses it is put, what different meanings it comes to carry.

Other questions come to mind when I watch children in the Philippines, for example, or China, using a few words of English as they pursue some video-camera-carrying tourists. Or the sight in so many places of students huddled over their books late at night, trying to study for the TOEFL exam. English seems to turn up everywhere. In a small village market near the border between China and Burma, a T-shirt declaring 'we are animal', or the sounds of Michael Jackson tumbling from a dusty stereo in a roadside restaurant. Conversations on buses and trains. Sitting in monasteries in Thailand and Tibet, talking about religion, repression and revolution. On a beach in the Philippines talking about Catholicism, contraception and poverty. Drinking Guinness in a hawker centre in Singapore and listening to a bitter tale of the limited opportunities in English-speaking Singapore for the Chinese-educated. Learning that the 'English Corner' in Changsha (Hunan, PRC) every Sunday was used by English teachers to distribute Christian literature. Finding the inscription 'I ♡ homosex' carved into a table in a small town in Malaysia.

Watching the thousands gather at a TESOL conference to talk about strategies, schemata and syntax. Walking into libraries around the world and being able to pick up a newspaper or journal in English. Listening to colleagues in a bar in Tokyo calling their students 'robots'. Sharing the pride and joy of setting up and seeing succeed a new intensive language programme in the Chinese countryside. Sitting in staffrooms, conferences, bars, coffee shops, talking and listening to earnest language teachers and our shared joys, concerns, hopes, worries. Walking along a muddy path between the rice fields in northern Hunan as the hectic work of harvesting, reploughing, and replanting is going on, talking to an old student of mine about Dickens and Hemingway. 'But what have these writers got to do with all this?' I ask. 'Much more than you will ever know', she replies with a smile. There are longer stories, too, but no space to tell them. I recall many conversations in China about families sent down to the countryside during the Cultural Revolution because of their connections to English, of their quiet work to ensure their children would be proficient in the same language that in the 1980s would take them back to prestigious jobs in Beijing, Guangzhou or Shanghai. English and English language teaching seem ubiquitous in the world, playing a role everywhere from large scale global politics to the intricacies of people's lives.

These moments and stories have all affected my thinking, my attempts to understand the roles of English in the world, my attempts to understand what it has meant for me to be standing in front of (or amid) groups of students in London, Munich, Tokyo, Montreal, Xiangtan, Toronto, Hong Kong teaching English. Indeed, despite the apparent commonality implied in the terms 'teaching/ learning English', I wonder whether these situations are not in fact so diverse that they can only be discussed in terms of their specific contexts. And as I have sought ways of thinking about these questions, I have been so often disappointed by what the 'experts', the applied linguists, have to say. While many people I have talked to share similar concerns to my own, it has been almost impossible to find any serious academic treatment of these questions. Of course, there is talk of 'English as an international language' and of local varieties of English but much of this seems to have served as a smoke screen that has obscured the underlying political, cultural and ethical questions around English and English language teaching.

Outline

What I have aimed to do in this book, then, is to seek out ways of thinking about the position of English in the world that will help myself and other teachers to understand our work differently. Although this project ranges over a wide area, from international relations to linguistics, from colonial history to postcolonial literature, there are nevertheless two principal themes. The first develops my concern with the limitations I see in the dominant ways of thinking about English language teaching in applied linguistics, which I have here called the *discourse of English as an International Language (EIL)*.[4] The second theme involves an attempt to think about the cultural and political implications of the spread of English, which I have termed the *worldliness of English*.

The next section introduces the discourse of EIL and suggests that this discourse tends to look at the spread of English as natural, neutral and beneficial. This will then be taken up in much greater depth in Chapters 3–5. Considerable space has been devoted to this attempt to locate the historical and cultural origins of this discourse because it is probably impossible to develop an alternative understanding of English language teaching without looking in depth at how the dominant understanding in mainstream applied linguistics has come to be constructed as it is. Chapter 3, therefore, looks at the colonial origins of this discourse, examines the debates between the colonial 'Anglicists' and 'Orientalists', and argues that colonial education policies were significant not only because of the spread of English that they brought about but also because of the increase in studies of English that they produced. This idea is developed further in Chapter 4, which argues that the key aspect of the development of linguistics and applied linguistics has been their status as *disciplines*, as academic fields of study that define and control language and language teaching. In Chapter 5 this discussion of the discourse of EIL is brought up to the present by showing how it has shifted in accordance with other global changes, and specifically how it has moved from a rhetoric of colonial expansion, through a rhetoric of development aid to a rhetoric of the international free market. English and English teaching in these terms has been considered intrinsically good for the world, a key aspect of global development, and a commodity freely traded on world markets.

In contrast to this view, Chapters 6–9 explore the cultural politics of English as an international language, or what I have termed the worldliness of English (a concept discussed in greater depth later in this chapter). Another aspect of this worldliness is developed in Chapter 2, which looks at ways of understanding international relations. If we are to pursue 'international' or 'global' questions, it is important to do so in the context of a carefully thought-out understanding of what we mean by 'international relations'. Chapters 6 and 7 try to make the idea of worldliness more concrete by looking in some detail at English in Singapore and Malaysia. The central argument here is that English is bound up in a wealth of local social, cultural, economic and political complexities. While it is important, therefore, to understand English globally, this must include the idea that 'global' here means not only *around* the world but also *in* the world, that English is embedded in multiple local contexts of use. Such an argument, however, runs the possible danger of reducing language to its material circumstances, of making language not only bound up with its particular contexts but also determined by them. Chapter 8, therefore, discusses aspects of resistance and human agency in appropriating English to its local contexts, by looking at *writing back*, at what is often termed 'postcolonial literature' in English. This chapter explores what it might mean to find a *voice* in English and how different *conditions of possibility* affect that process. Finally Chapter 9 returns to the key issue of teaching. While much of this book discusses the cultural politics of English as an international language, one of my basic challenges is how to come to terms with this pedagogically. In this last chapter, therefore, I discuss the implications of this view of language for teaching and, more specifically, try to suggest what a critical pedagogy for teaching English as a worldly language might look like.

THE NATURAL, NEUTRAL AND BENEFICIAL SPREAD OF ENGLISH

Otto Jespersen (1938/68) estimated speakers of English to have numbered four million in 1500, six million in 1600, eight and a half million in 1700, between twenty and forty million in 1800, and between 116 and 123 million in 1900. As we approach the end of the twentieth century, the number of speakers of English appears to have increased almost ten-fold since 1900. Today, rough agreement can be found on figures that put the total number of speakers of English at between 700 million and one billion. This figure can be divided into three roughly equal groups, native speakers of English, speakers of English as a second (or intranational) language, and speakers of English as a foreign (or international) language. It is this last group which is the hardest to estimate but clearly the fastest growing section of world speakers of English. Beyond these crude figures, a measure of the extent of the spread of English can be found by its varying uses around the world. For some time now, there has been circulating a range of descriptions of and statistics on the use of English, which have now become enshrined in the *Cambridge Encyclopedia of Language*:

> English is used as an official or semi-official language in over 60 countries, and has a prominent place in a further 20. It is either dominant or well-established in all six continents. It is the main language of books, newspapers, airports and air-traffic control, international business and academic conferences, science, technology, medicine, diplomacy, sports, international competitions, pop music, and advertising. Over two-thirds of the world's scientists write in English. Three quarters of the world's mail is written in English. Of all the information in the world's electronic retrieval systems, 80% is stored in English. English radio programmes are received by over 150 million in 120 countries. Over 50 million children study English as an additional language at primary level; over 80 million study it at secondary level (these figures exclude China). In any one year, the British Council helps a quarter of a million foreign students to learn English, in various parts of the world. In the USA alone, 337,000 foreign students were registered in 1983.
>
> (Crystal, 1987, p. 358)

There also seems to be fairly broad agreement on the reasons for and the implications of this spread. While perhaps not all would agree with Hindmarsh's (1978) bland optimism, his views nevertheless appear to represent a commonly-held view about how English has become so widely used: 'the world has opted for English, and the world knows what it wants, what will satisfy its needs' (p. 42). Although there are probably not many today who would overtly cling to the common nineteenth-century arguments (see Chapter 3) that England and the English language were superior and thus intrinsically worthy of their growing pre-eminence, it nevertheless seems that English is seen as beneficial to the world (which has freely chosen the language), and that the major danger may be to the language itself rather than to other people's languages or cultures. According to Crystal (1988), this view holds that 'while all mother-tongue speakers inevitably feel a modicum of pride (and relief) that it is their language which is succeeding, there is also an element of concern, as they see what happens to the language as it spreads around the world. . . . Changes are perceived as instances of deterioration in standards' (p. 10). Mazrui (1975a) sums up this attitude: 'In spite of the phenomenal spread of the language, the British at home seem to look on it at best as an amusing phenomenon, and at worst as something which is tending to pollute and corrupt the language' (p. 75).

The discourse of EIL

In linguistic and applied linguistic circles, however, such judgements are by and large eschewed (though they may indeed form the basis for the more conservative arguments for maintaining one standard), and the main focus is on description of the different types of English produced by its spread. The causes and effects of this spread are not generally considered and are relegated to a functionalist perspective not so different from Hindmarsh's opinion that the world has chosen English because it knows what it wants. By and large, the spread of English is considered to be natural, neutral and beneficial. It is considered natural because, although there may be some critical reference to the colonial imposition of English, its subsequent expansion is seen as a result of inevitable global forces. It is seen as neutral because it is assumed that once English has in some sense become detached from its original cultural contexts (particularly England and America), it is now a neutral and transparent medium of communication. And it is considered beneficial because a rather blandly optimistic view of international communication assumes that this occurs on a cooperative and equitable footing. Such views can be seen, for example, in the way in which Platt, Weber and Ho (1984) introduce the question of the 'new Englishes': 'Many of the New Nations which were once British colonies have realised the importance of English not only as a language of commerce, science and technology but also as an international language of communication' (p. 1). Similarly, Kachru (1986), who has been one of the most effective campaigners for the recognition and study of local varieties of English, argues that

English does have one clear advantage, attitudinally and linguistically:

it has acquired a *neutrality* in a linguistic context where native languages, dialects, and styles sometimes have acquired undesirable connotations. . . . It was originally the foreign (alien) ruler's language, but that drawback is often overshadowed by what it can do for its users. True, English is associated with a small and elite group; but it is in their role that the *neutrality* of a language becomes vital.

(pp. 8–9)

He goes on to suggest that 'whatever the reasons for the earlier spread of English, we should now consider it a positive development in the twentieth-century world context' (p. 51).

The main issue of debate is whether efforts should be made to maintain a central standard of English or whether the different varieties of English should be acknowledged as legitimate forms in their own right. The two ideologies – one or multiple standards – can be clearly seen in the title change of the leading journal on English as a world language: When its editorialship moved from W.R. Lee in Britain to Braj Kachru and Larry Smith in the United States, its title also changed from *World Language English* to *World Englishes*. In academic circles, the two leading figures in this debate have been Kachru (e.g. 1985) and Quirk (e.g. 1985), the former arguing, for example, that 'native speakers of this language seem to have lost the exclusive prerogative to control its standardization' (p. 30), and the latter, for example, that 'the existence of standards . . . is an endemic feature of our mortal condition and that people feel alienated and disorientated if a standard seems to be missing in any of these areas' (pp. 5–6).

Apart from the important work by Fishman, Cooper and Conrad (1977a) on the sociology of 'English as an additional language' (see also Fishman, 1982a), a comprehensive documentation of the spread of English which nevertheless has some surprising claims such as Fishman's (1977b) conclusion that English is not 'ideologically encumbered', the principal focus of work on English as an international language has been on questions of standards or on descriptions of varieties of English. The key issues, then, as represented in Kachru's important edited volume, *The Other Tongue: English across Cultures*, are questions of models, standards and intelligibility (e.g. Kachru, 1982a, b; Nelson, 1982), and descriptions of the new forms of English: Nigerian English (Bamgbose, 1982), Kenyan English (Zuengler, 1982), Singapore English (Richards, 1982), and so on. Similarly, a recent volume, *English Around the World: Sociolinguistic Perspectives* (Cheshire,

1991), although promising more, devotes a lot of space to questions such as variation of the use of 'after' in Dublin (Kallen, 1991), sociophonetic variation in Vancouver (Esling, 1991), /ae/ and /a:/ in Australian English (Bradley, 1991) or the pronoun system in Nigerian Pidgin (Bokamba, 1991). Indeed, so dominant has this focus become, *World Englishes* (which does at times deal with broader issues than these) has been joined by two more journals that focus almost entirely on varieties of English: *English World-wide: A Journal of Varieties of English* and *English Today: The International Review of the English Language*.

This view of the spread of English as natural, neutral and beneficial also seems to hold sway for many people more directly involved in English language teaching (ELT). Naysmith (1987) suggests that there is a 'cosy, rather self-satisfied assumption prevalent at successive national and international conferences that ELT is somehow a "good" thing, a positive force by its very nature in the search for international peace and understanding' (p. 3). My point here is not so much that intelligibility, standards or varieties are irrelevant questions (indeed, they are clearly of some significance) but rather that they have tended to become the only issues of debate and have thus obscured other questions. To the extent that debate on the role of English in the world is now framed between a conservative view on standards and a more liberal pluralist concept of variety, and to the extent that the primary concerns have become those of intelligibility and description, most people in English language teaching have been poorly served by academic work which fails to address a far more diverse range of questions that might encourage a reassessment of our role as teachers of English in the world. This is not surprising, however, since the view of the spread of English as natural, neutral and beneficial is central to the discourse of English as an international language.

THE SOCIAL, CULTURAL AND POLITICAL CONTEXTS OF ENGLISH

Recalling the abrupt shift from Chinese-medium elementary school to English-medium secondary school in Hong Kong, one of my students recently wrote: 'I had to speak and listen to English in all subjects except Chinese and Chinese History. It was a hard time for me indeed. . . . Every word looked like a monster, I wanted to kill them.' Another student wrote: 'Many students find difficulties in learning not due to their inferiority in learning ability, but the differentiation in their English proficiency. . . . Thus, students are subjected to the hindrance in studying through a second language.' Reading such remarks and discussing these issues with my students, it seems to me that the questions that emerge here have little to do with the structure of English or whether there are now acceptable forms of Hong Kong English, but rather with the worldliness of English, its relationship to class, education and culture, the materiality of its imposition on these students at secondary school, the complex implications of their eventual success in and through English. Certainly, it could not be said that English here has some sort of neutrality. And neither does it make much sense to consider its presence natural. As for being beneficial, in some ways it has been for my students – they are the successful ones who have 'made it' to Hong Kong University – but to see this as automatically beneficial is to see things only in terms of social and economic advantage within the colonial context of Hong Kong. We need to acknowledge the problem that this 'access' to English is anything but beneficial for the majority of Hong Kong students, and that even among these 'successful' students there are deep ambivalences in their relationship to English.

Sorely lacking from the predominant paradigm of investigation into English as an international language is a broad range of social, historical, cultural and political relationships. First, there is a failure to problematize the notion of choice, and therefore an assumption that individuals and countries are somehow free of economic, political and ideological constraints when they apparently freely opt for English. It is this failure to look critically at global relations that allows for a belief in the natural spread of English. Second, there is a structuralist and positivist view of language that suggests that all languages can be free of cultural and political influences; and, more particularly, there is a belief that by its international status English is even more neutral than other languages. And finally, there is an understanding of international relations that suggests that people and nations are free to deal with each other on an equal basis and thus, if English is widely used, this can only be beneficial.

Similar shortcomings can be found in much educational theory, where, as Giroux (1983) suggests, the predominant 'culture of positivism' allowed for analysis only of questions of efficiency in learning and teaching, and not for questions such as the extent to which 'schools acted as agents of social and cultural reproduction in a society marked by significant inequities in wealth, power, and privilege' (p. 170). As English language teachers, then, we have had little help in trying to understand our work, being obliged to draw on a specialist body of knowledge in applied linguistics that has operated with a very limited view of the world. As Phillipson (1988) suggests, the 'professional training of ELT people concentrates on linguistics, psychology and education in a restricted sense. It pays little attention to international relations, development studies, theories of culture or intercultural contact, or the politics or sociology of language or education' (p. 348). These, then, are the types of question I want to raise with respect to the global spread of English.

Beyond the issues outlined above, dealing with questions of standards and descriptions of new forms of English, a number of writers have pointed to a far broader range of cultural and political effects of the spread of English: its widespread use threatens other languages; it has become the language of power and prestige in many countries, thus acting as a crucial gatekeeper to social and economic progress; its use in particular domains, especially professional, may exacerbate different power relationships and may render these domains more inaccessible to many people; its position in the world gives it a role also as an international gatekeeper, regulating the international flow of people; it is closely linked to national and increasingly non-national forms of culture and knowledge that are dominant in the world; and it is also bound up with aspects of global relations, such as the spread of capitalism, development aid and the dominance particularly of North American media.

Linguistic genocide

Cooke (1988) has described English as a 'Trojan horse', arguing that it is a language of imperialism and of particular class interests. Both he and Judd (1983) draw attention to the moral and political implications of English teaching around the globe in terms of the threat it poses to indigenous languages and the role it plays as a gatekeeper to better jobs in many societies. First of all, then, English poses a threat to other languages. This process is what Day (1980; 1985) has called 'linguistic genocide'. In his study of the gradual replacement of Chamorro in Guam and the North Marianas, Day (1985) concludes pessimistically that 'as long as the Marianas remain under the control of the United States, the English language will continue to replace Chamorro until there are no native speakers left. This has been American policy and practice elsewhere, and there is no reason to believe that Guam and the North Marianas will be an exception' (p. 180). In a number of instances, therefore, English poses a direct threat to the very existence of other languages. More generally, however, if not actually threatening linguistic genocide, it poses the less dramatic but far more widespread danger of what we might call linguistic curtailment. When English becomes the first choice as a second language, when it is the language in which so much is written and in which so much of the visual media occur, it is constantly pushing other languages out of the way, curtailing their usage in both qualitative and quantitative terms.

Social and economic prestige

The second major issue raised here is the extent to which English functions as a gatekeeper to positions of prestige in a society. With English taking up such an important position in many educational systems around the world, it has become one of the most powerful means of inclusion into or exclusion from further education, employment, or social positions. In many countries, particularly former colonies of Britain, small English-speaking élites have continued the same policies of the former colonizers, using access to English language education as a crucial distributor of social prestige and wealth. Ngũgĩ (1985) describes his experiences in Kenya, where not only was his native language proscribed with humiliating punishments[5] but English became '*the* main determinant of a child's progress up the ladder of formal education' (p. 115):

Nobody could go on to wear the undergraduate red gown, no matter how brilliantly they had performed in all the papers in all other subjects, unless they had a *credit* (not even a simple pass!) in English. Thus the most coveted place in the pyramid and in the system was only available to holders of an English-language credit card. English was the official vehicle and the magic formula to colonial elitedom.

(p. 115)

Tollefson's (1986; see also 1991) study of leftist opposition to English in the Philippines gives further evidence of these connections between English and the social and economic power of élites. While many studies of English language use in the Philippines have concentrated on questions such as integrative or instrumental motivation, leftist policies on language suggest a different orientation in the support for English or Pilipino. The increased emphasis on English during the Martial Law restrictions from 1972 to 1983, Tollefson argues, underlined the degree to which English plays a major role in 'creating and maintaining social divisions that serve an economy dominated by a small Philippine élite, and foreign economic interests' (p. 186). What emerges here is the clear suggestion that we cannot reduce questions of language to such social psychological notions as instrumental and integrative motivation, but must account for the extent to which language is embedded in social, economic and political struggles. Arguing against the standard interpretation of the language situation in the Philippines, therefore, which tends to ascribe instrumental value to English while Pilipino struggles to maintain a symbolic and integrative role, Tollefson makes it clear that 'consistent leftist opposition to English in the Philippines should not be viewed as an effort to adopt Pilipino as a symbol of national unity and identity, but rather as part of a program to change the distribution of political power and material wealth' (p. 186).

Similar conditions obtain in India, where, as Pattanayak (1969) observes, 'English serves as the distinguishing factor for those in executive authority, no matter how low the level is, and acts as a convenient shield against the effective participation of the mass of the people in the governmental process' (p. 43). In recent years, there has been an increase in anti-English activity in the northern states of India, where the *Angrezi Hatao* (Ban English) movement, led by Mulayam Singh Yadav, the Chief Minister of Uttar Pradesh, has been urging far more widespread use of Hindi. This, however, has been met by fierce opposition from some southern states, notably Kerala and Tamil Nadu, where there has long been support for English (including violent demonstrations in the 1960s), largely out of resentment at the perceived imposition of the North Indian language, Hindi. It is against this background that writers such as Kachru (see above) have claimed a certain 'neutrality' to English, arguing that it rises above such 'local' concerns. Such arguments, however, fail to acknowledge both how English is embedded in local political and economic relations (there is something strangely awry, for example, in the claim that English is simultaneously used by a 'small and élite group' and also 'neutral') and how, as the dominant international language, it is bound up in a multitude of international relations (international capitalism, for example, is not in some way more 'neutral' than local relations of production).

The extent to which English is involved in the political, educational, social and economic life of a country is clearly a result both of the historical legacy of colonialism and of the varying success of countries since independence to ward off the threats of neocolonialism. The different roles of English and Swahili in Kenya and Tanzania, for example, need to be seen both with respect to their colonial pasts and to the different educational and development policies in the two countries (Zuengler, 1985). In Tanzania, Swahili has become widely used as the national and official language due in no small part to Nyerere's insistence on 'Education for Self-Reliance', a policy which emphasized the need for each stage of schooling to be complete in itself and to prepare Tanzanians in the socialist development of the country. In Kenya, by contrast, English is more widely used and enjoys greater prestige, largely because 'Kenya's capitalistic system, whose success depends on foreign investment, creates a climate for dependence on the English language' (Kanyoro, 1991, p. 415). The power of English in the world, however, has made it virtually impossible for a country like Tanzania to maintain policies favouring Swahili over English, and just as countries such as China and Malaysia reverted to more pro-English policies in the 1980s, so Tanzania has also been obliged to reconsider its stance.

Alexandre (1972) has suggested that in postcolonial Africa, social class may be distinguished more clearly along linguistic than economic lines. The group of speakers of the colonial languages, predominantly English or French, he argues, 'is separated from the [majority] by that monopoly which gives it its class specificity: the use of a means of universal communication, French or English, whose acquisition represents truly a form of capital accumulation' (p. 86). Resistance to the spread of the colonial languages also had its effects. Thus, while one effect of Muslim resistance to the imposition of European languages in North Africa was the preservation of a stronger sense of religious and linguistic cohesion, this also led to a degree of isolation and their slowness in gaining power after independence while English- or French-speaking African élites gained ascendancy (Laitin, 1977). A similar condition can be seen in Malaysia, where, under British colonial rule, the Malays were able to maintain their language, culture and religion but found themselves thereby excluded from social and economic power within the country (see Chapter 6).

Professional distance

A further dimension to the spread of English is the effects it has within specific domains. Maher (1986), for example, examining the development of English as an international language of medicine, found that the dissemination and exchange of medical information in English had become not only an *inter*national but also an *intra*national phenomenon, so that 'in countries such as Germany, Japan, and France, information is being regularly published in English for domestic "consumption" ' (p. 216). While this is clearly an important observation in terms of the influence the use of English may have on the education of doctors and on the type of information that is disseminated, Maher suggests a further implication of the expanding use of English in medical discourse. Drawing on the research that has shown how the use of medical terminology in doctor–patient interviews serves to reinforce the unequal power relations between doctor and patient (e.g. Shuy, 1974), Maher suggests that the use of English in certain clinical contexts could also be 'instrumental in making the "ownership" of medical information equally one-sided' (p. 215).

  Such observations start to show not only that the effects of the spread of English can be seen on a large scale in education and other systems and institutions, but also that its spread reaches and has implications for interactions at many points in different societies. Given the many domains in which such unequal positions of power operate in conjunction with a specialized form of language, such as medical interviews (e.g. Treichler, Frankel, Kramarae, Zoppi and Beckman, 1984) or in the courtroom (e.g. Wodak-Engel, 1984), and given the predominance of English in these professional domains, the use of English may have quite far-reaching effects in terms of exacerbating problems of the inaccessibility of information. In Malaysia, for example, where the move to replace English by Bahasa Malaysia as the language of the courts has been a long and often postponed process (see Mead, 1988), many issues arise over the differential access to justice posed by the continued dominance of English in the legal profession. Gibbons (1990) has also shown how police language use in Australia clearly disadvantages second-language speakers.

The international gatekeeper

Thus far, this section has been concentrating on the implications of the spread of English within countries, but clearly its global position also has numerous effects internationally. If English operates as a major means by which social, political and economic inequalities are maintained within many countries, it also plays a significant role as a gatekeeper for movement between countries, especially for refugees hoping to move to the English-speaking countries. In his extensive studies of the English language programmes in the South East Asian Refugee Processing Centres, Tollefson (1988, 1989) argues that they 'continue to limit refugees' improvement in English language proficiency, capacity for cultural adaptation, and pre-employment skills, thereby contributing to the covert goal of ensuring that most refugees will only be able to compete effectively for minimum-wage employment' (1988, p. 39). These programmes, then, while ostensibly providing immigrants with English language education to prepare them for their immigration into the United States, serve as centres for the preparation of a workforce to suit the US economy. They are constantly oriented towards the Americanization of immigrants, a process that assumes that American society has little or nothing to learn from immigrants' cultures and that 'immigrants' primary civic responsibility is to transform themselves by adopting that society's dominant values, attitudes, and behaviors' (1989, p. 58).

Significant here are the close links between, on the one hand, the English language and global relations of economic dependency and exploitation, and, on the other, between English and various forms of culture, in this case aspects of North American culture.

Linking the English Only movement in the United States to anti-immigration sentiment, Crawford (1989) argues that language politics has become a substitute for racial politics:

> The English Only movement, an outgrowth of the immigration-restrictionist lobby, has skilfully manipulated language as a symbol of national unity and ethnic divisiveness. Early in this century, those who sought to exclude other races and cultures invoked claims of Anglo-Saxon superiority. But in the 1980s, explicit racial loyalties are no longer acceptable in our political discourse. Language loyalties, on the other hand, remain largely devoid of associations with social injustice. While race is immutable, immigrants can and often do exchange their mother tongue for another. And so, for those who resent the presence of Hispanics and Asians, language politics has become a convenient surrogate for racial politics.
>
> (p. 14)

Thus, as Tollefson (1991) suggests, following Marshall (1986), 'the agenda of those who support the ELA [English Language Amendment] must be something other than language, namely, restricting access of non-English speakers to economic resources and political institutions' (p. 128).

Popular culture and academic knowledge

Although historically English has been closely tied first to British cultural forms and later to the cultures of an expanded circle of English-speaking countries (as in the example above), of more significance today may in fact be the connections between English and various forms of culture and knowledge that are far less readily localizable. Most important in this respect is the dominance of English in the domains of popular culture, international academic relations, and other forms of international information transfer. As Flaitz (1988) has shown, it is through popular music that English is making a major incursion into French culture. As this study also shows, there is a deep split between the attitudes of various members of the French élite, with their constant attempts to lessen the effect of English on the French language, and those of a broader section of the population, who welcome the conjunction of popular culture and English. Thus, just as Frith (1983) argues that in the 1920s the Americanization of popular culture in Britain was a threat to the cultural hegemony of Britain's intellectuals and produced hostile reactions from the likes of Orwell and Leavis, so Flaitz (1988) shows how the more recent incursion of American popular culture into France through English poses a threat to the cultural hegemony of the French cultural élite. More generally, Flaitz's study clearly shows how English is closely connected to the global spread of popular culture through music and films and thus that it is hard to maintain, as does Fishman (1977b), that English is not 'ideologically encumbered' (1988, p. 201).

In international academic relations, the predominance of English has profound consequences. A large proportion of textbooks in the world are published in English and designed either for the internal English-speaking market (UK, United States, Australia, etc.) or for an international market. In both cases, students around the world are not only obliged to reach a high level of competence in English to pursue their studies, but they are also dependent on forms of Western knowledge that are of limited value and of extreme inappropriacy to the local context. As Jernudd (1981) suggests, for example, the modern discipline of linguistics, with its very particular ways of studying formal properties of language, generally serves needs different to those of many Third World countries, where diverse questions concerning language use are often far more appropriate. Yet, as he explains, linguistics is often exported to and taken up in those countries 'because it is an internationally visible, modern approach to the study of language (and that not the least because it is available through the medium of English), and because the new countries' universities model themselves on Western counterparts' (p. 43). Pattanayak (1986) similarly argues that language planning policies in India have often been inappropriate and destructive because they have been based on ideas developed by an English-educated élite. These English-educated language planners 'plan for reduction of variation, thus creating confrontation among groups using different languages. They then prescribe so-called neutral languages to be used at different levels among the many groups seeking self-fulfillment through symbolic or token functional recognition of their languages. These societies are then made permanent parasites on the developed countries for knowledge and information' (p. vi). Altbach (1981) also suggests that much technological expertise in India has been inappropriate because 'much of Indian science is oriented toward metropolitan models, because of the use of English, because of the prestige of Western science, and because of the foreign training of many key Indian researchers' (p. 613).

What emerges here, then, is a complex set of relationships between English and what types of culture and knowledge are given international credibility. Access to prestigious but often inappropriate forms of knowledge is often only through English, and thus, given the status of English both within and between countries, there is often a reciprocal reinforcement of the position of English and the position of imported forms of culture and knowledge. This problem often permeates down through education systems, and indeed Pattanayak (1969) argues that English in India 'stands as a barrier between the student and a meaningful education', that 'English education bestows maximum advantage in acquiring position, rank, wealth and consequent power to the few who worship it and thus perpetuate the circle of intellectual aristocracy', and that ultimately 'the study of English remains a purposeless pursuit excepting as a passport to a degree and a convenient ladder to a job and consequent privileges' (p. 44). But therein, of course, lies one of the central difficulties: while from one perspective learning English is a 'purposeless pursuit', from another perspective it is anything but purposeless as long as it provides access to social and economic prestige.[6]

International capitalism

Finally, some writers have suggested connections between the spread of English and more general issues in global relations. Ndebele (1987, p. 4) suggests that 'the spread of English went parallel with the spread of the culture of international business and technological standardization'. Naysmith (1987) argues that English language teaching 'has become part of the process whereby one part of the world has become politically, economically and culturally dominated by another' (p. 3). The core of this process, he argues, is the 'central place the English language has taken as *the* language of international capitalism' (ibid.). Such a position, which suggests that English is an integral part of the global structures of dependency, has been explored at length by Robert Phillipson (1986; 1988; 1992). Phillipson's aim is to establish a connection between imperialism in general – global structural relations that maintain and reproduce economic and other inequalities between countries – and what he calls 'English linguistic imperialism'. English linguistic imperialism, a subtype of general linguistic imperialism, operates when 'The dominance of English is asserted and maintained by the establishment and continuous reconstitution of structural and cultural inequalities between English and other languages' (1992, p. 47).

Most significantly, Phillipson's work clearly demonstrates the limitations of arguments that suggest that the current position of English in the world is an accidental or natural result of world forces. Rather, through his analysis of the British Council and other organizations, Phillipson makes it clear that it has been deliberate government policy in English-speaking countries to promote the worldwide use of English for economic and political purposes. The British Council report for 1960–61, for example, draws a direct parallel between the advantages of encouraging the world to speak English (with the help of American power) and the history of US internal policies for its immigrant population: 'Teaching the world English may appear not unlike an extension of the task which America faced in establishing English as a common national language among its own immigrant population' (British Council Annual Report 1960–61, p. 16). Ndebele (1987) also suggests that 'The British Council . . . continues to be untiring in its efforts to keep the world speaking English. In this regard, teaching English as a second or foreign language is not only good business, in terms of the production of teaching materials of all kinds . . . but also it is good politics' (p. 63). Given the connections outlined above between English and the export of certain forms of culture and knowledge, and between English and the maintenance of social, economic and political élites, it is evident that the promotion of English around the world may bring very real economic and political advantages to the promoters of that spread. Indeed, Skutnabb-Kangas and Phillipson (1989) conclude that 'it has been British and American government policy since the mid-1950s to establish English as a universal "second language", so as to protect and promote capitalist interests' (p. 63).

Clearly, then, a more critical analysis of the global spread of English reveals a broad range of questions about its connection to social and economic power within and between nations, to the global expansion of various forms of culture and knowledge, and to various forces that are shaping the modern world. Such relationships can clearly be seen in Hong Kong, 'a monolingual (Cantonese-speaking) and ethnically homogeneous (98 per cent Chinese) society' (So, 1987, p. 249) in which English plays a disproportionately large role. While Cantonese is not threatened with linguistic genocide, it certainly encounters 'linguistic curtailment' because of the dominance of English in academic, professional and legislative domains. This, in turn, leads to a circular argument whereby Cantonese is then claimed to be linguistically unable to perform in these domains.[7] Clearly, English is the language of social and economic prestige in Hong Kong: 'English is the passport, it is the prestige, it is the profession, and parents want their children to get on the boat early and to stay there' (Fu, 1987, p. 29). The position of English in areas such as education and law also exacerbate difficulties of access to such domains for many people. In fact, the predominance of English in education – around 90 per cent of secondary education is in English – is clearly detrimental to the large majority of students (see, for example, Yu and Atkinson, 1988). As So (1987) remarks, 'there is much evidence indicating that EM [English medium] instruction has created learning problems for many students' (pp. 264–5). This dominance of English in the academic sphere also, of course, continues to promote inappropriate and irrelevant domains of knowledge for many students. Fortunately, one result of the burgeoning Cantonese popular music and film industries has been a clear domain of resistance to the incursion of English-connected cultural forms.

If on the one hand, then, it seems clear that there is a range of issues to be explored here, it also seems clear, on the other hand, that there is a dominant discourse on English as an International Language which tends to ignore many of these issues. In the light of many of the points discussed above, a view that holds that the spread of English is natural, neutral and beneficial needs to be investigated as a particular discursive construct. To view the spread as natural is to ignore the history of that spread and to turn one's back on larger global forces and the goals and interests of institutions and governments that have promoted it. To view it as neutral is to take a very particular view of language and also to assume that the apparent international status of English raises it above local social, cultural, political or economic concerns. To view it as beneficial is to take a rather naively optimistic position on global relations and to ignore the relationships between English and inequitable distributions and flows of wealth, resources, culture and knowledge.

To the extent that this discourse of EIL has permeated much thinking on English language teaching, there is an urgent need to investigate the construction of this discourse and its relationship to English language teaching. From his own particular perspective, Phillipson (1986) states that a primary purpose of his work is to gauge 'the contribution of applied linguists and English Language Teaching Experts in helping to legitimate the contemporary capitalist world order' (p. 127). As I have argued elsewhere (Pennycook, 1990b), it is incumbent on us as teachers and applied linguists to discard ways of thinking about ELT as if it were some neutral enterprise and, instead, to start exploring the interests served by our work. If we start to accept some of the critical perspectives outlined here, we must surely start to raise profound questions about our own theories and practices.

THE WORLDLINESS OF ENGLISH

While the critical orientations outlined above raise a number of far more significant questions than have been posed by the predominant paradigms of linguistics and applied linguistics, they also leave us with a number of difficult theoretical issues. A key part of this book, therefore, is concerned not so much with trying to describe the global spread of English or trying to present a theory that can explain it, but rather with trying to come to terms with the difficulties in understanding its diverse implications. The discussion in the last section showed how English is connected to social and economic inequalities both within and between countries and how it is bound up with various forms of culture and knowledge that are increasingly dominant in the world, but this still leaves us with certain questions concerning what 'connected to' or 'bound up with' mean. How can we make more concrete the connections between language and social, economic, cultural, political and historical contingencies? And how can we avoid a view that places language on one side of the equation and society, culture, politics or the economy on the other?

While there has clearly been a rejection of connections between language and its contexts in much of mainstream linguistics (there are of course exceptions to this, such as Halliday), it is at the same time clear that to many people who have not been caught up by the reductions and rejections of linguistic thought, these connections are of great significance. Thus I want to find ways of taking seriously such comments as Franz Fanon's that 'To speak means to be in a position to use a certain syntax, to grasp the morphology of this or that language, but it means above all to assume a culture, to support the weight of a civilization' (1967, pp. 17–18). Or Lloyd Fernando's comment on the use of English in South East Asia: 'It is not British culture which should be feared in South East Asia. . . . It is rather certain Western habits of thinking which are now deeply infused into the language to which we must be much more alert' (1986, pp. 89–90). Or Ndebele's (1987) suggestion that in South Africa 'the problems of society will also be the problems of the predominant language of that society. It is the carrier of its perceptions, its attitudes, and its goals, for through it, the speakers absorb entrenched attitudes. The guilt of English must then be recognized and appreciated before its continued use can be advocated' (p. 11). To pursue such questions, to take seriously the idea that to speak can be 'to assume a culture' or that 'habits of thinking' can be 'deeply infused into the language', or that we can talk of 'the guilt of English', it is necessary to look beyond much standard linguistic theory, especially in its dominant structuralist mode.

Unfortunately, to those trained in the structuralist traditions of linguistics and applied linguistics, the kind of questions raised here are either completely dismissed or put into boxes such as 'sociolinguistics' or the 'Sapir–Whorf hypothesis'. This is not the place to engage in a long debate on these perspectives, but I want to suggest briefly why I want to distance myself from such labels. The first problem here is exactly in this type of labelling and boxing: issues in applied linguistics are often seen as either sociolinguistic or psycholinguistic, a tendency which severely limits the scope of applied linguistics. Furthermore, sociolinguistics itself has generally come to be very narrowly conceived. It has, first, failed to explore the whole question of social class against which linguistic features are correlated (see Fairclough, 1989; Mey, 1985); second, it has frequently only seen language as a passive reflector of rather than an active agent in social relations (see Stewart, 1986); and third, it has continued to operate with, indeed to reinforce, the divide between the individual and society that is so central to structuralism (see Urwin, 1984). As for the so-called Sapir–Whorf hypothesis, the problems here are, first, that any attempt to discuss language, culture and thought gets instantly labelled as ascribing to this view and is then fatuously dismissed; second, Whorf's work, though important, was limited by his structuralist approach that concentrated on language as structure rather than on language in use; and third, Whorf's ideas are often misrepresented and, as Fishman (1982b) suggests, the political implications of his struggle to support a view of difference and diversity in the face of Anglo-American genocide and disregard of Native people's languages and cultures are frequently overlooked.

In trying to find ways to think about how to understand language and its connections to its many contexts, Edward Said's (1983) attempts to find a way of dealing with the 'worldliness' of texts is a useful way forward. 'Is there no way', he asks, 'of dealing with a text and its worldly circumstances fairly?' (p. 35) What Said is trying to do here, as a politically-engaged literary critic, is find a way of dealing with a text that does not leave it as a hermetically sealed textual cosmos with no connection to the world, but which also avoids reducing a text to its worldly circumstances. The key point here is to find a space between, on the one hand, a structuralist view of language as an idealized, abstract system disconnected to its surroundings, and, on the other hand, a materialist view of language that reduces it to its contexts and therefore sees language use as determined by worldly circumstance. To make this idea of worldliness useful, however, there are a number of other aspects of language that need to be discussed.

The language myth

The first important question worth raising concerns the very status of the notion of a language. Unfortunately this question is infrequently raised and, when it is discussed, it is rarely taken far enough. Lyons (1981), for example, after discussing various definitions of language, suggests that there is indeed a difficulty with the fiction of whole, homogeneous languages but, he suggests, if we follow this questioning to its logical conclusion, we end up with a position that acknowledges only difference: 'In the last resort, we should have to admit that everyone has his[8] own individual dialect' (p. 27). Thus, we are left here with an argument that hinges on the supposed opposition between universality and relativism: if we give up our universal construct of language, we will be left only with individual difference. Corder (1973) pursues this question a bit further and points out that there can be no linguistic definition of 'a language'; rather, we need to look to social psychology for a definition: 'The concept of "a language" is a matter of social psychology. A speech community is made up of people who *regard themselves* as speaking the same language' (p. 53). This certainly raises some interesting questions but still leaves us with the proposition that mutually unintelligible speakers nevertheless speak the 'same language' because they 'accept the same norm. They both regard themselves as English speakers' (p. 54).

It is interesting that in one of the first published discussions of the concept of English as an International Language, Strevens (1980) also takes up this question when he refers to the 'fiction of "English" ' (p. 79). Unfortunately he then backs away from this position and insists that we have to assume some form of commonality between the disparate forms and usages. What is commonly argued, then, is that although there is no clear way in which English can be defined, there is nevertheless something in common between the various international 'dialects' of English. It is then stressed that, in common with other structuralist approaches to language that discuss the 'equality' of dialects, these dialects of English should enjoy equal linguistic status with each other, as equal parts of a larger system. Although this emphasis on the equality of dialects has been an important egalitarian move that counters linguistic élitism and purism, it has tended to overlook another sense in which dialects are anything but equal. As Mey (1985) puts it:

> Abstract considerations of 'uniform structures' and general postulates about 'equal rights' of dialect speakers can easily lead the way to potentially manipulatory notions about 'linguistic democracy'

and similar things. Against this, I want to emphasize that linguistic models, no matter how innocent and theoretical they may seem to be, not only have distinct economical, social, and political presuppositions, but also consequences. . . . Linguistic (and other) inequalities don't cease to exist, simply because their socio-economic causes are swept under the linguistic rug. The veil of linguistic manipulation that is drawn across the consciousness of the underprivileged, can only hide, not abolish the existing state of social inequality.

(p. 26)

It is indeed interesting to observe the hierarchy implicit in Strevens's tree diagram of Englishes (1980, p. 86), with 'English' at the top, followed by 'British' and 'American English' and branching out into all the other 'dialects' of EIL.

There is, then, a fundamentally important question to be asked about the very assumptions contained in the term 'English as an International Language', assumptions that do not disappear by arguing that if the reality of the concept of a language is not acknowledged, we may slip into complete relativism, or that we can assume that speakers believe themselves to belong to the same 'language community' and therefore follow the same norms, or that we can avoid the problem by acknowledging some parity between all the 'dialects' of English. All these arguments seem to resolve themselves into the same a priori belief that the very existence of the term 'English' or 'English as an International Language' must imply some commonality, some shared system and norms, an argument that seems to recapitulate the seventeenth-century ontological argument for the existence of God (there could not be a concept of a perfect being were there not an ultimate referent for the concept). What is not acknowledged is that 'English' may indeed be fragmented, struggled over, resisted, rejected, diverse, broken, centrifugal and even incommensurable with itself. The point here is that the wrong questions are still being asked. When the impossibility of linguistic definition is raised, the question then switches to how else a top-down definition of a language can be arrived at. By contrast, my search is not for a definition but for a bottom-up way of understanding language, not for a description of language structure but a way of looking at the creation of meanings through English.

Harris (1981) is useful here in his call for a 'demythologised linguistics' that would involve an 'investigation of the renewal of language as a continuously creative process' (p. 164). He points to two central fallacies in modern linguistics, namely the idea that language transparently reflects either a real world or the thoughts of a person and the belief that language communities share a fixed code through which they communicate similar meanings to each other. This 'language myth', Harris suggests, 'is a cultural product of post-Renaissance Europe. It reflects the political psychology of nationalism, and an educational system devoted to standardizing the linguistic behaviour of pupils' (p. 9). (For further discussion, see Chapter 4.) The notion of *a* language, therefore, is a very particular cultural and historical construct; it may be more useful to start with a notion of language as constant change. Le Page (1985) has also challenged the assumptions made about categories such as language, race and ethnicity. Most Western linguists, he argues, are heavily influenced by, but largely unaware of, the ideological underpinnings of their view of language, influenced as it is by their own prescriptive educations, their belief in a concordance between language and nation-state, and by the monolithic grammars which claim to represent 'English', 'French' and so on. Linguistic behaviour for Le Page, then, is better understood in terms of 'a series of *acts of identity* in which people reveal both their personal identity and their search for social roles' (Le Page and Tabouret-Keller, 1985, p. 14).

By following this deconstruction of the notion of language, it is possible to start not with mainstream linguistic's version of language as a formal system for study, with priority always given to *langue* and competence while *parole* and performance are relegated to a position of fleeting aberrations, but rather to start with the utterance, with language in everyday life, with language use as a social, cultural and political act. This, then, is not merely a reversal of the performance/competence distinction (and hier- archy) but a questioning of the very nature of this dichotomy. Language is located in social action and anything we might want to call *a* language is not a pregiven system but a will to community. Having made a case for understanding language in terms of difference, in terms of individual acts that move towards community, however, it is important not to adopt some voluntaris- tic conception of language acts in which individuals freely do and say as they please. Rather, we need to understand the ideological or discursive constraints on language use. Once we start with a view of language in terms of difference, the next step is to consider how it is that meanings are created and produced in language.

This is the next crucial stage in developing a notion of worldliness: if I have successfully argued against a view of language as an abstract and isolated system, the next step is to find ways to think about how we come to use language and make sense that does not leave individuals as completely free and random actors in the world but that also does not deterministically tie us to our worldly circumstances.

Discourse and dialogue

Here the notions of dialogue and discourse in the writings of Bakhtin, Vološinov,[9] Pêcheux and Foucault, are useful. For Bakhtin, like Harris and Le Page, it is important to understand language and metalanguage (linguistics) as particular to their social, cultural and political contexts. He also draws attention to the process by which the concept of a unitary language arose as part of the centralizing movement of European state-building, of the centripetal forces that created a notion of a unitary language, which 'at every moment of its linguistic life . . . is opposed to the realities of heteroglossia' (1981, p. 270). Vološinov's (1973) wide-ranging critique deals, like Harris's, with the move, especially by Saussure and his followers, to construct a linguistics based on a view of language as an abstract system, to stress *langue* (the system) at the expense of *parole* (everyday utterances), and to remove language from its contexts and its ideological formation. 'Abstract objectivism', Vološinov argues, gives precedence to stability over mutability of form, to the abstract over the concrete, to systematization over historical actuality, to the forms of elements over the form of the whole, to the reification of isolated elements over the dynamics of speech, and to the singularization of word meaning over the living multiplicity of meaning and accent. Language is taken to be a ready-made artifact handed down from one generation to another and cannot account for creativity or difference (1973, pp. 77–82).

Stewart (1986) comments that the tendency of structuralist linguistics to 'silence the diversity of the powerful "unsaids" of actual speech in favour of an opaque and universal form of language is to strip language of its ideological significance – a stripping that is itself strongly and univocally ideological' (p. 44). It is Vološinov's development of the ideological dimension of language and of the sign as a site of multivocality and struggle that is most significant here. 'The divorce of language from its ideological impletion', Vološinov comments, 'is one of abstract objectivism's most serious errors' (1973, p. 71). For Vološinov, language and the sign must always be seen as forged in the contested domain of social interaction: 'The forms of signs are conditioned above all by the social organization of the participants involved and also by the immediate conditions of their interaction' (p. 21), and 'linguistic creativity cannot be understood apart from the ideological meanings and values that fill it' (p. 98). Such a view, then, takes language out of the abstract domain of the systems posited by the 'abstract objectivists', out of some idealized liberal notion of the individual, and into the social and political domain. Meaning becomes multiple, mutable and struggled over. Meaning can never be monological; it must always be dialogical. Similarly, Pêcheux (1982) argues that

> The *meaning* of a word, expression, proposition, etc., does not exist 'in itself' (i.e. in its transparent relation to the literal character of the signifier), but is determined by the ideological positions brought into play in the socio-historical process in which words, expressions and propositions are produced (i.e. reproduced) . . . *Words, expressions, propositions, etc., change their meaning according to the positions held by those who use them*, which signifies that they find their meanings by reference to those positions, i.e. by reference to the *ideological formations* . . . in which those positions are inscribed.
> (1982, p. 111; emphasis in original)

The importance of these ideas for an understanding of the worldliness of English is that it is now possible to consider language and meaning not in terms of a language system (English as an International Language) and its varieties (the New Englishes) but rather in terms of the social, cultural and ideological positions in which people use language. At this point, however, it is worth making a few comments on the notions of discourse and ideology, since throughout this book Foucault's concept of discourse will be preferred to the concept of ideology.[10] By and large, this is because it avoids notions of false consciousness (and, therefore, 'true consciousness') refrains from positing some underlying cause of social relations (usually taken to be socioeconomic relations), and always allows for the possibilities of counter-discourse. Discourses, in this sense, are relationships of power/knowledge that are embedded in social institutions and practices. They are ways of organizing meaning that are both reflected and produced in our uses of language and the formation of our subjectivities. Importantly, the focus in this poststructuralist sense of discourse is on 'seeing historically how effects of truth are produced within discourses which in themselves are neither true nor false' (Foucault, 1980a, p. 118). Here, then, we can start to see how using language is never simply an act that can be considered in terms of a linguistic system, the volition of an individual in cognitive isolation or an ideological trap determined by material relations. Rather, to engage in the social practice of language use is always an act situated within some discourse.

My insistence on the centrality of a notion of worldliness to my thinking should indicate that, if my stance is a poststructuralist one, it is not concerned centrally with the endless play of meaning, as deconstruction tends to be, but rather is concerned on the one hand with a challenge to the dominant dichotomies of structuralism (the individual and society, *langue* and *parole*, synchronic and diachronic linguistics, and so on), and on the other with an understanding of language and discourse in the world, with the relationships of power and knowledge. This is not, therefore, an attempt to find a relationship between the individual or language and society, but rather to suggest that they are inseparably intertwined. This is not an attempt to focus attention on *parole* instead of *langue* but rather to argue that language as system is only interesting as a by-product of language in use. This is not an argument for a historical rather than a contemporary analysis of language but rather an argument that the past is ever-present in language. Poststructuralist thinking has claimed a more fundamental role for language in human life than has been the case with the reified and compartmentalized version of language constructed by structuralist linguistics, and thus allows me to pursue my questions in a far more comprehensive way. 'Language', Weedon (1987, p. 21) argues, 'is the place where actual and possible forms of social organization and their likely social and political consequences are defined and contested. Yet it is also the place where our sense of ourselves, our subjectivity, is *constructed*.' This notion of the discursive construction of subjectivity immediately gives us a way of taking Fanon's assertion that 'to speak means ... to assume a culture, to support the weight of a civilization' (1967, pp. 17–18) more seriously, for as Weedon later asserts, 'To speak is to assume a subject position within discourse and to become *subjected* to the power and regulation of discourse' (p. 119). We do not, therefore, need to try to correlate linguistic systems with assumed social or cultural systems, but rather can focus on the discursive location of the speaker.

There is clearly a complex interweaving here of language acts and both local and global discourses. The relationship between 'English' and global discourses of capitalism, democracy, education, development, and so on, is neither a coincidental conjunction – English just happens to be the language in which these discourses are expressed – nor a structural determinism – the nature of English determines what discourses are spoken, or the nature of discourses determines what language they are spoken in. Rather, there is a reciprocal relationship that is both historical and contemporary. Colonial discourses and discourses of contemporary world relations have both facilitated and been facilitated by the spread and construction of English. English and a range of local and international discourses have been constituted by and are constitutive of each other, both through the history of their connections and their present conjunctions. Particular global and local discourses create the conditions of possibility for engaging in the social practice of using 'English', they produce and constrain what can be said in English. At the same time, English creates the conditions of possibility for taking up a position in these discourses. Clearly, then, language can never be removed from its social, cultural, political and discursive contexts and, to return to Fanon or Fernando or Ndebele – with a changed perspective on what is meant by 'language' or 'culture' – to speak *is* to 'assume a culture', habits of thinking *are* 'infused into the language', English *can* be called 'guilty'.

It is now possible, finally, to return to the notion of the worldliness of English and to suggest more clearly what I take this to mean. I believe that it is a felicitous term for what I want to deal with here because it points both to the global position of English and to English being embedded in the world. I do not intend to try to provide a firm definition of this term (such a proposition, in any case, would be somewhat contradictory to my discussion of meaning above), but will suggest some key aspects to this notion of worldliness. First, and in the most obvious sense, English is worldly by dint of its vast global expansion. Second, English is worldly in the sense that a person may be called worldly: it has been and is constantly in the process of being changed by its position in the world. And third, it is in the world, it is part of the world; to use English is to engage in social action which produces and reproduces social and cultural relations. The worldliness of English refers both to its local and to its global position, both to the ways in which it reflects social relations and constitutes social relations and thus the worldliness of English is always a question of cultural politics.

It is the tendency in much of mainstream linguistics to locate meaning as centred in the core countries, institutions and linguistic/cultural systems (see Chapter 4) that this notion of worldliness attempts to counter by suggesting that language be viewed as a social practice. This view suggests that language use is always 'situated', which is not to argue that context or participants determine meaning but rather to argue that language is always located within larger discursive frameworks and is always part of the cultural and political moments of the day. The issue, then, is not so much how 'using English as an international language' involves the users in various syntactical, phonological or lexical diversity from central English norms, but rather how those acts of language use always imply a position within a social order, a cultural politics, a struggle over different representations of the self and other.

The importance of the language under consideration being English, then, is not so much an issue of structural diversity, of trying to establish what syntactical or phonological norms and divergences occur as English spreads across the globe; rather, the issue is one of considering how using English implies certain relationships to certain discourses. The global position of English means that it is situated in many contexts that are specific to that globalization: to use English implies relationships to local conditions of social and economic prestige, to certain forms of culture and knowledge, and also to global relations of capitalism and particular global discourses of democracy, economics, the environment, popular culture, modernity, development, education and so on. The particular position of English suggests that these relationships, both local and global, will be very different from those between other languages and discourses. The worldliness of English, in both its global and local senses, implies relationships to the larger world and to the local context different from those of other languages. Given the dominant position of English in the world and its connections both to inequitable economic systems and to the dominance of certain forms of culture and knowledge, there are inevitable questions to be asked here concerning language and inequality.

CONCLUSION

In this chapter I have laid out some of the principal preliminary concerns of this book. Taking questions about the cultural and political implications of the global spread of English as my starting point, I argued that the dominant discourse on EIL, which is of particular significance for English language teaching, considers this spread to be generally natural, neutral and beneficial and is concerned more with questions of linguistic description than of language, culture and politics. By contrast, a review of some of the more critical work on English in the world has shown how it is linked to social and economic power both within and between nations, to the global diffusion of particular forms of culture and knowledge, and to the inequitable structures of international relations. Peirce's (1989; 1990) explanation of the differences between considering *People's English* in South Africa merely as a variety of English and viewing it as a locus of political struggle is a clear example of the difference between working from a traditional-structuralist approach to language and working from a politically-informed critical standpoint:

> To interpret People's English as a dialect of international English would do the movement a gross injustice; People's English is not only a language, it is a struggle to appropriate English in the interests of democracy in South Africa. Thus the naming of People's English is a political act because it represents a challenge to the current status of English in South Africa, in which control of the language, access to the language, and teaching of the language are entrenched within apartheid structures.
>
> (Peirce 1990, p. 108)

To pursue the issue of the cultural politics of English as an international language, I introduced the notion of the worldliness of English, a term which is intended to refer to the material existence of English in the world, its spread around the world, its worldly character as a result of being so widely used in the world, and its position not only as reflective but also as constitutive of worldly affairs. By deconstructing the notion of a language, furthermore, it is possible to take further the two central questions of this book. Thus, by viewing language use in terms of discursively mediated social action, rather than in terms of a fixed system for analysis, it is far more possible to explore the cultural and political implications of language use. Not only is the reinsertion of language in general into daily life a necessary step in understanding the worldliness of English, but we must also start with a deconstruction of the whole notion of 'English' and of 'English as an International Language'. Thus, rather than according some a priori ontological status to English in the world, English as an International Language can be understood as a discursive construct; rather than being some objective descriptive category, it is a whole system of power/knowledge relationships which produce very particular understandings of English and English language teaching (see Chapters 3–5). This helps us to make sense of Ndebele's (1987) comment that 'the very concept of an international, or world, language was an invention of Western imperialism' (pp. 3–4).

NOTES

1. From the BBC series *The Story of English*. See also McCrum, Cran and MacNeil (1986).
2. My thanks to Roger Simon for bringing this song to my attention.
3. My thanks to Roger Bradshaw for mentioning and locating this example.
4. Although this sort of labelling (ESL, EFL, ESP, EAP, EST, SLA, LAD, L1, L2, etc.) is what I see as both the cementing of complex ideas into simplistic and rigid categories and the attempt by applied linguistics to constitute itself as a science (see Chapter 4), I have abbreviated this clumsy term for convenience. As will become clear, however, I do not wish to signal my acceptance either of the standard understanding of EIL nor of the tendency to make such neat formulations.
5. Ngũgĩ's account of the system of informants and punishments to

prohibit the use of native languages in Kenyan schools echoes in painful fashion similar stories of the brutal repression of native languages and imposition of English among Native Canadians.

6. My thanks to Arleen Schenke here, who asked the key questions 'Purposeless for whom?' and 'Purposeless in what sense?'.

7. My thanks to Tse Lai Kun for our discussion of this and other issues related to English in Hong Kong.

8. After a great deal of consideration, I have decided to drop my former practice of marking all 'inappropriate' pronoun usage in quotations with [sic]. My feeling now is that this convention, although extremely important, has now become too formalized a practice to be useful. I suspect the same is the case with 'he or she', which has now become a formalized convention that does little to change gender relations in language. This misgiving is coupled with two other concerns: (1) that this practice has tended to follow a representationalist view of language (for a discussion of the complexities of gender, pronouns and representationalism, see Black and Coward, 1990); and (2) that, along with gendered pronouns, there are many other terms that we may find problematic (especially in terms of race, ethnicity and ethnocentricity in colonial documents). Rather than highlight an ever-increasing number of words and phrases with [sic], I have chosen to let them stand, in the hope that readers will see for themselves the problematic discourses at play.

9. There is a problem with attribution of authorship here. For simplicity, however, I am referring to Marxism and the Philosophy of Language as Vološinov (1973), whether or not its real author or coauthor was Bakhtin.

10. A great deal more could be said about this but I feel this is not the place to do so. In general, too, Foucault's thinking has been central to many of the ways I have approached this project, not only in terms of his work on the disciplining of language and distribution of discourse (1970; 1972), but also in terms of his methodological and political projects (1980a). Thus, I shall pursue genealogical, archaeological and ethical concerns. A genealogical focus will attempt to show how inquiries into the past can be of political relevance to the present by unravelling the historical construction of unquestioned assumptions. An archaeological focus will seek to investigate more closely the formation of discourses themselves, the historical conditions of possibility that gave rise to them, and the conditions of possibility that they in turn engender. An ethical focus will seek to draw connections between theoretical work and political struggles (see Gordon, 1980, p. 233).

TWO

Discourse and dependency in a shifting world

It is extremely difficult for a society to practise free flow of media and enjoy a national culture at the same time – unless it happens to be the United States of America.

(Smith, 1980, p. 53)

Our world does not follow a programme, but we live in a world of programmes, that is to say in a world traversed by the effects of discourses whose object (in both senses of the word) is the rendering rationalisable, transparent and programmable of the real.

(Gordon, 1980, p. 245)

The politics of diversity and plurality, by rendering the mainstream monolith irrelevant, becomes the foundation of an alternative post-modern era of action and knowledge.

(Kothari, 1987, pp. 279–80)

INTRODUCTION: RETHINKING INTERNATIONALISM

One of the several weaknesses with the notion of English as an International Language is that not only has there been a tendency to ask rather a narrow set of questions around 'English' and 'language' (see Chapter 1), but much of the work done under this rubric has also failed to give any consideration to what is implied by the notion 'international'. Rather than assuming that 'the world', 'global', or 'international' are unproblematic constructs, I believe we need to develop careful understandings of how culture, language and discourse operate within global relations of power. It is now fairly commonplace to talk of international or global issues; a frequently heard phrase these days, for example, suggests that 'the world is getting smaller'. As a TV advertisement for the BBC

World Service puts it: 'The world is a very large place, but it *is* getting smaller. . . . For fact, not fiction, 24 hours a day. . . . One Service for one world. The BBC. A world service.'[1] This phrase, apparently used without alarm or dismay, seems to suggest that because more people are able to travel to more places around the world and because global media are reaching further and further into people's homes, this is somehow a positive change. What does not seem to get asked here is: Who is doing the travelling? Whose media are expanding across the globe? What is the language of international travel and global media? If the world is indeed shrinking (a proposition that we might want to question since a more optimistic view could suggest that it is expanding), then it is being shrunk in a very particular direction. This seems to call for critical investigation, not casual celebration.

A rather bland optimism seems to operate in discussions of international affairs. Both the national – that comfortable place of flag, language, and culture – and the international – that exciting arena where men in suits gather to discuss global issues, and where the world tunes in to CNN – are accepted as 'givens' of the modern world. The nation seems to be taken as an unquestioned norm that takes care of our local concerns, a generally positive entity that forms part of our collective and personal identity. Meanwhile, the need to communicate between nations, to settle the 'inevitable' disputes that arise, and to foster 'mutual understanding' and respect is the domain of the international diplomat and global communications. There are a number of limitations with this understanding of internationalism. Most glaringly problematic are the profound inequalities in the world that render any easy talk of internationalism as equally oblivious to these inequalities as are simplistic discussions of 'equal opportunities' within any society. Easy talk of equality and global communication will not do much to address the vast disparities of wealth and power both within and between nations. Information in the world flows in a very particular direction (from wealthy to less wealthy countries), which is, not coincidentally, the opposite direction to the net flow of wealth. When organizations such as TESOL speak happily of internationalism – the TESOL logo is a picture of the world – they tend to do so without considering the massive inequalities inherent in that term, or that when they have 'international' conferences, they expect the world to come to them. Thus, it is the United States which sets the agenda for this 'international' organization, with input from other countries in proportion to their wealth and status (Canada, Britain, Australia and then a long list of 'others' with less and less influence). The theme for the 1993 TESOL conference was 'Designing our world'. Who, I want to know, is implied by the 'our'? Who is doing the designing? And for whom?[2] Is it time for some redecoration following George Bush's declaration of a 'New World Order'? TESOL offered a morning excursion to 'Atlanta's Global Villages', the headquarters of CNN and the World of Coca-Cola. Should we go along and celebrate the conjunction between these global powers and English or should we be raising critical questions about 'global villages'?

A more extensive exploration of international relations suggests they need to be understood in terms of the massive inequalities that exist between different regions of the world and in ways that go beyond a simple dichotomy between nationalism and inter-nationalism, between the nation and the world. There are moral, social, cultural, economic and political questions to be pursued here, dealing with poverty, starvation, tourism, pollution, migra-tion, multinational companies, the global diffusion of certain forms of knowledge and culture and much more. What are we to make of the vast flows of people, capital and information that move daily around the globe? What role do transnational corporations and international organizations play in world affairs? How do those of us that live in the wealthier countries deal morally and politically with the vast inequalities between different parts of the globe, when the major nutritional problems in North America relate to problems of overeating while 40,000 children die every day in the Third World?[3]

In order both to make sense of our daily lives and to start to theorize the place of English in the world, therefore, it is worth devoting considerable time and space to a discussion of questions of international relations. This chapter, then, will look at how different conceptions of the world imply very different under-standings of development, education and communication in a global context: first, the dominant (traditional) mode of analysis and its particular construction of the 'modern' and 'developed' as opposed to the 'traditional' and 'undeveloped'; second, a more critical view of world relations that takes inequality, imperialism and dependency as its key points of analysis; third, an understand-ing of the world that raises language, culture and discourse to a far more central role than they are often accorded.

DEVELOPMENT, AID AND MODERNIZATION

The noble savage and the savage noble

There have been many speculations over the centuries on how the world (whatever was meant by that term) works. Central to how the world in the late twentieth century is theorized, however, are the European origins of thought on international relations and the predominant paradigms that have informed both academic work and political process as defined by the dominant institutions of the West. An argument dear to Enlightenment thought, which has echoed through international relations theories ever since, is based on the opposition between Hobbes's view that 'man' was naturally aggressive and Rousseau's view that the inherently pacific nature of the 'noble savage' was corrupted by society. In the Hobbesian view, war was the natural result of natural human aggression, the history of European warfare being but an inevitable expression of nature, and the soldier simply being an example of 'natural man'. For Rousseau, however, war was more a result of societal conflicts, the soldier being an example of the citizen not the noble savage. This debate and this central concern with war and its causes was to set the agenda for many years.

Unlike Hobbes's deterministic pessimism, both Rousseau's belief in a possible social contract between nations, and Kant's belief in the possibility of a global community of republics stressed the importance of the type of political regime, favouring republics and criticizing princely despotism as a major cause of war. Thus, if there was no hope of a return to the edenic state of the noble savage, there was at least the possibility of curtailing the actions of the savage noble. These views laid the foundation for the optimism of eighteenth- and nineteenth-century liberalism. As Bentham was to argue in his 1789 *Plan for Universal and Perpetual Peace*, for example, the essential question in international relations was how different types of political regimes contributed to war or peace. Bentham attributed war to the passions, ambitions and desire for power of autocratic leaders. While some current analysts of international relations have suggested that the pessimistic concerns with 'power politics' of the 'traditionalists' and the more optimistic interventionalist policies of the 'liberals' should be separated,

Holsti (1985) suggests that they can be grouped together as the traditionalist or 'realist'[4] paradigm, which has been – and by and large still is – the predominant way of viewing the world.

Holsti (1985) characterizes this dominant view as taking war, peace and security as the foremost concerns, viewing the principal actors to be nation-states, and conceiving of the globe as a society of competing nations. This view has held sway in both the academic domain and the world political scene: government policy-makers, military strategists, diplomats, and so on, have taken the world to be comprised of antagonistic nation-states and their principal concern to be one of strategic defence. The study of international relations becomes an interest in how 'international power politics' work, in how nations move from a state of war to one of peace and back again. Morgenthau, for example, argues that 'as long as the world is politically organized into nations, the national interest is indeed the last word in world politics' (1952, p. 48). This, he argues, does not mean that war is therefore inevitable, but rather that 'it assumes continuous conflict and threat of war, to be minimized through the continuous adjustment of conflicting interests by diplomatic action' (p. 53).

The traditional and the modern

Closely associated with this view of the world is a range of assumptions about 'development' and 'modernization'. These issues emerged particularly after the Second World War, when, in the optimistic aftermath of the massive devastation and loss of life of the war, and with many former European colonies demanding independence, the question of how to help other nations to 'develop' came to the fore. Although we can identify certain differences in the approaches to this question, the principal one within the traditionalist/realist paradigm – or what Preston (1986) labels the 'bourgeois–liberal theories' – is 'modernization theory'. This view is essentially evolutionist, suggesting that modernization is a linear path of upward progress, moving from one side of a series of dichotomous constructs – traditional, undeveloped, agricultural, rural – to the other – modern, developed, industrial, urban. These distinctions in turn are used to explain the ultimate opposition between traditional/undeveloped and modern/

developed societies. These dichotomies could be resolved, these gaps could be closed, it was argued, through a process of 'modernization'.

Works such as Rostow's (1960) *The Stages of Economic Growth*, which outlined the stages of development through which nations passed, became highly influential since, as Preston (1986) suggests, it corresponded to establishment thinking on development by detailing a theory that explained the state of the developed countries and showed how the development of the under-developed countries could be carefully and rationally planned for. Furthermore, with its clearly stated anti-Marxist agenda (the subtitle is *A Non-Communist Manifesto*), it plainly illustrated how development needed to follow the Western model of capitalism. It is important to note that development theory grew up during the Cold War era (see Gendzier, 1985); 'aid' was very much part of a policy to secure political allies, either in the name of 'socialism' or of the 'free world'. Preston (1986, p. 174) characterizes moderniza-tion theory as 'offering an elaborated authoritative interventionist ideology of development, where the idea of development . . . rests upon a concern for economic growth'. While current views have shifted somewhat from the Keynesian interventionist policies of the 1960s to the *laissez-faire* marketplace orientations of monetarism, this central paradigm that bifurcates the world into developed and undeveloped and prescribes an economic package for moderniza-tion has stayed much the same in many circles (see, for example, Schultz, 1980).

Significant in the 'aid' that was sent to the 'undeveloped' countries were large educational programmes. Modernization theory, and particularly that aspect of it known as 'human capital theory', stressed the importance of investment in the 'improve-ment' of the workforce through education. With the passing of the classical, cyclical view of progress (both the multicyclical Greek view and the unicyclical Augustinian view), the Enlightenment era came to develop a view of constant upward progress, and to articulate a faith in education as a very important means of helping individuals and society along that upward path. By the nineteenth century, a close conjunction had started to emerge between a faith in unbounded upward human progress, industrial and technologi-cal advances, and formal, institutionalized education. It made good sense, then, that an essential part of development aid was the provision of formal education. Modernization theorists argued for the importance of education not only in training a workforce (the human capital side of the argument) but also in inculcating 'modern' beliefs, values, and behaviours in the population, a process considered by some essential for modernization. Thus, Inkeles and Smith (1974) argue that 'mounting evidence suggests that it is impossible for a state to move into the twentieth century if its people continue to live in an earlier era' (p. 3). This process, they argue, can be achieved through education.

Communication was also seen to play an important role in this process. Two of the major changes that occurred after the Second World War were, first, a massive increase in the technological means for mass communication in the industrialized countries, and, second, a rapidly increasing flow of information from the industrialized countries to the Third World. The predominant view of communication and its connection to development saw an important contribution of the mass media to the promotion of development and modernization. This view, which Meyer (1988) terms the 'conservative' and Boyd-Barrett (1982) the 'missionary', claimed that mass media could break down the 'traditional' values that were taken to be inimical to the process of modernization. Thus, Lerner's (1958) highly influential study suggested a causal link between media exposure and modernization, identifying the development of 'empathy' as the crucial element in this process. 'Empathy', Lerner (1958) argued, 'endows a person with the capacity to imagine himself as the proprietor of a bigger grocery store in a city, to wear nice clothes and live in a nice house, to be interested in "what is going on in the world" and to "get out of his hole" ' (p. 234). Other arguments suggested that mass media could play an important role in the development of national identity, in the dissemination of technical skills, or as a means to enhance educational expansion.

In the postwar years, then, a reasonably coherent paradigm concerning development, education, and communication grew up, based on the traditionalist view of the world as a society of antagonistic nation states. Whatever label we choose to give this view – traditional, realist, bourgeois-liberal, conservative, missionary – it appears to share certain common beliefs about the world. It divides the world into developed and undeveloped nations and further characterizes this distinction as one between modern and traditional. This gap can be breached through modernization, a process that involves the rapid industrialization of the country.

This, in turn, can be greatly helped by investment in the education of the workforce and inculcation of modern values through education and mass media. Although this view has been the predominant one, it has certainly also been challenged in certain circles, and it is with such criticisms that the next section deals. A note of caution is due here, however, for moving from one paradigm to another should not be taken to mean that these reassessments present some linear path of progress themselves, or that one view has replaced the other. Rather, different views coexist and, further, enjoy different status in different domains. Thus, while some academic discussion and much Third World political thinking has come to discredit the predominant model, it still maintains a strong influence over much popular and political culture in the First World.

DEPENDENCY AND IMPERIALISM

Doubts about the dominant model of the world and its concomitant views of development, education and international communications started to emerge for a number of reasons. The United States, the dominant nation both in the participation in development programmes and in the theorizing about international relations and development, entered a period of turmoil in the 1960s and early 1970s, a crisis in consciousness emerging in the civil rights movements within the country and as a result of the calamitous foreign engagements from the Bay of Pigs to the Vietnam War. These upheavals led to a considerable re-evaluation of, amongst other things, the intellectual paradigms that informed much academic work, especially since many of these had been clearly formed during the Cold War era. A further problem in the academic world was the revelation of the complicity between academics and various CIA operations (see, for example, Gendzier, 1985). Thus the stance of 'objectivity' claimed by social scientists came to be regarded with much greater suspicion. Most important, however, was the clear evidence that the development policies were not working. Third World nations were not developing as planned and there was in fact growing evidence that conditions in those countries were worsening. Indeed it became evident that most supposed development aid was based on the economic and political interests of the donor country rather than the recipient. The strongest criticisms of these policies came, not surprisingly, from Third World countries themselves: 'The Third World itself began to experience a measure of disenchantment, when it discovered that development aid was not really aid, but a business investment camouflaged to look like development aid' (Gibbons, 1985, p. 40).

Economic dependency

Out of these Third World criticisms and the shifting views of Western academics emerged a new critical paradigm based far more on Marxist than on liberal analyses of the world. The principal concerns were with the problems of modernization, exploitation and inequality, examined through an analysis of the relationship between capital and labour. But, while Marx and Lenin had been essentially optimistic about the consequences of the spread of capitalism (as an inevitable stage in the progress towards communism), the neo-Marxist paradigm was essentially pessimistic. In Holsti's (1985) terms, the view of the world changed from one of competing nation-states to one of a world capitalist system. The publication of Paul Baran's (1957) book, *The Political Economy of Growth*, was followed by a number of other works, especially from writers such as Raoul Prebisch and André Gunder Frank. This work started to articulate the concept of *dependency*, the underlying assumption being that within a global capitalist system, development and underdevelopment are inversely related within and between societies. Thus dependency refers to the causal relationship between the development of the central/metropolitan areas and the concomitant underdevelopment of the peripheral/ satellite areas. Frank (1966) argued that the expansion of the capitalist system over the past centuries had effectively reached even the apparently most isolated sectors of the underdeveloped world. Within this world-embracing metropolis/satellite structure, the metropoles tend to develop and the satellites to underdevelop, this relationship being stronger in proportion to the closeness of the ties between metropolis and satellite. Galtung's (1971) structural theory of imperialism similarly suggested that economic, political, military, communication and cultural imperialism were all results of the unequal relationship between *Centre* and *Periphery*.

While some of this work continued to focus only on economic relations, more broadly critical work led to a rethinking of the notion of modernization. It came to be seen that the bifurcation between traditional and modern was highly problematic, an ethnocentric and monoparadigmatic understanding of change. And clearly, if the notion 'modern' was based on a very particular understanding of the world, the other half of this equation, 'traditional', was equally problematic, a residual category defined principally in negative terms, that is, defined by how it deviated from the normative and unquestioned 'given', 'modern'. The modern/traditional dichotomy also denied history to Third World nations: only the developed nations had progressed from some assumed primordial state to the present. It also implied that 'traditional' societies were static and homogeneous and that the 'traditional' and the 'modern' were mutually exclusive, the only way of effecting change being through the replacement of the one by the other. A critical investigation of the concepts 'modern' and 'traditional' revealed them not only to be conceptually weak but also empirically unsound: on the one hand, various 'modern' traits appeared to be quite harmful in many contexts, and on the other, so-called traditional societies such as Japan were clearly developing without necessarily shedding their traditions.

In terms of development theory, this more critical view of the world suggested that the barriers to development were not so much internal (traditional barriers to be overcome) but, rather, external (derived from the structural characteristics of the global capitalist system). Change, then, was no longer seen to be accounted for by the neo-evolutionary theories of the liberals but was to a large extent exogenous, a result of the world capitalist system. This critical stance also questioned the ethnocentricity of the traditional model of modernity and pointed to how this notion of modernity was linked to the West's vested interests in the global expansion of capitalism. The understanding of politics changed from the conservative and liberal emphasis on the maintenance of order to a more radical view of democracy. The dichotomous analytic procedure based on the traditional/modern distinction was replaced by a form of historical materialism based on political economic analysis of the global system. Theories of economic growth and either economic interventionism or *laissez-faire* monetarism were discarded in favour of a critical analysis of capitalism. Finally, the focus shifted from an analysis of political élites as the primary agents of change to a view of change determined by class dynamics within the system of Centre–Periphery relations (Preston, 1986).

Education and dependency

Once these fundamental questions were raised about notions of development and modernization, the role of education in this process also came under scrutiny. The assumed causal link between education and development was rejected not because the possible benefits of education itself were doubted but because a critical analysis of the role of education in capitalist societies suggested that it was a crucial factor in reproducing social and cultural inequalities. One cannot, it was argued, look at the link between development and education without looking at the role of education within the world capitalist system. In a similar vein to the reproduction theories of Bowles and Gintis (1976) and Bourdieu (1973), which argued that education reproduced the social and cultural inequalities of societies, it was maintained that educational systems perpetuated inequalities in and between countries. Thus, Carnoy (1974), for example, argued that many education systems in Third World countries are forms of neo-imperialism and neocolonialism, continuing to serve the interests of the former colonizers and Central nations.

Altbach (1981), relating Galtung's (1971) theory of structural imperialism to universities, argues that the current intellectual Centres have a massive influence over the international academic system, providing educational models, publishing academic books and journals, setting the research agenda, and so on. The peripheral universities, while often playing extremely important roles in their own countries as central institutions, are often, according to Altbach (1981, p. 602), little more than 'distributors of knowledge' from the centre. He highlights five particular aspects of this process: first, the models of research and the forms of education are often inappropriate to the local conditions; second, the common use of Western languages (especially English) has particular implications since 'universities are automatically cut off from the majority of the population' (p. 608); third, these universities become consumers not producers of knowledge; fourth, the means of communication – journals, books, etc. – are in the hands of the industrial nations; and finally, many well-trained people leave the peripheral nations in what is commonly termed the 'brain drain'.

Mazrui (1975b) argues that the universities are analogues to multinational corporations. The African university, created by Europeans to serve European interests, continues to do so. Masemann (1986, p. 18) has also shown how the evolutionary model of development permeates much educational thinking, replicating the traditional/modern dichotomy with its simple assumptions that education passes from 'rote' to 'structural' to 'open'. Looking at the overall implications of Western educational expansion, Masemann (1986, p. 22) suggests that 'it is not difficult to view the diffusion of Western education internationally as part of a massive deskilling process of Third World populations in terms of indigenous systems of language, symbols, art, folklore, music, and knowledge itself'.

Communication and dependency

If the critical paradigm that emerged around dependency theory had a major effect on thinking about development and education issues, so too did it have a major effect in the domain of communication studies. In 1975, the demands for economic decolonization by Third World countries led to a demand from the UN for a 'New International Economic Order' (NIEO). The Brandt Commission that was set up to investigate these demands published its influential report, *North–South: A Program for Survival* in 1980. In that same year, there also appeared another report, prepared by the MacBride Commission, *Many Voices, One World*. This report was in response to the demand made to UNESCO by the non-aligned countries for a 'New International Information Order' (NIIO) (later, the 'New World Information and Communication Order': NWICO). This report focused on a number of issues in the global communication system, including Third World dependence on industrialized countries for nearly all their communications equipment, technology, skills and hardware; their inscription into a world system dominated by multinational corporations whose vast communication networks had no other goal than securing increased financial profit; the reduction of information from a basic right to a commodity; the overwhelming imbalance in the flow of news, television programmes, magazines, books, and so on; the biased portrayal of the Third World in the international media; and the impending dangers that this situation would further deteriorate with the growth of computer data banks and networks and new satellite technology (see Traber, 1985). These problems were seen as posing serious threats to indigenous cultures and to development.

Despite the fact that it was this 'politicizing' of communication and information that led the United States, closely followed by the UK, to withdraw their support from UNESCO (still disingenuously trying to proclaim the rights of all people in the world to 'freedom of information'),[5] Meyer (1988) is undoubtedly correct in classifying the MacBride Report as more within a 'reformist', or what Boyd-Barrett (1982) calls a 'pluralist', rather than a neo-Marxist orientation. Thus, while questioning the ethnocentricity of the modernization models, and trying to relate mass media to different models of development, this report nevertheless tends to see such issues in isolation rather than relating them to a broader framework of dependency. Indeed, Galtung (1985, p. 16) has suggested that, rather than *One World, Many Voices*, a more appropriate title might have been *One Voice, Many Worlds*. To feel the real significance of this struggle over world communication, it is worth quoting Gibbons (1985) at some length:

> The Third World sees that a broad attack must be made against the supports of the world system: Information and the channels through which it passes, is a target for assault: radio, television and film, the channels of communication, which daily attack their living space; the news agencies, which they hold accountable for interpreting news about them with little sympathy or understanding; the advertising agencies, whose messages leave them vulnerable to foreign influences and distant reality; cheap books and magazines, which occasionally expose them to ridicule; above all, the transnational corporations with their infinite resources of sophisticated communication systems from data banks, computers to satellites supported by governments.
>
> (1985, pp. 49–50)

From a more neo-Marxist, structuralist perspective, Galtung

(1980; 1985) argues that there is a causative link between communication imperialism and cultural imperialism. Drawing on his broader theory of structural imperialism, he argues that with the massively unequal flow of information from the Centre to the Periphery, the Centre comes to define what is considered newsworthy, which in turn starts to erode the cultural identity, national sovereignty, and political independence of developing states. Schiller's (e.g. 1985) main concern is with the effect of transnational corporations on international media. 'Transnational corporations (TNCs)', he argues (1985, p. 19), 'today are the dominant elements in the international economic order. And national media systems increasingly are being enlisted to provide the infrastructure for disseminating TNC economic and ideological philosophy.' This can have a devastating effect on a society, since the mass of Western programming and advertising results in the 'continuous construction of an economic order and value system in which the acquisition of consumer goods and services, to the near total disregard of the needs of the social and public sphere, is repeatedly emphasized with the most skilled communication techniques ever devised' (p. 20).

The studies of world information systems fall, roughly speaking, into two broad categories: those concerned with the extent and direction of the flow of information, and those concerned with the content and images of that flow. Within the first category, a major focus of attention has been on the flow of international news. Mowlana (1986) gives the following figures for the daily output of the 'big four' press agencies: of a total of 32,850,000 words per day, Associated Press (AP) produces 17,000,000; United Press International (UPI) 11,000,000; Agence France Presse (AFP) 3,350,000; and Reuters 1,500,000. In contrast, the combined German, Italian, Spanish, Yugoslavian and Inter-Press Service output is about 1,090,000 words per day. Of significance, too, is not only the quantity of output but the spheres of influence: Reuters has a very powerful influence throughout the Commonwealth, for example. Associated Press serves 1,320 newspapers, 3,400 broadcasters in the United States and 1,000 private subscribers; UPI serves 7,079 newspapers, 2,246 clients outside the Unites States and thirty-six national news agencies; AFP serves 12,000 newspapers and sixty-nine national agencies; and Reuters serves 6,500 newspapers (in 147 different countries) and 400 radio and TV stations (Smith, 1980, p. 108). With these few agencies dominating the world news market, many Third World countries obtain at least 70 per cent of their news through these agencies, and may indeed, as Galtung (1985) points out, have to rely on them for news of their neighbours. Similar figures can be found to show the massive imbalances in exports of television programmes (with the USA dominating the market), films (figures for 1974 show that 90 per cent of all films shown in Thailand, for example, were American [Smith, 1980, p. 43]), books (80 per cent of all books are published in the industrialized nations), magazines, radio, and so on. According to *Fortune* magazine (31 December 1990), American movies, music, television programming and home video produce a trade surplus of about US $8 billion a year, a figure second only to the aerospace industry. Seventy per cent of the U.S. $20 billion-a-year music business comes from outside the United States. Meanwhile, with the development of direct satellite broadcasting, the predominance of the Western media has become even more enhanced. The Atlanta-based Cable News Network (CNN) is now broadcasting directly into more and more homes around the world.[6]

The studies of the content (rather than the quantity and direction) of the international information flow have also provided real reasons for concern (Galtung, 1985; Gibbons, 1985; Mowlana, 1986; Smith, 1980). Looking particularly at international news, criticisms have focused on the Western-centric nature of the interests and reporting; the constant presentation of the Third World in negative terms through the reporting only of disasters and the constant emphasis on poverty, political instability and so on; the shallow and oversimplified nature of news reports, with an emphasis only on events rather than on the background and causes (Gibbons also mentions here the system of rotation of foreign correspondents, so that in the name of mythical 'objectivity', they do not lose their 'perspective'); and the concentration on political élites and individuals at the expense of more complex analysis of society and change. Meyer (1988) also points out the fundamental schism between the ideological bases of news: the Western industrial emphasis on up-to-the-minute information that is short, 'factual', and 'objective', as opposed to many Third World emphases on news as 'social good', an orientation that sees news as a positive element in the portrayal of development. The images carried by news programmes, films, advertising, and so on, concentrate on Third World poverty, disease, despotism and depravity and represent the industrial nations as white, wealthy and middle class. Gallagher (1985) has also pointed out the gendered nature of these representations: 'The entire structure, organization, and output of the communication and information industries reflect, feed, and perpetuate a worldview in which women and women's interests are subordinate' (1985, p. 37).

This more critical approach to global relations, then, raises deep concerns about development, dependency, education and communication. The dominant paradigm discussed in the last section, although divided by some writers into conservative/traditional and liberal/pluralist orientations, can by and large be considered as one (see Holsti, 1985; Preston, 1986), characterized by its conception of the world as made up of competing nation-states and its centring of war, peace and security as the primary concerns. Along with this view there has generally been a set of commonly held assumptions about development, communication and education. Dividing the world into developed and under-developed/developing countries, it has tended to prescribe a set of ameliorative procedures based on the notion of states competing equally in a global economy (economic policies have ranged from Keynesian interventionism to *laissez-faire* monetarism) and on the perception that to bring about such development, populations need to be changed from their traditional to more modern ways of life. This orientation has also implied a very particular understanding of culture and knowledge (see next section).

The more critical paradigm outlined in this section emerged in response to a number of problems with the predominant paradigm, whether in its views on modernity and development, which took the developed West as an unquestioned central norm, or in its economic and political policies, which ultimately could be seen to be based far more on self-interest than any concern with the countries involved (the net flow of wealth remains from the Third to the First World). Starting with a view of the world as comprising one large economic system, it stressed the ways in which parts of the world were interlocked in relationships of dependency. From this standpoint, different analyses of communication and education started to emerge which suggested that while economic and material resources were continually being drawn from Third World countries, these countries had also become dependent in terms of education and communication, with a massive flow of information, culture and knowledge from the

First to the Third World. Thus, barriers to development came to be seen not as nation-bound issues of internal modernization but as linked to a global capitalist system, in which culture, knowledge, communication and education were all ultimately bound up with First World capitalist exploitation of the Third World. Once again, this view has very particular implications for an understanding of culture and knowledge.[7]

CULTURE, DISCOURSE, DIFFERENCE AND DISJUNCTURE

According to Holsti (1985), a third view of the world is espoused by those working on world order models, especially the World Order Models Project (WOMP) based in Delhi and New York. Using his framework of distinguishing features – problematics, actors and worldviews – Holsti suggests that the WOMP paradigm is significantly different from the traditional and neo-Marxist. First, the problematic is expanded both from questions of war, peace and security, and from questions of the global political economy, to include human rights, ecological balance, income inequality, food distribution and malnutrition, overpopulation, energy scarcity, resource exploitation, and so on. Second, the principal actors are taken to be a wide diversity of transnational organizations, including multinational corporations, governmental organizations, institutions such as the World Bank and the UN, international federations, and so on. Finally, the view of the globe is one of complex interdependence, in which tourism, mail flows, international academic, business, and religious conferences, international sports events, and so forth all play a role. Whether this indeed represents a new paradigm remains a moot point – Blasius (1984) suggests that WOMP work can be seen as a radical discourse within a liberal ideology – but to the extent that these thinkers are raising a range of previously disregarded issues and especially to the extent that they have started to deal with a more complex understanding of the world, with culture and knowledge starting to play a more central role, their work remains significant. Certainly, to the extent that they allow us to go beyond the reductionism of international relations to competing nation-states or socioeconomic relations, they indicate some new directions for pursuit.

A major limitation of the critical work discussed in the last section is its reduction of international relations to a form of economic determinism. The globe is described within a structuralist framework in which people's lives are determined by economic relations. While this view has crucially focused attention on the deep-seated inequalities in the world, it does not provide sufficient space for considering how people live their lives within and against structures of global inequality. Culture and knowledge cannot be treated as if they are items of international export like coffee or coal; rather, they need to be considered as part of people's lived experiences and understandings of their lives. Thus, we need to bring to the fore essential questions about how the construction of meanings around our lives occurs within complex global relations. Bearing in mind the central focus on language in this book, it is of great importance to raise questions about how people's representations of themselves can and do occur within a global context.

Walker (1984) argues that the study of world order is part of a 'pervasive metatheoretical contradiction', namely that 'while grasping at a global or universal phenomenon, it does so almost entirely with one culturally and intellectually circumscribed perspective' (p. 182). He is here taking issue with the limitations of Western intellectual thought and especially with respect to its frequent assumptions to be able to universalize its conclusions. Specifically, Walker draws attention to the positivist basis of social scientific thought. Thus, while we may discuss at length the differences between the traditional and the neo-Marxist orientations, it is nevertheless inescapable that the move from the state-centric to the dependency model has remained firmly ensconced within a social scientific orientation. Essentially, Walker (1984, p. 191) argues, irrespective of which paradigm informs the work, there is a 'radical reduction of all human action to the same common denominators required by a positivist conception of knowledge'.

Gibbons (1985) suggests that a problem with both traditional and critical paradigms is that they treat people in the Third World as if they were a *tabula rasa*. In the traditional view, development was a question of inscribing modernization on to these blank slates; education and mass communication could supposedly help replace the useless 'traditions' of a society with the valuable qualities of modernity. A neo-Marxist perspective, however, is often little better, suggesting on the one hand that capitalist values were being ingrained into these malleable Third World minds through education and the media and that, on the other hand, critical education and different media could correct such 'false consciousness'. While the global spread of capitalism, the dominance of world communications by Western media, and the massive influence of the Western institutions in academic circles are fundamentally important issues, we cannot understand their implications unless we also open up a space to understand how these are interpreted, how people actively deal with and interpret their lives. Thus we need to be cautious about talking of universities as only 'distributors of knowledge' lest we thereby cast students around the world as nothing but passive receptors of knowledge. Or, as Boyd-Barrett (1982, p. 193) suggests with respect to international communication, 'much more attention needs to be given to the processes by which individuals and groups interpret, translate and transform their experiences of foreign culture to relate to more familiar experiences'.

This is where I feel there is a major shortcoming in Robert Phillipson's (1986; 1992) extensive documenting of 'English linguistic imperialism'.[8] He is concerned with the threat to people's linguistic human rights by the linguistic imperialism of the English language. The key concept of 'linguicism' here refers to 'ideologies and structures where language is the means for effecting or maintaining an unequal allocation of power and resources' (1992, p. 55). While his work on the institutions that promote this linguistic imperialism is of great importance, and while he has performed a valuable service by putting the phrase 'linguistic imperialism' into play in ELT circles, his adherence to a version of structural imperialism leaves us at a problematic impasse. The unfortunate conjunction between structuralism and neo-Marxism in world order theory has tended to reduce human relations to a reflection of the political economy, assuming that culture, language or knowledge can be handled like any other commodity. Thus, discussions of culture from this viewpoint (e.g. Wallerstein, 1990) tend to reduce it to an ideological reflex of the global economy. Similarly, Phillipson amply demonstrates how and why various governments and organizations have promoted the spread of English but rarely explores what the effects of that promotion may be apart from maintaining global capitalism. And when he does, it tends to be in terms of deterministic impositions: 'What is at stake when English spreads is not merely the substitution or displacement of one language by another but the imposition of new "mental structures" through English' (p. 166). English linguistic imperialism, in conjunction with other forms of imperialism, remains the end point of analysis and leaves little space for consideration of how English is used in diverse contexts or how it is appropriated and used in opposition to those that promote its spread.

Knowledge and modernity

In looking for a way to go beyond a reductive theory of imperialism, then, it is important to find ways of thinking about language, culture and knowledge that allow for broader possibilities of difference, challenge and diversity. Along with the need to look specifically at how resistance and appropriation may occur (see particularly Chapter 8), therefore, there seem to be two crucial issues that need further examination. First, we need to go beyond a positivistic and universalizing form of knowledge. This can be pursued through critiques of knowledge and modernity both from within the West and from outside. Second, there is the need to understand culture in a way that avoids reducing it to a high/low dichotomy, to essentialized versions of national and ethnic cultures or to superstructural reflections of infrastructural realities, and instead looks at culture in terms of how people make sense of their lives and thus how human agency operates within global structures of inequality.

A useful place to start here is by looking at critiques of modernity and positivist knowledge, at anti-foundationalist or anti-essentialist critiques of modernity that go to the very core of Western theorizing and its effects. Some of this – the critique from within – may be subsumed under the rubric of postmodernism, if by postmodernism we mean not so much parody or a play of images on images (as it is often understood) but rather postmodernism as 'a task of critical remembrance' that seeks to reread and rewrite modernity (Kearney, 1988, p. 26). As Rust (1991) suggests, 'The most popular competing theoretical orientations to modernization, such as dependency theory and world-systems analysis, are themselves, in fact, committed to the basic language and assumptions of the modern age, and postmodernism poses as much a challenge to these theories as it does to modernization theory itself' (p. 613). Crucial here is the questioning of the metanarratives of modernity, those claims to universal and objective understanding of the world. More particularly, this questioning puts under scrutiny the belief in a transcendent form of rationality (the rational and the logical transcend culture and language), the belief in history as a linear upward path (the modern comes after the premodern and is intrinsically better), and the belief that it is possible to gain objective knowledge of the world (the knowing subject stands distinct from the world of objects).

If part of this critique has come from the inside, as it were, a kind of epistemological implosion, other parts have come from different degrees of 'outsiders', from those who have been marginalized, excluded or have been the objects themselves of this knowledge. One part of this challenge has come from a wide diversity of feminist thinkers. If a postmodernist challenge to modernity has posed general questions about rationality, progress and objectivity, a great deal of feminist thinking has located that challenge in the specific struggles around gendered representations of the world.[9] Meanwhile, writers such as Ashis Nandy (e.g. 1983), Rajni Kothari (e.g. 1987), and Ali Mazrui (e.g. 1986), amongst many others, have pointed out the limitations and dangers of monoparadigmatic Western thought. Kothari (1981; 1987) points to the myths and confusions inherent in the nexus of scientific, modernist, progressivist thinking. Human progress, Kothari suggests, has been conflated with development, development with modernization, and modernization with Westernization. Science has been conflated with technology. Together with the myth of value neutrality, the splitting of religion and morality from scientific questions, and the ever-increasing autonomy and primacy of technology, these conflations have led to policies and practices that ultimately justify ecocide and ethnocide. Once Western science came to be used as a secular justification of Western dominance, other forms of Western thought also came to be seen as superior, leading to a massive process of cultural and epistemological colonization, privileging one form of culture or knowledge over others. 'Modern science', argues Kothari (1987), 'in delegitimizing the notion of plurality of paths of truth, threatens to overwhelm mankind with an homogenizing monoculture of the mind' (p. 284).

It is on the universalizing tendencies of much of the modernist project that many of these criticisms focus. In modernism, Richard (1987) identifies a three-fold wish for unity through rationalization, belief in progress as a universalist project, and an assumption of the objective consciousness of an absolute meta-subject:

> This threefold foundation of modernity's universalism suffices to show the link to the totalizing tendency of a hegemonic culture bent on producing and reproducing a consensus around the models of truth and consumption that it proposes. With regard to its economic programme and its cultural organization, this concept of modernity represents an effort to synthesize its progressive and emancipatory ideals into a globalizing integrative vision of the individual's place in history and society. It rests on the assumption that there exists a legitimate centre – a unique and superior position from which to establish control and determine hierarchies.
>
> (p. 6)

Nandy (1983) shows how these hierarchies are established within the modern world around a set of polarities such as the modern and the primitive, the secular and the nonsecular, the scientific and the unscientific, the expert and the lay, the normal and the abnormal, the developed and the underdeveloped, the vanguard and the led, the liberated and the savable. It is by countering these dichotomous constructions, the foundations of modernity's universalism, that a counter-politics of difference can be established. 'The politics of diversity and plurality', Kothari (1987, pp. 279–80) argues, 'by rendering the mainstream monolith irrelevant, becomes the foundation of an alternative post-modern era of action and knowledge'.[10]

Another aspect to this rethinking of knowledge in the world is to understand knowledge as discourse. Key here is Said's (1978) significant work on Orientalism, which he describes as:

> a Western style for dominating, restructuring, and having authority over the Orient. . . . [W]ithout examining Orientalism as a discourse, one cannot possibly understand the enormously systematic discipline by which European culture was able to manage – and even produce – the Orient politically, sociologically, militarily, ideologically, scientifically, and imaginatively during the post-Enlightenment period. Moreover, so authoritative a position did Orientalism have that I believe no one writing, thinking, or acting on the Orient could do so without taking

into account the limitations on thought and action imposed by
Orientalism. . . . This is not to say that Orientalism unilaterally
determines what can be said about the Orient, but that it is the whole
network of interests inevitably brought to bear on (and therefore always
involved in) any occasion when that particular entity 'the Orient' is in
question.

(p. 3)

The first important point that Said's genealogy of Orientalism
raises is that domination and authority are not just questions of
social, economic or physical control but rather are also effected
through discourse (power and knowledge). Discourse, it should be
noted, does not imply some necessarily false position or some
infrastructural base (socioeconomic relations) that determines how
people think and act. The second important point is that in order
to avoid reinscribing people within a new academic discourse, it is
crucial to seek to avoid essentializing representations of the 'Other'
(The Arabs, The Chinese, and so on) and for the 'Other' to find
ways of achieving representation outside these discourses. A
central question for this book concerns how such discourses
restrict and produce certain representations and thus how people
are represented and can represent themselves through English.

The effects of such global discourses have also been explored by
Escobar (1985; see also DuBois, 1991), though in this case with
respect specifically to development. Echoing Said, he suggests that

Without examining development as discourse we cannot understand
the systematic ways in which the Western developed countries have
been able to manage and control and, in many ways, even create the
Third World politically, economically, sociologically and culturally; and
that, although underdevelopment is a very real historical formation, it
has given rise to a series of practices (promoted by the discourses of the
West) which constitute one of the most powerful mechanisms for
insuring domination over the Third World today.

(1985, p. 384)

Escobar's work, then, seeks to investigate the formation of this
discourse of development, how development is 'put into discourse'. The discourse of development, Escobar (1985, p. 388)
argues, 'has been successful to the extent that it has been able to
penetrate, integrate, manage and control countries and populations
in increasingly detailed and encompassing ways'. Importantly, for

Escobar, in order to enable countries to follow different paths of development, it is essential that the discourse be dismantled, and that strategies of resistance and counter-discourse be articulated. This suggests, then, an alternative strategic response to the global spread of Western knowledge. Rather than viewing this spread as an export of knowledge and culture within the global economy and thus assuming that the central strategy of opposition must be in terms of opposing the global capitalist system, this view suggests that it is the discourses themselves, whose power is related to but not determined by economic forces, that exert domination over people. Opposition, therefore, needs to be carried out on the level of 'discursive intervention' (see Chapter 9).

Culture and difference

What all these criticisms of Western knowledge and modernity point to is the need, on the one hand, to understand the extreme power and importance of these forms of knowledge and, on the other, to find ways of opposing them. It is not enough merely to show how the First World is constantly making the Third World economically dependent, for it is not only in the economic domain that these relationships occur. But is equally insufficient to then build a model of imperialism and to suggest that culture and knowledge are simply thrust upon people as reflexes of international trade. Rather, it is essential to see how these discourses of development, modernity, education and so on operate and to find ways in which they can be dismantled or countered. On the one hand, then, postmodern critiques of modernist universals and an understanding of the central role that discourse plays in the world form part of this rethinking of global relations. On the other hand, there is a need to understand culture as an active process by which people make sense of their lives. Just as it is important to understand the power of knowledge in the world, so it is equally important to understand the role of culture. Ngũgĩ (1985, p. 118) argues for the importance of understanding international relations in terms of culture:

Colonialism imposed its control of the social production of wealth through military conquest and subsequent political dictatorship. But its most important area of domination was the mental universe of the colonized, the control through culture, of how people perceived themselves and their relationship to the world. Economics and political control can never be complete or effective without mental control. To control a people's culture is to control its tools of self-definition in relationship to others. For colonialism this involved two aspects of the same process: the destruction, or the deliberate undervaluing of a people's culture, its art, dances, religions, history, geography, education, orature and literature; and the domination of a people's language by that of the colonizing nation.

Culture is a difficult concept, however, and indeed Williams (1976) has suggested that it is one of the two or three most complicated words in the English language. We may identify a number of different meanings (see Walker, 1984; Williams, 1976; Worsley, 1985): culture as a set of superior values, especially embodied in works of art and limited to a small élite; culture as a whole way of life, the informing spirit of a people; culture as a set of values imposed on the majority by those in power; and culture as the way in which different people make sense of their lives.

The first sense of culture, as a set of higher aesthetic principles embodied in works of art, informed much of the traditionalist thinking. For some realist/traditionalists, this led to a dismissal of the relevance of culture to world relations. Morgenthau (1973, p. 513), for example, argues that 'the problem of world community is a moral and political and not an intellectual and aesthetic one'. For him, institutions such as UNESCO have little relevance since the real issues for the world are constituted by power politics, and there is little or no connection between the cultural and the political. The Germans, for example, while 'steeped in classical culture' nevertheless 'throughout most of their history have been nationalistic and warlike' (1973, p. 510). Ultimately, the question of culture can be reduced to questions such as whether 'Russians would take to Mark Twain as Americans would take to Gogol' (1973, p. 513). But many other thinkers within this paradigm maintained a faith in the importance of education in 'high' culture. This unitary sense of culture that demands instruction in a prescribed canon of cultural knowledge is still powerful today; indeed it has been regaining ground under the agenda of the New Right in the United States and the UK. Thus, the views of Bloom (1987) and Hirsch (1987), amongst others, with their emphasis on 'The Great Books' or 'cultural literacy' have once again stimulated calls for a national curriculum. Great Britain is currently embroiled in a major battle over the imposition of just such a national curriculum and just such a view of culture. It is this view of culture that has certainly been dominant throughout most colonial and neocolonial education programmes and has led to attempts to establish what amounts virtually to a parallel 'international curriculum'. It is at the heart of many of the tenets of modernization theory, especially to the extent that it is dismissive of all other forms of culture, which are either taken to be the 'low' culture of working people within the industrialized nations or the 'primitive' culture (superstitions, rituals, and so on) of non-industrialized nations.

Perhaps equally important in the thinking on international relations, however, has been the social scientific view of culture. In this view, while culture is expanded to both a plural concept (cultures) and to a much broader domain (often some sort of 'informing spirit' or underlying set of behavioural principles of a people), it tends to remain secondary to other aspects of the human world. Thus, within the classic social scientific subjective/objective divide, culture is relegated to the subjective domain and is therefore much less amenable to objective investigation, or is seen as determined by other factors, whether societal, economic or biological. As Wuthnow et al. (1984, p. 5) put it, 'in standard social scientific discussions of culture the human world is divided in two, objective social structure on the one hand, subjective thoughts and perceptions on the other, and the cultural part is defined as the most fluid, unconstrained, and least observable category of non-behavior'. This view is probably at its strongest in Marxist views of culture as a superstructural phenomenon determined by the socioeconomic 'realities' of the infrastructure. Culture in this view is closely linked to ideology and often then seen as 'false', an obfuscating set of values and beliefs imposed on people by the hegemonic class ('mass culture'). Worsley (1985, p. 60) points to the shortcomings of this view when he suggests that in looking at culture we need to avoid 'not only the assumption that the "cultural" is a *separate* sphere, but that it is causally *secondary* (merely "superstructural")'. Whether within the traditionalist view of development or within the neo-Marxist view, this social scientific reduction of culture to a secondary position in human analysis has led to a tendency to ignore the ways in which people live and understand their own lives.

There are, then, two crucial questions that emerge in an attempt to develop a critical understanding of culture. First, and this ties in very closely with my discussion of worldliness in the last chapter, how do we avoid reducing culture (or language) to a deterministic reflection of other 'realities'? And second, how can any cultural representation avoid essentializing the Other? Walker (1984, p. 209) raises these difficulties when he suggests that a 'well-intentioned attempt to take the differentiation of cultures as a serious issue in the study of world politics ends up as an imposition of distinctly Western categories on other cultures'. Thus, if we wish to elevate a concept of culture to an important position in our understanding of international relations, the question that emerges here is whether it is indeed possible to 'escape procedures of dichotomizing, restructuring, and textualizing in the making of interpretative statements about foreign cultures and traditions' (Clifford, 1988, p. 261). How can we talk of culture without reinscribing the Other into yet another essentializing category? In trying to transcend the dichotomizing and essentializing notion of culture, Clifford suggests that it may have 'served its time. Perhaps, following Foucault, it should be replaced by a vision of powerful discursive formations globally and strategically deployed' (1988, p. 274).

This point comes very close to the discussion of language in the previous chapter: perhaps language – and particularly English as an International Language – should also be replaced by a vision of powerful discursive formations globally and strategically employed. Clifford also argues (pp. 273–4), however, that if we avoid all essentializing modes of thought, we can nevertheless hold on to some conceptions of 'cultural' difference, especially when culture is seen not as organically unified or continuous, not as simply received from tradition, language or environment, but as 'negotiated, present process', as *made* in new political-cultural conditions of global rationality'. This is similar to the point I made about language, namely that we need to start not with an essentialized notion of *a* language but rather with an understanding of how language as social practice occurs within particular discourses.

It is, then, important to raise culture to a highly significant position in international relations for this allows an understanding of how people make sense of their lives. Viewing culture as subordinate, as Archer (1990) suggests, is what defines an 'industrial society theorist' with his or her limited 'industrial imagination' that conflates structure with culture, instrumental rationality with morality and technical advance with social progress (p. 117). But the different orientations towards the world that I have been discussing generally imply very different understandings of culture. First, it is important to avoid the traditionalist-conservative high–low culture divide, a view that is particularly insidious when applied to a division between advanced/developed on the one hand and traditional/primitive on the other. Such a position articulates nothing but disdain for cultural practices that diverge from those of the Centre. While a liberal pluralist view may allow for greater tolerance of difference, it again presents problems in terms of often maintaining the same high/low distinction as the conservative view or an essentialized version of culture that is too simply equated with a notion of nationality. Finally, the view of culture commonly associated with more critical views of the world is all too often reductionist and deterministic, since it relegates culture to a position both separate from and secondary to socioeconomic 'realities'.

While maintaining a politics that is highly critical of world conditions, and indeed still drawing on many of the useful critiques of global relations discussed in the previous section, we need to be careful not to reduce the world to nation-states or the world economy, but to see culture and discourse as fundamentally important in how the world is structured and how people understand their lives. Furthermore, we need to consider the complexities of Clifford's (1988) arguments for an understanding of multivocality rather than a belief that human diversity can be dealt with in terms of fixed, independent cultures. As Appadurai (1990) suggests, 'The new global cultural economy has to be seen as a complex, overlapping, disjunctive order, which cannot any longer be understood in terms of existing center-periphery models' (p. 6). Notions such as the 'East' and the 'West' start to collapse both from an understanding of how these became constructs of Orientalism and from an understanding of how, in a complex world, Japan or Hong Kong, for example, may be as much disseminators of the 'West' as is Europe.[11] Once we start to deal with the local, the incommensurable, the disjunctive, within a world in which discourses construct and regulate subjectivities, offering new and old subject positions to ever-changing populations, and once we see culture as constructed and produced within local conditions of power, then the ways in which we approach issues of global relations become very different.

This view of culture connects closely with the understanding of the worldliness of English. In the same way that language can be seen as local, social acts that move towards community only through the cultural and political relationships of daily life, so culture can be seen as local practices of meaning-making. Culture here refers to people's ways of making sense of their lives, where such sense-making is understood in terms of productive signifying practices that are organized in various conventionalized ways. Such practices occur always within particular social and historical relations of power, and thus we are able to speak of *cultural politics* as a struggle over different meanings. This highlighting of a sense of culture as productive meaning-making practices always located within relations of power (cultural politics) brings to the fore two key issues that have particular import for the spread of English, issues of representation and distribution. Looking at the spread of English and its constant interweaving with local and global discourses (see Chapter 1), difficult questions emerge about how people around the world are represented and how they can come to represent themselves in the contested terrain between their own cultural locations and the conditions of possibility that arise through English and its connected discourses. With unequal access in any society not only to material goods but also to languages and discourses, this also raises the question of distribution: who has access to the significant means to make particular meanings in English?

[handwritten annotation: Power struggle. Who determines education use.]

CRICKET, ENGLISH AND CULTURAL POLITICS

The arguments about culture and discourse have been long and complex. Before concluding, therefore, it may be useful to make a short detour. One implication of the arguments above is that not only are global relations not reducible to the political economy (or competing nation-states), but that we need to understand how power operates through a multiplicity of cultural relationships and thus how diverse cultural practices may be the site of cultural imposition, struggle, resistance and appropriation. Ashis Nandy, in his book *The Tao of Cricket* (1989), for example, suggests that 'some arguments about colonial, neo-colonial, anti-colonial and post-colonial consciousness can be made better in the language of international cricket than that of political economy' (p. ix). Indeed, the history of international cricket forms a very interesting parallel with the history of international English. First of all, it spread with the empire, and, as Searle (1990) puts it, cricket was 'an integral part of an imperialist culture that was designed to create a class of colonized Indians fashioned as English mimics and devotees of the empire' (p. 31). As part of imperialist culture, it was also a vehicle for instilling the ideologies of empire. Both Nandy and Searle dwell, for example, on the Indian aristocrats, Ranjitsinhji and Duleepsinhji, who, after following the prescribed aristocratic path of education from India to England and Oxbridge, ended up playing cricket for England. For the English, these players represented the exotic Orient, but as Nandy shows, not only was Ranjitsinhji an exoticized object of Orientalist discourse, he was also a 'shameless apologist of the raj' (p. 108).

The struggle against the institutionalized racism and colonialism of cricket, however, has mirrored the anti-racist and postcolonial struggles of more recent times. Searle (1990) suggests that the struggle of Caribbean cricketers both in the Caribbean and England 'has been a major factor in transforming cricket from a game played and controlled by white English and colonial élites, to a sport carrying the aspirations of national independence and democratic ownership' (p. 34). Other themes common to the postcolonial era emerge. Nandy (1989) looks at the change from cricket as a strange and rather mystical game played at a gentle pace over several days to its incorporation into big business and the politics of nationalism. Searle concentrates on racism in the game, and the shift from the acceptance of the exotic Indian princes in England to the struggles against racist abuse by modern players of Afro-Caribbean and South Asian origin. He suggests close parallels between the British media campaign to vilify the victorious Pakistani bowlers in the summer of 1992 and racial attacks on South Asians during the same period (Searle, 1993). Of particular significance for the issues of this chapter is the extent to which this odd British game has changed from a cultural imposition under colonialism to a major form of indigenous cultural and political expression in the post-colonial world. Searle (1990) describes Caribbean cricket as 'a cricket of resistance and assertion, which mirrored an entire people coming into their own, rejecting colonial divisions imposed upon them and bringing a new confidence and will for cultural construction' (p. 36). The long struggle against colonialism and racism by West Indian cricketers has been described in detail by C.L.R. James (1963), who points out that West Indians watching international cricket matches 'bring with them the whole past history and future hopes of the islands' (p. 225). Indeed, when Nandy points to the pressure on Indian players, who 'are expected to recover the self-esteem of 800 million Indians and undo – in both the everyday and psychoanalytic senses of the term – colonial history in the southern world' (p. 108), it is worth observing that cricket may form a far more important practice of popular cultural struggle, refusal, abrogation and appropriation than does the postcolonial literature discussed in Chapter 8.[12]

This brief discussion of the cultural politics of cricket suggests that while critical paradigms which point to the inequitable structures of global relations have far more to say than the conservative or liberal analyses of international relations, it is nevertheless essential that we understand the roles of discourse and culture in the world. Discourses, as systems of power/ knowledge relationships that increasingly limit and produce the ways in which people around the world can think about questions of democracy, education, modernization, development, religion, freedom, justice, and so on, play a key role in constructing and reconstructing international relations. Cultures, as socially and historically located ways of making meaning of our lives, always involve us in struggles over meaning. It is *this* that makes for the particularity of the worldliness of English, for English is always bound up in these cultural politics.

Work such as Phillipson's (1992) has significance for helping us understand how and why the global dominance of English has occurred. Furthermore, his attempts to define and have accepted a code of international linguistic rights may be of great benefit to many minority language speakers. His point of intervention, therefore, is principally in the domain of language planning (though he is also concerned with views on language teaching that constantly promote the further spread of English), in trying to find policies that will allow languages other than English to survive. While accepting the importance of this battle, my work operates with a different focus and starts with an understanding that, following Luke, McHoul and Mey (1990): 'While language, in the sterile sense linguistics has attached to it, can be "planned", discourse cannot' (p. 39). My point of intervention is not so much in the domain of language planning, but in the realm of teaching, in an attempt to pursue a form of critical pedagogy that could intervene between English and the discourses with which it is linked. This requires a view that on the one hand makes language more central to global relations (more worldly) but on the other allows for struggle, resistance and different appropriations of language, opening up a space for many different meaning-making practices in English.

There are a number of reasons for taking up this stance against deterministic theses that define the spread of English as a priori imperialistic, hegemonic, or linguicist. First, this is part of a general struggle against all deterministic theses; whether we are dealing with a biological or sociobiological definition of women's roles, a psychoeducational deficit theory to explain minority students' 'failure' at school, or a fundamentalist understanding of creation and morality, we are dealing with views antithetical to questions of social change. Second, it is in reaction to the totalizing tendencies of much critical theory, which, in its views on ideology, hegemony, superstructure, historical materialism, class structure, 'the masses', the oppressed, or the dominant group, leave little or no space for struggle, resistance, change, human agency or difference. Third, it is in response to the more specific location of those who have learned and benefited from English; for many who have learned English, the experience has opened up new possibilities of personal gain and communal interaction, and to dismiss their learning and using of English as a colonization is to position them within a new academic imperialism. Finally, it addresses the need to develop some other space for those of us who teach English, for while it is important to do so with a critical awareness of the implications of the global spread of English, it is also crucial that we can establish some way of teaching English that is not automatically an imperialist project.

By taking up this anti-deterministic stance I feel I can pursue in greater depth how the spread of English sits in a complex reciprocal relationship with both global and local discourses that have facilitated and been facilitated by the spread and construction of English. The position outlined at the end of the last chapter, where languages were seen as constructs in complex discursive spaces, coupled with the view of the production and reproduction of global inequalities through the operation of global discourses suggested in this chapter, allows for an understanding of the worldliness of English. The arguments in favour of local differences and cultural politics as struggles over meaning have opened up a space for a non-deterministic view of the spread of English. This issue will be taken up particularly in Chapter 8, which deals with ways in which English is taken up and appropriated for different political goals. While Chapters 6 and 7 will be explorations of the worldliness of English in the context of Singapore and Malaysia, the next three chapters (3, 4 and 5) will address the other primary concern of this book, the construction of the discourse of English as an International Language.

NOTES

1. This advertisement was shown on the Star TV network in Hong Kong many times in 1993.
2. At his plenary address at TESOL '93 Henry Widdowson raised similar concerns about the way this conference was framed.
3. I do not, of course, use the term 'Third World' comfortably or unproblematically. 'Developed' or 'developing' have been rejected because of their unwarranted assumptions about development and its direction (see later in this chapter). 'Underdeveloped' is a possibility if it is used in the active sense (i.e. certain countries have been underdeveloped by others) or in contrast to 'overdeveloped', but this term still leaves unchallenged some of the basic premises of the notion of development; to be acceptable, it would have to be taken to refer only to the economic/industrial domain. Thus, while searching for a better term, I am left with 'Third World', for which I make no claims to neutrality or suitability, but which I hope can be taken to reference all the problematic issues in world relations that I am trying to deal with.
4. This term comes from the distinction made by E.H. Carr (1946) between 'realists' and 'idealists'.
5. As Smith (1980) puts it, 'It is extremely difficult for a society to practise free flow of media and enjoy a national culture at the same time – unless it happens to be the United States of America' (p. 53).
6. It is interesting to speculate whether, since George Bush's description of the military dominance of the world by the United States as a 'New World Order', there will be, in a sad echo of the 1980 calls for new world economic and information orders (see above), a call for a CNN-dominated 'New World Information Order'.
7. In trying to deal with what is now a vast body of literature on

international relations, global communication, development and so on, and in concentrating more on the epistemological frameworks for analysis rather than the details and implications of development aid, etc., I am aware that I have obscured a number of important differences. Certainly many of the thinkers I have discussed here would not necessarily subscribe to the purer models of economic determinism within which I have been casting their work, and indeed a number of the writers on global communication start to raise questions about the effects of the global spread of culture and knowledge rather than leaving the issue simply as one of structural imperialism. Nevertheless, since I am suggesting that it is crucial to explore in greater depth questions of culture, discourse, difference and disjuncture, I would prefer to leave issues in alternative development, grassroots activism, implications of the spread of particular forms of culture and knowledge, and so on, to the next section.

8. Throughout this book I make a number of criticisms of Robert Phillipson's (1992) *Linguistic Imperialism*. While I hold to these criticisms, I do not want it to appear that I am trying to distance myself completely from his work. The phrase 'linguistic imperialism' can now be heard in many contexts and serves as an excellent place to start discussing the broader concerns that both of us share. Robert has also been helpful in clarifying my thinking and indeed served as external examiner for my doctoral dissertation.

9. I am of course glossing over a vast range of work here. For issues in philosophy and postmodernity, see especially Baynes, Bohman and McCarthy (1986). For a broad collection of feminist work, see de Lauretis (1986). For a discussion of the problems in theorizing the relationship between postmodernism and feminism, see Nicholson (1990).

10. I have been cautious here to avoid the dangers of subsuming this work under the rubric of postmodernism. Not only are there very real concerns, as Richard (1987) points out, with a postmodernist dismantling of such distinctions as Centre and Periphery, and the concomitant nullification of the significance of these relationships, but there is also the danger that to term this work postmodern is to reinscribe it once again within a Western epistemological framework. While this work has great significance for a postmodern critique, therefore, it is important not to reincorporate these critiques into a notion of postmodernism.

11. For an interesting, though not unproblematic, book that takes as its topic the complexities of the presence of the 'West' in the 'East', see Pico Iyer's (1988) *Video Night in Kathmandu and Other Reports from the Not-so-far East*.

12. Interestingly, too, there are linguistic correlates of such struggles.

When the West Indian team routed the England side a few years ago, the term 'blackwash' (from 'whitewash') was coined. More recently, the dominance of Indian spin bowling has produced the new term 'spinwash'. The practice of displaying signs in English at Indian cricket matches is also worthy of study in itself. A sign referring to the 1993 defeat of the English team by India, announced: 'England rule from 1641 to 1947, India rule in Calcutta and Bombay'. Once again the anti-colonial sentiment is unmistakable.

THREE

English and colonialism: origins of a discourse

The English language is travelling fast towards the fulfilment of its destiny . . . running forward towards its ultimate mission of eating up, like Aaron's rod, all other languages.
(Thomas de Quincey, 1862, pp. 149–50)

I am not in favour of extending the number of 'English' schools except where there is some palpable desire that English should be taught. Whilst we teach children to read and write and count in their own languages, or in Malay . . . we are *safe*.
(Frank Swettenham, *Perak Government Gazette*, 1894)

As pupils who acquire a knowledge of English are invariably unwilling to earn their livelihood by manual labour, the immediate result of affording an English education to any large number of Malays would be the creation of a discontented class who might become a source of anxiety to the community.
(E.C. Hill, Straits Settlements, 1884)

INTRODUCTION: THE COMPLEXITIES OF COLONIALISM

This chapter sets out to explore the colonial origins of the discourse of English as an International Language (EIL).[1] A key argument here is that the discourse of EIL had its origins in colonialism, but not so much in terms of an expansionist drive as in terms of a will to description. This will involve an analysis of what have been termed the Orientalist and Anglicist ideologies of colonialism. A common assumption appears to be that Orientalism (policies in favour of education in local languages for both the colonized and the colonizers) was replaced by Anglicism (policies in favour of education in English), which led to the widespread use of English under colonialism and thus its current position in the globe. Conservative interpretations of this moment see it as a decisive move towards the long and painful process of 'development', the moment when the British finally came to terms with their moral imperative to civilize the world. More liberal interpretations point to this imposition of English as a negative moment in colonial history, a moment only rectified by many peoples' subsequent decision to 'choose' to learn English in the postcolonial era. More critical views interpret this moment as one of the crucial early steps in the long colonial and neocolonial history of Anglicist 'linguistic imperialism' (e.g. Phillipson, 1992). While this documenting of more recent English expansionism makes a significant contribution to the rewriting of the historical record, my own exploration of colonial language policies suggests that the whole question is somewhat more complex.

It seems that rather than Anglicism replacing Orientalism, the two ideologies in fact operated alongside each other. This observation goes beyond a redressing of an understanding of colonial education and language policies because it suggests, first, that promotion of education in local languages was as much part of colonialism as was the promotion of English and, second, that the denial of access to English may have been as important for colonialism as the insistence on English. This, in turn, raises the question as to whether, in looking at the relationships between language and inequality, there is not a danger of focusing too much on 'linguistic imperialism' and expansionism, rather than trying to understand the implications of both insistence on and denial of a language within larger structures of inequality. My point here is not, of course, to suggest that the world has freely 'chosen English' but rather that, given the broader inequitable relationships in the world, people have little choice but to demand access to English. The problem here lies partly in concentrating on the imposition or non-imposition of a language as if it were an object disconnected to all the other political and cultural forces around it (see Tollefson, 1991). The reduction of colonial language policy to a battle between the imposition of English and the denial of English obscures the extent to which such policies were part of a far more complex set of policies and relationships dealing with broader (and sometimes conflicting) political, religious, educational, cultural, social and economic agendas. The notion of the worldliness of English applies as much to the colonial era as it does to the present day.

Second, this suggests that a crucial part of the colonial process is not only the material domain of physical and economic exploitation but also the discursive domain of cultural definition. Edward Said's (1978) exploration of Orientalism as a colonial definition of the Other opens up an analysis of Orientalism here not as a benevolent precursor to Anglicism but as a different site of colonial oppression (see Chapter 2). As Tejaswini Niranjana (1992) suggests, 'Since the practices of subjection/subjectification implicit in the colonial enterprise operate not merely through the coercive machinery of the imperial state but also through the discourses of philosophy, history, anthropology, philology, linguistics, and literary interpretation, the colonial "subject" – constructed through technologies or practices of power/knowledge – is brought into being within multiple discourses and on multiple sites' (pp. 1–2). This concept of discursive regulation leads on to the final argument of this chapter, that the implications of the growth of Anglicism had more to do with a massive increase in the study of English than with the spread of English.

ANGLICISM AND ORIENTALISM: TWO SIDES OF THE COLONIAL COIN

The early policies of the British in India encouraged the colonial officers and administrators to develop a better understanding of Indian political structure, language and culture in order to establish a sound basis for British rule and administration. In 1800, Governor-General Marquess Wellesley established the College of Fort William in Calcutta, the aim of which was to educate and train East India Company officials in Indian languages, culture, legal systems and so on (see Kopf, 1984). Interestingly, it was often the Indian bourgeoisie who opposed these policies, feeling themselves excluded from access to social, political and economic advancement, which they saw as dependent on an education in English. Thus the Bengali bourgeoisie, for example, frustrated at their exclusion from the institutions of British rule, set up their own college, The Hindu College, in 1816, which was designed to provide an education in English language and literature, Western philosophy and the social and natural sciences. As Rahim (1986) remarks, 'English and Western education became a powerful agent of change at the initiative of the Bengali middle class in Calcutta who found it essential in gaining advantage in their unequal power relationship with the British' (p. 235). What is immediately worth observing here is that it was not so much that British policy actively pursued the expansion of English, but rather that the local élites demanded it because of its links to social and economic prestige. As I shall show later with respect to Malaya, the British authorities themselves were indeed often very reluctant to provide education in English.

Towards the middle of the nineteenth century, however, there were a number of important shifts in colonial policy, resulting not so much from an improvement in methods of colonial administration as from a major shift in the ideological climate in Britain. Stamford Raffles, the 'founder' of Singapore, observed this shift in a letter in 1821:

> It is very certain that on the first discovery of what we term savage nations, philosophers went beyond all reason and truth in favour of uncivilised happiness; but it is no less certain, that of late years, the tide of prejudice has run equally strong in the opposite direction; and it is now the fashion to consider all who have not received the impression of European arms and laws, and the lights of Revelation, as devoid of every feeling and principle which can constitute happiness, or produce moral good.
>
> (Raffles, 1835, p. 193)

This discursive shift is clearly illustrated in Brantlinger's (1985) genealogy of the 'dark continent', in which he shows how the romanticism of the anti-slavery discourse, which had led to the banning of all slavery from British territory in 1833, centred upon a notion of the 'noble savage'. It was assumed that once the evil influence of European slavery was removed from Africa, the native people could return to their edenic life. This view changed dramatically with the growth of imperialist discourse in the middle of the nineteenth century: 'Africa grew "dark" as Victorian explorers, missionaries, and scientists flooded it with light, because the light was refracted through an imperialist ideology that urged the abolition of "savage customs" in the name of civilization' (1985, p. 166). As the rapidly industrializing Britain started to change its economic relations to the colonies, as imperialism started to take over from earlier forms of colonialism, as new philosophies such as utilitarianism emerged, and as forms of Darwinism combined with forms of racism, new and very different attitudes emerged towards Indian and African people: 'By mid-century, the success of the antislavery movement, the impact of the great Victorian explorers, and the merger of racist and evolutionary doctrines in the social sciences had combined to give the British public a widely shared view of Africa that demanded imperialization on moral, religious, and scientific grounds' (1985, pp. 167–8).

This shift had important implications for the provision of education in English since the moral imperative to imperialize came to include a moral imperative to teach English. Nevertheless, while this moral imperative to educate in English (Anglicism) was an extremely significant new development in the discourses of colonialism, it did not replace the earlier view of the 'noble savage' (Orientalism) but rather started operating alongside it. It is commonly held by those who have dealt to some extent with the history of the spread of English under colonialism (e.g. Kachru, 1986) that Macaulay's famous Minute in 1835 marked the victory of those who espoused education in English (commonly termed the 'Anglicists') over those who espoused education in the vernacular (the 'Orientalists'). Phillipson (1992), for example, suggests that 'Macaulay's formulation of the goals of British educational policy *ended* a protracted controversy which had exercised planners both in India and in the East India Company in London' (p. 110; emphasis added). While this period indeed saw a major discursive shift in terms of the development of a view in which English education could be taken up as a moral imperative, however, it is essential to recall that this was only ever intended for a small part of the population, that it was inevitably constrained by economic and practical concerns and that, perhaps most importantly, Anglicism never really replaced Orientalism, but rather operated alongside it. As Clive (1973) suggests, the issue is in fact far more complex than the simplistic version of Macaulay's role in the educational controversy, whereby he is supposed to have arrived in India, written the Minute on education and then departed with English now firmly ensconced in the colony. Rather, it is important to understand that Macaulay articulated a position that had already been discussed for a long time; that Anglicism and Orientalism ultimately concerned far more than a mere battle over which languages should be used; and that both ideologies continued to have a great deal of influence. And finally, it is essential to understand Orientalism not merely as a series of language policies but rather as Said (1978) has described it (see previous chapter), that is, as a discourse which has had particular effects in producing and regulating the colonial Other.

First, then, it is worth noting the brief caveat before Macaulay's oft-quoted remark on the creation of 'a class of persons Indian in blood and colour . . .':

> It is impossible for us with our limited means to attempt to educate the body of the people. We must at present do our best to form a class who may be interpreters between us and the millions whom we govern – a class of persons Indian in blood and colour, but English in tastes, in opinions, in morals and in intellect.
>
> (Macaulay's Minute of 2nd February 1835; Macaulay, 1835, p. 249)

Macaulay clearly recognized that it was not possible to do more than educate a small portion of the society. Those who quote this passage starting at 'a class . . .' (e.g. Kachru, 1986, pp. 5, 35) may give the impression that this English education was intended for a much larger population than was in fact the case. According to the 1919 *Report of the Calcutta University Commission* (cited in Nagle, 1928), the effects of the pendulum swinging in favour of Macaulay and the Anglicists has often been misinterpreted: despite favouring English as the language of higher education and supporting increased Westernization of education, the colonial authorities still encouraged vernacular education. Indeed, as the records of colonial educational policies in the Straits Settlements and Federated Malay States (see next section) clearly show, in many parts of the empire vernacular education and Orientalist discourse predominated into the twentieth century. Clive's (1973) study of Macaulay also shows that rather than Macauley's Anglicism coming to predominate, Orientalism in fact remained very firmly established in India. According to Loh Fook Seng (1970), 'that it is part of the white man's mission to teach the native in his own native tongue was an abiding article of faith of European missionaries, humanitarians and orientalists of the nineteenth century in spite of Macaulay's Minute' (p. 108).

Macaulay, 'whose incomprehension and contempt for traditional Hindu scholarship were alike profound' (Harris, 1987, p. 118), was clearly one of the more extreme Anglicists, proclaiming that 'a single shelf of a good European library was worth the whole native literature of India and Arabia' (Macaulay, 1835, p. 241), that 'all the historical information which has been collected from all the books written in the Sanscrit language is less valuable than what may be found in the most paltry abridgments used at preparatory schools in England' (p. 241) and that 'sound Philosophy and true History' should not be sacrificed for 'medical doctrines which would disgrace an English Farrier – Astronomy, which would move laughter in girls at an English boarding school – History, abounding with kings thirty feet high, and reigns thirty thousand years long – and Geography, made up of seas of treacle and seas of butter' (pp. 242–3).[2] And yet, it is worth noting that, on the one hand, he claimed that such views were in fact supported by Orientalists and, on the other, the practical dictates of providing education in British colonies and the practical needs for only a small class of people to act as intermediaries between the colonial administrators and the rest of the population militated against any widespread provision of such education. Furthermore, the move towards greater provision of English-language education had its origins in the demands of the Indian bourgeoisie as much as in an imposition from British missionaries and educators: 'the movement towards Anglicization originated in missionary and Hindu quarters before Macaulay had begun to sharpen his pen and select his epithets in the land of "exile" whose culture he was to traduce' (Mayhew, 1926, p. 13). Given the conditions already imposed on India by colonial rule, the spread of English might well have proceeded without Macaulay's 'singularly tactless and blundering championship' (ibid.). It is important, therefore, to maintain a clear distinction between the discourse on English as it was constructed by men such as Macaulay and the actual causes and extent of the spread of English.

It is also important to understand these Anglicist and Orientalist positions not so much as competing positions, with the former winning out over the latter, but rather as complementary discourses within the larger discursive field of colonialism. Loh Fook Seng (1970) argues that Macaulay's dismissal of Indian culture and scholarship should not be seen as oppositional to the Orientalist position: 'They are but two sides of the same colonial coin sharing the same rationale, to bring light into the native darkness as well as facilitate the exigencies of trade and government' (p. 108). Similarly, Viswanathan (1989) suggests that the two positions should be seen 'not as polar opposites but as points along a continuum of attitudes toward the manner and form of colonial governance' (p. 30). Ultimately, she suggests, 'both the Anglicist and the Orientalist factions were equally complicit with the project of domination' (p. 167). This point has great significance, both for an understanding of language and education policies during the colonial era and for the implications of modern versions of Anglicism and Orientalism today. To explore these issues further, I shall now turn to look in more detail at colonial policies in Malaya.

ENGLISH FOR THE FEW: COLONIAL EDUCATION POLICIES IN MALAYA

The British first started to exert their influence in the region in the late eighteenth and early nineteenth centuries, establishing a series of colonial settlements along the coast (Penang in 1786, Singapore in 1819 and Malacca in 1824) in order to secure a greater hold over the lucrative spice trade, growing tin markets and the key trade route between India and China. In 1826 Penang, Singapore and Malacca were combined to form the Straits Settlements, which were administered successively by the East India Company, the Governor of India and, from 1865, the Colonial Office. Although the East India Company had originally ceded control of the settlements to the government because they were seen as an unprofitable drain on the company's resources, by the second half of the nineteenth century the growing prosperity of the Straits Settlements and the neighbouring Malay states was engendering increased commercial interest.

In 1874, ostensibly to calm unrest among local leaders over tolls for tin, and to settle disputes between Chinese tin-miners, the British Governor-Designate, Sir Andrew Clarke, signed the Pangkor Treaty, installing a British Resident[3] in the Malay state of Perak. As Caldwell (1977a) points out, while standard histories of this and subsequent moves by the British have tended to accept uncritically the arguments that the British were interested solely in restoring 'law and order', the real motives appear to have been largely commercial. The growing industrial threat to Britain's world economic supremacy posed by Germany and the United States, the recent opening of the Suez Canal, and the fear of other colonial rivals in the region, especially Germany, greatly influenced the British attempt to gain control over a new area of natural resources. Subsequent policies in the area to free indentured Chinese labourers from their slave-like conditions in the tin-mining industry and to lessen the power of the Chinese tin-mining bosses were aimed not so much at the creation of law and order or a more equitable society as they were at breaking the Chinese monopoly on tin production and freeing cheap Chinese labour for the new British commercial interests. As Sir Andrew Clarke himself commented in 1875, 'it only wants the protection and assistance of a civilised power here to fill all these empty waste lands with industrious and thriving settlements' (quoted in *The Straits Times*, 9 January, 1875).

By 1896 British Residents had been appointed in the states of Selangor, Negri Sembilan and Pahang, and these had been combined with Perak to form the Federated Malay States. By the early twentieth century, there were three separate groupings, the British Colony of the Straits Settlements, the Federated Malay States and the Unfederated Malay States (made up of the remaining states of Malaya), all of which were falling increasingly under the control of the colonial government in Singapore through the system of Residents and Advisers. The region was also changing demographically, due to a massive increase in immigration to the area in order to service the growing colonial economy. Chinese immigrants had been settling in the peninsula for centuries, though with the growth of the predominantly Chinese-controlled tin-mining industry, this flow increased considerably.[4] Meanwhile, there had been a constant flow of Indians to the peninsula, especially from the southern states of Tamil Nadu and Kerala, brought about mainly by the need for cheap labour on the British and other European plantations. By 1911, of the total population in Malaya of about 2,620,000, there were some 1,437,000 Malays, 916,000 Chinese and 267,000 Indians (Hall, 1964). By 1941, the 2,379,000 Chinese outnumbered the Malay population of 2,278,000, and with an Indian population of 744,000, the Malays were rightly concerned that not only had colonial rule disenfranchised them economically and politically, but they had also even lost demographic superiority. It is also important to observe that, apart from some Malay aristocrats and some wealthy Chinese merchants and mine-owners, the growing prosperity of the region, due to increased world demands for rubber and tin, did little to benefit the local inhabitants, whatever their ethnic origin: 'Tamil tapper, Chinese coolie, and Malay poor peasant suffered rather than gained from the process of "development" ' (Caldwell, 1977a, p. 33).

The educational policies of the British during this period must be seen both in the context of the economic and political interests of colonialism and as part of the shifting discourses on colonialism. Thus, they need to be seen within the context of educating a workforce to suit the commercial needs of the colonial power, of educating with a missionary zeal to bring 'enlightenment' and 'civilization' (the Anglicist discourse) and of educating to maintain an idealized way of life (the Orientalist discourse). Such policies should not be seen as mutually exclusive or oppositional to each other. Macaulay's Anglicist concept of 'diffusion', whereby a small group were to learn English and diffuse this to the rest of the population, remained, not surprisingly, a project with limited effect, and that predominantly in the domain of higher education. Meanwhile, the Orientalist approach had much more effect on the elementary levels, bringing education in the vernacular to larger sections of the population. Such policies, therefore, served colonialism quite well by providing an English-educated élite and a vernacular-educated population better able to participate in a colonial economy. These policies also need to be understood relative to other colonial policies – the Straits Settlement 'development' occurred some time after similar moves in India – and also in their practical context of limited resources and bureaucratic inefficiency.

Raffles

The founder of Singapore, Stamford Raffles, had arrived with high goals for education. He immediately set about trying to set up a college, laying the foundation stone of the Singapore Institution (later Raffles Institution) in 1823. In his original grandiose conception, the institution would have had literary and moral departments for Chinese, Malay and Siamese, plus a scientific department, and would be influential not only over the Malay peninsula but also as far as China, Japan and India (see Raffles, 1835). He also did a great deal in those early years to encourage both Malay vernacular education and missionary work. According to Chelliah (1947), Raffles was 'the embodiment of the new humanitarianism that was beginning to influence a large and growing body of public opinion in England, led by men like Wilberforce, who advocated the theory that commercial inter-course with the backward races involved not mere exploitation of them but a moral obligation toward them to help them to advance in civilization and its moral and intellectual welfare' (p. 12). Although Raffles's plans in fact came to little, and he cannot really be said to have had much influence over the education of the region, the unquestioning championing of his cause by colonial historians (such as Chelliah), and his powerful position as the founder of Singapore (Singapore still echoes with his presence, from the proud white statue by the river to Stamford Road and Raffles Place), suggest that it is worth taking a slightly more critical look at this 'embodiment of the new humanitarianism'.

In dealing with the educational officers in the colonial admini-stration, it is important not to confuse their apparently 'good intentions' with the location and effects of their work within colonialism. Reading Raffles's letters and memoirs (Raffles, 1835), for example, can give us one story, of a man of intelligence, conviction and vision; a sad story of the death of three of his four children from tropical diseases, of the deaths of other friends and relatives, of the loss of years of work recording local history, culture, geography and fauna destroyed in a shipboard fire on the homeward voyage; of an early death at forty-five. These are stories of some interest, but they are also the stories that have dominated in the history of colonialism, histories that need to be read against the grain, and histories that need to be pushed aside to allow the multiple subjugated voices of the colonized to speak.

First, the writing on Raffles derives from a long history of colonial writing, a body of texts that has continually sung the praises of these exemplary figures of colonialism. Alatas (1971) points to the 'strong ethnic bias of British historians and biographers in favour of Raffles' (p. 2). Second, on reading his diaries, it becomes clear that he was indeed a great believer in the whole process of colonialism, and thus we cannot speak of his 'humanitarianism' without seeing it in the larger context of the effects of colonialism, and thus, as Viswanathan (1989) puts it, as 'the creation of a blueprint for social control in the guise of a humanistic program of enlightenment' (p. 10). And third, although it was perhaps true that Raffles was more enlightened than some of his contemporaries, his humanitarianism is less clear when judged in the light of other contemporary reform movements which objected to imperialism, child labour and the appalling living and working conditions of many workers in and beyond Britain. Thus, viewing Raffles's life within the broader contexts of British colonialism, it becomes evident that 'being civilized in Raffles' sense was to serve British mercantile capitalist interest' (Alatas, 1971, p. 43). Ultimately, Alatas (1971) concludes that Raffles's 'entire conduct was not dominated by a broad love for humanity . . . but by the fanatical glorification of the English at the expense of other nationalities. . . . The political philosophy of Raffles is the ideology of imperialism *par excellence*' (pp. 46–7). This reassessment of Raffles is not in order to put a few smears on the gleaming white figure by the Singapore River, but to start this overview of educational policies on a note that questions the received histories that have been written of the era and the region, and to start to look more critically at how Orientalism was as much part of colonial exploitation and control as was Anglicism.

Playing safe

In the early years after Raffles, there was little educational provision in the region beyond the already extant informal Malay schools based around the teaching of the Qur'an. In 1854 the dispatch from the Court of Directors of the East India Company to the Governor-General of India marked a new era in educational policies (Chelliah, 1947, p. 23; Wong Hoy Kee and Ee Tiang Hong, 1971, p. 9). This dispatch spelled out in clear terms the goals of education in the colonies:

> This knowledge will teach the natives of India the marvelous results of the employment of labour and capital, rouse them to emulate us in the development of the vast resources of their country, guide them in their efforts and gradually, but certainly, confer upon them all the advantages which accompany the healthy increase of wealth and commerce; and at the same time, secure to us a larger and more certain

supply of many articles necessary for our manufacturers and extensively consumed by all classes of our population, as well as an almost inexhaustible demand for the produce of British labour.

(Quoted in Rahim, 1986, p. 236)

Recognizing that education was a 'sacred duty' on behalf of the British Government, the report recommended extended provision for elementary education in the vernacular. The official education reports for these early years show the growth of three types of school (Straits Settlements, 1860–70): 'Free' schools, missionary schools, and Malay vernacular schools. Free schools were few in number and it was the missionary and vernacular schools that dominated. The 1874 report by the Straits Settlements Inspector of Schools (Straits Settlements, 1874) lists fifty Malay vernacular schools with an enrolment of 1,222 students, a significant increase from the sixteen schools with 596 students in 1872. The inspector also visited nineteen English and 'Anglo-vernacular' schools with an enrolment of 1,761 students. It was the vernacular schools that were expanding more rapidly, however, with eighty-five schools (2,230 students) by 1882, and 189 schools (7,218 students) by 1892 (Straits Settlements, 1882–92). Malay elementary education was also growing fast in the Federated Malay States and eventually widespread compulsory elementary education became the norm (see Cheeseman, 1931), although the regulations were in fact rarely strictly enforced. One important result of the provision of free education for Malays and their reluctance to send their children to the Christian schools was that the vast majority of students attending the missionary or free schools were Chinese, Indians, Europeans or Eurasians. The 1884 Straits Settlements report gives the figure of Malay enrolment in English schools at only 8 per cent. This, as will be seen later, was to have major repercussions.

In the 1884 report on education (Straits Settlements, 1884), E.C. Hill, the Inspector of Schools for the colony, explained his reasons for not increasing the provision of education in English:

The objections to teaching English in all the Malay schools would be – (1) that the cost would be very great; (2) that it would be impossible, at once, to obtain teachers with the necessary qualifications; (3) that as pupils who acquire a knowledge of English are invariably unwilling to earn their livelihood by manual labour, the immediate result of affording an English education to any large number of Malays would be the creation of a discontented class who might become a source of anxiety to the community. A certain number of Malays educated in English are of course required to fill clerical appointments and situations of the kind which do not include manual labour.

(p. 171)

While the first two problems are no doubt valid (though not, of course, insurmountable), it is the third argument that is of more interest. Later, Hill points out that he is in no way against education in English: 'On the contrary, I believe a thorough knowledge of English is of the greatest benefit to all who acquire it, and I should be glad to see English take the place generally of Native languages' (p. 172). Hill, then, appears to be quite capable of taking up a position in the Anglicist discourse, a position quite different from a number of other administrators, whose support for Malay education is based far more on an Orientalist view of the Malays. Hill would quite happily see English replace local languages – and indeed seems to think that this could only benefit those who learnt the language – but nevertheless warns against pursuing such a policy because of the benefits that an English education could now bestow on its recipients, benefits that had nothing to do with the language itself or its cultural associations but everything to do with its position at the centre of political and economic power in the colony. To allow more than those needed for administrative jobs to have access to English could be a major destabilizing element in society.

These views are echoed by the influential figure of Frank Swettenham, Resident of Perak (later, Sir Frank, High Commissioner of the Federated Malay States and Governor of the Straits Settlements), when he commented in the *Perak Annual Report* for 1890 that 'the one danger to be guarded against is an attempt to teach English indiscriminately. It could not be well taught except in a very few schools, and I do not think that it is at all advisable to attempt to give to the children of an agricultural population an indifferent knowledge of a language that to all but the very few would only unfit them for the duties of life and make them discontented with anything like manual labour' (p. 16). Four years later in the *Perak Government Gazette* (6 July 1894), he wrote: 'I am not in favour of extending the number of "English" schools except where there is some palpable desire that English should be taught. Whilst we teach children to read and write and count in their own languages, or in Malay . . . we are *safe*' (emphasis in original). Both

Hill and Swettenham, therefore, seem very aware of the dangers of providing local people with English education. Thus, it was not so much the widespread use of English that gave it its power as it was the position of social, economic and political prestige that it attained.

It is also important to locate these views relative to those in other colonies, especially India. While the effects of Anglicism were limited, it is nevertheless clear that there was some concern in India from about 1870 onwards that English had been too widely taught. It was felt that too much money was being spent on English education, producing too many English-educated Indians to take up the limited number of jobs available in the colonial administration, and that insufficient time and money were being devoted to education in the vernacular. As H.B. Collinge, in the report quoted at length below, put it: 'It is the mere smattering of English and English ideas that is harmful, and which in India causes the country to "swarm with half-starved, discontented men, who consider manual labour beneath them, because they know a little English" ' (cited by Hill in Straits Settlements, 1894). Furthermore, as Viswanathan (1989) suggests, it was felt that instead of producing the docile colonial subjects that they had hoped for, English education was in fact producing a new group of people armed with a sense of 'moral autonomy, self sufficiency and unencumbered will that caused more problems for British rule than expected' (p. 143). By the early 1900s, Lord Curzon, Governor-General of India, had started to reverse the trend by providing greater support for vernacular education and less support for education in English. Such changes in the key colony of India naturally had effects on colonies such as Malaya, both because of the formal connections through the Colonial Office and the less formal connections between colonial administrators in the two countries.

There was another aspect to the role of languages in the distribution of social, economic, and political power in the Malay peninsula. While there was broad agreement that English should only be taught to a certain few, there was, as we have already seen, support for elementary vernacular education for Malays. This policy can be seen as clearly complementary to the limitations on English. In his 1884 report on education, Hill goes on to quote H.B. Collinge, the Inspector of Schools for the State of Perak, on his views on vernacular education. These comments by Collinge, a much respected Inspector, were reprinted in the *Perak Government Gazette* (4 January 1895) and were frequently quoted and referred to in subsequent reports (e.g. *Reports on the Federated Malay States*, 1901). They are worth quoting at some length:

> Thousands of our boys are taken away from idleness, and whilst learning to read and write their own language, to cipher a little, to know something of geography, to write Malay in the Roman character, and to take an active interest in physical exercise and manly sports, they at the same time acquire habits of industry, obedience, punctuality, order, neatness, cleanliness and general good behaviour.... After a boy has been a year or two at school, he is found to be less lazy at home, less given to evil habits and mischievous adventure, more respectful and dutiful, much more willing to help his parents, and with sense enough not to entertain any ambition beyond following the humble home occupations he has been taught to respect.... The school also inspires a respect for the vernacular; and I am of the opinion that if there is any lingering feeling of dislike of the 'white man', the school tends greatly to remove it, for the people see that the Government has really their welfare at heart in providing them with this education, free, without compulsion, and with the greatest consideration for their mohammedan sympathies.
>
> (p. 177)

Here, then, is the other side of the coin. Vernacular education is intended to inculcate habits of industry, obedience and punctuality, to prevent students from entertaining any ambitions above their humble station in life, and to encourage them to feel thankful rather than resentful towards their colonizers. Such policies Caldwell (1977a) has described as 'consciously seeking to ossify Malay rural society' (p. 25). The stress on cleanliness, order and punctuality can be frequently found; Swettenham, again, in a speech in 1896, argued that 'nothing but good can, I think, come of teaching *in the native languages* what we call the three R's; and of greater value still are the habits of orderliness and punctuality, and the duties inculcated by teachers in the hope of making good citizens of their pupils' (Swettenham, 1896, p. 186).[5] Most important, however, was the view that Malays were inherently and incurably suited to their agricultural life and that the purpose of vernacular education was to maintain this way of life. George Maxwell (Chief Secretary to the Government of the Federated Malay States, 1920–26), for example, argued in a speech in 1927 that while on the one hand 'an English-educated boy draws a far higher salary than a boy who only knows his own language, and has an opening for an advancement which is closed to the other', the principal aims of education in Malaya were 'to improve the bulk of the people and to make the son of the fisherman or peasant a more intelligent fisherman or peasant than his father had been' (Maxwell, 1927, p. 406).

While this desire to preserve the status quo of the Malay peasantry was clearly functional in terms of educating against social change, it should also be seen within the context of Orientalism. Orientalist and Anglicist discourses were complementary aspects of colonialism rather than different attitudinal stages as many writers seem to have suggested. The significance of Orientalism was in its construction of the Malay Other as innocent and happy and in the consequent educational policies designed to preserve the state and status of the Malays. Savage (1984) argues that just as an earlier view had portrayed indigenous people as 'noble savages', so the 'British administration in the early halcyon days of colonialism in Malaya pictured the Malays as "noble peasants" ' (p. 289). In fact, the view of the noble peasant was maintained right through the early part of the twentieth century. This view may have been more extreme in Malaya than in other colonies, although, as Clive (1973) suggests, Orientalism was also very widespread in India, in spite of men such as Macaulay. The reasons for this seem to lie first in the different forms of racist discourse that operated within the discursive field of colonialism. There were clearly differences in how Africans, Indians and East Asians were viewed, generally with the latter being spared some of the more vehement denigration and derision that was aimed at African peoples. Second, this was also combined with a more exoticized view of the Orient that tended to elevate Asian cultures to a position deemed worthy of preservation. Finally, the relative size and remoteness of Malaya, compared to India for example, possibly led to a larger proportion of Malay scholars to take up positions in the colonial administration. Raffles, Swettenham, who 'earned his Knighthood on the strength of his ability to understand the ignorant unspoilt Malays' (Loh Fook Seng, 1970, p. 114), Hugh Clifford (Resident of Pahang), R.J. Wilkinson (Inspector of Schools for the Federated Malay States), George Maxwell (Resident of Perak), and the influential R.O. Winstedt (Straits Settlements Assistant Director of Education from 1916 to 1921 and Director from 1924–31) were all acclaimed scholars and writers about the region.

Their view of the noble peasant was often coupled with what Alatas (1977) has called the 'myth of the lazy native', a view of local people as lazy (relative to cultural capitalism) and thus justifying exploitative policies. Hugh Clifford, in his essay 'At the heels of the White man' in his 1898 book *Studies in Brown Humanity*, thus lamented on the one hand the effects of colonial rule for the changes it had made to Malay peasant life: 'It is worth considering how far we are morally responsible for the evil that is daily done in our name by those that follow at our heels' (p. 138). On the other hand, he lamented that the Malay 'never works if he can help it, and often will not suffer himself to be induced or tempted into doing so by offers of the most extravagant wages' (1927, p. 19). Swettenham's view was that 'the leading characteristic of the Malay of every class is a disinclination to work' (1907/1955, p. 136). Or as W.H. Treacher, Resident-General of the Federated Malay States, remarked in 1902: 'The Malay, with his moderate wants, and rooted disinclination to steady work of any kind, will give his labour neither to Government undertakings nor to mines or plantations' (*Reports on the Federated Malay States*, 1902). This last quote clearly shows how the construction of the 'lazy native' was in the context of the Malays' refusal to engage in the exploitative labour of tin mines and rubber plantations.

These views of the Malays as noble but lazy peasants helped the implementation of the education policies aimed at maintaining the inequitable structures of colonial rule: 'Much of the primitive Malay education that continued to be supplied by the British Government was in no small degree due to this attempt to preserve the Malay as a Malay, a son of the soil in the most literal sense possible' (Loh Fook Seng, 1970, p. 114). Under Winstedt's fifteen-year period as Assistant and then Director of Education, these views led to the continued championing of Malay vernacular education, his refusal to entertain the possibility of Malay secondary education,[6] and finally his strong emphasis on a 'vocational' element in Malay education, including an almost fanatical devotion to basket-weaving (see, for example, Straits Settlements, 1926).

This education for social and cultural stasis was clearly divided along ethnic lines, but it also had its gendered dimensions. While the reports make frequent disapproving reference to the reluctance of Malay families to send their daughters to school, and while they celebrate the slow increase of girls in the vernacular schools as a sign of clearly more enlightened thinking, such 'progress' must also be seen within the context of education for social maintenance. Thus, the education for the girls was, like that for the boys, aimed at making them more capable at performing their daily tasks as determined by the colonial administration, positioning Malay women not only within the exploitative and racist elements of colonial discourse but also within the gendered premises of this discourse. The Director for Education commented in 1934 that 'The curriculum of the girls' schools is no longer dead and uninspiring. Cookery, clay-modelling, paper-cutting, drawn-thread work, hygiene taught by Lady Medical Officers, are romantic subjects for the little Malay girl compared with what her elder sisters learnt a few years ago' (Straits Settlements, 1934).

Two final developments in education in the early part of the twentieth century are worthy of note. The first was the founding in 1905 of the Malay Residential School (the Malay College from 1909) in Kuala Kangsar (Perak). With full boarding facilities, a British headmaster, and teachers with a British public school background, the school catered almost entirely for the children of the Malay aristocracy in a replica of a British public school. The second was the founding of the Sultan Idris Training College in 1922, aimed at preparing Malay primary school teachers. On the one hand, then, the children of the Malay aristocracy were given an élite education in English and prepared for further study at Oxford or Cambridge and privileged positions within the colonial administration. On the other, the more able children of the Malay peasantry were trained to return to their villages as teachers in the vernacular schools. Once again, English education was carefully rationed and conferred as a privilege to a selected few. Such policies maintained and possibly increased social divisions between the Malays themselves, enhancing the status of the aristocracy and maintaining the position of the ordinary Malay.

Clementi

The language and education policies of the colonial administration were, in many respects, similar in the twentieth century, maintaining the basic policy of limiting access to English and promoting

Malay elementary education. A good example of this can be seen in a debate that occurred between the Governor, Sir Cecil Clementi, and some of the members of the Legislature in 1934. Clementi had been struggling to maintain control over the growing number of private Chinese schools and had started trying to limit their development and encourage the Chinese population to take advantage of the free education in Malay. Clementi now saw the purposes of education as to 'Malayanise the children of the permanent population, i.e. to make them true citizens of Malaya', to develop a sense of patriotism, and to produce 'a law-abiding thrifty and industrious population' (Clementi, quoted in *The Straits Times*, 13 February 1934). Thus, while the dropping of grants to Chinese schools was in part an economic measure in the face of slumping world tin and rubber prices brought on by the world economic recession of the 1930s, it was clearly also a political move to try to deal with the dangers of a large and politically active Chinese community by attempting to foster a sense of common nationalism. Interestingly, as an administrator in Hong Kong some years before, Clementi had fought a similar battle against the growth of Chinese nationalism. In Hong Kong, however, he had approached the problem by attempting to promote 'traditional' Chinese education – he was instrumental in founding a high school and setting up the Chinese Department at Hong Kong University. Thus, he tried to defuse the threat of Chinese nationalism by promoting traditional Confucian loyalties (Luk Hung-Kay, 1991). Such examples clearly point to how the promotion of certain forms of education, language and culture were inextricably bound up with colonial rule.

In a fierce debate in the Legislature (as reported in *The Straits Times*, 13 February 1934), Tan Cheng Lock, Member for Malacca, welcomed Clementi's notion of 'Malayanization' but hoped fervently that it did not imply that non-Malays should adopt the Malay language and culture. He went on to argue that 'English should be the best common basic language to serve as a bond between the different sections of its permanent population'. English, he argued, was already the most widely spoken language in the world, was already becoming the common language in Singapore and other towns in Malaya, and was 'well on the way to securing universal currency in this country and in the whole of the East'. Furthermore, English was essential for economic advancement, since all advanced education in agriculture, technology, commerce and industry was conducted in English. Therefore, he concluded, to establish a united Malaya, without distinction of race, class or religion, English should become the common language, and the government should, on the one hand, support Chinese vernacular education, and, on the other, provide free education in English.

These comments are interesting for a number of reasons. First, they attest to the fact that although there is clearly some exaggeration in the claim that English was 'securing universal currency . . . in the whole of the East', it was at least perceived by some as the most useful language for wider communication in the country, the region and beyond. Second, English was clearly tied to educational and economic advancement. Third, English was claimed to be a language that could be used to bridge ethnic, class or religious differences. Finally, these comments illustrate again that the demand for English education by local people was frequently far stronger than the colonizers' desire to teach it. As discussed above, it was often through the initiatives of local people that greater provision for English education was made. Once English was established as the language of power and prestige, many people, despite their reservations about the connections between English and an alien cultural and religious order, realized that an education in English was the best means for their children to achieve a measure of social and economic prestige. By this time, this was also true of the Malays, who had started demanding more provision for education in English. Winstedt, in his education report for 1920, had already noted this trend: 'The awakening of the Malay race to the advantages of education, vernacular and English, has been rapid and widespread. Education is the daily topic of the Malay press. In every state, Malays seek admission to English schools in increasing numbers, and take full advantage of the Government scholarships' (*Federated Malay States Annual Report* for 1920). Indeed, according to Asmah Haji Omar (personal communication), one of the first groups after the aristocracy to start sending their children to the English schools were the Muslim religious leaders.

To these demands for more English education, A. Caldecott, the Colonial Secretary, replied that English should be limited because of its commercial value: 'So long as it possesses a rarity value, so long as it is associated in the public mind with the idea of an open sesame to sweatless livelihood, so long would it be criminal folly to make it the basic language of free primary education.' Clementi then made a long defence of policies that favoured Malay education and limited English. First, he argued, Malay was the most widely used language in the peninsula;[7] second, that education in English cost about five times more per student than education in Malay; third, that primary education in English in India, Ceylon and the Philippines had produced a discontented body of unemployed who 'had acquired a distaste for their ancestral methods of earning a livelihood'; and finally, that the teaching of English would pose grave dangers to the traditional way of life, and that they should avoid 'Westernizing' *kampongs*.[8] Once again it was a question of limiting English instruction for economic and political reasons.

Social implications

Chai Hon-Chan (1964) argues that to the extent that the British policies left a wide gulf between the vernacular-educated, who remained as a substratum of Malay life, and the English-educated, who formed either an aristocratic élite or an urban middle class, there is strong evidence to support the argument that these were deliberate policies to divide and rule: 'The vernacular educated remained as a substratum of the new Malayan society; while the Malay aristocracy learned that their duty was to get on in the world created by the British, the mass of Malays remained untouched by Western culture and had no share in the enormous wealth produced by the country' (p. 278). One effect of these policies, then, was to increase class and ethnic divisions in the country, dividing the different ethnic groups and developing a more inequitable social structure in which the only ones encouraged to overcome ethnic divisions through education formed a small élite who were, by and large, cut off both culturally and economically from their own backgrounds. These policies were also particularly harmful to the Malays, whose education effectively ensured that they remained bound to the land and unable to take advantage of some of the benefits of a growing economy. According to Caldwell (1977a),

by enhancing the formal status of the Malay Sultans (and enriching them); by co-opting much of the Malay aristocracy . . . and by restricting the bulk of the Malay population to the rural areas and rural subsistence occupations (and by attempting to restrict their mental horizons to deference and basket-weaving), the British consciously sought to secure and ensure socio-political hegemony and some kind of minimally plausible ideological underpinning for it.

(p. 27)

It would seem too that the almost complete negligence of Chinese and Indian education again served the British well, producing a small English-educated middle class that cut across ethnic lines, but otherwise leaving the ethnic groups sharply divided.

If Malays wished to progress to the exclusively English-medium secondary schools, they were at a clear disadvantage when compared with Chinese and Indian children who had received their elementary education in English at missionary schools. By 1920 English was firmly established in business and administration in Malaya, but nevertheless restricted to a small élite. These early effects of colonial education and language policies were to have a major effect on life in Malaya up to the present day. The language of education had become one of the most significant markers of social prestige, so that by the 1930s, 'while it was clear that birth was still of fundamental importance in determining status and privilege, education – English education in particular – had emerged as a new basis for the achievement of élitist status' (Loh Fook Seng, 1975, p. 85).

In addition to these clearly pragmatic bases of British colonial policy, however, it is important to understand these policies in light of the both competitive and complementary discourses of Anglicism and Orientalism. The one emphasized the superiority of English and the moral compunction to enlighten the 'native' through an English education. The Anglicist discourse was tempered, furthermore, not only by the pragmatic and economic constraints of colonial administration, but also, I suspect, by a belief that something as fine as the English language could only be taught to a princely or scholarly class. In fact, this discourse, with a few notable exceptions such as Macaulay, was of more significance in Britain itself than in the colonies it ruled (see next section). Anglicism was balanced and complemented by the Orientalist discourse, which appears to have predominated in Malaya, especially through the series of Malay scholars who held various influential administrative posts. Their view of an idyllic Malay peasant, tempered by a belief that Malays were lazy, led to a constant emphasis on elementary (and only elementary) vernacular education, with an orientation towards 'vocational' education in order to make (to cite Maxwell again) 'the son of the fisherman or peasant a more intelligent fisherman or peasant than his father had been' (1927, p. 406). Within the broader context of colonialism, with English established as a powerful but élite language, it was this Orientalism that was disenfranchising for many colonial subjects.

ANGLICISM AND ENGLISH STUDIES

This review of colonial policies in Malaya has supported my earlier argument that the crucial aspect of colonial language policy was not so much the winning out of Anglicism over Orientalism but rather the operation of both in conjunction. It was Orientalism that supported 'the idea of the lazy native to justify compulsion and unjust practices in the mobilization of labour in the colonies' (Alatas, 1977, p. 2). What emerges, then, from the period of nineteenth-century colonial policies is an educational orientation aimed at improving the work proficiency of the new labour force. In line with arguments in Chapters 1 and 2, economic and political exploitation should not be seen as the sole determinants of colonial policy, since the cultural and the ideological need to be considered as primary and not reducible to the social and economic. Thus, while acknowledging the extreme importance of seeing colonial policies within the context of capitalist exploitation, it is also essential to see the cultural, ideological or discursive shifts in Britain and the colonies as equally significant and not necessarily reducible to the material domain. Thus, in trying to understand colonial discourse – 'the body of knowledge, modes of representation, strategies of power, law, discipline, and so on, that are employed in the construction and domination of "colonial subjects"' (Niranjana, 1992, p. 7) – Anglicist and Orientalist discourses can be seen to play complementary roles. On the one hand, there was an Anglicist zeal tempered by pragmatic concerns, aimed at providing education in English as part of the coopting of the aristocracy and to provide sufficient translators and clerks to run the colonial administrative bureaucracies, and on the other hand, the Orientalist discourse, which supported educational policies to maintain the social status and conditions of the majority of the population while educating them against their 'laziness' to become better workers and consumers within colonial capitalism.

English and the panopticon

Describing the shift in educational policies in the middle of the nineteenth century, Rahim (1986) suggests a parallel between Foucault's (1979) description of the development of disciplinary society in nineteenth-century Europe and the development of colonial modes of control. Foucault uses as a central metaphor the *panopticon*, Bentham's design for prisons in which 'by the effect of backlighting, one can observe from the tower, standing out precisely against the light, the small captive shadows in the cells of the periphery' (1979, p. 200). This new orientation, Foucault argues, reversed the principle of the dungeon in which prisoners were deprived of light and hidden away, for now they were lit from behind and constantly observed. Ultimately, the prisoner subjected to this field of visibility, 'becomes the principle of his own subjection' (p. 203). Thus Foucault charts the 'formation of disciplinary society in this movement that stretches from the enclosed disciplines, a sort of social "quarantine", to an indefinitely generalizable mechanism of "panopticism" ' (p. 216).

The connections between Foucault's description of the emergence of European disciplinary society and my interest in the emergence of a discourse of EIL during the same period could be explored at far greater length than is possible here, but it is worth making a few significant points. First, there are clearly interesting parallels to be drawn between the shift from the darkness of dungeons to the light of the panopticon and the idea discussed earlier in the chapter of how Africa 'grew dark' as the missionary and colonial light flooded across the country. Second, this becomes an even more interesting image when we compare the notion of the central tower and the backlit prisoners on the periphery with the notions of centre and periphery discussed in the last chapter. What is interesting here is that this notion of panopticism can help us understand the relations of power in colonial language use not in terms of English being thrust upon all subject peoples but in terms of English becoming the language of colonial panopticism. 'English', Rahim (1986, p. 237) suggests, 'was the eye of the power apparatus of disciplinary society.' Finally, and this is perhaps the crucial issue, the parallel that Foucault then draws between this mode of social control and the growth of the social sciences as *disciplines* points to the importance of the emergence of scientific discourses. Central to this discussion of the discourse of EIL is the development of linguistics and applied linguistics as disciplines, for this 'shedding of light' on language and language teaching has had very much a disciplinary effect.

Although the expansionist zeal of Anglicism was much tempered by both practical and ideological concerns in the colonies, this period was nevertheless crucial for the position of English in the world. While the position that English attained at the centre of the colonial empire was in itself by no means insignificant (though not a necessary precursor to its current global expansion), of more significance was that this position of English occasioned a massive expansion of studies on English, and thus the birth of the discourse of EIL. The importance of Anglicism, therefore, was not so much in spreading the English language throughout the empire but rather in occasioning a massive body of study of English. Orientalism operated as a mode of social control, as a means of defining and creating the colonial Other through a vast new body of knowledge. The colonial enterprise had produced a great wealth of studies of other languages, cultures, religions and so on, and this Orientalist knowledge had become crucial in the establishment of colonial authority. The Anglicist side of the colonial equation had in many ways been less successful: the teaching of English had in many instances had a destabilizing effect. What was ultimately lacking was a greater body of knowledge about English language and literature, which could become part of the means of governance over meanings available to the English-learning colonial subjects.

Anglicist rhetoric in Britain

Anglicism had produced a great deal of expansionist rhetoric in England. The English language, it was suggested, was destined to replace all other languages. English was superior to other languages both in terms of its own qualities and of the culture which it represented. In much of Britain, this was a period of great optimism as Britain secured its new position as the pre-eminent industrialized nation in the globe. This confidence translated into a desire to see the English language and culture spread with the nation's economic expansion. In 1838, looking at this new spread of English, Guest suggested that English

> is rapidly becoming the great medium of civilization, the language of law and literature to the Hindoo, of commerce to the African, of religion to the scattered islands of the Pacific. The range of its influence, even at the present day, is greater than ever was that of the Greek, the Latin, or the Arabic; and the circle widens yearly. Though it were not our living tongue, it would still, of all living languages, be the one most worthy of our study and our cultivation, as bearing most directly on the happiness of mankind.
>
> (Guest, 1838/1882, p. 703)

Similarly, George (1867, p. 6) suggested that 'other languages will remain, but will remain only as the obscure Patois of the world, while English will become the grand medium for all the business of government, for commerce, for law, for science, for literature, for philosophy, and divinity. Thus it will really be a universal language for the great material and spiritual interests of mankind.' Trench (1881, p. 44) quotes Jacob Grimm, the German linguist, as stating in 1832 that 'the English language ... may with all right be called a world-language; and, like the English people, appears destined hereafter to prevail with a sway more extensive even than its present over all the portions of the globe'. For some writers, such as de Quincey, this was a matter of destiny: 'The English language is travelling fast towards the fulfilment of its destiny ... running forward towards its ultimate mission of eating up, like Aaron's rod, all other languages' (de Quincey, 1862, pp. 149–50).

An important aspect, therefore, of the shift in mid-nineteenth century thinking – the confidence in the Empire, the belief in the pre-eminence of Britain as an economic power, the growth in social Darwinism and thus an evolutionary model of cultural development – was that the British people, language and culture were considered superior to all others. This cultural superiority was then considered to be reflected in the English language. Writers such as Archbishop Trench felt that a parallel could be drawn between the liberal institutions of Britain and the liberalism of the language: 'we may trace, I think, as was to be expected, a certain conformity between the genius of our institutions and that of our language' (quoted in Crowley, 1989, p. 75). This assumption that the superiority of the language reflected the superiority of the nation could be used in two different ways: on the one hand, the superiority of the British culture and institutions must be reflected in the English language, thus justifying its superiority; on the other, the English language was evidently of such quality that it could only have derived from a superior culture. Thus, some argued that since Britain was the home of liberalism, democracy and freedom, so too was the language: 'As the mind grows, language grows, and adapts itself to the thinking of the people. Hence, a highly civilized race, will ever have, a highly accomplished language. The English tongue, is in all senses a very noble one. I apply the term noble with a rigorous exactness' (George, 1867, p. 4). Others argued that the frequency of borrowed words in English, for example, reflected the openness not only of the language but also of the British people. This second type of argument can be seen as Trench, looking at the language as an ancestral inheritance, poses the rhetorical question:

> What can more clearly point out their native land and ours as having fulfilled a glorious past, as being destined for a glorious future, than that they should have acquired for themselves and for those who came after them a clear, a strong, a harmonious, a noble language? For all this bears witness to corresponding merits in those that speak it, to clearness of mental vision, to strength, to harmony, to nobleness in them who have gradually shaped and fashioned it to be the utterance of their inmost life and being.
>
> (Trench, 1881, p. 3)

Meanwhile, religious views had also been influenced by the whole missionary project and commonly articulated a position strongly in favour of the spread of English. Indeed, the two predominant philosophies that supported much of the Anglicist drive were Utilitarianism and Evangelicism (Clive, 1973). The connection between English and Christianity was a crucial one, for it suggested ultimately that English was in itself Christian. Viswanathan (1989) argues that the general tendency of the colonial administration to avoid religious instruction in order not to offend the colonized peoples led to a search for another means by which the laws of social order and morality could be inculcated. This medium, she argues, was English literature. Indeed, Viswanathan suggests that 'the discipline of English came into its own in the age of colonialism' (p. 2), and the development of English literature in India in fact served as a trial run in social and political control before it was taken up in Britain. It would seem, however, that not only was it English literature that was seen as this embodiment of Christian thought, but also the language itself. In 1792, Charles Grant had stressed the learning of English in his evangelical project: 'The use and understanding of the English language would enable the Hindus to reason, and to obtain new and better views of their duty as rational and Christian creatures' (Clive, 1973, p. 345).

Indeed, many of those who were consumed by Anglicist zeal were also men of the church. Trench was not only a scholar of the English language but also Archbishop of Dublin. Another man of the church, the Reverend James George, started his lecture on the mission of Great Britain to the world by suggesting that it is God's will that certain nations should rise up and spread at certain points in history; the time had now come for Great Britain to sit 'as a mighty teacher – and while she sits in her matchless powers of political supremacy, commerce, wealth and literature – these influences will combine to diffuse the language, with all the excellences kindred to it throughout the whole world' (p. 8). Thus, he suggested, the nation had been 'commissioned to teach a noble language embodying the richest scientific and literary treasures' (George, 1867, p. 4). Not only was the spread of English the will of God, however; it was also a means of rectifying the sins visited on humans after Babel. Thus, the punishment of speaking in many tongues, George argues, could be assuaged when 'our English speech shall become the universal speech of all men' (p. 7). Thus the messianic spread of English could be seen both as a chosen act of God so that the 'rich freightage with which this Argosy is so majestically sailing down the stream of time' could be borne to all people, and as a means of combating the evils the Lord had brought on humans after the building of the Tower of Babel.[9]

What is of great significance is that this zeal around the nobility of English is indicative not so much of a massive expansion of the English language but rather of a massive increase in interest in English. As Crowley (1989, p. 71) points out, 'the more the English nation extended the boundaries of its empire, the more the English language was praised as a superior language and subjected to extensive study'. As Ashcroft, Griffiths and Tiffin (1989) remark, 'the study of English and the growth of Empire proceeded from a single ideological climate and ... the development of the one is intrinsically bound up with the development of the other' (p. 3). Thus, although Anglicism has probably been given too great a prominence as the central ideology of colonialism, one crucial effect of the expansion of English in the empire was to occasion an ever-growing body of studies of the English language. This work, linked as we have seen to the discourses of colonialism and the moral imperative to educate in English, tied up with questions of standardization (see next chapter), and eventually given the solemn blessing of the scientific discourse of linguistics must be seen as emerging within a very particular set of social, cultural, political and economic conditions in the late nineteenth century. It might be more accurate to say, therefore, that this period witnessed not so much the expansion of English as the expansion of the discourse of English as an international language.

Alongside the knowledge produced by Orientalism as part of the colonial enterprise, therefore, there started to grow a new body of knowledge produced by Anglicism. Orientalism was, in many ways more tolerant, pluralist and sympathetic towards local languages and cultures than Anglicism, which in its strongest versions could be utterly contemptuous of anything but English (or European languages). Nevertheless, there are a number of other things to be considered here. First, as the debate between these two factions shows, 'there was no dispute between Orientalists and Anglicists about the superiority of Western to Eastern literature and learning' (Clive, 1973, p. 356). Second, despite the immense scholarly activity produced within Orientalism, Warren Hastings' original formulation of the doctrine, as Viswanathan (1989) points out, clearly stated that it was part of a process of social and political control. Thus, although Orientalism favoured the study of Oriental languages, it was still a means to exercise social control over the populace and to inculcate Western ideas. According to Niranjana (1992), 'the famous Orientalist attempt to reveal the former greatness of India often manifests itself as the British or European task of translating and thereby *purifying* the debased native texts. This Romantic Orientalist project slides almost imperceptibly into the Utilitarian Victorian enterprise of "improving" the natives through English education' (pp. 16–17).

CONCLUSION

The common assumption that Macaulay's Minute signalled the victory of Anglicism over Orientalism serves several views. First, it has permitted the belief that the spread of English was due to a few misguided fanatics in the nineteenth century, rather than being a long process which only started developing to its current scale within the neocolonial structures of world relationships after the Second World War. Second, it reinforces the view that the key issue is only one of imposing or not imposing a language on other people, rather than seeing this question within the larger context of the complexities of colonial rule. And third, it supports a view that Orientalism was somehow a good and innocent project that only had the rights of colonized people at heart. The implications of this, especially for a view of the colonial or neocolonial history of English as simply the imposition of English on colonized people, are several. First, both Anglicism and Orientalism operated alongside each other; second, Orientalism was as much a part of colonialism as was Anglicism; third, English was withheld as much as it was promoted; fourth, colonized people demanded access to English;[10] and finally, the power of English was not so much in its widespread imposition but in its operating as the eye of the colonial panopticon. This view of colonial education policy also has significant implications for current battles between the English Only movement and supporters of multiculturalism and bilingualism.

The other significant outcome of this discussion is that, in looking for the origins of the discourse of EIL in the colonial era, it seems that more significant than the spread of English itself was the massive expansion of studies on English. The teaching of English in India, as Viswanathan (1989) suggests with respect to literature, can be seen as an experiment in the use of English language teaching as a form of social, cultural and political control. This experiment was not a great success since it produced a class of people who were often simultaneously alienated from their own languages and cultures and discontented with colonial rule. As Mazrui (1975a) and Clive (1973) both suggest, anti-colonial activism originated most often from among the ranks of the English-educated. While Orientalism had produced a massive body of work which, as Said (1978) argues, played a key role in defining and 'disciplining' the constructed Oriental, Anglicism lacked such a body of knowledge. While English remained as the language at the eye of the colonial panopticon, the relative failure of the colonial English experiment occasioned a massive emphasis on studying English, producing both English Studies, with the primary focus on literature, and Linguistics and Applied Linguistics as they developed in the Anglo-Saxon world, with the key focuses on the structure and the teaching of English. Although the spread of English had produced quite a range of expansionist rhetoric, such as de Quincey's belief that it was the destiny of English to 'eat up' all other languages, it also produced the need to define and to control the language, to produce a body of knowledge that held the language and its desired meanings firmly in the hands of the central colonial institutions. It is this growth of linguistics and applied linguistics that is the focus of the next chapter.

NOTES

1. From my discussion of the notion of discourse in the last two chapters, it should be clear that it is being used here to refer not to a piece of text or conversation but rather, in Foucault's (1980b) terms, as that place in which 'power and knowledge are joined together' (p. 100). This use of discourse is akin to, though in my view preferable to, a notion of ideology (see Pennycook, in press). Thus, it is a political understanding of knowledge, a view that sees knowledge as socially constructed and related to questions of power, but does not imply either a notion of false consciousness or some necessary socioeconomic cause. Discourses are organizations of knowledge that have become embedded in social institutions and practices, a constellation of power/knowledge relationships which organize texts and produce and reflect different subject positions. Thus, I take the discourse of EIL to be a particular and predominant way of understanding and articulating the position of English in the world, a discourse that affects how linguists, applied linguists and teachers, amongst others, view, carry out, and talk about our work. Such discourses do not simply emerge, however; rather, they are the result of protracted struggles over the worth, and thus the inclusion or exclusion of different knowledges. It is to an exploration of the complex historical conditions of production of such discourses and to the insurgent possibilities of knowledges that have been cast aside in this process that Foucault's notion of genealogy turns. While I cannot hope to

conduct an exhaustive genealogy of the discourse of EIL here, I shall nevertheless be attempting to make this genealogical sketch, in Foucault's (1979) terms, a 'history of the present'.

2. Similar contempt for non-European languages and cultures can be found in many contexts, including of course North America. Ashcroft (1979) quotes the Federal Superintendent of Indian Affairs, who, in 1895, argued that 'If it were possible to gather in all the Indian children and retain them for a certain period, there would be produced a generation of English-speaking Indians, accustomed to the ways of civilized life . . .' (p. 27). An official document on native education in the United States in 1888 had this to say on native languages:

> These languages may be, and no doubt are, interesting to the philologist, but as a medium for conveying education and civilization to savages they are worse than useless; they are a means of keeping them in their savage condition by perpetuating the traditions of carnage and superstition. . . . To teach the rising generation of the Sioux in their own native tongue is simply to teach the perpetuation of something that can be of no benefit whatever to them. . . . I sincerely hope that all friends of Indian education will unite in the good work of teaching the English language only, and discourage in every way possible the perpetuation of any Indian vernacular.
>
> (Quoted in Hymes, 1983, p. 208)

3. The Residential system was a means by which the British could give an appearance of indirect rule of the Protected Malay States by appointing an adviser (Resident) to the Sultan, supposedly at the request of the Malay rulers. The Resident then appointed a State Council of about ten individuals who met about once every seven years. With the power of the Sultans much reduced and these rulers coopted and given large allowances, the Residents became the effective rulers of the states (see Andaya and Andaya, 1982, pp. 172–5).

4. It is important to note that a large part of the major influx of Chinese and Indian immigrants in the nineteenth century were deliberately imported to Malaya to work as cheap indentured labour in the tin mines and on the rubber plantations. A problem with some of the histories of the region is that they fail to acknowledge the contribution of this background to the growing ethnic mix in Malaya. Thus, in the disappointing historical introduction to Platt and Weber (1980) – considered generally to be a key work on English in Singapore and Malaysia – it is suggested that it was the arrival of Chinese and Tamils that *caused* the rapid expansion of the tin and rubber industries. Rather, as Caldwell (1977a) outlines, Chinese workers were recruited, shipped and controlled largely by the Chinese secret societies and tin

mine owners, and Indian workers were imported by the British from South India and Ceylon to work on the rubber plantations. If the colonial capitalist goals of the British are hidden behind a belief in their maintaining law and order, and if the immense exploitation of Chinese (often by other Chinese) and the Indian workers (Caldwell gives the figures of annual deaths among plantation workers as 200 per thousand, as opposed to ten per thousand for Europeans) is not understood, then neither can the colonial era in Malaya nor its legacies be properly understood.

5. These views on schooling as moral and social regulation should be seen within the broader context of nineteenth-century education in Britain and its orientation towards the production and regulation of desired and undesired behaviour and expression (see, for example, Corrigan, 1987).

6. Loh Fook Seng (1975) describes this as 'an enigma' (p. 122), but I would suggest it is perfectly explicable in the light of the argument that these Malay scholars and Orientalists on the one hand bore a true affection for and interest in the Malays, but on the other hand felt that these 'noble peasants' should remain unchanged.

7. This does not necessarily contradict Tan Cheng Lock's view. Malay was presumably the most commonly used language, although English enjoyed a special status in the towns and between various groups.

8. *Kampong* is Malay for village, a word that has a long history as part of local English.

9. With such fundamentalist rhetoric echoing around the United States in the 1980s and 1990s, it would be interesting to know to what extent many of the Christians who rode on the back of the English language teaching boom to China and other countries were fuelled by such an anti-Babel mission. Rather than English language teaching being simply a means of Christian proselytism, therefore, it may also be a goal in itself.

10. Niranjana (1992) points out, however, that this demand for English was also a colonial construct, i.e. the colonizers constructed a view of local people crying out for English in order to justify their promotion of the language.

FOUR

Spreading the word/disciplining the language

The linguistics introduced by Saussure placed theoretical constraints upon the freedom of the individual speaker no less rigid than the authoritarian recommendations of the old-fashioned grammarian pedagogue.

(Harris, 1981, p. 46)

I am very much interested in the question of Basic English. The widespread use of this would be a gain to us far more durable and fruitful than the annexation of great provinces.

(Winston Churchill, 1943)

What types of knowledge do you want to disqualify in the very instant of your demand 'Is it a science?'

(Foucault, 1980a, p. 85)

INTRODUCTION: ANTI-NOMADIC DISCIPLINES

In this part of the book (Chapters 3–5), which focuses on how the spread of English has been theorized and described in the dominant discourses of the Western academy, the previous chapter dealt with an overview of colonial language and educational policies. A key conclusion of Chapter 3 was that ultimately the most significant effect of the colonial spread of English may have been not so much the Anglicist insistence on education in English but rather the Anglicist-inspired study of English. While Orientalism had produced a vast body of knowledge about the colonial Other, the growing pre-eminence of English required that the language be more clearly defined, understood and regulated.

While the word spread, the language needed to be disciplined. This chapter will look most closely at how the discourse of EIL has its origins in a key area of this growth of English studies, the broad discursive fields of linguistics and applied linguistics. Thus, following Simon's (1992) argument that, given 'the integral connection between knowledge forms and forms of power ... in order to trace the effects of theory, it is necessary both to historicize its production and contextualize its distribution' (p. 85), this chapter will seek to historicize the production of and contextualize the distribution of linguistic and applied linguistic theories and practices insofar as they are connected to the discourse of EIL.

There is a crucial period in the nineteenth century during which several key elements came together to produce a very particular orientation towards language. From amidst the context of rapid industrialization and standardization of the workforce, the massive expansion of the British Empire, social Darwinism, and the beliefs in the absolute supremacy of scientific methods, a body of thought arose that was to have a major disciplining effect first on language and then on language teaching. According to Foucault (1979), 'one of the primary objects of discipline is to fix; it is an anti-nomadic technique' (p. 218). The development of linguistics and applied linguistics as disciplines had the same effect; while the English language was embarking on its great nomadic voyage, linguistics and applied linguistics developed as anti-nomadic techniques, disciplines interested in the controlling and disciplining of the language.

The word 'discipline' here needs to be understood in a Foucauldian sense; that is to say that the construction of the *discipline* of linguistics and the *discipline* of applied linguistics had a *disciplining* effect (cf. *surveillance* in French) on the construction of knowledge about language teaching. As Foucault (1979) puts it, 'disciplines are techniques for assuring the ordering of human multiplicities' (p. 218). A key focus here will be on the establishment of knowledge about language and language teaching as scientific knowledge, as an ordering of the human multiplicities possible in language and language teaching. Foucault (1980a) argues that, in light of the dominance of scientific knowledge in industrialized societies, genealogies (see Chapter 3, note 1) are almost inevitably and precisely 'anti-sciences' (p. 83), and thus are concerned with 'the insurrection of knowledges that are opposed primarily ... to the effects of the centralizing powers which are linked to the institution and functioning of an organized scientific discourse within a society such as ours' (p. 84). This project, therefore, aims both to look at the knowledges *included* in the formation of the scientific discipline of applied linguistics and to suggest what knowledges may have been *exluded* in this process. As Foucault (1980a) puts it, 'in contrast to the various projects which aim to inscribe knowledges in the hierarchical order of power associated with science, a genealogy should be seen as a kind of attempt to emancipate historical knowledges from that subjection, to render them, that is, capable of opposition and of struggle against the coercion of a theoretical, unitary, formal and scientific discourse' (p. 85).

THE DISCIPLINING OF LINGUISTICS

The spread of English under colonialism occasioned a massive increase in studies of the language. While English had become the language at the eye of colonial discipline, the question remained as to who would discipline the language – *quis custodiet ipsos custodes*? This section will deal with the growth of linguistics with two very particular issues in mind: first, the question of standardization, the development of standard English as a very particular construction of the nineteenth century, one that has been held in place by the discipline of linguistics; second, the extent to which linguistics is a very particular European cultural form. From the cultural politics of linguistics has emerged a view of language as a homogeneous unity, as objectively describable, as an isolated structural entity; meaning is taken either to reside in a world/word correspondence that is best articulated in English or within the system itself (and typically in the brain of the native speaker); monolingualism is taken to be the norm; and speech is always given priority over writing.

It is no easy task to establish where to start with a discussion of linguistics. In *A Short History of Linguistics*, for example, Robins (1979) argues against the fallacy which takes science as a slow accumulation of truth and which therefore privileges the more recent science of linguistics as the real arbiter of truth about language. Instead, he suggests that we should see different investigations into language as serving different purposes at different times; accordingly, he starts his history of linguistics with the Greeks (while acknowledging the importance of other traditions such as the Indian). Many books claim, however, that modern linguistics started with Saussure, though there have also been successive rival claims to have developed a more scientific linguistics, so that some might see Bloomfield in the 1930s, or Lado and Fries in the 1950s, or Chomsky in the 1960s as the true originators of the modern discipline. It is exactly these claims to science and rigour that are of interest as different linguists have sought to establish their views over those of their predecessors. The key period in this process is the late nineteenth century (out of which Saussure's work emerged), with the commonly made claim that the development at this time of a new science of linguistics marked the end of *prescriptive* grammars and the beginning of *descriptive* linguistics.[1]

My contention, by contrast, is that although there was indeed a great deal of prescription in earlier years, the effect of the growth of linguistics as a scientific discipline was an even more rigorous *disciplining of the language* than that which had gone before. Furthermore, this disciplining of the language was intimately connected to the *spreading of the word* through imperial expansion. With the spread of English across the empire, the issue of the standardization of English became not merely one of cultural politics within Great Britain but increasingly one of imperial cultural politics. The putting into discourse of a view of a global standard English was to become a key tenet of the discourse of EIL. The significance of a process of standardization should not be overlooked for it is connected both to the construction of social difference (by privileging one form of language over others and giving people differential access to that privileged form) and to the denial of forms of social difference (by regulating the forms of expression available in the language). Shapiro's (1989) discussion of 'language purism' expresses this well.

> At many levels, a society's approach to the Other is constitutive of the breadth of meaning and value it is prepared to tolerate. Language purism is a move in the direction of narrowing legitimate forms of meaning and thereby declaring out-of-bounds certain dimensions of otherness. It is not as dramatic and easily politicized as the extermination of an ethnic minority or even so easily made contentious

as the proscription of various forms of social deviance. But the Other is located most fundamentally in language, the medium for representing selves and other. Therefore, any move that alters language by centralizing and pruning or decentralizing and diversifying alters the ecology of Self–Other relations and thereby the identities that contain and animate relations of power and authority.

(p. 28)

Standardizing the language

In his discussion of the relationship between early language standardization and the growth of the nation state, Illich (1981a; 1981b) compares the effects of Christopher Columbus's voyage to discover new trade routes with the effects of Nebrija's *Gramatica Castellana*, printed fifteen days after Columbus set sail (3 and 18 August 1492, respectively). Illich argues that while both were offering their services to a new type of empire building, Nebrija's proposal for a grammar was more significant. Columbus was merely proposing to expand trade routes and the political influence of Spain; Nebrija argues for influence over a totally new domain: 'state control over the shape of people's everyday subsistence' (1981b, p. 21). His grammar was written, Illich suggests, 'as a tool for conquest abroad and as a weapon to suppress untutored speech at home' (p. 7). Language, Nebrija argued, 'has always been the consort of empire, and forever shall remain its mate', and as he explained in his petition for support to Queen Isabella, his grammar would be a 'tool to colonize the language spoken by her own subjects' (p. 6). While the extensive critical attention drawn to the history of European colonization of the Americas by the 500th anniversary of Columbus's voyage was a welcome commentary on this history of genocide and abuse, there was perhaps an irony here that the colonizing process that Nebrija put in motion was largely overlooked.

Although, as Howatt (1984a) suggests, the 'fixing of the language' was a long process that can be traced back through the seventeenth and eighteenth centuries, it was the relationship between standardization of the language and standardization of education that was to prove crucial in the cultural and political context of the nineteenth century. Of great importance here, however, is the understanding that such changes and standardizations of the language were not merely movements towards randomly chosen rules but rather reflected other societal changes. Martin (1987) observes that the period around 1800 marked a point in medical science when devastating attacks were made on the previously held belief that men's and women's bodies were analogously structured, leading to a whole series of studies aimed to show fundamental biological differences between the sexes. Within this context of a major regrouping in relationships between men and women, it is not coincidental that, as Bodine (1975) shows, this period also saw the proscription of the singular use of 'they', culminating in the 1850 Act of Parliament that legally replaced 'he or she' with 'he'. If such changes were particularly gendered, others were based more in class relationships.

In her study of the politics of language around the end of the eighteenth and the beginning of the nineteenth centuries, Smith (1984) shows how attitudes towards language served to justify and maintain the harshly inequitable social divisions during this period. These ideas were based on the belief that language reveals the mind and that to speak the common or 'vulgar' language demonstrated that one belonged to the vulgar classes and thus that one was morally and intellectually inferior. A clear dichotomy was constructed between the 'refined' language, in which noble sentiments and higher intellectual ideas could be expressed, and the vulgar language, in which only base passions and expression of sensations was possible. To maintain such a distinction, Smith suggests, required a great deal of work to construct a refined version of the language which was as different as possible from the vulgar, hence the unprecedented intensity of study of the language during the period.

Smith's (1984) work clearly illustrates how English was constructed in very particular ways to serve very particular cultural political goals. Those who spoke the refined version of the language were considered to be rational, moral, civilized, and capable of abstract thought, while those who spoke the vulgar version were allegedly irrational, controlled by emotion, materialist, and unable to transcend the immediate concerns of the present. Thus a fundamental series of dichotomies was established, marked by linguistic differences: using one form of the language or another could bestow on the speaker either desirable or undesirable qualities. This construction of the language was to have great significance when taken up within the discourses of colonialism and their particular construction of colonizers and colonized. Indeed, once a notion that to speak a certain type of English bestowed qualities such as civilized, educated and so on became part of the discourse of EIL, learning, speaking and teaching English came to have very particular connotations.

This work on the English language, coupled with the growth of standardization in education, was to lay the ground for a new era of linguistic standardization. It was based on the belief in *standard English*, which, as Crowley (1989) and Harris (1988) have convincingly argued, was itself a creation of the mid to late nineteenth century. As various historians (e.g. Hobsbawm, 1983) have demonstrated, the Victorian era was a period characterized by the wholesale invention of traditions. With Britain going through massive social upheavals as it became increasingly industrialized and the pre-eminent global power through its colonial activities, there were numerous attempts to establish continuity with a suitable historic past, an attempt to structure some parts of life as unchanging and invariant. As Ranger (1983) puts it in his essay on the invention of tradition in colonial Africa: 'The 1870s, 1880s and 1890s were the time of a great flowering of European invented tradition – ecclesiastical, educational, military, republican, monarchical. They were also the time of the European rush into Africa. There were many and complex connections between the two processes' (p. 211). As Ranger suggests for Africa and Cohn (1983) for India, the invention of traditions became a crucial part of colonial rule as the British sought to justify their presence and redefine the colonized societies in new terms.

It is important to understand the development of a standard language within this larger framework. Thus, as Harris (1988) argues, the myth of standard English was originally formulated in the Victorian era and was consolidated in the period between the wars, especially with the publication of the *Oxford English Dictionary* in 1928. Indeed, as Harris points out, the *OED* quoted its own proposal for the writing of the dictionary in 1858 as the first use of the phrase 'standard English'.[2] 'There can hardly be a more remarkable example in intellectual history' Harris (1988, p. 17) suggests 'of quoting one's own claim as evidence to establish the validity of what was claimed.' It is worth looking in more detail, then, at the creation of this myth in relation to the development of Victorian Britain and the British Empire.

Towards prescription

In Crowley's (1989) extensive investigation of the development of a notion of standardization, he first points out yet another myth associated with linguistics. This oft-repeated belief is that there was a major shift from the eighteenth-century social and rhetorical concerns with language to an objective and scientific approach in the nineteenth and twentieth centuries. This shift, a commonplace assertion in most linguistics texts, is usually stated in terms of a move from prescription to description, from the attempts to stipulate what *should* be spoken, what counted as 'good' English, to purely descriptive accounts of the language that considered language from an objective and scientific viewpoint. Yet, as Crowley's study shows, no such shift from prescription to description in fact took place: 'The objectification of language . . . is a construction of the history of the study of language in Britain that cannot be supported by the evidence . . . a discursive construction that serves particular social and rhetorical purposes' (1989, pp. 13-14). This discursive construction was to become a key tenet of the discourse of EIL, for it has long been a cherished belief of linguists and applied linguists that their work involves only the objective description of language rather than any prescription or proscription of language forms. Such a position, Crowley suggests, is not tenable.

> Amongst linguists there was a clear shift *towards* (rather than away as most accounts would have it) prescription and proscription. That is, a clear discrimination between various forms of language *and* the banishment of certain forms. . . . Certain forms were to be prescribed (the educated, cultured, good), others proscribed (the vulgar, rude, coarse), and the language was again to be divided in terms of social class.
>
> (1989, p. 157)

Indeed, Harris (1980) argues that this constant attempt by modern linguists to claim descriptive neutrality for their work and to distance themselves from their supposedly more prescriptive predecessors will eventually be seen as one of the most salient and most misguided features of twentieth-century linguistics: 'When the history of twentieth-century linguistics comes to be written, a naive, unquestioning faith in the validity of this distinction will doubtless be seen as one of the main factors in the academic sociology of the subject' (p. 152).

Crowley suggests that although Foucault (1970) is correct in general in his assertion that the appearance of historicity is the major factor in the shift that took place in linguistics (and other fields) around the beginning of the nineteenth century, it is dangerous to overgeneralize this tendency and thus to assume that European and British linguistics developed in the same way. Comparative philology, the study of the history of *language*, indeed became the predominant interest of European linguists. In Britain, however, the focus was much more on the history of *the language*, i.e. English. This study, this attempt to fix a standard form for English and to trace it back through British history, was a reaction to particular shifts in the political, economic and cultural discourses of early and mid-nineteenth-century Britain, especially Chartism and other workers' movements in Britain, and the rapid expansion of the empire. Thus, the particular work being done on the English language at this time should be seen perhaps not so much as part of a general epistemological orientation in Europe, but rather as another instance of the worldliness of English, of the very particular social, cultural and political battles that were being fought.

On the local level, the attempt to establish a standard was part of a more general reaction to labour unrest. Within the context of stricter labour laws and the rapid standardization of education, moves were also made to standardize English in order to operate more centralized control over education, language, printing, reading and, possibly, thought. As Harris (1988, p. 19) puts it, 'the dubious marriage of historical lexicography with educational reform produced the even more dubious offspring of a "standard language" '. This standard was based on a concept of a *standard literary language*, a language based on the literary canon. Significantly, of course, this was also the era of the creation of the literary canon, and Crowley suggests that the canon was, in fact, a direct result of the attempt to develop a standard language: 'The reason for the marked appearance of the canon of English literature at this period was quite simply its previous nonexistence and the need for it that had been produced by the work of the linguistic historians' (1989, p. 123). The drive to develop a standard version of the language based on literary texts and with historical validity, then, was a major factor in the development of the literary canon, which has only recently started to be deconstructed (see, for example, Batsleer et al., 1985; P. Widdowson, 1982).

The nineteenth century saw the tracing of a standard literary language as a historical phenomenon by the linguistic historians as it emerged into its role as the national, uniform, written language. There was also a process of defining the standard spoken form, whose value was defined not so much by its uniformity but by the social status of its speakers. This second definition was based on clear regional, gender and class criteria. The commonly accepted norm for the spoken form of the language was that spoken by men who had been educated in the public schools of the South. Le Page (1985) points out that the emergence of this 'Received Pronunciation' (RP) was due to a number of connected developments: the shift from entry into the Civil Service by patronage to entry by examination, the reforms at Oxford and Cambridge Universities so that they became training grounds for these civil servants, the public school reforms so that they in turn became avenues of entry to the universities, and the recruitment of public school teachers only from these two universities. 'A new self-perpetuating élite was established, to which admission was through similarity of education proclaimed by similarity of linguistic behaviour' (Le Page, 1985, p. 32).

The particular type of work done on the English language in the nineteenth century was linked not only to cultural and political concerns within Britain, but also to the expansion of the empire. As Harris (1987; 1988) and Crowley (1989) suggest, the standardization of English was a very particular construction of the Victorian era. 'To conjure up a "standard English" as the "national language" of English-speaking people was to invent a sociolinguistic fiction' (Harris, 1987, p. 115). This nexus of views on language was framed within, on the one hand, attempts to combat growing labour unrest in Britain by greater standardization through education, and, on the other, the attitudes towards the spread of English in the globe. 'Given sufficient optimism, it was perhaps understandable that the equation of standard English with national norm, and that in turn with dominant international language, should be treated as a foregone historical conclusion' (ibid., p. 119). Crowley's work, furthermore, has illuminated not only the construction of the standard language and its links to social control and imperialism but also the myth of objectivity to which linguistics has laid claim. This standardization of English had major ramifications for the construction of the discourse of EIL, especially when we consider Harris's suggestion that an equation between standard English and the dominant international language was seen as an inevitable historical process.

Linguistics as a European cultural form

If a key connection in the growth of linguistics, and ultimately the discourse of EIL, was with the formation of a version of standard English, equally important was the construction of linguistics as a European cultural form. It is important here to understand the construction of the concept of language as it has grown up in Europe and North America, since it was these European origins that gave rise to the 'givens' of modern linguistics. There are at least two important reasons for engaging in such an investigation: to historicize our view of linguistics, showing the philosophical tenets and shifts that gave rise to various views on language and communication; and to show that the views held by most Western linguists (and therefore, alas, by many others) are but the legacy of very particular political and cultural circumstances in Europe. Thus, just as we may argue that different languages cut the world up differently, so it may also be reasoned do different languages cut themselves and each other up differently. There is no Archimedean point from which we can regard either the world or language; linguistics is obliged to study language through language. Linguistics, like language, has been forged in the contested terrains of cultural politics, a fact which has particular ramifications for the discourse of EIL since linguistics and applied linguistics form such key elements of this discourse.

First, we should acknowledge that the notion of language as it grew up in Europe was intimately tied to the growth of the nation state. 'Is it accidental', asks Fairclough (1989, p. 22), 'that the emergence of the notion of *langue* occurred during a period when the myth of the "national language" was at its height – the turn of the twentieth century?' As emerging post-Renaissance states sought to wean their citizenry away from the church and to strengthen their hold over diverse groups of people by developing the concept of a homogeneous ethnicity, so the fundamentally important notion of *a language* as a shared means of communication between this homogeneous national/cultural group was born. Illich (1981a, b; and see previous section) gives a detailed account of Nebrija's arguments to Queen Isabella of Spain for funding his new grammar of Castillian. He argues that this first attempt to describe Spanish dialects as a uniform, standardized entity would be a crucial tool both in creating a notion of homogeneity within the nation and as a tool of linguistic colonization beyond the shores of Spain. Governmental control over the language, he insisted, could also greatly limit the dangerously diverse reading that was at that time occurring across the country.

This political construct was to take on even greater significance in the nineteenth century with the coming of industrialization and colonialism. This era saw the attempts to establish mass education and a standardized language (see above) and to use these further to subjugate not only the people within one country but also those in the growing empires. As Harris (1981) suggests, the construction of the modern European myth of language was a cultural product of post-Renaissance Europe, reflecting the political psychology of nationalism and the devotion of the education system to a desire to standardize the linguistic behaviour of its pupils. This notion of a language as a homogeneous unity shared by the inhabitants of a nation state was finally to be taken up and given a 'scientific' blessing as the twentieth century witnessed the emergence of linguistics in its modern form. Thus, 'the orthological dogma of Renaissance nationalism was finally reinstated as the official doctrine of twentieth-century linguistics. What had started out as a patriotic aspiration was eventually given the solemn blessing of modern science' (Harris, 1980, p. 167). The connections among Saussure's particular conception of '*la langue*', his idealization of the community of the nation state, and the political crises of the European states in the early part of the twentieth century cannot therefore be ignored.

This European development of a notion of language also brought with it a series of understandings of language and communication that can be seen to be once again specifically European in their cultural origins. An important aspect of this is the specific ways in which meaning has been understood, either in terms of a representationalist or of a structuralist view of language (see Harris, 1980; 1981; Morgan, 1987). In the first view, which has been called variously representationalism, correspondence theory, surrogationalism and expressivism, language is held to be a transparent medium which represents the material world in a one-to-one correspondence or which expresses thought in a similarly transparent way. In this view, therefore, meaning is said to lie in the linguistic representation of a prelinguistic material reality or in the prelinguistic thoughts of an individual. Although challenged by Saussure's structuralism, this view has been at the very heart of a great deal of European thought, from St Augustine to Bertrand Russell.

There are a number of shortcomings with this view – such as its reduction of language to a passive mirror of reality and its denial, therefore, that language may play a role in creating reality – but there is a particularly significant aspect of this understanding of language when applied to English. An example can be found in the works of the influential grammarian/linguist Otto Jespersen. It is worth observing in passing how Jespersen's discussions of English often reflect to a remarkable degree the Anglicist rhetoric illustrated in the previous chapter. In one work, Jespersen (1938/ 1968) argues that English is a 'masculine' language since English consonants are 'clearly and precisely pronounced' (p. 2). After analysing consonant clusters in the first ten stanzas of Tennyson's *Locksley Hall*, he is able to conclude that 'the English language is a methodical, energetic, business-like and sober language, that does not care much for finery and elegance, but does care for logical consistency and is opposed to any attempt to narrow-in life by police regulations and strict rules either of grammar or of lexicon. As the language is, so also is the nation' (p. 16). Clearly, such a description of English has less to do with some notion of scientific description than it does with discursive production, here the production of an English that is superior to other languages, masculine, logically consistent, sober, energetic, businesslike and free. And while the tone and style of such rhetoric have changed, this discourse lives on in much of the more soberly celebratory writing on the spread of English.

Of greater interest than such constructions of English, however, are the implications for the status of English from some comments made by Jespersen a few years earlier. With respect to lexical diversity in 'primitive languages', Jespersen (1922/1969) argues that the presence in Zulu of many words for 'cow' or in Lithuanian of many words for 'grey' illustrates the fact that 'primitive man did not see the wood from the trees' (p. 430). There are at least three important elements worth noting in this view. First, it is assumed that there is a necessary correspondence between the world and language. Second, it is assumed that there is an evolutionary process from primitive and partial representation of the world (in 'primitive' languages) to developed and full representation (in 'advanced' languages). And third, it is assumed that such a correspondence has truly been arrived at only in the most advanced of all languages, namely English. Fernando (1986) has pointed to the full significance of this view with respect to the position of English in the world.

> Because a major proportion of the modern extensions of knowledge have been conducted and recorded in English, far too many people have fallen victim to two serious fallacies: one is the influential and peculiarly Western notion that 'Language' is capable of describing the whole of nature alone: nature can be put entirely and completely into words. The other submerged assumption is that English, particularly, is capable of doing this, that other languages – usually Asian ones – do not have the full range of concepts necessary for the purpose.
>
> (Fernando, 1986, p. 108)

Not only has this belief that language is a simple representation of reality become a key assumption about language within the powerful scientist[3] discourse on language – linguistics – (with all the questions about effects of claims to truth that such an observation entails), but the effects of so much work having been done in and on English itself (see, for example, Kachru, 1990) have led these assumptions to take a very particular direction with respect to a world-object correspondence and a fixed community of users. There is, therefore, a key assumption within the discourse of EIL that the world as described by English is the world as it really is and thus to learn English is essential if anyone wants to understand the modern world.

The representationalist view of language came under attack from Saussure, among others (e.g. Wittgenstein), in his argument that meaning was not dependent on a correspondence with an outside world but was dependent on *internal* structural relationships. Nevertheless, it would be wrong to conclude that this structuralist view of language replaced a representationalist view; rather, they have continued to operate alongside each other. The structuralist view of meaning was to have even greater implications for the global position of English, for it is here that we can see most clearly one of the centralizing effects of linguistics. Once meaning is assumed to reside in the linguistic system itself, and as long as the convenient fiction can be maintained that this English as an international language is indeed one distinct linguistic system, then clearly the definition of meanings resides in the describers of the language.

This centralizing of meaning is reinforced by Saussure's view of language as a fixed code shared by a homogeneous speech community as the guarantor of shared meanings. Languages are taken to be fixed and agreed-upon codes for 'language communities' to express their ideas. This model of communication, then, holds that 'individuals are able to exchange their thoughts by means of words because – and insofar as – they have come to understand and to adhere to a fixed public plan for doing so' (Harris, 1981, p. 10). This suggests, therefore, that there is some kind of tacit agreement on meanings in English that is shared by speakers the world over as they develop 'competence' in the language. The continuation of such beliefs can be found most clearly in the generativists' concept of a homogeneous speech community and its 'communicative cripple' (Harris, 1981, p. 33), the 'ideal speaker–hearer'.

Saussurean structuralism had a number of further significant effects for the discussion here, notably the emphases on monolingualism, linguistic competence and phonocentrism, as well as a belief that language could be dealt with entirely in terms of its internal structure and thus without reference to its cultural, social, historical and political contexts. One product of this thinking, then, which has great significance to the issues of this book, is the way that thought on linguistics from Saussure through to Chomsky and beyond has taken monolingualism to be the norm, a view clearly rooted far more in the language myths of Europe than in the multilingual contexts in which most people in the world live. 'Saussure evidently saw the linguistically "normal" individual as being a monoglot, and the linguistically "normal" community as being a monoglot community. Bilingualism or multilingualism are apparently "unnatural" conditions for Saussure, and he never discusses them' (Harris, 1987, p. 112). Such an assumption not only has major implications for linguistics but has had a very particular influence on applied linguistic work in language planning and language teaching (see next section).

The centring of these beliefs around the 'linguistic competence' of the individual led to the reinforcement of a notion of a standard language, thus dismissing other forms of language as incorrect. As Harris (1981, p. 46) points out: 'The linguistics introduced by Saussure placed theoretical constraints upon the freedom of the individual speaker no less rigid than the authoritarian recommendations of the old-fashioned grammarian pedagogue. But instead of the rules being imposed by the educational pedants, they were envisaged as being imposed from within the language itself.' As Bourne (1988; and cf. Harris, 1987) suggests, the increasing awareness of linguistic diversity in the 1960s was countered by Chomsky's move to internalize the notion of a fixed, unitary language as an innate system, relegating all variation to the random vagaries of performance. Second language acquisition research further applied the notion of a homogeneous language to performance data and 'thus bolstered the notion of a unitary, homogeneous, national standard English, as a code in which meaning stands in a fixed unproblematic relationship to form, not simply by social consent, but by mental programming' (Bourne, 1988, p. 88).

A further key tenet of linguistics as it started to develop in the late nineteenth century is its phonocentrism, or its insistence on the primacy of speech over writing. While there appear to be some particular causes for this new obsession with the spoken language during this period – the advent of better technology for the analysis of sounds for example, or the reaction of this new generation of linguists against the text-based analyses of the philologists – this emphasis appears to have deeper significance than these technological or academic arguments would suggest. The dogmatic insistence on the primacy of oral language can be seen as part of the structuralists' refusal to deal with the social and cultural implications of language. Linguists may adduce numerous arguments in favour of the priority of speech; Lyons (1981), for example, argues that speech has historical priority (in the course of human development it appears that spoken language has always developed before written), structural priority (writing is a visual representation of speech), functional priority (spoken language has more uses than written) and biological priority (spoken language emerges first in the child, who may in fact be biologically 'pre-programmed' to produce speech) (pp. 12–15). As Harris (1980) suggests, however, these arguments miss 'the vital point that although *homo loquens* is undoubtedly the precursor of *homo scribens*, the emergence of *homo scribens* makes a radical and henceforward irreversible difference to what a language is, irrespective of the media employed' (p. 14). The point here is that the advent of writing fundamentally changed the nature of language, society and culture and to insist on the priority of spoken language is to deal with language in some idealized abstracted context.

Derrida (1974) goes further in his analysis of this phonocentrism, suggesting that there was 'at the very moment by which linguistics is instituted as a science, a metaphysical presupposition about the relationship between speech and writing' (p. 28). He compares Saussure's views with those of Rousseau, who argued that 'Writing is nothing but the representation of speech; it is bizarre that one gives more care to the determining of the image than the object' (cited in Derrida, 1974, p. 36). What emerges from this comparison is that Saussure's belief that the normal, the natural and the undisguised form of language is in its spoken form recapitulates Rousseau's belief not only in the 'noble savage' but in the 'noble oral savage'. This phonocentrism, then, becomes a kind of Orientalism (see Chapters 2 and 3), a belief that speech reveals the pure unsullied thoughts of our primitive selves. Derrida's argument, therefore, is not intended to reverse the speech/writing hierarchy, but rather, on the one hand, to deconstruct this hierarchy itself and, on the other, to show that the centrism implied in phonocentrism is part of what he sees as the larger Western tendency towards logocentrism, that belief in ultimate causes and origins in God, the Word or the Unitary Self. This phonocentrism also has major implications for many of the underlying assumptions of language teaching.

Positivism and structuralism

Two other key aspects of linguistics are its claim to being a science and its adherence to structuralist principles. This insistence on linguistics being the science of language (see, for example, Lyons, 1981) has long been essential to the discipline of linguistics: 'that linguistics is a science is certainly the claim made for it by all its practitioners since Saussure' (Robinson, 1975, p. 1). Derrida (1974) suggests that of all the human sciences, 'linguistics is the one science whose scientificity is given as an example with a zealous and insistent unanimity' (p. 28). What is of significance here is not whether linguistics is or is not a science, but what the effects of such claims to truth may be. To constitute thought as a scientific discipline on the one hand excludes other possible knowledges, and on the other hand gives this particular discourse extreme power (see Foucault, 1980a). One of the significant effects of nativism, with its positing of an innate language acquisition device, was that it allowed linguists to make even greater claims to be engaged in an empirical science. Unlike Saussure's psychologistic notion of the sign (which was in any case to be rejected later by Bloomfield in favour of a more empirically amenable notion of language behaviour), nativists could now claim to be investigating a biological reality, a physical part of the human brain available to empirical analysis. It is interesting to note that within linguistics and applied linguistics, Chomsky and his followers are often considered to have forsaken structuralism because of Chomsky's critique of the behaviourist base of North American structuralism. As Robinson (1975) suggests, however, the claims to a Chomskyan revolution will in time be recognized as 'only another episode in the history of the long and desperate effort to reduce thought about language to an exact science' (p. 186).

Another part of the Saussurean legacy is the dominance of the structuralist belief that language is an objective and fixed system amenable to analysis (for a criticism of this view, see Chapter 1), which excludes all social, cultural or political implications of language use. Such a position allows for the tendency to ignore, for example, the multiple social, cultural and political effects of literacy. Chapter 1 focused on numerous other ways in which language cannot be taken up from a structuralist perspective. One further aspect of this view is to insist on a form of linguistic universalism, whereby it is assumed that languages represent basically equivalent means of expression with only superficial surface differences. With language being split from culture, some of the more extreme differences between languages are then explained away as 'cultural differences'. Thus it is never considered that languages and concepts of language are constitutive parts of any culture and that there may indeed be incommensurability between languages. Instead, difference is explained away as 'cultural' and linguists can adhere to a belief in linguistic universality.

Linguistics as it has developed this century is, first of all, a very particular cultural form. Thus, the linguist, despite claims to objectivity and universality, is as locked into a certain world view as any of us. As Harris (1987, p. 130) puts it, 'far from having the (largely illusory) objectivity of the natural sciences (which it likes to claim), modern linguistics constantly projects into its analysis of language the biases and assumptions of a particular cultural tradition, even while overtly disavowing them'. Similarly, Le Page (1985) comments that 'Most Western linguists today are strongly influenced in their theoretical approach by their own prescriptive education, by their concept of the relationship between national language and nation-states, by doctrines of correctness, and by monolithic grammars which seek always to represent all varieties of English as based upon a central English grammar' (p. 31).

Now one might, as does Harris (1981), go on to suggest that the limitations of linguistics render it inadequate as a science of language: It is according to the criterion of its ability to deal with language in its communicative contexts rather than as an abstract phenomenon 'that the orthodox tradition of modern linguistics, from Saussurean structuralism down to contemporary generativism, must be judged; and must be found to fail' (p. 166). This is not merely a question of omission, Harris suggests, but rather a refusal to deal with the essential elements of language: 'The sterility of modern linguistic orthodoxy is precisely that it relegates the essential features and conditions of language to the realm of the non-linguistic' (ibid.). Important though this failure is, however, it is not the central concern of my writing here. I am more interested in the *truth effects* of the discourses of linguistics than the *truth* itself (whatever that might mean). That is to say, my concern is not so much with the descriptive adequacy of linguistics (though clearly there are many problems here) as with the effects of its claims to descriptive adequacy.

As a dominant informing discourse to the discourse of EIL, linguistics on the one hand has a very particular normative and prescriptive basis, despite its constant attempts to claim scientific status and objectivity, and on the other hand, through its claims to scientific status and the discovery of objective, universalizable language laws, has come to embody a very particular set of views on language that derive from a specific cultural politics. The two dominant conceptions of meaning, either representationalism (meaning is dependent on a relationship to an objective world) or

structuralism (meaning is dependent on internal structural relationships in language), leave meaning not in the hands of the users, as
a point of contestation, as an issue of cultural politics, but in the
hands of those in the centre, in the first case through an assumed
reciprocal connection between English and the best representation
of the world (see Fernando, 1986), and in the second case through
an assumed linguistic system (English) from within which
meanings are defined. Furthermore, as Derrida (1974) suggests, the
phonocentrism of linguistics is not merely a fascination with the
sound but, rather, is part of the logocentrism at the heart of
Western philosophy, which once again posits a series of core
meanings and truths that are not in the hands of the everyday
language user. Thus, from a position that claims legitimacy
through its status as a Western science, linguistics distances itself
from questions concerning society, culture and politics – the
worldliness of English – and at the same time prescribes both a
particular view of language (monolinguistic and phonocentric) and
particular forms of that language.

THE DISCIPLINING OF APPLIED LINGUISTICS

As with the discussion of linguistics in the last section, this
treatment of applied linguistics will be a very partial one, a
reading against the grain that differs in a number of ways from
other histories. Applied linguistics should be seen not so much as a
gradual accumulation of scientific knowledge, not so much as a
linear progress that has moved ever closer to an articulation of
some truth about language teaching and learning (a belief
frequently reiterated in applied linguistic texts). Rather, applied
linguistics has emerged as a remarkably cohesive and powerful
discourse on language education (and other domains of applied
linguistic work). The principal concern here, then, is how the
discourse of applied linguistics has been constructed, how it has
increasingly come to exert power over language teaching, and how
it has gradually developed as an autonomous discipline. From a
secondary position as an area of 'applied' or 'practical' work that
was seen as inferior to its theoretical parent, linguistics, it has
emerged as a discipline in its own right, an emergence that can be
seen in terms of the development of its own hierarchy between

theory and practice. The point here is not to show the shifts and changes in applied linguistics, to demonstrate how it has gone through paradigm shifts and upheavals,[4] but rather to show the consistencies in the development of applied linguistics. Thus, just as Foucault (1980b) argues that the nineteenth and twentieth centuries are marked more by commonality in terms of the 'putting into discourse' of sexuality rather than by disjuncture between nineteenth-century proscription and twentieth-century libertarianism, so it is more important to grasp the commonality to the putting into discourse of a range of issues around English language teaching, rather than concentrating on some apparent disjuncture between different eras in the nineteenth and twentieth centuries.

This is not, therefore, an attempt to show that English language teaching theory has been inherently expansionist, an argument made by Phillipson (1992), but rather, while not refuting these expansionist tendencies, to look at the formulation of applied linguistics as a discourse which plays a dominant role in the larger domain of the discourse of EIL. The issue, then, as with the discussion of linguistics, is how a dominant discourse both controls and produces thinking about language teaching. To paraphrase Said (1978, p. 3; and see Chapter 2) somewhat, it might be said that without examining applied linguistics as a discourse one cannot possibly understand the enormously systematic discipline by which British and American culture has been able to manage – and even produce – English language teaching politically, sociologically, culturally, ideologically and scientifically since the end of the nineteenth century. Moreover, so authoritative a position has applied linguistics had that I believe that no one writing, thinking or acting on language teaching could do so without taking account of the limitations on thought and action imposed by applied linguistics.

Pygmalion and applied linguistics

Applied linguistics as a formal, named discipline emerged after the Second World War. Howatt (1984a) gives the first instance of its public use as 1948, in the subtitle of the Michigan University journal *Language Learning – A Quarterly Journal of Applied*

Linguistics. While this acknowledgement of applied linguistics as a formal discipline clearly marks an important point, we would doubtless miss a great deal if we took this first naming of applied linguistics as synonymous with its origins. On the other hand, to look at all instances of the application of linguistic thought to language teaching as applied linguistics (thus including, for example, the pedagogical grammars of the seventeenth century) would be to cast our net too broadly. The focus here is on the development of applied linguistics as a 'science' towards the end of the nineteenth century and then its changing configurations in the twentieth century.

It is to the work of such writers as Henry Sweet (1845–1912) that we can most usefully turn, since this era saw the development of positivist approaches to language and their similar application to language teaching. An interesting aside here is that George Bernard Shaw's *Pygmalion* was in part a mockery of the nineteenth-century efforts towards standardization. Professor Higgins, the cold and callous phonetician who succeeds in his brutal experiment of turning Elizah Doolittle's speech into that of the upper classes, was intended as a parody of Henry Sweet, for whom 'all scholars who were not rabid phoneticians were fools' (Shaw, 1983, p. 7) . If Henry Sweet is taken as one of the originators of applied linguistics, and if Shaw's depiction of a man intent on scientific experiment and standardization overriding class, gender and other basic human considerations is taken as symptomatic of this era, a very particular image of applied linguistics as a discipline starts to emerge.[5] As with linguistics, both the origins and the contemporary practices of applied linguistics are ultimately prescriptive.

Sweet established himself as a major figure and published widely in the field of phonetics. Howatt (1984a, p. 182) remarks that Sweet had two main passions in life: phonetics and England. It is important to observe once again this connection between linguistics and fierce nationalism. As Sweet commented in 1884, 'This science [phonetics] in its practical application is the indispensable foundation of the study of our own and foreign languages, of dialectology, and of historical and comparative philology. It is of the greatest importance to England' (quoted in Howatt, 1984a, p. 182). Sweet was dedicated to the development of a scientifically trained professional body of teachers who could help spread their perfectly enunciated English. Here, in the early applied linguistic writing, the same combination of scientism and nationalism that emerged in the previous section is evident. And as Shaw's parody of Sweet so clearly suggests, the applied linguists' job was to mould the non-standard speakers into the newly prescribed standards. If linguistics, then, had emerged as a discipline engaged in the careful regulation of English, applied linguistics was starting to emerge as the discipline engaged in the implementation of the new standards.

The early twentieth century saw the continuation of the work on phonetics, particularly by Daniel Jones (1881–1967), and the development of various forms of the Direct Method, particularly by Harold Palmer (1877–1947). The partnership between these two in the 1920s was further to consolidate phonetics at the core of applied linguistics. Palmer's significant work exemplifies three of the crucial orientations of this period which have come to form the very core of applied linguistics and thus to play a significant role in the discursive construction of English as an International Language: the attempt to develop forms of simplified English as a particular type of standardization, the emphasis on oral language as primary, and the call to make the study of language teaching scientific. Palmer's development of the Direct Method and subsequent work with Michael West (1888–1973) led to the development of the 'New Method', based on the latter's work on simplified word lists. This applied linguistic form of simplification and standardization is worth examining in a little more detail.

Simplified Englishes

Undoubtedly the most significant attempt to create a simple and standard form of English was the development of Basic English. In 1930 the Cambridge philosopher C.K. Ogden developed what he called 'BASIC' English, an acronym for British American Scientific International Commercial. Basic English was made up of only 850 carefully selected words and a much simplified grammar. As I.A. Richards, who was a great supporter of Basic English and whose intellectual prominence was often used to accord it greater academic legitimacy, explained: 'Basic English, though it has only 850 words, is still normal English. It is limited in its words and its rules, but it keeps the regular forms of English. And though it is designed to give the learner as little trouble as possible, it is no more strange to the eyes of my readers than these lines, which are in fact in Basic English' (Richards, 1943, p. 20). Ogden was a philosopher with a particular interest in the utilitarianism of Jeremy Bentham, the man who gave the English language both the word 'panopticon', which Foucault (1979) uses so effectively as a general metaphor for forms of social and self discipline (see Chapter 3), and the word 'international', a connection which may not be as coincidental as it at first seems. There are significant connections between the incursion into many domains of daily life of rational-technical thought (see Habermas, 1984) – with its origins in pragmatism, positivism and utilitarianism – the new formations of disciplines and modes of social and personal subjection (see Foucault, 1979), and the effects of international discourses (see Chapter 2). In passing, it is also worth noting that Ogden developed a 'word wheel' for teaching sentence formation, which he called the *Panopticon* (Ogden, 1968, p. 40).

The title of the revised edition of Ogden's work (1968) is *Basic English: International Second Language*, and we should have no doubts about the implications of this 'International Second Language'. According to Ogden, the goals of Basic English were to 'form an International Auxiliary Language, i.e. a *universal second language*, for general communication and science; but . . . also [to] provide the best first step, complete in itself, to any form of wider English, and an educational instrument of great value' (p. 5, emphasis added). A number of influential people took a great deal of interest in the possibilities of this language, including Winston Churchill, F.D. Roosevelt and, according to Churchill, Joseph Stalin. On 11 July 1943, Churchill wrote to Sir Edward Bridges, the Secretary of the War Cabinet: 'I am very much interested in the question of Basic English. The widespread use of this would be a gain to us far more durable and fruitful than the annexation of great provinces. It would also fit in with my ideas of closer union with the United States by making it even more worth while to belong to the English-speaking club' (reprinted in Ogden, 1968, p. 111). Churchill went on to propose the setting up of a committee of ministers to examine the use of Basic English, including the Minister of Information, the Colonial Secretary, the President of the Board of Education, and a representative from the Foreign Office. In a speech at Harvard later that year (September 1943), Churchill praised the Americans, and especially F.D. Roosevelt, for taking an interest in Basic English. The Americans, he said 'are the headstream of what might well be a mighty fertilizing and health-giving river. . . . Such plans offer far better prizes than taking away other people's provinces or land or grinding them down in exploitation. The empires of the future are the empires of the mind' (reprinted in Ogden, 1968). These far-sighted comments, spoken at the height of the grimmest and most bloody war in human history, are highly significant. They presage the new order that was to emerge from the battlefields of Europe and the rest of the world, an order in which colonialism and open physical exploitation were to be replaced by more subtle forms of exploitation in which language, and especially the English language, was to play a very large role.

During the 1930s, something of a battle raged between different versions of simplified English, most notably between Ogden and Michael West. West himself was one of the great exponents of the development of a simplified vocabulary of English. He argued that there are many different types of words that 'the foreigner can dispense with' (1934, p. 166), such as 'ceremonial words' (expressions of emotion or degrees of formality), or 'subjective words'. 'The foreigner is concerned only with *la langue*. His linguistic plaything, his means of self-expression, is his mother tongue' (1934, p. 166). West argued for great caution in compiling this sort of limited vocabulary, however, since it 'will not help mankind if the English language gains the whole world and loses its own soul' (p. 165). Ultimately, then, the key is to develop a simplified version of the language that maintains a balance between wide accessibility and cultural content. 'This heritage of the English speaking peoples is something of stupendous importance to the world. We believe that it is more important that mankind should learn to think Englishly than that it should learn merely to speak English' (1934, p. 172). Once again, it can be clearly seen that such applied linguistic work had as its primary goal both the spread of English and the spread of English culture. It is also worth speculating on the extent to which such simplified versions of English on the one hand assumed an inability to learn the full English language (unsimplified English was too diverse and complex for speakers of other languages) and, on the other hand, aimed to circumscribe the ability of learners to use the language.

Although applied linguistic reductions of English have developed in different directions in recent years (see the discussion in the next chapter of communication and content in English language teaching), attempts to produce a version of English with simplified lexis and grammar have by no means stopped. In his debate with Kachru over the question of the need for one or many standards of English, Quirk (1981; 1985) asks whether, in the face of such diversity, we should 'abandon hopes for the universality of English' (1981, p. 154). In order not to abandon such a goal, Quirk proposes what he calls 'nuclear English', a grammatically simplified version of the language that could serve as an international medium. Thus, he suggests either that we need a simplified version of English or that we need to maintain global standards of English. Indeed, he even goes as far as to suggest that the need for standards is part of the human condition.

> The existence of standards (in moral and sexual behaviour, in dress, in taste generally) is an endemic feature of our mortal condition and . . . people feel alienated and disoriented if a standard seems to be missing in any of these areas. Certainly, ordinary folk with their ordinary common sense have gone on knowing that there are standards in language and they have gone on crying out to be taught them.
>
> (1985, pp. 5–6)

There are a number of problems with this position. It legitimates a notion of standardization by universalizing it and locating it as part of the human condition, as something 'natural', thus ignoring all questions of power and the interests served by the setting of such standards. To then suggest, perhaps somewhat condescendingly, that 'ordinary folk' are crying out to be taught these standards flies in the face of much evidence that the cultural and ideological conflicts fought out in many schools between school curriculum (standards) and student culture and knowledge (what 'ordinary folk' do and think) are the source of much student anger, resistance and failure (see, for example, Giroux and Simon, 1989). Following the lead of Prince Charles's attack on declining standards of English, Quirk has since registered his dislike of 'liberation linguistics' and suggested that 'Black English' is as absurd a proposition as 'British French', and that the new conservative climate in Britain should be welcomed since it is now possible once again to call something 'bad English' (see Sutherland, 1989, p. 1332). To suggest that there can be different standards of English he sees as 'misleading, if not entirely false' (Quirk, 1988, p. 234). With such pronouncements being given considerable credence, it is worth also giving credence to Mukherjee's (1986) comment that 'ESL has become the political arm of Standard English' (p. 46).

Post-war shifts

If one path to be followed is from Churchill's advocacy of Basic English to modern attempts at standardization and simplification, another path leads from his recognition that the United States was indeed to be the major global power to the flourishing of applied linguistics after the war. As already noted, the first use in print of the term appears to have been in 1948. Although I argued that this formal naming should not be seen as indicative of the birth of applied linguistics, it would also be a mistake to ignore the significance of this moment, for it clearly marks a new status for applied linguistics, namely the start of its progress towards becoming a relatively autonomous discipline. Such a move, especially within the context of ever-increasing claims to have developed a science of language teaching, would signal a new relationship, no longer between linguist and applied linguist, but now between theoretical applied linguist (predominantly male academics in the Western academy) and practising applied linguist (predominantly women teachers, including ever-growing numbers in the classrooms on the periphery of international power). Of great significance, too, is the fact that this naming occurred in the United States, for the postwar period also marked the firm establishment of the United States as the pre-eminent world power. Thus, the emergence of applied linguistics as a formal, named discipline co-occurs with a major shift in global relations, the start of the 'Cold War', new concepts of development and modernity, and new visions for the role of language(s) in the world.

An important reason for the quick growth and consolidation of applied linguistics after the war was Defense Department spending and, later, money from the new National Defense Education Act of 1958, a response to a crisis in US confidence after the 1957 USSR launching of Sputnik.[6] As with Churchill's comments discussed above, in which he argued that battles in the post-war era were to be fought over people's minds, with language playing a key role, so post-war policy in the United States reflected a similar interest in languages. As Mortimer Graves, the Executive Secretary of the American Council of Learned Societies, a major source of research funding, stated in 1950:

> Ideological World War III has started and there is no certainty that it is well won yet. In spite of the fact that this is a war for men's minds, there exist no Joint Chiefs of Staff planning such a war, no war production authority concerning itself with material for such a war. These questions are by and large, in our society, left to the private initiative of the type that one sees in the Georgetown Institute of Languages and Linguistics.
>   In this war for men's minds, obviously the big guns of our armament is competence in languages and linguistics.
>
> (Quoted in Newmeyer, 1986, p. 56)

It is instructive to observe the similarities here between these remarks and those of Churchill cited above. What they make abundantly clear is that the shrewder political thinkers realized that the postwar era was no longer one of military dominance or direct economic exploitation through colonialism. Rather it would be a period in which 'development' and aid and a restructuring of the global economy would predominate; and in this process that stressed ideological coercion more than direct material exploitation, language and language learning would play a crucial role. Thus, the growth of applied linguistics after the war must be understood in this context of the search for new means of social and political control in the world. Although it was an interest in learning languages other than English that gave applied linguistics this important boost, it was soon to be English which enjoyed chief status once again as it started its prodigious spread in the postwar era and as US foreign policy and the giant 'philanthropic' organizations (Ford, Rockefeller, Carnegie; see Arnove, 1982a) reacted to the needs for cultural and linguistic expansion. It is surely no coincidence that the TESOL organization itself grew out of Georgetown University.

The main implication to be drawn from these connections between post-war politics and the growth of applied linguistics is that while it might at first appear overstated to draw close parallels between the growth of applied linguistics and American expansionism or the Cold War, it has become clear that applied linguistics cannot be divorced from its cultural and political contexts and accorded some 'neutral' status. The involvement of American social scientists (especially anthropologists) in US covert foreign policy in Chile (the 'Camelot Project'), Thailand and elsewhere has been well documented (see, for example, Mey, 1985, pp. 345–9). More significant than this direct cooperation, however, is the more general observation revealed by studies of the role of university-based social scientific research that it tends to support the vested political and economic interests of the state both with respect to the internal interests of the nation (e.g. Popkewitz, 1984; Silva and Slaughter, 1984) and to its global interests (e.g. Gendzier, 1985; Joseph, Reddy and Searle-Chatterjee, 1990).

Phonocentrism and monolingualism

A further tenet of applied linguistics from its inception was its adoption of the contemporary linguistic belief in the primacy of spoken language over written, an assumption that has remained almost unchallenged in both linguistics (see previous section) and applied linguistics to the present day. In the same way that linguistic phonocentrism appears to have arisen both out of a long philosophical tradition and out of immediate academic struggles at the turn of the century in Europe, applied linguistics seems to have adopted this emphasis partly because of linguistics and partly because there were now better scientific tools available for the analysis and teaching of the sound system. However, it must also be seen, as the discussion of standardization in the previous section revealed, as part of a process to make a very particularly classed and gendered accent into what would then be considered *the* standard accent.

This phonocentrism has a number of other implications. As suggested in the brief discussion earlier of *Pygmalion*, one of the central focuses of early applied linguistics was on phonetic training. While the practice of this type of language teaching has changed, an emphasis on oral language learning as primary has remained a key focus of much of applied linguistics. Apart from a post-Chomskyan hiccough and various reading- and writing-based approaches, applied linguistics this century, whether in the form of the Direct Method, with its emphasis on oral explanation, of post-war Audiolingualism, with its oral drilling, or of the later 'communicative approaches', with their emphasis on 'humanistic' or communicative activities, has tended to emphasize oral language as primary and prior to written language. This has been justified by arguments similar to those for linguistics: oral language is ontogenetically prior (the child learns it before written language), structurally prior (writing is a representation of speech) and functionally prior (speech has more uses than writing). Such arguments ignore the fact that most people learning English as a second language are already literate in a first language and therefore capable of very different operations on and through language from someone who is learning their first language orally; that writing is a far more complex social and cultural practice than a representation of speech; and that while speech may have many more purposes than writing, it is in order to deal with the written text that many people study English. Furthermore, if Derrida's (1974) critique of phonocentrism as part of the more general Western tendency towards logocentrism is taken into account, the applied linguistic obsession with oral language appears to have even greater implications. It is, in some ways, an appeal to an essentialist view of meaning, an appeal to the unsullied truth of oral language as an expression of our inner desires. It ignores the complex social and cultural implications of literacy and, perhaps most crucially, the possibilities that reading and writing open up for more reflexive and more numerous interpretations of meaning. And in the emphasis on second language learning as a process akin to first language learning, it leads to an inevitable trivializing of both the learners and the learning process.

The close connections between linguistics and applied linguistics led not only to a belief in the primacy of oral language but also to the post-Saussurean belief in monolingualism as the norm. As suggested in the previous section, an almost unquestioned premise of Western linguistics has been that monolingualism is the norm both for communities of speakers and for individuals, with bi- or multilingualism taken as an exception and often stigmatized through its connections to minority groups, the Third World and ESL learners. Meanwhile, applied linguists, although obviously having levels of bilingualism as their goal, had declared that classroom teaching should be monolingual, bilingualism and translation being inefficient or 'unnatural' (cf. the Natural Method).

As Kachru (1990) puts it, 'multilingualism is an aberration, and monolingualism is the norm' (p. 16). Increasingly, the belief in monolingual teaching, the proscription of translation and the belief in oral communication before all else were backed by the power of a scientist discourse. Given the stigmatism attached to bi- or multilingualism in many 'ESL' contexts (where English is a second language for immigrant peoples), this monolingualism and the concomitant elevation of the native speaker and proscription of first languages seem on the one hand to be linked to an ardent belief in the importance of English, and on the other to a disrespect for other languages and cultures.

Applied linguistics as a science

Alongside the particular applied linguistic interests in standardization, simplification and oral language, a major development in the growth of applied linguistics has been its emphasis on its scientific status. Returning to Palmer's influential work early this century, this emphasis starts to emerge alongside his interest in simplification and phonetics. In 1917 he argued that despite many advances, despite the prevalence of the application of scientific phonetic principles to language teaching, 'evidence of various kinds shows that this subject has not yet attained the scientific stage, but is so far in the experimental or empirical stage' (1917/1968, p. 1). Palmer insisted that since 'definite and complete answers' did not exist to such questions as What is the function of the teacher? What is understood by Grammar, Semantics or Direct Method? or How many types of exercise exist, and how may they be classified? the scientific study of language teaching did not yet exist. 'It is time', he goes on, 'that language study should be placed on a scientific foundation' (p. 3). This Palmer then sets out to do, outlining linguistics (phonetics, phonology, orthography, etymology, semantics and ergonics[7]), linguistic pedagogy (including curriculum design), developing standard and specialized programmes (akin to the more recent ESP programmes), and the functions of teachers and students. Thus, Palmer endeavoured to outline a new science of language teaching based on linguistics, psychology[8] and pedagogy.

This move towards making a scientific discipline of applied

linguistics was widespread. A report on modern language instruction in Canada in 1928 attests to this increasing positivism.

> The educational world of to-day is governed by the statistical psychologist, who insists that problems must be submitted to experiment in such a way that all factors can be controlled.... Though the science is new in its application to foreign language study, it is obvious from a consideration of the large body of literature that already exists on the subject, and the growing use of the new methods, that subjective opinion in educational matters is yielding to conclusions reached by objective experimentation.
>
> (American and Canadian Committees on Modern Languages, 1928, pp. xi–xii)

Meanwhile, because of the adherence to structuralism as a dominant mode of analysis, many social, cultural and political dimensions of language learning and teaching were discarded. A good example of this can be found in that area of applied linguistics known as 'language planning'. Working with the view of language outlined earlier and from within the limited understandings of social scientific positivism, language planners by and large construed their work as ideologically neutral, focusing on corpus planning (the description of languages) and status planning (the analysis of the social status and use of languages). Absent from this work has been any useful analysis of the social, cultural and political implications of its practice (see Tollefson, 1991). According to Luke, McHoul and Mey (1990, p. 25), 'many language planners embrace the discursive strategies of what Habermas (1972) has called "technicist rationality": the presupposition that the linear application of positivist social science could transform problematic, value-laden cultural questions into simple matters of technical efficiency'. They go on to argue that:

> In the absence of a critical analysis of the complex dynamics of economics, politics and culture, language planning has aspired to a technicist value-free neutrality, only to be viewed by many of its practitioners and sceptics alike as a formalization and legitimation of politically preordained developments, policies which with uncanny consistency concur with or reinforce extant relations of power and authority.
>
> (p. 41)

This reluctance to deal with the political contexts and implications of language planning has had other repercussions, especially the application of inappropriate models of language to diverse contexts (see Jernudd, 1981; Pattanayak, 1986). This in turn, as Kachru (1990) has pointed out, is a result of the problem that the majority of applied linguistic work on second or first language acquisition, sociolinguistics, lexicography, translation, and general- izations about supposed linguistic universals has been predomin- antly based on the English language. 'The field of linguistics and its applications', suggests Kachru (1990, p. 5), 'are closely linked to one major language of our time, English.'

At the end of his extensive history of language teaching, Kelly (1969) concludes: 'That the expert in language teaching acts with the purity of motive and design expected from a scientist is demonstrably untrue. Discoveries are filtered by social and educational needs, and what suits the circumstances is what is considered proved' (p. 407). It is not just that applied linguistic research always reflects the cultural and political contexts in which it is done, however, but also that the knowledge it produces is always connected to larger interests. As Phillipson (1991) com- ments with respect to claims made by applied linguists to be engaged in a neutral, objective endeavour:

> With the political agenda which legitimated the activities in question, namely the promotion of British and American interests in order to keep Third World countries in the Western sphere of influence, it must be rather sobering for anyone brought up on a diet of the 'non-political' or 'neutral' nature of academic research to realise that our profession, at least in its contemporary guise, was established in order to ensure that Third World countries did not leave the capitalist fold or harm those with investments there.
>
> (p. 50)

Wartime interest in language learning had led to the develop- ment of a new relationship whereby linguists wrote comparative descriptive grammars and applied linguists prepared materials for the teachers to implement in the new 'GI', 'Mim-mem' (mimicry- memorization), or later audiolingual teaching approaches. Whereas with Palmer's call for a more scientific analysis of language teaching, the emphasis had been on how to conduct research in order to rationalize a range of pedagogical decisions, now the emphasis came to be on the descriptive linguist at the top of a hierarchical model, followed by the applied linguist, whose job it was to grade and select items to be taught and then to provide teaching materials to be handed down to the teacher. With the constant call for scientific analysis, authority moved centrally to what was taken to be the most scientific area (linguistics) and secondarily to its slightly less scientific partner, applied linguistics. In line with the general process of deskilling teachers (see, for example, Apple, 1986; Giroux, 1988), control of teaching theory, and to a large extent practice too, moved away from teachers and into the hands of the linguists and applied linguists.

As applied linguistics grew, there were increasing attempts to establish itself as an autonomous discipline. Thus, by laying claims to scientific theories of language use (sociolinguistics) and language learning (psycholinguistics), applied linguists were able to clamber out from under the shadow of linguistics and claim to have formed a scientific discipline in its own right. It was now at the top of its own hierarchy, using linguistic theory where needed, but otherwise drawing on its own growing body of theory and practice in order to determine both linguistic content and teaching style. As I have suggested elsewhere, a typical example of the positivism, progressivism and prescriptivism of applied linguistic thought has been the concentration on a concept of Method in language teaching (Pennycook 1989a). This concept not only has particular implications for the political economy of texts and the inequitable relations between academics (often men) and teachers (often women), but also has major effects on teaching around the world as teachers are increasingly positioned within the expanding discourses of applied linguistics. This is clearly a significant aspect of the discourse of EIL since it concerns not only the English language but also teaching practices connected to the language (see Chapter 5).

One of the major problems here is the ease with which applied linguists can make claims by recourse to the power of their positivistic discourse. An excellent example of this can be found in Krashen's and Terrell's (1983) claims for their new approach to teaching. In *The Natural Approach*, while acknowledging that their approach is in many ways very similar to the nineteenth-century Natural Method (see Howatt, 1984b, for convincing evidence that they are indeed very similar), they nevertheless claim their approach is superior because of its rigorous scientific backing, based as it is 'on an empirically grounded theory of second language acquisition, which has been supported by a large number of scientific studies in a wide variety of language acquisition and learning contexts' (1983, p. 1). Similarly, Titone (1968) suggests that the grammar-translation approach of the nineteenth century was in fact a *deviation* from the proper oral approaches and that this 'deviation can most probably be explained by the inevitable lack of linguistic and psychological knowledge on the part of the language teachers in those days; and the traditional inertia or routine-addiction of the school practitioners, who did not care for change or improvement of their teaching habits' (pp. 1–2). Here Titone argues for his scientifically backed oral approach (and note the prevalence of arguments for oral-based approaches) by comparing it with some previous era of unscientific teaching. In the international context this comparison becomes particularly insidious since other cultural practices are classed as backward, primitive and unscientific.

THE SPREADING AND DISCIPLINING DISCOURSE OF EIL

The emergence of linguistics and applied linguistics was linked to both the spreading of the word and the disciplining of the language. This process has had serious implications for the discourse of EIL since it too has its origins in nineteenth-century colonialism and is also intimately tied to the discourses of linguistics and applied linguistics. The view of the spread of English as natural, neutral and beneficial is made possible by the dominance of positivism and structuralism in linguistics and applied linguistics, since these paradigms have allowed for the concentration only on a notion of abstract system at the expense of social, cultural or political understandings of language. The dominance of positivism and structuralism has had other effects, too, especially in terms of the power accorded to such scientist discourses and the knowledges that they exclude in their construction.

Despite claims that there is an important disjuncture between nineteenth century prescriptivism and twentieth-century descriptivism, this analysis of the disciplining effects of linguistics and applied linguistics has suggested that there is far more submerged prescriptivism in this discourse than is at first evident. As the discussion of language and colonialism illustrated, with English going through a major process of standardization within Britain, its position as the eye of a new system of colonial control saw not so much a vast spread of the language across the world but rather a vast increase in the production of knowledge about English. In its assumption of a unitary language (English as an International Language) within which variation may occur (or shouldn't occur, in the conservative view), the discourse of EIL assumes an a priori homogeneity and a hierarchized series of variations. In its use of Western linguistic concepts of language, the discourse also takes meaning as either controlled by the nature of the system itself and lodged in the heads of monolingual native speakers, or linked to a representation of the world which is best articulated through English.

These various aspects of the construction of applied linguistics have a number of significant implications for the discourse of EIL. Not only have many English-language teachers been presented with a view of language that denies any notion of the worldliness of language, but they have also been trained within a discipline that has taken as its central concerns various 'psycholinguistic' abstractions. Strangely, for a discipline which purports to be involved in teacher education, there is extremely limited considera-tion of educational issues, let alone any means of raising questions about the social, cultural and political contexts of education in any critical fashion.[9] Thus for many English language teachers, especially those trained in North America (but increasingly those trained elsewhere too as the power of the scientific discourse of applied linguistics infiltrates more and more domains), to consider the role of English and English language teaching in the world is to have available only questions of linguistic structure and decontextualized teaching practices.

The growth of this discourse, as with the establishment of the larger discursive fields around linguistics and applied linguistics, cannot be isolated from the cultural and political contexts in which it occurred. From its origins in nineteenth-century expansionism, through its emergence in the postwar era amid discourses of development, modernity, communism, capitalism, fundamen-talism, and so on, it has always been a worldly discourse. And yet, with the dominance of structuralism and positivism, it has always been a discourse that denies its very worldliness. The next chapter continues to explore further issues around the discourse of EIL, dealing particularly with how this discourse has shifted in response to notions of development and an international market-place, and the significance of understanding English language teaching practices as cultural practices.

NOTES

1. My argument here is that linguistics emerged out of a particular context in the nineteenth century. Some may object to this or query, for example, my reference to Jespersen as a linguist (see later). However, many of these objections are, I would like to suggest, a product of the writing of linguistic histories that have tried to make particular claims to the objective and scientific nature of linguistics and to write various people into the histories while writing others out.
2. This was, however, later updated, giving the 1858 citation as the second use of the term.
3. I use the word 'scientist' here, rather than 'positivist', since, as Williams (1976) observes, the term positivist is no longer used by those following what we may term a positivist approach to knowledge, leaving the argument often irrelevant to those against whom it is aimed. His suggestion that 'scientific' be substituted is also problematic, however, since its reference is less to the ideological framework of science than to its methods. I have chosen to use the less common 'scientist' as an adjective from 'scientism', referring to the inappropriate transfer of physical scientific approaches to the human domain.
4. Such arguments are often made particularly with respect to the concept of Method, an issue that I have discussed at length elsewhere (Pennycook, 1989a).
5. As for Shaw, he himself was an advocate of a *laissez-faire* approach, arguing that the world language would probably ultimately be 'Pidgin English, the *lingua franca* of the Chinese coolie, the Australian black boy, and the traders and seafarers who employ them. It gets rid of the incubus of much useless grammar' (Shaw, 1950, p. 62). It might be objected that my use of Shaw's *Pygmalion* here as a demonstration of the prescriptivism of applied linguistics is a bit far fetched. It is my feeling, however, that such images, while they clearly do not constitute any sort of proof, are nevertheless worth taking very seriously.
6. 1957 also saw the setting up of the School of Applied Linguistics at Edinburgh University. It was also, though I suppose quite coinciden-tally, the year of my birth.

7. Ergonics was roughly equivalent to what later came to be called functions.
8. His subconscious/conscious distinction pre-empted Krashen's acquisition/learning distinction by over fifty years.
9. I have discussed this question of applied linguistic alienation from education and particularly critical education theory at greater length elsewhere (Pennycook, 1990c).

FIVE

ELT *from development aid to global commodity*

There is a hidden sales element in every English teacher, book, magazine, film-strip and television programme sent overseas.
(British Council Annual Report, 1968–69, pp. 10–11)

ELT is a service industry, supplying people with a service – English language teaching – and a commodity – the English language.
(White, 1987, p. 221)

It hardly needs pointing out that the presumptuous, ethnocentric spirit of westernization readily finds its way into EFL instructional materials and instructor opinions, attitudes and approaches.
(Casewit, 1985, p. 12)

The main aim of this chapter is to conclude this broad attempt to describe the discourse of EIL by looking at how it has shifted according to changes in the position of English in the world and to changes in other global discourses. While Chapters 3 and 4 documented the origins of the discourse of EIL in colonial history and tried to show how the growth of linguistics and applied linguistics as custodians of the language and of language teaching produced the conditions of possibility for the emergence of this discourse, this chapter attempts to avoid the teleological trap of suggesting that its origins determine its current form. Discourses are made and remade within their current circumstances, a process which is particularly true when they achieve a degree of autonomy, as has the discourse of EIL. As questions of English in the world are increasingly 'put into discourse', the discourse itself is increasingly put into the world, which on the one hand solidifies and institutionalizes the discourse but on the other opens it up to influences from other discursive and non-discursive practices.

The three principal areas on which this chapter focuses are, first, the institutions that have promoted the spread of English, such as the British Council. That such institutions have been unabashedly Anglicist (see Chapter 3) is clear (see Phillipson, 1992); what is of greater interest to my argument here is the ways in which this promotion of English have shifted over time, from the discourses of pre-Second World War 'cultural propaganda' through the postwar discourses on English language teaching as 'development aid', to the more recent understanding of English as a 'global commodity'. Second, it looks at how English language teachers have taken up positions within these various discourses and thus have frequently been able to understand English Language Teaching (ELT) as a fundamentally 'good thing' by appeal to a view of ELT as development or ELT as determined by the global market. Finally, it examines ELT practices as cultural practices. The point here will be to show not so much that ELT theories are inherently expansionist nor merely that ELT practices are largely inappropriate when transported to different contexts; but rather, how the teaching practices themselves represent particular visions of the world and thus make the English language classroom a site of cultural politics, a place where different versions of how the world is and should be are struggled over. Important here is the reciprocal relationship between the spread of English and the spread of English teaching practices.

FROM CULTURAL PROPAGANDA TO GLOBAL BUSINESS: THE BRITISH COUNCIL

Chapters 2 and 4 discussed the importance of the postwar philosophical and political shifts with respect to international relations. This was to be a new era in which battles were to be fought for people's minds and in which language and culture were to play an ever greater role. It was to be the era of organizations such as the British Council and the Ford and Rockefeller Foundations. This growing emphasis on language had started before the war. A major cause of increased overseas activity came in response to the highly efficient propaganda systems of the German and Italian states in the 1930s. The British felt that through promotion of British culture, language and political system, they could counter the spread of European fascism. It was prompting from the business world, however, which finally led to the setting up of 'The British Council for Relations with Other Countries' in 1934. This committee, made up of educational experts and businessmen, aimed to help spread the English language and develop an understanding of British culture. At the official inauguration of the British Council (as it was renamed) in 1935, the Prince of Wales (later Edward VIII) outlined the goals of the new organization.

> The basis of our work must be the English language . . . [and] we are aiming at something more profound than just a smattering of our tongue. Our object is to assist the largest number possible to appreciate fully the glories of our literature, our contribution to the arts and sciences, and our pre-eminent contribution to political practice. This can be best achieved by promoting the study of our language abroad.
>
> (Quoted in White, 1965)

Beneath some of the idealistic rhetoric about the mission of the Council to increase 'cultural understanding', there is a constant recognition of its commercial and political role. Its goals, as published in the foreword to the collection of speeches given at the inaugural meeting, were centred around the need to 'promote abroad a wider appreciation of British culture and civilization, by encouraging the study and use of the English language, and thereby, to extend a knowledge of British literature and of the British contributions to music and the fine arts, the sciences, philosophic thought and political practice' (Donaldson, 1984, p. 1). The original memorandum sent to overseas missions by R.A. Leeper in 1934, however, had been more explicit, bearing the title 'cultural propaganda' (see Coombs, 1988; Donaldson, 1984). In public, the British Council has always eschewed reference to such phrases as cultural propaganda and has denied involvement in anything that could be construed as 'political activity', but it is clear that such claims are not only highly questionable from the theoretical orientations of this book (i.e. that the cultural is always a struggle over ways of understanding our lives and is therefore always political), but are also questionable when one looks at the activities of the Council itself.

Around the period of the Second World War, a protracted battle was fought over whether the Council should be taken over by the Ministry of Information. It was the Minister of Information (Duff

Cooper) himself, however, who made the clearest argument against this move in a strongly worded letter to the Prime Minister, Winston Churchill: 'The supposition is that the British Council exists only for cultural and not for political propaganda, but this at the best of times was mere camouflage since no country would be justified in spending public money on cultural propaganda unless it had also a political or a commercial significance' (quoted in Donaldson, 1984, p. 78). The Council itself, in its annual reports, has generally been similarly clear about its purpose: 'The Council does not pretend to dispense charity: in all its work it aims to further the long-term interests of Britain' (*Annual Report*, 1963–64, p. 18).

A major shift in British Council policy occurred after the war, especially with the publication of the Drogheda Report, in which it was suggested that the Council should shift its emphasis from 'cultural' to 'educational' affairs and from 'developed' to 'developing' countries. Such a shift was clearly in line with the overall move from colonialism to development aid, from exploitation through direct government to exploitation through global markets, outlined in Chapter 2. For Britain it became especially useful to have at its disposal a 'non-governmental' agency for continued cultural and political influence in the face of the demise of the colonial educational service. According to the Drogheda Report, the value of the British Council's work centred upon the nature and extent of British political and commercial interests. Essential here was the ability to influence the attitudes of educational élites towards Britain. Significant, too, was the extent to which the Council's work was intended to lessen the threat of communism, especially among intellectuals (see Donaldson, 1984, pp. 183–4). Central to all these concerns remained the teaching of English, for despite many difficulties in the Council's history, despite cutbacks and policy changes, as Donaldson puts it, 'it has nevertheless always possessed one golden egg – the English language' (p. 35).

ELT as development aid

From this point on, then, the emphasis of the Council's work moved from cultural exchanges with largely European nations to educational aid for Third World nations, especially former colonies. Its goals remained steadfastly expansionist, however. The 1968–69 report of the British Council discusses the development of English as a world language and ways in which the Council can contribute to its expansion. In the same laudatory prose that can be found in the Anglicist discourse of the nineteenth century (see Chapter 3), the report suggests that 'we have come to accept as natural that television interviews with a Swiss banker, a Dutch harbourmaster, a German journalist, a Norwegian statesman, should reveal them with an easy colloquial command of English. And it is almost certain to be the language of space' (p. 7). In answer to possible concerns that this spread could be counter-productive since it is the language of Chinese and Soviet propaganda and of German and Japanese business, the report argues that 'we should welcome this as furthering English as the language of international commercial promotion, opening the world more readily to our salesmen. There is a hidden sales element in every English teacher, book, magazine, film-strip and television programme sent overseas' (pp. 10–11).

Not only is this export of English useful commercially, the report argues, but it also carries with it cultural and political messages. 'The British teacher of English', the report suggests, 'cannot help being a teacher about Britain' (p. 11). Finally, having argued that Britain does indeed 'gain political, commercial and cultural advantage from the world-wide use of English' (p. 11), the report goes on to outline what is being done to promote the expansion of English. First, it acts as a coordinator with other British organizations such as the BBC and with US organizations such as the Peace Corps, the Center for Applied Linguistics and the Ford Foundation. There had been a series of conferences between Britain and the United States after the war, with a view to exploring means to cooperate in promoting the global spread of English. The British Council Report for 1960–61 draws attention explicitly to the need for mutual assistance, suggesting a parallel between US internal policies on English and those for the rest of the world.

> America, with its vast resources, its prestige and its great tradition of international philanthropy, no less than because it is the largest English-speaking nation, is one of the greatest English-teaching forces in the world today. Teaching the world English may appear not unlike the extension of the task which America faced in establishing English as a common national language among its own immigrant population.
>
> (p. 16)

Second, the Council provides support for university departments, conferences and research on English language teaching. It had helped start the journal *English Language Teaching* in 1953 and had also helped in the foundation of the first British Department of Applied Linguistics in Edinburgh in 1957. Coordinated by the English-Teaching Information Centre (now defunct), which has 'the world's largest library and archives devoted to the subject' (British Council Report 1968–69, p. 13), the Council was able to claim in the 1974–75 report that 'the Council with its home and overseas bases has established its position as the world authority on TEFL/TESL and through it Britain is generally acknowledged to be the world centre for the provision of goods and services for this speciality' (1974–75, p. 23). Third, the Council helps maintain the spread of English through its links overseas, by teaching English in its centres, offering teacher training courses, sending British experts around the world, and offering scholarships for people to study in the UK. Fourth, it supplies a great many teaching materials, especially books, which, as the report states, 'is at once both a major contribution to maintaining English as a world language and a major export' (p. 16). According to the report for 1959–60, 'Her Majesty's Government is now giving increased support to British books and periodicals overseas in recognition of the vitally important contribution they make to the dissemination of British ideas' (1959–60, p. 19). Finally, the Council is involved in examinations and inspections aimed to maintain standards of English teaching. With regard to local variants of English, the report has this to say: 'the unremitting efforts of native-English-speaking countries will be needed to keep local variants of second-language English within limits of comprehensibility' (p. 9).

Despite its claims to independence and autonomy, then, the British Council is clearly an institution supportive of British commercial and political interests. It has always had the goal of spreading the English language as far as possible and this has been for clear political and commercial reasons. Phillipson's (1986) analysis of British Council policies and practices suggests that its activities stand in a complex relationship to British foreign policy and trade. He undermines the claims to independence and autonomy and shows how the British Council has been a major force in the promotion of English in the world: 'The ideological significance of the notion of autonomy is that it serves to strengthen the myth that the Council's work is non-political' (Phillipson, 1986, p. 205). My main concern here, however, is not so much to prove that the British Council is not autonomous and neutral but rather to explore the ways in which the Council has been able to make such a claim to neutrality and autonomy. One of the important aspects of the discourse of EIL is the way in which it presents the spread of English as natural, neutral and beneficial. This analysis of the British Council has made it possible to see how this view is constructed beyond the domains of linguistics and applied linguistics by appeal to notions of 'cultural exchange' and 'development'. Thus, the Council has worked in a complex reciprocal relationship to this discourse, both locating itself within the discourse of EIL (and therefore being able to claim that the spread of English is a good thing), and helping to construct this discourse by linking the spread of English and English language teaching to 'cultural exchange', 'development aid', and by appeal to a view of the global marketplace as a site of equal and innocent transaction.

Turning more explicitly to the relationship between the British Council and its promotion of English Language Teaching, it can be seen that just as the overall promotion of English is clearly part of British Council ideology, so the promotion of particular approaches to teaching has been firmly institutionalized. An early example is what became known as the 'Madras Snowball', a massive project aimed at retraining 27,000 Indian teachers (Smith, 1962). Using a system common to British Council practice, which in many ways is reminiscent of Macaulay's 'diffusion' model for the spreading of English in the nineteenth century (see Chapter 3), twenty teachers were trained in a situational-structural syllabus with an oral presentation methodology and were then sent back to train other teachers (hence 'snowball'). This project, as Widdowson (1968) shows, was a collossal and also disturbing failure. It failed because the oral methodology (see Prabhu, 1987, p. 119) which, as suggested in the previous chapter, seems to have been an axiomatic belief of applied linguistics, was neither relevant nor sustainable in the context of Madras schools. Perhaps the very inappropriacy of the metaphor of the 'snowball' to the context of Madras is indicative of such a misguided project.

While the 'Madras Snowball' seems to have settled quietly into the dust of English language teaching history, another British Council project has remained more in the public eye and is of particular interest because of the connections it reveals between the British Council, English teaching practices, book publishing and academics. The 'Bangalore Project', or 'Communicational Teaching Project', ran from 1979 to 1984 under the guidance of the Madras British Council Officer, N.S. Prabhu, and was an attempt to explore the belief that the development of second language competence requires not so much systematized second language input as conditions under which learners cope with communication through a 'procedural syllabus' (see Prabhu, 1987). It has been suggested[1] that this project was once again of little relevance to an Indian context. Of the eighteen teachers who participated, nine were teacher trainers, two university lecturers, three members of the British Council specialist staff, and only four regular teachers. According to Beretta's (1990) critical evaluation, furthermore, these regular teachers were among those who never came to terms with the demands of the project, and he suggests that the project 'would not be readily assimilable by typical teachers in South Indian schools' (p. 333). While this project has been virtually ignored in the United States, it has received inordinate coverage in the UK, especially from the various prestigious applied linguists who were invited to visit Bangalore (including Keith Johnson, Dick Allwright, Christopher Brumfit, Douglas Barnes, S. Pit Corder and Alan Davies; and see e.g. Beretta, 1990; Beretta and Davies, 1985; Brumfit, 1984; Greenwood, 1985; Prabhu, 1987, 1990). It appears that the British Council interest here was to gain acclaim for its promotion of communicative language teaching, an orientation that has been so strong in the British Council that it suggests powerful economic (textbook and course sales) and ideological underpinnings. Teaching practices need to be seen as cultural practices, and thus the promotion of particular teaching approaches is closely linked both to the promotion of English and to the promotion of particular forms of culture and knowledge.

US philanthropy

The British Council is the main mediator of ELT projects from Britain, coordinating book publishing, teaching projects, video and television programmes, and so on. By contrast, there is no such clearly central institution coordinating US policy, though it would be an error to assume that the United States has therefore played a less significant role. First of all, it is worth observing that when the United States was directly involved in colonialism, its policies were strongly in favour of widespread education in English. 'Aware that language, as history, is also intimately tied to a people's consciousness', suggests Walsh (1991, p. 7) with respect to Puerto Rico, 'the United States instituted English as the language of government, of education, and of public life.' In the Philippines, Foley (1984) argues that 'the American regime was committed to making a showcase Asian democracy, and school, English, and a literate citizenry were central to this goal' (p. 50). According to Sibayan (1990), 'of all the language planning decisions ever made in the Philippines the use of English in the controlling domains of language has had the most profound and far-reaching effect on Philippine life and thought' (p. 55). In Guam, an editorial in the *Guam Recorder* (a US Navy-run paper) in February 1925 stated that 'This is American territory. It is American to have public schools where only English is taught. Americans have an obligation and such they have never shirked' (quoted in Day, 1985, p. 175; see also Underwood, 1989, p. 78).

The greatest influence of the United States, however, has been in the post-war era and thus as more of a neocolonial than as a colonial power. More responsive to a world of global economic (inter-)dependency and large-scale development initiatives than the British, the United States consolidated its power through a vast array of institutions – political, economic, academic and cultural. Fullbright awards (administered by Department of State), and others from the Ford, Rockefeller, Carnegie and other Foundations, plus involvement by the Agency for International Development, the US Office of Education, the Defense Department and the Peace Corps have all contributed to the global spread of English, American ideology, capitalism and US power (see Marckwardt, 1967; Berman, 1982).[2] One of the most interesting involvements here has been the role of the great 'philanthropic' foundations. Brown (1982) argues that the 'humanitarianism' of these institutions 'was shaped by their ethnocentrism, their class interests, and their support for the imperialist objectives of their own country. By the time their humanitarianism was expressed in programs, it was so intertwined with the interests of American capitalism as to be indistinguishable' (p. 139). As the studies in Arnove (1982a) show, the foundations constantly supported the social and political status quo and various capitalist enterprises, and this was as true in their overseas ventures as it was domestically. Arnove (1982b) summarizes their role as 'the principal architects of international networks of scholars and agencies involved in the production and dissemination of knowledge' (p. 5). The foundations, he suggests, form 'an international network of corporate interests, philanthropists, and policymakers who increasingly coordinate activities to their advantage' (p. 11).

The combined impact of these foundations and other US agencies, departments and organizations outweighs the influence of the British Council, notwithstanding its carefully maintained post-colonial connections. American policy was concentrated through these comprehensive networks on many different fronts, with English carefully interwoven but rarely as a primary objective. While on one level US foreign policy has been simplistically militaristic – supporting despotic right-wing regimes and invading countries that stepped out of line – other policies more closely matched the emerging global structures of the postwar/neocolonial era, since they were centred not so much around the former 'missionary' model as around an understanding of an interconnected global market. While the British were still ambiguously caught up in a mixture of prewar imperialist discourse and postwar development discourse, the Americans, less bound up with the discursive constructs of prewar colonialism, had more quickly forged a new relationship between English and development, modernization, capitalism, democracy and education.

ELT as business

The English language is so widely used today that a new dynamic has entered the economics of EFL. While the commercial value of language teaching was recognized early this century by Berlitz, the spread of English has put a new complexion on the business of ELT. The idea that ELT was not only good for business but was good business itself was signalled as long ago as 1956 in a key Ministry of Education document. This *Report of the Official Committee on the Teaching of English Overseas* is worth quoting at some length:

English is a commodity in great demand all over the world; it is wanted not only for reasons of friendship and trade with the English-speaking countries but also for other reasons not necessarily connected with any desire to imitate British ways or to understand British history and culture. We are, therefore, looking at the language mainly as a valuable and coveted export which many nations are prepared to pay for, if it can be supplied in the right quantities, and which some others would be glad to have on subsidised terms if they cannot pay the full price. English is, moreover, an export which is very likely to attract other exports – British advisers and technicians, British technological or university education, British plant and equipment and British capital investment. There are clear commercial advantages to be gained from increasing the number of potential customers who can read technical and trade publicity material written in English.

(Ministry of Education, 1956, para. 10)

According to a study for the Economist Intelligence Unit (EIU) (McCallen, 1989), it is estimated that the world market for EFL/ ESL training in 1988, not including expenditure by public authorities, was worth around £6.25 billion (about US$9.5 billion). Of this figure, just over £1 billion (16.4 per cent) was accounted for by the British market, £2 billion (32 per cent) by the North American market, another £2 billion (32 per cent) by Australasia and the Far East, and £1 billion (16 per cent) by Europe. The North American market is dominated by its internal ESL requirements and the concomitantly large textbook sales. Another important contributor to this market is the money from overseas students, the top ten countries in 1985/86 being Japan, South Korea, Saudi Arabia, China, Mexico, Indonesia, Colombia, Iran, Malaysia and Taiwan. The East Asian market is dominated by Japan with its thousands of private language schools and large-scale company investment in English teaching. The rapidly expanding economies of South Korea, Taiwan, Malaysia, Indonesia and Hong Kong further add to this figure.

Over half of the British market derives from the 600–800 language schools around the UK, the second major source of income being the large-scale export of EFL textbooks, estimated to be worth anything from £70 to £170 million. Around 500,000 students were estimated to have taken courses in 1987, the majority of those being from Western Europe, particularly France and West Germany. Indeed, the British Invisible Export Council rated English language courses as the sixth highest source of invisible exports for the UK in 1985 (behind financial institutions, tourism, shipping, civil aviation and telecommunications and postal services). The report concludes that not only is EFL a large market but it is also a growth industry. A conservative estimate of the growth in the UK would project an increase from £1 billion in 1988 to £1.5 billion in 1992. The report was written before the upheavals in Eastern Europe, which have caused a scramble to secure this vital new market. The British Council's corporate plan for the early 1990s indeed includes a major emphasis on securing the Eastern European market. The report also warns that the main rival for the British share of the market is not North America but rather other European countries such as Germany and the Scandinavian countries.

Another significant aspect of the global EFL market is the EFL examination market. In 1987 it was estimated that about 452,000 examinees at more than 1,100 centres in 170 countries and areas took the TOEFL exam, generating an income for the US-based organization of some £9.5 million (about US$14 million). The British examination boards accounted for a further income of about £6 million (US$9 million). The countries of origin for students taking TOEFL are dominated by Asia: Taiwan (88,401 examinees in 1984/86), Hong Kong (64,417) South Korea (64,030), Japan (62,659), Malaysia (41,451), China (39,219), India (32,021), Indonesia (22,499), Thailand (22,471) and Pakistan (14,415). Recently, TOEFL has tried to enter the European market with its new 'Eurocert' examination, a move which has been met by a counter-proposal by the University of Cambridge testing services (UCLES) to enter the US market. It is also worth considering the effects of examinations such as the TOEFL within countries, since it is increasingly used as a measure of competence for jobs involving English, and has spawned a whole series of schools and publications dedicated to training people specifically for this exam.[3]

Once ELT is seen as a business, there is another potential shift in the discourse of EIL. The EIU report sums up by arguing that 'The reality of the situation appears to be that English has become a commodity and one which has developed into a very large and frequently lucrative international market' (McCallen, 1989, p. 117). The size of this market clearly has major implications for the promotion of standards and the marketing of EFL books, courses and teachers. If, for example, British English can continue to be successfully marketed over its other competitors in Europe and other parts of the world with which Britain has close connections (Singapore and Hong Kong, for example), this has major economic implications for Britain. And if certain views of language teaching promoted by applied linguistics can gain ascendancy, this may have major financial implications if some new approach or method can be successfully marketed. Of most significance to the theme of this chapter, however, is that it is not only as a means to support broader political and commercial interests that the English language is being forcefully exported around the world, but also as a product in itself. Thus, as will be further discussed later in this chapter, it is possible to see ELT as a massive service industry, supplying 'English for Special Purposes' (ESP) such as English for Science and Technology (EST), English for Oil and Petroleum (EOP), English for Medical Purposes (EMP), and so on. This has the effect of further neutralizing the possible implications of the spread of English by appeal to market forces and the technical domain of service industries.

Such a shift can be seen in the way the British Council now discusses its ELT operations. *The British Council Corporate Plan* (British Council, 1990) for 1991/92 to 1993/94 is illuminating in this respect. In a number of ways, the statement of its goals has remained much the same: 'The Council believes that its own and Britain's strategic interests are best served by seizing every opportunity to expand its involvement in bilateral and multilateral cultural relations' (p. 15); and 'Its offices in ninety countries overseas each offer a single point of access for all aspects of British culture, science and education' (p. 3). What appears to have changed is the new note of competitive business: 'The Council aims to secure a substantial share of agency markets for educational and cultural services overseas' and to do so 'on a full cost-recovery basis' (p. 15). Direct Teaching of English (DTE) 'is managed as a global business by Central Management of Direct Teaching (CMDT)', principal objectives being to 'improve business performance', 'invest in DTE growth', and 'establish DTE in Eastern Europe' (p. 11). Its goals are not only to promote 'a wider knowledge of the English language abroad' but also 'to increase the demand for British examinations in English as a foreign language' (p. 11). The International English Language Testing System (IELTS; now taken over by UCLES) which was launched in 1989 is being 'promoted as an international alternative to the American Test of English as a Foreign Language' (TOEFL), and the report promises that 'a global business plan for EFL and other examinations will be agreed during 1990' (p. 11). What is interesting here is that along with the expansionist rhetoric (with particular emphasis in this report on getting into eastern Europe as quickly as possible), there is now a view of English language teaching as a global business. The importance in promoting its spread is not only as an indirect aid to British economic and political goals, but is now an economic goal in itself.

This new orientation marks an important shift in the discourse of EIL. Starting from its nineteenth-century origins (see Chapter 3), this discourse grew out of Victorian imperialism and soon became connected to British expansionism and linguistic standardization. With the rise of linguistics and applied linguistics, a new positivistic and structuralist version of English as an international language emerged, in which language was construed as a neutral medium for communication, a language divorced from social, cultural or political concerns, and a language in which speakers all over the world had equal rights. During the postwar period, through its connections especially to North American power, this discourse became interwoven with global discourses of development, modernization and capitalism, allowing for a view of English not only as a neutral medium of communication, but also as a generally 'good thing' that could help countries 'develop'. Most recently, however, the changing position of English and its relationship to global economic forces, coupled with changes in international economic discourse from interventionism to monetarism, has brought about a new marketplace element to this discourse. Now English is a 'global commodity' to be bought and sold on the world market.

'THE WEST IS BETTER . . .': DISCOURSES OF ELT

It is not, of course, only organizations such as the British Council that have reacted to and produced this shift in the discourse of EIL. Very similar discourses can be found within other areas of ELT. This section will concentrate specifically on how language teaching has often been infused by the ethnocentric spirit of notions such as development and modernization. The connections made between English and modernization provide a discourse for

English language teachers going overseas in which we can see ourselves as bringing advanced ideas to backward regions of the world. As Casewit (1985) remarks:

> The potentially negative ramifications of the relationship between modernization and the English language are also intrinsic to the EFL learning situation itself and can easily be intensified with unfortunate affective results. It hardly needs pointing out that the presumptuous, ethnocentric spirit of westernization readily finds its way into EFL instructional materials and instructor opinions, attitudes and approaches.
>
> (p. 12)

Just as there was a shift in this discourse from development aid to marketplace forces, however, so a discourse has increasingly become available to teachers in which we can see ourselves as involved in the marketing of English as a global commodity.

The dominance of the Western academy in defining concepts and practices of language teaching is leading to the ever greater incursion of such views into language teaching theory and practice around the world. The export of applied linguistic theory and of Western-trained language teachers constantly promotes inappropriate teaching approaches to diverse settings. It is of fundamental importance to acknowledge that different ways of teaching and learning are embedded in social, political, philosophical and cultural differences. It is not surprising, then, that conflicts often occur; as Porter (1987) suggests with respect to contact between Chinese and Western educators, they 'evolve from such different cultural roots that it is no wonder conflicts and misunderstandings dominate historical and modern attempts by foreigners to impact Chinese education' (p. 369). This cultural difference is exacerbated, however, by the discursive construction of language teaching as development aid. That is to say, such differences do not merely occur in isolation from other power/knowledge relationships, but rather are related to particular views on what is developed, modern, efficient or scientific, as opposed to what is backward, traditional, inefficient or unscientific. Thus, a crucial aspect of the discourse of EIL is the view of English and English language teaching as developed, modern, efficient and scientific.

Following Said's (1978) work on the construction of Orientalism (see Chapters 2 and 3), my own experiences of teaching in a number of countries have led me to believe that non-native[4] English language teachers frequently take up positions within similar discourses. Thus there is, for example, a discourse on China that is both reflected and constructed through various forms of writing on China. This operates principally through a process of dichotomizing ('we' and 'they') and essentializing the resultant Other ('The Chinese'), creating a series of stereotypes within a discourse that constitutes China as dirty, backward, dull, and ruled by a tyrannous communist government, yet also mysterious, exotic, paradoxical and inscrutable. Such discourses – and similar discourses exist for India (e.g. Burney, 1988), African countries (e.g. Mudimbe, 1988), Arabic countries (Casewit, 1985), and other parts of the world – become embedded in institutions and are constantly played and replayed through texts and conversations about these countries. It is not uncommon for Western teachers in China to take up subject positions within this discourse on China, with its varied implications for how teachers view themselves relative to their students, colleagues and hosts. Two published examples of teachers' experiences in China may serve to illustrate this point.

The discourse on China

Murray (1982), an American professor of English teaching in China, complains that there was a 'mighty resistance to the technique called "informal class discussion" ' (p. 58); that the lecturer faces 'a sea of glued-on smiles that do not even indicate whether the lecture is being understood',[5] and so on. To explain this, Murray develops the metaphor of the wall and argues that neither 'the wall between Chinese and foreigners' nor 'the one individuals set up to protect themselves seems to promote the modernization of education that the Chinese nation purportedly seeks',[6] and finally 'the wall between foreigners and natives is like the attitude of the ancient Chinese ... back in the Tang dynasty' (p. 58). Here Murray's notion of development makes itself clear: if China wants to develop (and clearly in his view it hasn't developed much since the Tang dynasty [seventh to ninth centuries AD]), it must open its doors fully and unconditionally to the West. 'Resistance' to supposedly superior and universalizable approaches such as 'informal class discussion' is defined merely as an act of backwardness, of the closed minds of the Chinese students.

Jochnowitz (1986), an American professor of linguistics, is clearer still. After explaining how much he enjoyed the year he spent in China, the complaints take on a familiar ring: 'I was happy in Baoding despite its backwardness'; '... there are three things that I think China should learn from America: bathrooms, telephones, and freedom' (p. 527). On finding that his students sometimes laughed at each other's errors in class,[7] Jochnowitz concludes that 'our [American] society's tolerance for error, I suspect, is one of the secrets of its wealth and productivity' (p. 524). Acknowledging that his Chinese students were in a number of respects much better than his students in the United States, he nevertheless manages to find serious problems: 'I personally consider independent thinking a virtue nurtured by bourgeois societies, not Marxist ones' (p. 525) and 'In order for the senior theses to be really good, China would have to be a different kind of society, one in which free classroom discussion and independent thinking were encouraged.' Finally, he explicitly states what Murray was hinting at in the limited relationships allowed between Chinese and foreigners: 'This fear of letting Chinese people fraternize freely with foreigners is an attempt to keep them ignorant of how good life can be elsewhere and therefore an admission that *the West is better*' (p. 526, emphasis added).

Casewit (1985) has described similar problems with respect to teaching English in the Islamic world. Locating this within the broader questions of 'the distorted and often derogatory image of Muslim societies painted by certain orientalists', Casewit points to the 'ethnocentric reactions of "progressive" Western observers to Islam which they perceive as an oppressive, inflexible religion' (p. 14). Many Westerners, he suggests, believe in some 'universal conception of individual liberty', from which standpoint they criticize the observance of Ramadan, the veiling of women,[8] and the belief in the omnipotence of God as an enslaving form of fatalism. He suggests that 'the culturally self-centred ignorance on the part of many native English speakers about Islamic culture' shows the low opinion that English-speaking communities have for Islam, which almost inevitably is reflected in instructional materials and classrooms. The discourse on Islam, which has received fairly extensive attention, clearly differs in a number of ways from the discourse on China, and with the recent shift of Western attention from its former foe (communism) to its new foe (Islam) it is now this latter which has come to take on some of the more ethnocentric and racist rhetoric that was reserved for 'Red China' after the war. Nevertheless, both share a great deal in their relationship to views on development and modernization and in their beliefs in the inherent superiority of the West.

We cannot stop, therefore, with an analysis of the wide cultural gaps between North American or European approaches to language teaching and those in other parts of the world. Rather, we have to understand these in relationship to one particular aspect of the discourse of EIL, namely the view of English language teaching as development aid, a view which often carries with it an unquestioned belief in the innate superiority of Western teaching practices and the innate inferiority of local practices. On the one hand, then, there is a belief that, for example, education has followed a developmental route from 'traditional', 'rote' teaching to 'modern', 'student-centred' teaching (see Masemann, 1986), and on the other, a deep-seated confidence in the current beliefs and practices of English language teaching. Wu Jing-Yu (1983) finds the high status accorded to foreigners one of the main sources of the problematic relationship:

> I would like to encourage foreign teachers to treat Chinese colleagues as fellow teachers on an equal footing. Perhaps because foreign teachers are referred to as 'experts' in China, some think they are the only ones who possess teaching expertise. Furthermore, the fact that they are teaching a language that is their mother-tongue gives some people a sense of superiority. Labeling expressions that are unfamiliar to them as 'not English' or as 'Chinglish' is resented by many Chinese teachers and students. Some EFL specialists, thinking that they have the best ideas and methods, are intolerant of ideas and methods different from their own.
>
> (p. 115)

According to Sampson (1984), three major problems emerge in the export of Canadian language teaching methods to China. The first stems from the 'fallacy of the unidimensionality of development' (p. 20), i.e. the fallacy that *everything* exported from developed to developing countries is advanced. Thus, by assuming that technical superiority in some domains bestows superiority in others, applied linguists and teachers feel justified in telling Chinese teachers and teaching experts that 'the methodologies they are using are old-fashioned and therefore should be replaced' (p. 22). The second problem stems from a 'confusion . . . between scientific and educational theories' (p. 21), i.e. an extension of positivism to educational theory. As Sampson points out, this conflation leads to the dominance of inapplicable 'scientific' theories in language teaching so that much of applied linguistics, especially in contexts outside Europe and North America, 'can only be regarded as irrelevant to educational practice' (p. 26). The third problem is a result of 'technocratic imperialism' (p. 21), i.e. the claim that educational goods are value-free and therefore appropriate for all contexts. One upshot of this view is that:

> It is often suggested to the Chinese ESL specialists that the new methods are wholly scientific. Sometimes they are proposed as a kind of modern technology of teaching. Because of this association of methods with modern technology (and hence science), both Canadian and Chinese ESL specialists unconsciously assume that the methods are value-free, and, as a result, applicable to all teaching situations.
>
> (p. 27)

From Sampson's description, two of the key aspects of the discourse of EIL clearly emerge: the role of applied linguistic positivism and the view of teaching as development. She gives an interesting example of the implications of this conjunction in the common criticism of memorization.

> That Western teachers respond to memorization by Chinese students with such derision and scorn is, I venture to suggest, not a mark of advanced scientific thinking, but the response of persons raised in a society used to the instant obsolescence of words. Perhaps Westerners need to reflect carefully on this matter and ask why there is apparently nothing worth memorizing in Western society today.
>
> (1984, p. 29)

The literary critic George Steiner suggests that 'the catastrophic decline of memorization in our own modern education and adult resources is one of the crucial, though as yet little understood, symptoms of an after-culture' (1984, p. 428). He argues that the plethora of discardable texts and the influence of other media have led to a 'post-literate' society in the West. While this is itself also something of a problematic and questionable claim, a critical view of the West as post-literate or overdeveloped may at least form a better starting point for educational interaction than the assumed superiority borne by many teachers.

Here we can see, then, how the scientist discourse of applied linguistics becomes linked through the discourse of EIL to a discourse of development, creating an extremely powerful conjunction which articulates disdain for local teaching practices as backward or old-fashioned while championing its own practices as scientific and modern. This discourse not only, therefore, favours the continued spread of English through the intimate connections between applied linguistics and the English language, but it also sanctifies a range of teaching practices which have their ideological underpinnings firmly based in other Western ideologies. There are, then, several complex relationships here, between English, applied linguistics and global relationships: ELT is supported and rationalized through the discourses of development and applied linguistics, which together produce a view of English as neutral and beneficial. The spread of English, in turn, also helps the promotion of such views of development and language teaching.

ELT as a service industry

The scientist discourses of applied linguistics allow only for a view of English and English language teaching as socially, culturally and politically neutral. A further way in which English language teaching can be construed as neutral is by appeal to the discourse of marketplace capitalism. Thus, within the context of the global EFL market discussed earlier in the chapter, it is also important to understand TEFL/TESL as firmly located within a capitalist, market-oriented philosophy. Brumfit (1985, p. 155) suggests that the whole emphasis on language interaction and on language as communication, especially in the terminology used ('transaction', 'tokens', 'exchange') is essentially mercantile. Furthermore, with the burgeoning of the field of ESP (English for Special or Specific Purposes), English teaching has started to be seen as a kind of service industry, providing English services for a range of specialized areas.

White (1987, p. 221) states the relationship between ELT and business explicitly: 'ELT is a service industry, supplying people with a service – English language teaching – and a commodity – the English language'. He goes on to argue that we should draw directly from the field of business studies to improve language teaching: 'All of us in ELT can benefit from the experience and theories derived from the commercial sphere, with whom we may be surprised to find that we have more in common than we thought' (1987, pp. 217–18). Yorio (1986) extends the relationship further:

> Second language programs can be viewed within this marketing framework. It is clear that we are suppliers of a product (or service) which consumers need and avail themselves of. Students are consumers who pay for our product directly (from their own pocket) or indirectly (through subsidies given to them or us). We are like 'corporations' which on the basis of certain management decisions produce a service which we hope will be purchased by many and which will please all buyers. We advertise the product (some of us more, others less), we hire personnel to deliver the project (teachers), and we build and administer the locations where the product changes hands (schools and classrooms).
>
> (p. 670)

The thinking of some applied linguists, then, has not been unresponsive to a view of English as a global commodity. Indeed, to judge by the evidence of the above quotations, there is an awareness of the similarities between international business and the global English market. This tendency to celebrate the market-driven expansion of English as an innocent, technical operation, reducing students to 'consumers', teachers to 'suppliers of a product', and schools to 'corporations', appears to be an increasingly common way in which teachers and applied linguists have been able to take up the global spread of English. Indeed, a whole new field of 'ELT Management' (e.g. White et al., 1991) deals explicitly with language teaching in these terms. A recent article (Bamforth, 1993) in *ELT Management* (the newsletter of the IATEFL Management Special Interest Group), for example, suggests that 'It is usual nowadays to refer to the EFL "industry" ', that 'language schools are not set up in order to further learning but rather to ensure an adequate profit margin', that 'language schools are no different from other service businesses such as banks, airlines, restaurants or office cleaning companies' (p. 2), and that 'If . . .

there are academically-minded teachers operating in a marketing context, they will have the same effect on the running of the school as would drops of water in oil for the running of an engine' (p. 4).

Such comments are problematic in a number of ways, not least of which are the naive celebration of international business, as if this were something we should be happy to emulate, and the reduction of the complexities of schools, students, teachers and curricula to a discussion of manufacturing. For the argument here, however, the key issue is the way in which this discourse of the marketplace once again fails to acknowledge the complexities and inequalities of international relations and education. Thus, just as the discourse of development produced a view of ELT as a necessarily good thing that could help raise countries from their 'backward' state, so the discourse of the marketplace produces a position from which ELT can be seen as something fairly traded. Crucially, both views disregard the inequitable global relations within which such 'exchange' occurs and perpetuate an understanding of language teaching practices as neutral.

ENGLISH LANGUAGE TEACHING PRACTICES AS CULTURAL PRACTICES

It is this issue of the neutrality of language teaching practices that is the main theme of this section. While the discussion in preceding chapters has highlighted the idea that language is never neutral – it is always involved in cultural politics – my argument here is that language teaching practices are equally non-neutral – they too are always involved in cultural politics. The issue here is not so much the *effect* of teaching (i.e. the learning of English) but rather the *process* of teaching. It is important to see language teaching practices not as some neutral aspect of classroom methodology or technology but rather as cultural practices. Furthermore, given the intimate relationship between the spread of English and the spread of applied linguistic knowledge, these particular cultural practices are constantly being supported as the newest and best ways to teach English.

Nayar (1989) lists a number of Western assumptions about teaching English 'that nearly have the strength of canonical truths in the West (particularly in the United States) [and] reveal an ignorance of and perhaps an indifference to the sociocultural, attitudinal, pragmatic and even economic realities of Afro-Asia' (p. 3). Kachru (1990) also strongly criticizes the 'evangelical zeal with which the pedagogical methods are propagated and presented to the developing Third World, often with weak theoretical foundations, and with doubtful relevance to the sociological, educational and economic contexts of the Outer Circle' (p. 15). They are clearly assumptions based on a particularly Western view of education and grounded in teaching practices in the comfortable surroundings of private language schools and university-based intensive English programmes. They include a view of classes as small and full of students who share similar approaches to learning, are self-motivated, find informal interaction comfortable and are from literate cultures. Teachers are expected to be informal, to enjoy their teaching, to have easy access to a range of teaching aids and technologies, and to be free from much outside pressure. The goal of EFL is frequently taken to be oral communication with native speakers of English (Nayar, 1989).

In Ożóg's (1989) study of attitudes towards English in the International Islamic University in Malaysia, he suggests that fears towards English are not only a legacy of a suspicion towards English as the language of Christian proselytization but are also a consequence of the methods and materials of English language teaching. The issue is a broad one concerning the fundamentally different types of knowledge in the West and in the Muslim world: 'English language teaching methodology is a product of the West, a secular society and is therefore seen as an undesirable product by many Islamic educators and students' (p. 399). What starts to emerge here, then, is that not only are many of the beliefs and practices of English language teaching based on a narrow set of teaching and learning circumstances and are thus largely inappropriate to much of the world, but these beliefs and practices also cannot be seen as 'neutral'. ELT practices cannot be reduced to a set of disconnected techniques but rather must be seen as part of larger cultural, discursive or ideological orders. In his discussion of the teaching of writing, for example, Berlin (1988) argues that 'a way of teaching is never innocent. Every pedagogy is imbricated in ideology, in a set of tacit assumptions about what is real, what is good, what is possible, and how power ought to be distributed' (p. 492). Similarly, Prodromou (1988) suggests we need to acknowledge 'the ideological nature of language teaching', by which he means 'that what we teach and particularly the *way* we teach reflects our attitudes to society in general and the individual's place in society, and that our own educational practice is an implicit statement of power relationships, of how we see authority in the classroom and by extension in society outside the classroom' (pp. 74–5).

What is at issue here, then, is more than just a question of inappropriacy. As applied linguists, often with the aid of agencies such as the British Council, spread their views of language teaching as scientific, modern, new, better, and so on, they make of the classroom a site of cultural politics, in which battles over social and cultural practices are fought within the context of English language teaching. This is true of both the content and the process of teaching. Thus, Candlin (1984) has pointed out that rather than a syllabus being merely 'an ordered sequence of selected items of content, it reveals itself as a window on a particular set of social, educational, moral and subject-matter values. Syllabuses seen in this perspective stand, then, for particular *ideologies*' (p. 129). Tollefson (1991) suggests that ELT practices 'must be examined for their impact upon the relationship between students and teachers, and for their ideological assumptions about the roles of teachers and students in society' (p. 102). And Auerbach (1993) argues that 'commonly accepted everyday classroom practices, far from being neutral and natural, have ideological origins and consequences for relations of power both inside and outside the classroom' (p. 29). This process is intimately tied up with the spread of English and the discourse of EIL, on the one hand because it occurs as a result of the global spread of English and the applied linguistic theorizing that accompanies it, and on the other because the discourse of EIL constantly promotes the view that both the spread of English and the teaching of English are natural, neutral and beneficial.

Monolingualism

Recalling some of the axiomatic beliefs of linguistics and applied linguistics discussed in the last chapter, it can be seen how an important constellation of practices has emerged from the beliefs in the primacy of oral language, the normality of monolingualism, and communication being the primary function of language. Language teaching methods, which have been exported to the world as scientific, modern and efficient, have constantly supported the belief in monolingual English teaching. The audiolingualism of the 1950s and 1960s and the communicative approach of the 1970s and 1980s have maintained as rigid dogma the proscription of any other language in the classroom. While the arguments of the 1960s and 1970s took issue with the behaviourist case for the use of English and only English (other languages would constitute interference and lead to bad habit formation), they only succeeded in replacing the behaviourist views in favour of monolingual teaching with an insistence on 'authentic' communication in the second language (English) as the only means to learn a language. Meanwhile, the research agenda of the 1970s, guided by a monolingual nativist view inspired by Chomsky (see Bourne, 1988), again stressed not only the importance of the second language but attempted to argue that the first language was all but irrelevant in learning the second language. Second language learning became a question of following a virtually predetermined path through the fixed system of the second language or the fixed patterns of a pre-wired brain. Such views should be seen in the context of a stress on monolingualism (especially when that language is English) which simultaneously disregards the significance of other languages and cultural practices. The English language classroom, as idealized in the discourses of Western ELT theory, is not a place in which languages can be freely used and exchanged but rather has come to reflect a dogmatic belief in a monolingualist approach to language learning. As Auerbach (1993) has suggested, it is not just the public and political face of the English Only movement in the USA that needs to be opposed but also the English Only movement as it exists in many ESL classrooms. She argues that:

> monolingual ESL instruction in the US has as much to do with politics as with pedagogy. Its roots can be traced to the political and economic interests of dominant groups in the same way that the English Only movement has been; the rationale and research used to justify it are questionable; and there is increasing evidence that L1 and/or bilingual options are not only effective but necessary for adult ESL students with limited L1 and schooling backgrounds.
>
> (1993, p. 29)

Communication and trivialization

Of significance here is not only the inappropriacy of certain views of teaching to the vast majority of language classrooms in the world or the optimistic universalism with which such views are acclaimed, but also the views of language, teaching and learning that it supports. The stress on informal interaction, enjoyment and functional communicative competence has a number of implications. Looking at the implications of using a communicative approach to language teaching in India, for example, Malshe (1989) questions its appropriacy, given the specific uses of English in India, the multilingual context of language use, and the sociolinguistics of Indian society. Since English serves mainly as the language of 'higher academics and of the highly organized areas of trade and commerce' (p. 46), it is unclear how a communicative approach would help the learning of English for this restricted domain. The monolingual tenets of communicative approaches also seem to fail to 'use the multilingual Indian situation as a resource' (p. 47). Since the central tenets of linguistics take multilingualism to be an aberration (Hymes, 1983; Kachru, 1990; and see Chapter 4), it is not surprising that communicative language teaching tends to view multilingualism as a problem rather than as a resource. Finally, Malshe questions the normative rules of appropriacy of communicative competence, since 'how much significance is to be attached to politeness in verbal behaviour will be decided by the learner, not by adopting the native speaker's values, but with reference to his own cultural values' (p. 48) The issue, then, is not merely one of inappropriacy but rather that the supposedly neutral notion of communicative competence is a very particular discursive construct. Not only can it lead to the transmission of fixed norms of appropriacy, but it supports wider views of language, communication and interaction.

Many other assumptions of a communicative orientation towards language teaching need questioning in a global context. Ożóg (1989) discusses the idea of the 'information gap', which is supposed to induce students to speak. 'Are we as Europeans', he asks, 'not making a cultural assumption that speakers the world over are uneasy in silence and that they have an overwhelming desire to fill gaps which occur in natural discourse?' (p. 399). Silence is a salient feature of conversation in the Malay world, he points out, a feature that has also been noted in Japan and a number of other cultures (see Loveday, 1982). Indeed, the whole question of requiring others to speak needs to be questioned in terms of both cultural and gender differences (see Schenke, 1991a, b). The point here is not to exoticize some notion of cultural difference, but rather to suggest that language is a cultural practice, that, as argued in Chapter 4, both language and thinking about language are always located in very particular social, cultural and political contexts. How language (including silence, paralanguage, and so on) is used, therefore, differs extensively from one context to another, and thus any approach to language teaching based on one particular view of language may be completely inapplicable in another context. If particular language teaching practices (advertised and exported as the best, newest and most scientific) support certain views of language, then such practices clearly present a particular cultural politics and make the English language classroom a site of struggle over different ways of thinking about and dealing with language. Communicative language teaching with its 'information gaps' identifies language and language learning with oral performance, thereby ignoring cultural, class, personal and gendered ways in which silence may be preferable to speech.

Two central issues in English language teaching are the problems of content and communicative competence. Communicative language teaching[9] is based on a belief that as long as a message of some sort is passed from A to B, learning could take place. To achieve this, a range of 'communicative' activities were devised, the majority of which attempted to stimulate language use through some sort of game. As Brumfit suggests, however, there are serious questions to be raised about the use of such games: 'whatever other weaknesses there were in the earlier emphases, they were not as inherently trivial as some of the games which are now so much encouraged, nor as flippant about serious issues as some of the current exercises' (1985, p. 155). The triviality of these activities, in conjunction with the emphasis on 'survival' English, has serious implications for the educational development of students: 'While the content of such courses is obviously important for "survival" in a second-language environment, it is of trivial educational value and has contributed to a narrowing and restricting of the content of language lessons and to a *diminishment* of language learners' (Tomlinson, 1986, p. 34). The implications of this trivialization of language teaching are not only educational, however; they are also social and political. Mukherjee (1986) states this most strongly when he suggests that:

In ESL the puerile structure of content was not and is not about
transmission of skills or critical understanding of concepts. It is geared
to receiving situational instructions and learning how to assimilate as
an 'object' into a structural order, into a value order, into a cultural
order, into a linguistic order and, above all, into a racist order.

(p. 46)

This trivialization of English language teaching should not be seen
as a coincidental byproduct of current teaching fads, but rather, as
Mukherjee suggests, as closely connected to issues of assimilation.
If attempts to develop simplified versions of English can be seen
both as part of the attempt to promote English and as part of a
derogation of learners of English as a second language (see
Chapter 4), the trivialization of content can be seen in a similar
light. As Candlin (1984) has pointed out, the emancipatory goals
implicit in early formulations of communicative language teaching
were soon superseded by the development of fixed syllabuses of
language functions that were ultimately 'mere re-labelling' (p. 137).
The emphasis on a reductionist concept of language in terms of
language functions, on the one hand, may facilitate wider and
quicker language learning but, on the other hand, reduces
possibilities for those learners, ignores key issues of social
inequality faced by many ESL learners, and treats education as a
pleasurable luxury that has nothing to do with the reproduction of
social and cultural inequalities, or with questions of racism and
exclusion. This implies a profound lack of respect for the lives and
cultures of students learning English.

As for communicative competence, not only can this notion be
seen as inappropriate in many language programmes around the
world, with its stress on functional language and a pragmatic
notion of ability, but the central issue of social appropriacy has
remained isolated from the question of the political desirability of
language forms. Bourne (1988) argues that functional language
teaching has reworked the diverse possibilities in the notion of
communicative competence into the transmission of fixed norms of
appropriacy. And Peirce (1989) has suggested that 'the teaching of
English for communicative competence is in itself inadequate as a
language-teaching goal if English teachers are interested in
exploring how language shapes the subjectivities of their students
and how it is implicated in power and dominance' (p. 406). If we
teach for communicative competence, therefore, without examin-

ing how language has been historically constructed around questions of power and dominance, we will once again be advocating a view of teaching that may have more to do with assimilation than with any useful notion of empowerment.

Another instance of the universalizing and the trivializing of ESL was the adoption in the 1970s of a number of ideas drawn from humanistic psychology. A selection of activities from Moskowitz's (1978) popular book illustrates well the particular focus on individualist self-interest that was at the core of this orientation: 'Accentuate the positive' (#89), 'I enjoyed, I enjoyed' (#114), 'What made me me' (#131), 'Step right up and see me' (#136), 'What I want from life' (#151), 'The best product – me' (#160), 'I hear happiness' (#180), 'Read all about me' (#214), 'From me to me' (#215), and so on. Ting YenRen (1987) points to the problems that such activities have within a communicative methodology, suggesting that Chinese students may feel they are not learning anything, are being treated like children, and that the teacher is making no effort to teach. There are further implications, however, since, as Ting YenRen also remarks, this labelling of Western language teaching as 'humanistic', somehow seems to imply 'the "inhumanity" of things non-Western' (p. 59). He goes on to argue that the use of many of the currently popular techniques in Western TEFL may fail to work because 'self-interest is chosen as the starting point. People assume that only the pursuit of self-interest is humanistic, and to many of them the assumption has become a mind-set.' Thus once again it is possible to see that such activities may not merely be impracticable in many contexts, but also carry a range of implications about the concept of the individual, self-interest as both a factor for motivation and a topic of discussion, and ultimately what is defined as 'humanistic'.

Both humanistic and communicative language teaching also need to be understood within the larger context of 'student-centred' education which has now become such a central dogma in many of the teacher-training institutes of the West. Student-centred education is not only inappropriate to many contexts in which student and teacher roles are defined differently, but it also supports a very particular view of the individual, development and authority. Edwards and Mercer (1987) point to a deep contradiction that emerges from student-centred pedagogy: if a teacher is advocating student exploration on the one hand but is nevertheless, on the other hand, working towards a fixed curriculum, there must be either a belief in an inevitable route which the student is bound to follow, or a degree of hidden coercion by which the teacher attempts to bring the students to the 'right' answers. This observation suggests that, as Walkerdine (1984) has pointed out, the developing student is a *product* rather than a *discovery* of the learner-centred classroom and that the discourse of learner-centredness masks the authority of the teacher (see also Candlin, 1984). Thus, for many learners, not only is such an educational approach inappropriate, in that it is very different from how they have learnt to learn, but it is also premised on a version of a universalized cognitive and linguistic path of development that ignores language as a social practice. It presents a version of masked authority that bears interesting similarities to ways in which authority is masked behind the facades of democracy in Western capitalist states. Moreover, if the communicative language learner is a *product* of communicative language teaching, rather than some natural beast waiting to be released by the modern pedagogies of the West, then once again it becomes clear how language teaching practices present a very particular cultural politics.

One final example of the cultural politics of teaching practices can be seen in the definitions of and reactions to 'plagiarism'. When it is acknowledged that there are questions of cultural difference to be explored here, this all too often stops at a recognition that the Other – the students – are culturally conditioned to behave as they do. Rarely is there consideration that the tradition of writing into which it is hoped these students are being assimilated is of course equally a cultural tradition. On the one hand, therefore, there is commonly a reductive version of the students' culture and, on the other, a preferable way of writing and thinking. Deckert (1992), for example, reduces Chinese cultural practices in general to such things as an 'absence of individualism' (to preserve 'social harmony'), and Hong Kong culture in particular to an immoral den of hi-tech illegal copying. Meanwhile, the tradition that these students should be adopting is decribed as 'normal academic practice' (p. 52) or 'genuine academic exchange' (p. 53).

There are two extremely important consequences of this. First, there is no suggestion that the teachers or the way of writing need to change. Deckert suggests that the Hong Kong school system is a bicultural tradition, combining British and Chinese elements.

When the students arrive at the tertiary institutions, they are not sufficiently prepared, presumably a consequence of the Chinese element of their schooling. Nowhere is there consideration of the possibility that these institutions are not prepared for the students that come to them. Secondly, these attacks on plagiarism ultimately start to justify the correctness of a very particular cultural politics. Once the argument is made that it is Chinese cultural traditions that are holding the students back, the next step is easy: the students have to be taught to think differently and to give up their cultural misdeeds. Deckert argues that the lack of 'individuality' in Chinese culture (he here makes the dangerous conflation of individuality and individualism) needs to be challenged so that in the final analysis learning to avoid plagiarism is only secondarily about 'facility in documentation'; primarily it is concerned with 'a new understanding of who they are' (p. 55). Thus, Deckert argues that the inherent individuality of Chinese students is denied them by the Chinese education process. Part of the process of teaching how to avoid plagiarism, therefore, is to enable these true selves to emerge: 'part of the educative process that helps catapult a student into genuine academic exchange is learning who one is and what one's own special perspective might be arising from personal experience and strengths' (p. 53). Not only does he therefore employ an essentialist humanist version of the inherent characteristics of the individual (thus suggesting that subjectivities are preformed rather than produced by education) but he also argues that humanism can help save these culturally stunted students.

The native speaker

Also tied to the monolingual belief is the figure of the *native speaker*, that idealized person with a complete and possibly innate competence in the language. The questions of whose version of the language gains sway, and whose interests are served by forms of control and standardization, are always political questions (see Chapter 4). Rampton (1990) suggests that the concepts 'native speaker' and 'mother tongue' support a very particular ideology of the primacy of those born into a particular language, conflating language as an instrument of communication with language as a symbol of social identification, and emphasizing the biological at the expense of the social. These concepts tend to imply that a language is inherited (genetically or by inclusion into a homogeneous social group), that there is a close correspondence between holding citizenship of a country and being the native speaker of one mother tongue, that the inheriting of this language automatically confers a high level of proficiency in all domains of the language, and that there is a rigid and clear distinction between being a native speaker and not being so. The version of the homogeneous language outlined in Chapter 4 has in many ways been embodied in the concept of the native speaker. In the international native-speaking English language teacher there is furthermore an embodiment of the homogeneous and monolingual beliefs around English that constitute a significant element of the discourse of EIL.

This stress on monolingualism and the native speaker is also closely tied to the political economy of global EFL, for as Rampton suggests, 'the supremacy of the native speaker keeps the UK and the US at the centre of ELT' (1990, p. 98). If claims can be made that English should be taught in English and by native English speakers, then once again the English-speaking centre is able to maintain a strong hold over the production of language textbooks and forms of English teaching. Unilingual EFL textbooks can sell universally, and the skills of the native speaker English teacher are applicable anywhere. Maintaining the native speaker as the preferred model also has clear implications for the maintenance of language standards derived from the central English-dominant nations. Thus, not only do native speakers tend to be dismissive of other possibilities, 'labeling expressions that are unfamiliar to them as "not English" ' (Wu Jing-Yu, 1983, p. 115), but they also stand as representatives of central language norms.

International textbooks

The question of international English language textbooks also has further implications. On the one hand, the global export of English, English language teaching, and English textbooks frequently leads to situations of cultural conflict where the norms presented in the texts are in direct conflict with local social and cultural norms.

Both Ożóg (1989) and Ellis (1990), for example, have pointed to the inappropriacy of many materials in Western textbooks for the Malay/Muslim world. Ellis (1990) argues that Western-produced textbooks remain ethnocentric and give little consideration to the sociocultural contexts in which they may be used. British coursebook writers, he suggests, suffer from ignorance, arrogance or indifference. Examples he gives from British textbooks that are incompatible with Muslim lifestyles include: social interactions between men and women, including living together, advertising for boy/girlfriends in personal ads (a favourite of textbook writers), and holiday romances; social settings, often 'boy meets girl' settings such as pubs and parties, where the dress, the social setting and the drinking of alcohol are all discordant with Islamic norms; and other topics such as rock music, astrology, gambling and revealing clothes (miniskirts, off-the-shoulder gowns, swim-suits) which all pose problems to Muslim audiences.[10]

On the other hand, the view of English as an international and therefore neutral language, a view central to the discourse of EIL, resurfaces in the form of a new 'international content' for ESL textbooks. Prodromou (1988) suggests that 'globally designed textbooks have continued to be stubbornly Anglo-centric: appealing to a world market as they do, they cannot by definition draw on local varieties of English'. He goes on to describe the content of these books as 'vacuous, empty of life. Even when the textbooks went technicolour, they were still marketing a black-and-white cardboard cut-out world' (p. 76). Of significance here, of course, is that this 'cardboard cut-out world' is not only trivial but also presents complexities of the world within a simplified 'Western' framework. Lubega (1988) points out the absurdity of the claim that EIL can 'express an international culture, which is non-descript' or that alternatively the cultures of all speakers of English will be fused into one language which will then function as an international language (p. 50). As Brown (1990) suggests, however, with the attempts by many publishers to sell books that somehow reflect this new concept of EIL, the content of many books has shifted to a new 'cosmopolitan' set of contexts, revolving around international travel and hotels. But the claims to neutrality and internationalism break down under scrutiny. This new 'cosmopolitan English', Brown asserts, 'assumes a materialistic set of values in which international travel, not being bored, positively being entertained, having leisure, and, above all, spending money casually and without consideration of the sum involved in the pursuit of these ends, are the norm' (p. 13).

English language teaching beliefs, practices and materials are never neutral, and indeed represent very particular understandings of language, communication, learning, education, and so on. Such understandings, in turn, are also not merely random views but rather are very much part of a broader range of discursive and cultural practices that emanate from the 'West'. The issue, therefore, is not only one of inappropriacy, nor only one of showing the non-neutrality of such views, but also of showing that language teaching practices are connected in a complex reciprocal relationship to the expansion of English and other forms of culture and knowledge. Teaching practices, techniques, approaches, methods are cultural practices that occur within specific discourses and imply particular understandings of language, of teacher and student roles, of the importance of (student-initiated) speaking in class, of what are desirable topics for speech, of the importance of structures or functions, of reading practices, of what constitutes a well-written text, of learning as a fun activity, of education as 'learner-centred' as opposed to 'teacher-centred' (this dichotomy being an interesting construction itself), of the importance of 'authentic' texts and activities, of motivation as an autonomous subject's desire to speak, of 'plagiarism' as an objectively describable and lamentable crime, of 'correctness' being less important than a will to speak, and so on.

On the one hand, these views on language, society, the individual and education derive from the same context from which discourses of modernization, development, capitalism, democracy and so on emerged. On the other hand, situated as they are within the discourse of EIL, they become bound up with notions of what is preferable, more modern, more scientific, and so on. This makes of the English language class and the teacher education class a site of cultural politics. It is not that as English language teachers we are necessarily either overt messiahs or duped messengers, but rather that the constant advocacy of certain teaching practices that have become bound up with the English language necessarily represents a constant advocacy for a particular way of life, a particular understanding of the world. Thus, in some ways, it might be said that the English language class may be less about the spread of English than about the spread of certain forms of culture and knowledge, and not only through the links between English and various discourses, but also through the very practices of English language teaching that have become part of the discourse of EIL.

It might be felt that the position argued for here remains frustratingly vague in that I have refrained from naming what such ideological practices support 'in the final analysis'. This has been deliberate, however, since I do not wish to suggest some simple relationship here, whereby ELT practices support the global spread of capitalism, for example, or are an instance of cultural imperialism that automatically supports the vested interests of Western nations. Phillipson's (1992, Chapter 7) analysis of the ideologies of ELT points to a fundamentally expansionist ideology: English is best taught as early as possible, as much as possible, and by monolingual native speakers. While such Anglicism is clearly significant, my arguments in Chapter 3 with respect to the dual ideologies of Anglicism and Orientalism, and the arguments developed in this chapter, suggest other complexities that need to be considered. The argument here is that teaching practices always imply larger visions of society and that the language and teacher education classroom must inevitably become a site of cultural politics. Thus, while English expansionism is one aspect of ELT, teaching practices and beliefs support a wider diversity of cultural positions on humanism, individualism and originality, and so forth. Certain beliefs about language, the individual, education or communication that emanate from the Western industrialized nations will inevitably be linked to the particular cultures and ideologies that have arisen at the same time. These represent a very particular view of the world and a powerful constellation of concepts that together may appear to present a very coherent and dominant world view. Nevertheless, there are also possibilities here for resistance, appropriation and change and although these views are thrust upon language teachers and learners around the world, the outcome of this process cannot be easily predicted.

CONCLUSION: THE COMPASS OF A DISCOURSE

This and Chapters 3 and 4 have focused on the compass of the discourse of EIL, in terms of its size, its direction and its ability to encompass other discourses. Important in this process were, first of all, its origins in an Anglicist reaction to colonialism; second, the conditions of possibility for this discourse that emerged through the very particular process of the formulation of the disciplines of linguistics and applied linguistics; and finally, the worldliness of this discourse that places it in particular relationships to discourses of development, global economics and English language teaching. This discourse has come to articulate a very particular view of the global spread of English and English language teaching, which does not serve English language teachers well in our quest to understand the significance of the position of English in the world and our position in teaching it. The positivist and structuralist basis of this discourse, along with its connection to development and more recently marketplace orientations, has constantly stressed the neutrality, beneficiality and normalcy of the spread of English while ignoring a range of social, cultural and political issues. Having dwelt at length on the construction and nature of the discourse of EIL, I now want to turn my attention elsewhere. In the next two chapters, I want to pursue once again the issue of the worldliness of English, by looking at English in the particular contexts of Singapore and Malaysia.

NOTES

1. I am indebted to Makhan Tickoo for his discussion of this project.
2. It is interesting to observe here the recent expansion into eastern Europe, Vietnam and, under the umbrella of the UN, Cambodia.
3. The TOEFL exam has wide-reaching implications throughout the world, setting curricula, spawning black markets, and so on. According to a report in *The Straits Times* (6 February 1991), a recent expression amongst Beijing students has been 'TDK', referring to the three central concerns of Chinese youth: TOEFL, dancing and kissing. Meanwhile, another article in *The Straits Times* (4 February 1991) reports a marked increase in Chinese students taking the exam (40,000) in 1990, following the suppression of the 1989 student movement. There are also reports of elaborate systems for cheating on the multiple choice sections and high fees for students with passing scores to sit the exam in the place of the original student. Raimes (1990) also cites the sad instance of a student jumping to his death at a TOEFL exam, under his arm a notebook with the words 'TOEFL, TOEFL, TOEFL, CONFIDENCE, CONFIDENCE, CONFIDENCE' (p. 436).

4. I use this term 'non-native' as a conscious echo of the frequently used terms 'native' and 'non-native speakers'. These terms, as I discuss later in the chapter, imply hierarchies of competence. My use of the term 'non-native teachers' is in part to suggest a reversal of this hierarchy by pointing to foreign teachers' lack of 'native' knowledge rather than local teachers' lack of 'native' (= English) competence. I have expanded at much greater length on the discourse of China elsewhere (1989c).

5. It is worth dwelling for a while on the implications of phrases such as 'glued-on smiles'. Such an expression is not merely derogatory; it also fails to acknowledge cultural difference and imputes insincerity. Insincerity, along with notions such as 'inscrutability', has long been part of the discourse on China and other Asian countries. Further-more, as Alice Pitt has suggested (personal communication), there are important issues around the gendered nature of smiling that could be usefully explored here and which are automatically overlooked by a culturally essentialist view that deals only in terms of 'The Chinese' or 'The West'.

6. The use of 'purportedly' here allows Murray to question the whole issue of development and modernization when it doesn't fit the model that he, as a knowledgeable, modern and developed Westerner, envisages for the country.

7. I would suggest that this is not particularly common. In any case, it may be interpreted very differently since smiling and laughing may have very different social functions in different cultures; a class of students in China is a group of people who study all day with each other and eat and sleep in the same dormitories, and are therefore a very different body of people from a class at a North American university; and there are particular ways of reacting to the commonly demanded 'performance' that one must often give before a group. Jochnowitz appears to have latched on to one instance in his class, to have failed to understand possible causes and differences in this instance, and from there to have generalized that China is a country with low tolerance for error while America's 'greatness' is based on its high tolerance.

8. This is, of course, a difficult question. The wearing of veils must be understood within the contexts of those societies in which it occurs but while I agree with Casewit's attack on the ethnocentricity of some criticisms of this practice, his reference to veiling as 'that form of modesty' also requires further critical investigation.

9. This reductive end-product of the development of communicative language teaching was certainly not what was envisaged by some of the originators of this movement, for whom it was a means of

challenging received norms and curricula. For Piepho (1981), communicative language teaching offered opportunities 'to overcome stock figures and social and national stereotypes' (p. 19); and for Candlin (1981), 'The social implications of communicative language teaching are such as to provoke concern about the establishment of norms, especially where all the evidence is that communicative meaning is signalled by culturally-specific formal signs. Communicative ability cannot sensibly be divorced from social, cultural and ethnic background' (p. 43).

10. As Alice Pitt has pointed out to me (personal communication), the depiction of women in such 'revealing' clothing should also raise questions for any of us, irrespective of whether or not we are Muslim.

SIX

The worldliness of English in Malaysia

There is nothing that the English language can do for us in terms of modernising our minds if its role is conceived merely, as we do now, in terms of understanding instructions from our multinational bosses on the factory shopfloor.

(Rustam A. Sani, *New Straits Times*, 16 April 1990)

Once we have achieved national integration, when the Chinese, Indians and Malays think, eat and sleep Bahasa Malaysia, then we can think of English.

(Dato Ismail Tom, *The Straits Times*, 5 March 1990)

Those opposed to the study of English will only succeed in making Malaysians backward. They are not true nationalists. They can harp on the need to develop Bahasa Malaysia, but without emphasizing the need for English, they would only prevent Malaysians from improving.

(Syed Hussein Alatas, *The Straits Times*, 5 March 1990)

CONTEXTS

In this and the next chapter, I shall look specifically at the worldliness of English in Singapore and Malaysia, at how English in both countries is intertwined with relations of class, ethnicity, religion, development, nationalism, popular culture, the media, academic work and education. These countries are interesting for a number of reasons: They share a similar colonial history (which I discussed in Chapter 3); they have diverged dramatically since that time so that the education system of one uses English as the first medium of instruction, while the other has established Bahasa Malaysia as the medium of instruction; and in both countries, the

topics of language, culture and education remain central points of
debate, with constant letters and articles in newspapers raising and
reraising these contentious issues. While Singapore and Malaysia
therefore present ideal contexts to pursue an understanding of the
worldliness of English, many of the issues that I raise here are
clearly of equal relevance to other contexts.

Taking up such a topic of investigation, however, presents
numerous problems: not only practical problems related to gaining
access to people and ideas, but also moral and political concerns.
Arriving in Singapore from the grey, drizzling skies and stiff
buildings of London (where I had been buried in the echoing
chambers of old libraries, sifting through musty colonial records), I
was struck once again by a deep sense of difference: the tropical
heat and monsoon rain, the thick vegetation, the slowly falling,
sweet-smelling Frangipani, the spread of a Rain Tree, the neat
rows of Malaysian rubber plantations and the clustered nuts of the
palm-oil trees; the flashes of colour as birds dip between the
foliage, the occasional song of a Merbok, the creaking of the
cicadas and the vague whirring of a ceiling fan, the scented
languor of a Hindu temple, the haunting dawn call of the muezzin
amid the gilded domes of a mosque, the incense drifting round the
slated roofs of a Chinese temple; steaming plates of Hokkien mee,
rows of grilling satay, curries eaten off banana leaves; the cries of
fruit-sellers in a market behind piles of rambutan, lung ngan,
starfruit, durian; the business of shopping on Orchard Road. . . .
My body reels amid these myriad sensations. And I am struck not
only by this rich sensuality, by the hectic pace of cities and sleepy
torpor of a midday kampong, by the pleasure at being back in
South East Asia, but also by an increased sense of otherness. What
is the 'English language' doing here so far from its insular origins?
What now am I doing here, chasing elusive questions about the
worldliness of English? In light of the discussion of Orientalism in
Chapters 2 and 3, what kind of knowledge will my 'occidental'
eyes produce? What can I now hope to know with honesty and
confidence in this context in which I descend as a privileged,
white, male, Western researcher?

While all of us from the English-dominant nations who work
'overseas' as language teachers, researchers, administrators, teacher
educators and so on, or indeed any of us anywhere involved in
research, need to address such questions, there are some ways in
which such work can be usefully contextualized. The first, key

question that needs to be asked concerns the larger political aims of the project. Rather than questions of methodology predominating, or research being justified with vague references to broadening knowledge, this question demands justification in terms of the interests served by the production of this knowledge. Is it research that is supportive of an inequitable status quo or is it aimed at social, cultural and political change? As part of a project aimed, to put it simply, at developing a critical pedagogy to deal with the worldliness of English, I believe this research is morally supportable. Second, if the way the knowledge is framed is not so much through those claims to universality and objectivity that are so much part of the Western academy's framework of research, but rather in terms of dealing with local specificities and struggles, then the knowledge produced may be seen as located in a specific context and thus usefully applicable both to that context and to whatever generalizable concerns seem possible.[1]

This concern with local contexts is also a key aspect of the term worldliness. The concept of the worldliness of English is not intended to suggest that in the global spread of English there are universal implications. Such a position would run the danger of constructing a new academic colonialism, of assuming a new (if critical) universality in a world in which we need to be attempting to understand difference. On the contrary, worldliness is intended to deal with the specificity of the relationship between English and its diverse contexts. Worldliness on the one hand points to the global spread of English, and on the other hand is concerned with English as it is caught up in everyday use in its own contexts. It is important, therefore, to avoid conclusions that suggest, for example, that the predominance of English in modern Singapore is but a direct and inevitable consequence of Singapore's lack of natural resources and consequent compulsion to become a trading centre within the global economy; or to argue that Malaysia's more determined opposition to the spread of English is a result of its greater natural wealth and consequent options over its development. Such arguments reduce the worldliness of English to a correlative relationship with the political economy of the two countries within the global economy and thus overlook the relationships among language, culture, discourse, national identity, ethnicity, religion, education, and so on.

While the social, cultural, economic and political changes and struggles within each country cannot be seen in isolation from international relations, neither should they on the other hand be seen as determined by them. From the different perspectives of different Malaysians, English may be seen as the most valuable legacy of colonialism (Asmah Haji Omar, 1982), as a remnant of Western imperialism, as a tool for social and economic advancement both within and beyond the country, as the language through which unequal distributions of wealth and power are allocated, as the language through which social criticism can reach a wider audience, as a threat to Bahasa Malaysia, Malay identity and Islam, as the language of universal scientific thought, as the language of modernity and popular culture or as the language through which Western culture makes its destructive inroads into the cultures of Malaysia. The rest of this chapter concentrates on some particular areas of these debates: English and Malay nationalism; English, class and ethnicity; English and Islam; and English and the media.

CULTURAL POLITICS AFTER INDEPENDENCE

The legacy of colonial language and education policies (Chapter 3) had deep implications for Malaysia. Provision of English education for a small élite, support of English education in missionary and free schools to cater for the needs of the colonial administration, provision of elementary education for Malays as part of a policy to maintain their social position, and neglect of Tamil and Chinese education followed by attempts to gain control of the growing private Chinese education system had profound effects. The society was deeply split along class and ethnic lines; parts of the Malay aristocracy and some of the new Indian, Chinese and, to a lesser extent, Malay middle class were closely linked, economically and culturally, to colonial rule; there was a growing Chinese and Indian merchant class in the bigger cities; and meanwhile in the rural areas, Tamil plantation workers and Chinese and Malay farmers lived in poverty. Malays wanted above all to reassert themselves culturally, politically and economically in the country they considered to belong to them by rights. Wealthier Indians and Chinese wanted to protect their wealth and position with increased political rights. And in the middle of all this, English remained as the crucial means to social and economic advancement. The years after the Second World War, however, were years in which both global relations and consequently English went through major changes. As the former colonizing nations and the United States scrabbled to establish different types of trading links, to implement programmes of 'development' for the poorer nations, and to redefine the world in terms of communism and capitalism, English started to take on a very different texture. No longer was English so tied to the discourses of colonial élitism, social Darwinism or missionary expansionism; now it was the language of development, modernization, capitalism, science, technology and even democracy.

English-educated élites

As the former colonial powers gave up their colonies, they were intent on negotiating economic and political terms that would remain favourable to them. In this process, there was an inevitable degree of collusion between the British and local élites, who were also intent on securing good terms for their continued economic and political control of the country. As Alatas (1977) points out, in Malaysia there was no protracted struggle for independence as took place in Indonesia, India or the Philippines, but rather a brief series of negotiations and a quickly reached settlement. The leader of UMNO[2] and the first Prime Minister of Malaya, Tunku Abdul Rahman, was an English-educated Malay aristocrat, and while he has played a key role in Malaysian politics – both in terms of his negotiations for independence and his later principled stances against UMNO and what he saw as increased extremism and polarization – he was in many ways very much a product of colonialism. Indeed, Shaharuddin Maaruf (1988) suggests that as a representative of the old feudal order, the Tunku's leadership reflects the reassertion of feudal values after the damage inflicted on them by colonialism.

The gaining of independence and the early assertion of Malay political power may also be seen, therefore, as both a reassertion of a previous Malay social order and as the installation of a government sympathetic to British interests. Thus, Lee Kam Hing (1981) points out that independence did not signal any significant change in the Malaysian political élites. Alatas (1977) maintains that 'there was no intellectual break with British ideological thinking at the deeper layer of thought' (p. 152) and that 'the existing ruling class in Malaysia forms an unbroken link with the colonial past' (p. 154). Shaharuddin Maaruf (1988) asserts that the new government in 1957, contrary to the hopes of many Malays, 'merely continued the development philosophy of the former colonial power and shared its biases and prejudices. There was no rethinking of the suitability and relevance of classical Western liberalism and capitalism to the Malaysian situation' (pp. 120–1). Such ideologies were not only in many ways inappropriate but were also directly harmful since they had been developed 'for the convenience and vested interests of foreigners' (p. 127). The problem here was not so much the intentions of the new leaders but rather the effectiveness of British colonial education. The distance of these new rulers from the lives and interests of the ordinary population, by dint of their class position and economic, political and cultural links to the British, was clearly bound up with their English language education. According to Shaharuddin Maaruf, 'Tunku's idyllic picture was partly influenced by the colonial myth of the lazy native' (1988, p. 122).[3]

Another aspect of this problem was the stress on ethnicity and the constantly reiterated view that the economy was dominated by the Chinese. While it was certainly true (and still is today to quite an extent) that a legacy of colonial rule was the economic imbalance between Chinese and Malays, the claim that Chinese dominated the economy obscures two issues. First, the vast majority of Malaysian wealth was in fact in the pockets of the British: 75 per cent of rubber plantation acreage, 61 per cent of tin production, and 75 per cent of all services and trade were owned by Europeans, the large majority of whom were British (Caldwell, 1977b). Second, the emphasis on Chinese economic power as opposed to Malay political power, which has dominated much of post-independence politics, excludes the fact that, as Husin Ali (1984) points out, it is only the *élites* of each ethnic group that have any real measure of economic or political power. Most Chinese or Malays have little of either. This misrepresentation, Husin Ali (1984) suggests, contributes once again not only to a tendency to ignore socioeconomic class as opposed to ethnicity, but 'also deliberately obscures the fact of foreign control or influence over the country's economy and politics' (p. 25).

The Chinese élite at independence also had a strong interest in working with the British colonial administration and UMNO in opposing Malayan Communist Party (MCP) activities: after the British, they were the major employers. In 1949, they formed the Malayan Chinese Association (MCA), which formed an alliance with UMNO, followed by the Malayan Indian Congress (MIC) in 1951. These groups shared a number of common interests and backgrounds, among which was the English education of many of the leaders. Lee Kam Hing (1981) points to the paradox that 'most successful political leaders, both Malay and Chinese, were English-educated and cosmopolitan, yet based their power on organizations that were exclusive and communal' (p. 254). Non-communal parties, such as the MCP and the Independence of Malaya Party (IMP; 1951) were defeated, the one by predominantly British troops through the protracted 'State of Emergency',[4] the other by the UMNO–MCA alliance. Communalism and English-educated élites were becoming defining elements of early political struggles. When the Alliance negotiated *merdeka* (independence) from Britain in 1957, it was willingly granted, since, according to Caldwell (1977b), it was 'to the satisfaction both of the élites of the Malay and Chinese communities and of the cream of British businessmen so deeply entrenched in the economy of this hand-made neo-colony' (p. 251).

Thus the Alliance which took over government of the country in 1957 was a coalition of largely English-educated élites from the Malay, Chinese and Indian communities. While these leaders had quite a lot in common by dint of their English education, their interests and connections in many ways were closer to those of the British than to those of the large majority of the population. The constitutional proposals of the Reid Commission were endorsed and 1957 saw the setting up of a bicameral parliamentary legislature, a prime ministerial and cabinet system, an independent judiciary, and a constitutional monarchy. The constitution enshrined Malay as the national language and English as an official language for ten years (1957–67), after which it would be gradually phased out. Despite the government's policies aimed at promoting general economic development, fostering a sense of national unity, and redressing the economic imbalances between the different ethnic groups, progress in all these areas remained slow. Indeed, there was growing unrest among a number of people about the efficacy of these policies. Meanwhile, enrolment at English schools rose from 48,235 in 1957 to 349,121 in 1967, leading Ożóg (1990) to suggest that during those years the government 'actively encouraged English' (p. 309).

It was clear that after ten years of independence many of the promised improvements had not come. In 1957–58, the mean monthly household income of Malays had been $144, compared with $272 for Chinese, and $217 for Indians; by 1967–68, Malay income had actually declined to $130 per month, while Chinese income had risen to $321 and Indian income to $253 (Zainudin Salleh and Zulkifly Osman, 1982, p. 143). Alongside these figures, however, it is also important to note that in 1957–58 the bottom 40 per cent of the population held 15.9 per cent of the total income, while the top 20 per cent held 48.6 per cent. By 1970 the holdings of the bottom 40 per cent had declined to 11.2 per cent, while the top 20 per cent now held 56.1 per cent (Osman-Rani, 1990). The social and economic inequalities left by the British increased rather than diminished in the first ten years of independence. Significantly, however, these inequalities tended to be defined predominantly in terms of ethnic difference rather than socio-economic class, which tended to obscure the extent of the continued presence of European capital and influence. The legacy of colonial education in English on a post-independence élite was proving effective for the British and that élite, but perhaps too much so. With a growing economic divide between rich and poor, and with that divide being defined principally in terms of ethnicity, with progress towards establishing Malay power within the country moving slowly, and with English education still growing, the scene was set for severe unrest.

It came on 13 May 1969, when violent clashes erupted in Kuala Lumpur (and elsewhere) between Malays and Chinese. Following Chinese celebrations of the victory of opposition parties over the MCA in the national elections, Malays were given permission for counter-demonstrations. Bloody clashes ensued, leaving many dead and causing extensive damage to property. Whatever actually happened on 13 May 1969 – and there is some cause to doubt the official version of events and to question the reasons for granting permission for the counter-demonstration – these events marked a watershed in Malaysian politics. May 13th has become a political icon: to invoke it is to raise the spectre once more of communal violence. To whatever extent the riots represented real underlying racial tensions, they have since been used as a central metaphor for ethnic divisions in the society.

When the dust settled, a number of changes had occurred. Tun Abdul Razak had taken over as Prime Minister from Tunku Abdul Rahman, who had resigned after his vision of a peaceful, multiracial society had been shattered. The Alliance was broadened and reformed as the Barisan Nasional (BN; National Front), leaving only the Chinese-dominated Democratic Action Party (DAP) in opposition. A New Economic Policy (NEP) was declared, aimed at redistributing wealth in the country by lessening foreign control of the economy, developing new sections of the economy, and favouring *bumiputras* ('sons of the soil', referring to Malays and other indigenous groups) through the establishment of employment and investment quotas. Coupled with the NEP was a new educational policy designed to dramatically increase the participation of *bumiputras* in tertiary education; and a strengthening of the National Language Bill, aimed at speeding up the conversion to the national language, Bahasa Malaysia. The *Rukunegara* (National Ideology) was also introduced, with an emphasis on belief in God, loyalty to the King and country, upholding of the constitution, the rule of law, and good behaviour and morality. Finally, the Constitutional Amendment Act made it illegal to question in public, state legislatures or parliament any matters pertaining to citizenship, the national language, the special position of the Malays, or the sovereignty of the rulers.

MALAY NATIONALISM AND ENGLISH

Perhaps more importantly, along with these policies aimed to speed up development and enhance the position of the Malays, there was also a shift in political power and political culture within the Malay community. The first three Prime Ministers, Tunku Abdul Rahman, Tun Abdul Razak, and Datuk Hussein Onn, all had connections with the Malay aristocracy, had studied in English and had trained as lawyers in the English system. While such leaders were to hold power for another ten years, and indeed presided over many of the policies that emerged in the 1970s, it was the newly emergent Malay middle class, with a much stronger sense of Malay nationalism, that was starting to make itself the dominant voice in Malay and Malaysian politics. Most notable of this new generation was Dr Mahathir Mohamad, who had been expelled from UMNO in 1969 for his criticism of government policies. He was soon reinstated, however, and became Deputy Prime Minister under Datuk Hussein Onn, and eventually Prime Minister in 1981, a post which he still holds. While the Tunku's liberal humanism and English-oriented interests had not perhaps been ideal for solving Malay problems, the ascendancy of this new group was to have profound effects, reshaping the cultural politics of Malaysia through their views on ethnicity and national culture. Kua Kia Soong (1985) suggests that the 1969 elections and riots had been fought around questions of language and culture, but now such questions were to take on a particular salience.

National culture

As I have already suggested, the tendency to view Malaysian society in terms of competing ethnic groups was not only a legacy of colonialism but was also reinforced by post-independence ideology. Ethnicity (or 'race') had come to be the principal division by which social difference was understood, rather than other divisions such as socioeconomic background or gender. Zakaria Haji Ahmad (1987) calls race an undeniable leitmotif of Malaysian political life, and suggests that 'there appears to be a tendency to interpret every issue in the country as racial even if its origins are non-racial' (1982, p. 88). In 1970, Mahathir published a book, *The Malay Dilemma*, in which he was highly critical of the pre-1969 government, accusing it of patronage and incompetence. He makes a strong argument for the special needs of the Malays, based on a very particular view of racial difference:

> Races are differentiated not merely by ethnic origin, but also by many other characteristics.... The Jews for example are not merely hook-nosed, but understand money instinctively. The Europeans are not only fair-skinned, but have an insatiable curiosity. The Malays are not merely brown, but are also easy-going and tolerant. And the Chinese are not just almond-eyed people, but are also inherently good businessmen.
>
> (1970, p. 84)

In a similar vein, he later suggests that 'the gleaming success of

South Africa as compared with the other African countries is a product of the different racial character of the immigrant white African and the indigenous black African' (p. 96) Thus, not only is 'race' taken as the primary division of society, but 'racial characteristics' are posited as a primary and deterministic explanation of social difference. Alatas (1977) points out that such views are echoed in a 1971 UMNO publication *Revolusi Mental* (Mental Revolution), which reinforces a similar stereotyped version of Malays.

What seems at first puzzling here is that the new Malay nationalism of the 1970s should appear to rest on a defeatist determinism based on racial characteristics: 'Mahathir is convinced of the racial inferiority of the Malays, in particular the rural folk' (Shaharuddin Maaruf, 1988, p. 139). The economic backwardness of the Malays is explained in terms of inherited characteristics, and capitalist success is associated with superior genes. But while the Orientalist discourse of the British, and to some extent of the pre-1969 government, led to a position that Malays should live in a domain separate from capitalist production because of their natural innocence and indolence, Mahathir uses similar arguments to justify special policies to enhance Malay participation in the capitalist economy. Thus, these racial arguments on the one hand justify the extent of the pro-*bumiputra* policies, since only by extreme measures can such inherited handicaps (or inherited benefits in the case of the Chinese) be overcome, and on the other ignore other forms of and reasons for inequality. Such views also signalled that this was no longer to be an era of *laissez-faire* tolerance as had been seen under the Tunku. And, as we shall see, part of this battle against the genes, would involve a struggle against English.

Meanwhile, another crucial aspect of the post-1969 shift was the move towards defining national culture. Asmah Haji Omar (1982) points out that although in the first years of independence language planning was seen as an immediate need, little attention was paid to 'culture planning' until the 1971 congress on national culture. From this congress, attended almost exclusively by Malays, a new orientation emerged which drew the question of national culture into the centre of Malaysian politics, and started to equate Malaysian culture with Malay culture. Thus the growing struggle for Malay ascendancy had two particular orientations: the implementation of educational and economic policies to favour

Malays, and the increasing use of Malay cultural and political symbols to represent Malaysian national identity (Tham Seong Chee, 1981a). The Malaysian constitution defines a Malay as one who habitually leads the Malay way of life, speaks the Malay language, and is a Muslim (Asmah Haji Omar, 1982, p. 13); increasingly, these aspects of Malay life, language and religion came to be presented as representative of Malaysian national culture. Thus, only literature in Bahasa Malaysia is considered 'national literature', all other literatures being considered 'sectional', and a long debate centred around the unsuccessful attempt to have the Chinese lion dance considered as part of Malaysian national culture (see Kua Kia Soong, 1987a; 1990). As Lim Kit Siang, leader of the opposition in parliament, said in a speech in 1982: 'Malaysia was never conceived to be a nation with "*one language and one culture*", as it will lose completely its distinctive characteristics as a multi-racial, multi-lingual, multi-religious and multi-cultural society' (Lim Kit Siang, 1986, p. 8). Crucially, however, for the position of English, the struggle for Malay cultural, economic and political ascendancy was a struggle against Chinese and Indian economic power and the language most closely connected to that power: English.

Casting English aside

At independence, the new government was left with the task of changing the hierarchical and divisive system left by the British. By and large, the education system could be ranked with English (primary, secondary and higher) on top, Chinese (primary and secondary) second, Malay (primary) third, and Tamil (primary) last. The languages of education had come to represent major social, cultural and economic divides in the country (see Watson, 1983), with only Chinese and English offering any hope of secondary education. The 1957 Education Ordinance, based on the Razak Report (Federation of Malaya, 1956), laid the groundwork for the establishment of a single national education system, with Bahasa Malaysia as the main medium of instruction, though with provision for National-type schools in which other languages would serve as the media of instruction as long as the schools followed the national curriculum. The later Rahman Report (1960), a review of the Razak Report, suggested that the flexibility of the Razak Report, which allowed for government support of Chinese secondary education, was incompatible with national policy.

Chinese schools were given the option of converting to the national system (either Malay or English at the time), failure to do so incurring the withdrawal of government support. Despite outcry from the Chinese community, fifty-five of the sixty schools converted, though, crucially, the majority converted to English-medium rather than Malay-medium schools. In 1960, enrolment in government-assisted secondary schools had been 72,499 (62.3 per cent) in English, 38,828 (33.4 per cent) in Chinese, and 4,953 (4.3 per cent) in Malay. Although Malay schools continued to expand, the conversion of the Chinese schools to English led in 1962 to 90 per cent (119,219) of secondary students being in English schools as opposed to only 10 per cent (13,224) in Malay schools (see Watson, 1983, p. 138). With English still operating as a key to wealth and prestige in the country, and with large numbers of Malays, especially in the rural areas, excluded from the language, 'English came to be regarded as a barrier to Malay social and economic advancement' (Ożóg, 1990, p. 309). Chai Hon-Chan (1971) suggests that 'the English language came to be regarded not only as the language of colonial domination but also, after independence, as an obstacle to the educational, social and economic advance of the majority of Malays' (p. 61)

Most significantly, then, the struggle for the ascendancy of Malay politics, language and culture had to be directed against the language that operated to convey social and economic power: English. The Malay nationalists were 'determined to replace the dominant position of English by Malay' (Watson, 1983, p. 140). Thus, as Mahathir Mohamad himself (1986) puts it, 'In the struggle to uphold their language, the Malays were forced to oppose and cast aside the English language' (p. 43). But this posed several problems. First, it was no easy process to remove English from its position embedded in the educational and administrative struc-tures of the society, and such a policy could only be carried out in conjunction with broader economic and educational policies. Second, it was important for Malaysia to remain linked to the global economy and thus for sufficient numbers of Malaysians to be proficient in English. And third, given the position of English both within and outside Malaysia, it was essential that certain Malays had a sufficient command of English to establish themselves economically. Citravelu (1985) poses the problem thus: 'In the conflict between the need to modernize using English as a language of wider communication . . . and the fear of substituting political colonization with cultural and economic colonization . . . what will the loading on modernization (and therefore English) be?' (p. 85). A key aspect of the 'Malay Dilemma', then, was how to promote their own interests in the face of the very worldliness of English.

After 1969 the urgency of the Malay programme increased, and between 1970 and 1983 the entire national educational system was gradually converted to Bahasa Malaysia medium, with the exception of Chinese and Tamil elementary schools. Four new universities were created, and *bumiputras* started to make up an ever larger proportion of the student population and to participate more widely in the economy. In 1967–68, Chinese students made up 56.1 per cent of students at the University of Malaya, Malays 30.7 per cent, and Indians 11.8 per cent (see Chai Hon-Chan, 1971, p. 27). Even more significant than these figures, however, were the subjects studied: almost 70 per cent of Malays were studying in the Arts Faculty, less than 1 per cent in engineering, 6 per cent in science, 5 per cent in medicine, and 11.35 per cent in economics and administration. Thus while the Malays dominated in the arts subjects, the Chinese were concentrated in the scientific and professional areas: 82 per cent of science students were Chinese, 70 per cent of medical students (Malays 18 per cent, Indians 11 per cent), and 90 per cent of engineering students (Malays 3.5 per cent, Indians 6.5 per cent). The causes of this were, as Asmah Haji Omar (1987) points out, to a large extent linguistic, since arts subjects could more easily be studied through Bahasa Malaysia, while the science subjects were predominantly in English. The effects were clear: Chinese (and to a lesser extent Indians) dominated in these professional domains.

Gradually, however, the new policies had their effect: In 1970, enrolment in university degree courses was 40.2 per cent *bumiputra*, 48.8 per cent Chinese, 7.3 per cent Indian and 3.7 per cent other. By 1980, this had changed to 66.7 per cent *bumiputra*, 26.2 per cent Chinese, 6.0 per cent Indian and 1 per cent other (*Fourth Malaysia Plan*). According to the *Fifth Malaysia Plan*, this over-representation of Malays had balanced out in 1985 to reflect more or less the ethnic make-up of the country: *bumiputras* made up 51.7 per cent of all certificate, diploma, degree and overseas students, Chinese 38.7 per cent, Indians 8.8 per cent and others 0.8 per cent. *Bumiputra* participation in technical and professional domains of education also increased. In engineering, for example, *bumiputra* enrolment rose from 1.3 per cent in 1970 (all universities) to 31.9 per cent in 1975, and in medicine from 17.2 per cent in 1970 to 39.1 per cent in 1975 (*The Star*, 31 August 1982). In employment, too, *bumiputras* were making gains. In 1970, they had represented only 22.4 per cent of administrative and managerial workers, compared with 65.7 per cent Chinese; by 1975, this proportion had shifted to 32.4 per cent and 55.2 per cent respectively (*Third Malaysia Plan*). *Bumiputra* mean monthly income increased from $172 (65 per cent of the national average) in 1970 to $384 (78 per cent) in 1984, and their share in the corporate sector grew from 4.3 per cent in 1971 to 17.8 per cent by the end of 1985 (*Fifth Malaysia Plan*).

ENGLISH, CLASS AND ETHNICITY

Despite these advances, a number of problems also emerged. While the stress on the need to redistribute wealth between ethnic groups was clearly benefiting the *bumiputra* group as a whole, it also had a number of detrimental effects. First, as Loh Kok Wah (1984) and Muzaffar (1984) point out, far from lessening ethnic tensions by equalizing economic differences, the stress on ethnicity as the principal division in society had in fact increased racial polarization, leading to what Tan Chee Beng (1984) refers to as the 'national cancer' of 'ethnicism' (p. 210). According to Maznah and Saravanamuttu (1990), 'To put it plainly, race has been the basis of governance and political mobilization in Malaysian politics. Even in the aftermath of the traumatic racial riots of May 1969, the Malaysian ruling élites have chosen to pursue this basic model of politics, albeit with drastic proscription and suppression of political freedoms with respect of ethnic mobilisation' (p. 101). Second, the constant stress on ethnicity at the expense of other ways of thinking about social difference, and the inequitable division of wealth overlooked other divisions within the society: 'The problem of poverty in this country is actually of a class nature, but very often it is presented as a racial or ethnic one' (Husin Ali, 1984, p. 30). Thus there has been a constant tendency to see poverty in terms of the different distribution of wealth between ethnic groups rather than in terms of class distribution. Osman-Rani's (1990) figures, for example, show that there is very little difference between ethnic groups in terms of share of wealth within each group: the top 20 per cent of Malays, Chinese, and Indians all hold about 50 per cent of the wealth of their ethnic group, a position which has not improved since independence. Since English use was in fact distributed much more in terms of class than in terms of ethnicity, the emphasis on ethnic difference tended to obscure the role of English in the country.

In one of the few studies that has looked at the effects of language planning policies in terms of class and ethnicity, de Terra (1983) found far-reaching implications for the non-Malay working class because there was insufficient support for them to learn Bahasa Malaysia: 'What language is for Bahasa Malaysia language planners is not what it is for working-class, non-Malay speakers' (p. 528). The language planners were too far removed from the realities of working people and provided insufficient help to learn: 'There are no literary programs at the village level; there is no pedagogy for these oppressed' (p. 529). Ultimately, she suggests that this lack of support for the implementation of the National Language policy indicates that other motives may be at play: 'By not implementing the plan, racial or ethnic divisions are maintained among the working class' (p. 529). Thus, ethnic differences are enhanced, especially among working people, while the class base of English is overlooked.

Furthermore, the move to increase *bumiputra* participation in the economy emphasized capitalist development and therefore tended to favour only a certain group of Malays. As a number of analyses of the effects of the New Economic Policy show (Ishak Shari and Jomo, 1984; Hing Ai Yun, 1984; Loh Kok Wah, 1984; Muzaffar, 1984), it was aimed to benefit the Malay middle class, 'to cater for the economic and political aspirations of middle-class Malays' (Muzaffar, 1984, p. 378). Kua Kia Soong (1987b) suggests that 'many of these policies – such as New Economic Policy, the National Education Policy – have not, by any means, solved the fundamental problems of the Malay poor. They have merely benefited a small handful of rich and well placed *bumiputras*' (p. 7). Thus, what seems to have developed from these policies is a battle between the entrenched Chinese middle and upper classes and the newly emergent Malay middle and upper classes: 'The largely Malay government is committed to the creation of a Malay middle and upper class. This class and its aspirations have brought it into direct conflict with an established non-Malay middle and upper class which grew out of the colonial era' (Muzaffar, 1984, p. 378).

Clearly, since much of the private sector still functions in English (Citravelu, 1985), this struggle between the Malay and Chinese and Indian middle classes involves a struggle around English. But it also poses the Malay dilemma of needing to promote Bahasa Malaysia as a symbol of Malay power and national unity, and the need to ensure that Malays are sufficiently competent in English to compete both with the Chinese within Malaysia and also in the global economy. An important upshot of the increased racial polarization is that, for many non-Malays, language and education policies are still perceived as Malay rather than Malaysian. Thus, according to Tan Chee Beng (1984), 'Malay as the national language has yet to transcend ethnicity' (p. 209). He suggests that two Chinese of different dialect groups will prefer to speak English or use a dialect that neither is conversant with rather than Malay, which both may know quite well.[5] Indeed, he suggests, many Chinese 'prefer to cut short the interaction rather than to proceed in Malay which both can speak' (p. 208).

Studying overseas

A further complication in education has been the vast numbers of students studying overseas. According to the *New Straits Times* (20 December 1981), there were about 40,000 students abroad, compared with about 30,000 in Malaysian universities (plus 18,000 in other Malaysian institutes of higher learning). Citravelu (1985) gives the figure of 58,000 overseas students compared with 55,072 in Malaysian universities. According to official government figures, there were about 60,000 students abroad in 1985 (*Fifth Malaysia Plan*). Of these, 22,684 were on degree courses, 6,113 on certificate courses and 5,738 on diploma courses; a further 10,700 were in secondary education in Singapore. There are two significant factors to be noted here. First, the large majority of these students were in English-speaking countries: of the 49,200 registered abroad, 10,300 were in Australia, 2,700 in Canada, 1,100 in New Zealand, 13,500 in the United States, and 3,400 in the UK. The secondary students in Singapore would also be studying in English. Second, the majority of these students were non-Malay: Of the 22,684 students on degree courses, 13,406 (59 per cent) were Chinese, 6,034 (27 per cent) Bumiputra, and 3,108 (14 per cent) Indian; of the total 34,535 on degree, diploma and certificate courses, 21,428 (62 per cent) were Chinese, 8,360 (24 per cent) Bumiputra, and 4,463 (13 per cent) Indian (*Fifth Malaysia Plan*).

Clearly, this situation is to quite an extent in response to the quota system at Malaysian universities (Kua Kia Soong, 1987b). Indeed, according to a recent study (*The Straits Times*, 5 March 1991), it is estimated that only about 20 per cent of qualified Chinese students enter local universities. More interesting, however, are the implications of this both for education in the country prior to students going abroad and for employment when they return. In the face of diminished opportunities for study in Malaysia (or at least perceived or relatively diminished opportunities, since despite the quota system, the rapid increase in university enrolment since 1970 has in fact given all communities greater access to higher education), the Chinese and the Indian middle and upper classes have used their economic resources to continue to provide a privileged education for their children. Significantly, most students study in English-speaking countries, because these are seen as offering the best education and because both the prior educational experiences of the students in English and the opportunities for work in English make a university education in English, rather than in Bahasa Malaysia, a highly desirable option. Thus, schools from which students are likely to go abroad need to emphasize the English skills of their students. The headmaster of one private school estimated that between 30 per cent and 40 per cent of his sixth-form boys go overseas each year (*New Straits Times*, 31 March 1985). There has also been a burgeoning of private language schools, from the courses run by the British Council in Kuala Lumpur and Penang to tiny one-room schools in smaller towns.

The other side of this overseas education in English may have significant implications for employment. Although the pro-*bumiputra* policies were successful in attracting *bumiputras* to areas such as architecture, medicine, the law, and engineering in university, in 1984 they made up only 15.6 per cent of architects

(Chinese 81.9 per cent), 8.9 per cent of accountants (Chinese 82.8 per cent), 25.2 per cent of engineers (Chinese 67 per cent), 16.7 per cent of doctors (Chinese 41.8 per cent, Indians 38.7 per cent), and 16 per cent of lawyers (Chinese 48.7 per cent, Indians 32.8 per cent) (*Fifth Malaysia Plan*). As Citravelu (1985) points out, there is now a major split between the public and private sectors, the former functioning predominantly in Bahasa Malaysia, the latter in English. What appears to be happening is that the locally educated Malays are tending to go into public and government service, while the English- and overseas-educated Chinese and Indians are still taking up the majority of jobs in the English-dominant private sector (Muzaffar, 1984). With by and large the cream of Malaysian students and/or the children of the already privileged going abroad (including also government- and privately-funded Malays), those educated in the Malaysian university system tend to be regarded as second-class students, and thus have more difficulty finding top jobs, especially in the private sector, while the overseas-educated remain a social and economic élite. Mead (1988) comments that 'this university education overseas, and particularly in the English-speaking world . . . served to protect privilege and to create the conditions for economic advancement available to only a small minority' (p. 37). Once again, because of both its international saliency and its connections to local divisions of society, English has remained as an important guardian and provider of privilege in Malaysia.

English and educational equality

An irony for the Malaysian Government is that despite the need to oppose English in order to promote the national language, they have also had to promote the widespread teaching of English as the 'second most important language'. In part, of course, this has been because English poses less of a threat to the promotion of Malay rule than would the promotion of Chinese or Tamil. But it is also a recognition that to participate in the world economy it is essential to have a sufficient number of people proficient in English. As Prime Minister Dr Mahathir Mohamad said recently:

'We have to trade with Europeans and Americans more and more. We need to communicate effectively with them. If we can only speak Bahasa Malaysia, who is going to ever understand us?' (Quoted in *The Star*, 26 June 1990). Given the need to maintain levels of English competence, and the democratization of the education system to provide in theory equal opportunities for all, English has now spread far further than it ever did before. Asmah Haji Omar (1987) points out that English is no longer limited to an élite few, since every child in Malaysia now has the opportunity to learn English. 'English', she says, 'has now reached out to the masses' (p. 67). Such a view seems rather optimistic, however. First of all, it is inevitably still caught up in difficult relationships to Malay culture and the national language. Second, as with any education system, there are more complex questions to be asked here about the extent to which education systems, and therefore English, indeed open up possibilities for everyone. And finally, there are questions to be asked about resistance to English and its connections to various forms of culture and knowledge.

With respect to the first issue – the relationship between English and Bahasa Malaysia – many of these problems appear on the face of it to have been solved. The recent calls for more emphasis on English, by Prime Minister Mahathir Mohamad and Education Minister Anwar Ibrahim (see *The Star*, 7 October 1988; 18 June 1989; *New Straits Times*, 24 January 1990) come in the light of a confidence that Bahasa Malaysia is now firmly established as the language of education, government, and administration. Nevertheless, Ożóg (1990) points to the problem that 'if English is important then their people must have access to it, and yet, to admit its importance undermines, in their eyes at least, the status of the National Language' (p. 313). There is, then, always a degree of struggle around the status of English and its relationship to Bahasa Malaysia.

The second issue – a question of English and equality – is more complex. Any critical understanding of schooling points to the many ways in which, rather than offering diverse opportunities for social and economic mobility, education systems tend to reproduce social, cultural and economic disparities. Toh Kin Woon's (1984) study of the Malaysian education system found that class inequality not only affected access to education but also success in the school system. Thus, children from a higher socioeconomic background had better access to education, stayed longer in education and performed better. Toh Kin Woon (1984) concludes that 'the formal educational system in Malaysia has been utilised more as a mechanism for the intergenerational transmission of economic status by high status families rather than as a vehicle for the social advancement by the poor' (p. 260). There must be doubts, therefore, whether the 'reaching out to the masses' of English can in any real sense be in the service of equality. The Malays, furthermore, have felt the need to discourage English amongst non-Malays and promote the national language, and at the same time to provide the opportunities for a Malay élite to be fluent in English. Thus, as Mead (1988) suggests, on the one hand 'the national élite – and in particular the Malay élite – must be encouraged to include English in their arsenal of languages', but on the other hand 'the masses – and in particular the non-Malay masses – must be directed away from English culture and towards the goal of a Malay-speaking polity' (p. 30). Such a tension may have broad implications for equality within the education system.

With the entire population obtaining, at least in theory, a certain competence in English, it is now the level of competence in English that has become the more crucial divider. Mead (1988) argues that although the political and economic system makes a knowledge of Bahasa Malaysia a prerequisite for upward mobility, it offers 'only the small high-flying minority the incentive to add specialized English to their other language skills' (p. 31). According to Rajah (1990), since a high proficiency level in English gives students a head start over others academically and therefore economically, 'there are chasms existing within the educated élite caused by the different competence levels in English' (p. 115). Thus, she goes on, 'sociopolitical changes have therefore created an emerging educated élite united by the national language, Bahasa Malaysia, but divided by the "second language", English' (p. 115).

A persistent problem in providing widespread English education has been the difficulty in supplying rural areas with competent teachers and other resources. As with many national education programmes, however, there are also problems of relevance, motivation and resistance. In one study, Asmah Haji Omar (1990) has concluded that 'it is not just an impression but a foregone conclusion that Malaysian students are in general positive towards learning English' (p. 28). Since the students she studied were all at the University of Malaya, however, this is not such a surprising finding since it does not deal with questions of class or rural poverty. Furthermore, her arguments are framed very much within the discourses of linguistic and applied linguistic thought discussed in Chapters 1 and 4: 'The fear that English may have a negative effect on their religious beliefs, ethnic culture, and nationalism is very minimal. If there is any occurrence at all in real life to illustrate such a fear, it can be interpreted as an isolated one. The Sapir-Whorfian theory . . . does not seem to apply here' (p. 28). Such a framework for analysis overlooks the very connections around the worldliness of English that I have been trying to explore. An earlier study of attitudes towards English (Mariam Zamani, 1983), by contrast, found that students of low socioeconomic status and living in rural areas tended to be more favourable towards Bahasa Malaysia, while students from high socioeconomic backgrounds and urban areas favoured English. In fact, it seems that there may indeed be quite real resistance to English in many sections of the Malaysian population, but particularly among the Malay rural poor. Aminur Rahim (1992) suggests with respect to Muslim Bengal that an apparent apathy to English may be more a product of social and economic disparities between Muslims and Hindus than a resistance based on religion. Although the same case could be made in terms of the Malay rural poor, there also seem to be important reasons for exploring the difficult relations between English and Islam.

ENGLISH AND ISLAM

There is of course a long history of conflict between the Western/ Christian world and the Muslim world, from the Crusades of the Middle Ages to recent confrontations between the United States and Iran, Libya and Iraq, or even the 'Rushdie Affair'. Indeed, it is important, I think, to see the struggles around Salman Rushdie's *Satanic Verses* as, in part, a struggle between English and Islam. Referring to this battle, Harris (1991) argues that 'English is not just a language, any more than Islam is just a religion. . . . The names *English* and *Islam*, whatever else they may be, are names of two very big battalions when it comes to the international power struggle for control of the Middle East' (p. 90).[6] The notion of worldliness suggests that such a protracted history of conflict could not but leave its traces on the discourse/language nexus that forms between English and various discourses. For many colonized people, a strong relationship was felt between English and Christianity, since the first contact with the language was through Christian missionaries, and two of the most obvious signs of cultural expansion under colonialism were the spread of religion and the spread of the language. The same can be said for Malaysia (see Mahathir, 1970), where many Malays were suspicious of the missionary schools (Chapter 3). The struggle for independence from colonialism in the Muslim world frequently involved strong appeals to Islam as a unifying force around which people could join in the battle against European domination (Casewit, 1985). Independence movements, therefore, often involved a revival of Islamic consciousness with a concomitant stress on local languages and a rejection of Christianity and English (or other European languages). But as Laitin (1977) points out, the strength of the Islamic opposition to colonialism often left Muslims least able to participate in independence politics. Thus, as was the case with Malays, Muslim people often emerged after colonialism with a strong sense of religious and linguistic identity that was in vehement opposition to the language and religion of the colonizers, but they also emerged as the disenfranchised within their own country.

This Islamic consciousness has been undergoing a period of revival, perhaps in part in conjunction with or in opposition to what seems to be a global trend towards religious fundamentalism, perhaps also as a response to the threats posed by the spread of Western technology, knowledge and culture. Kamal Hassan (1987) suggests it is reasonable to expect Islamic 'revivalism' or 'resurgence' to continue to spread through the Muslim world, given its present momentum and, amongst other things, a growing crisis in confidence in Western models of government and development, the reaction to increased Christian missionary work, and the weakening of autocratic and dictatorial rule in Muslim countries. According to Ożóg (1990), in the same way that many Muslims in the Middle East are rethinking many aspects of their religious, cultural and political lives, so 'the Malays are re-evaluating much of their lives and, in so doing, are rejecting many Western ideas and practices' (p. 314). Ożóg goes on to argue that this strengthening of Islamic feeling has reinforced the idea that English is a Western language with little place in the lives of Malays. Thus, he suggests, 'a view expressed by many, although not yet publicly by a politician, is that English is a *kafir* (non-Islamic) language' (p. 314)

Secular and religious knowledge

Asmah Haji Omar (1987) points out that the Malay word *barat* (the West) evokes both positive and negative reactions, suggesting on the one hand progress, modernization, knowledge, science, technology, and so on, and on the other, moral permissiveness and degradation. But there is a more fundamental connection between rejection of things Western and the Islamic religion, namely in terms of the different conceptions of knowledge. As Mohd. Nor Wan Daud (1989) explains, an Islamic worldview has a number of implications for knowledge and education. Since knowledge is an aspect of divinity, seeking knowledge and teaching are fundamentally important acts of divine worship and a lifelong process. Knowledge is an integrated concept, formed of *revealed* knowledge (the *Qur'an* and *Sunna* of Muhammad) as well as *acquired* knowledge of both the external world of nature and the internal world of human experience. 'The proper and sincere application of knowledge in one's personal and collective life forms the foundation of the only criterion of human excellence in Islam, *taqwa*' (p. 113). The concept of knowledge in Islam, then, is fundamentally important, in part because revealed knowledge comes from the Scriptures and in part because its pursuit is considered a facet of a properly religious life. Significant here is that there is a profound difference between Western secular thought embodied in technological–rational knowledge and the holistic concept of divine knowledge embodied in Islamic thought. Significant, too, is the close connection between the spread of English and the spread of Western secular thought.

According to Mohd. Nor Wan Daud (1989), however, the distinction between secular/Western and Islamic/religious knowledge is not so clear cut, since much of what is taken to be Western actually has its origins in Islamic and Arabic thought. Furthermore, since, as Mahathir Mohamad (1986) suggests, Islam 'encourages the pursuit of all knowledge' (p. 30), or as Asmah Haji Omar (1990) says, 'knowledge should be sought from anywhere in the world' (p. 10), there may be no Qur'anic justification for such a separation:

It is indeed an injustice to history and to the true spirit of Islam that some Muslim activists (and many Western scholars also) equate Islamization with an anti-Western philosophy. Muslims are urged in the *Quran* to benefit from the signs of God in *all* parts of the world; and learning from the West, whose rise to prominence can be attributed significantly to its contact with the Muslim world, should be positively regarded as a reciprocation of a magnificently creative process.

(Mohd. Nor Wan Daud, 1989, p. 120)

Nevertheless, others, such as Ashraf (1987) and Ali (1987), argue that Western secular thought is a direct threat to the tenets of a Muslim society. In her study of the problems posed by Western forms of knowledge in higher education in Bahrain, Zahra Al Zeera (1990) compares the 'Western-imposed models' to the Trojan Horse (cf. Cooke, 1988) and suggests that Bahrain 'is being torn between poles, fragmented between the secular and the religious' (p. 336). She argues that:

Western secular programs are at the root of the most serious problems at the university and in the society. Problems of coeducation and secular education, Arabization, English-language domination of the job market, motivation, and bilingual, bicultural issues are all based in modernization projects. What is happening at the university is a reflection of what is happening in the society. A unidimensional, secular theory of knowledge introduced into Bahrain's higher educational institutes is causing a crisis at different levels: linguistic and language, economic, social, cultural, academic, psychological and religious.

(p. 322)

Mohammad Shafi also connects this split to the teaching of English, and argues that 'in the Muslim countries there is a great disparity between the objectives of teaching English and the ultimate aim of Muslim education' (p. 33). Mahathir Mohamad (1986), the Malaysian Prime Minister, suggests that this debate is indeed alive in Malaysia today: 'The perception of the education and the knowledge brought by the British as "secular" or "Western" shaped Malay attitudes to such an extent that they became ingrained in the Malay psyche. To this day opposition to so-called "secular" education still exists and the debate continues on the merits and demerits of education other than "religious" '

(p. 22). A study by Ożóg (1990) at the International Islamic University in Malaysia found that all of the fifty students interviewed 'were concerned that English was the main avenue through which Western, that is non-Islamic or even anti-Islamic, culture entered the country' (p. 314).

With the strengthening of Islamic feeling in Malaysia and the need to win votes from the Islamic PAS party, which has been gaining strength especially in the rural North, the government has been faced by yet another dilemma: how to support the learning of English for 'pragmatic' scientific, academic, business, and political reasons while at the same time supporting the Islamization of the country, which for many may seem a process incompatible with the learning of English. Clearly, whether there is an inherent tension between Western and Islamic knowledge or not, there is a strong feeling that English is connected to forms of knowledge and culture that are oppositional or even threatening to an Islamic way of life. Once again, the difficulties of dealing with the national and international cultural politics of English can be seen. To the extent that students are wary of some of the possible implications of learning English, a useful oppositional politics can be formed, but to the extent that English is an important means by which social and economic privilege is apportioned within the society, a general resistance to learning English, especially in rural areas, can serve to maintain ethnic and class inequalities.

An Islamic approach to TEFL

Mohammad Shafi's (1983) view that there is a disparity between the objectives of teaching English and the aims of Muslim education has led him to argue for an 'Islamic approach to teaching English as a foreign language'. This implies 'learning English which is based on the Islamic faith, thought and conduct and excluding anti-religious and irreligious ideologies' (p. 34). He suggests that to avoid the 'sad and precarious' situation of Muslim youth, who, 'after being educated through the medium of English ... are transformed into split personalities', there is the 'utmost need to make English language teaching truly Islamic' (pp. 36–7). This would involve a whole reassessment of teaching methods, so that 'each lesson in the teaching of English should be based on behavioural objectives having Islamic concepts to be taught according to Islamic objectives to be achieved' (p. 38). It would involve the retraining of teachers, the teaching of lexical items and Islamic concepts in context, rewriting syllabuses and textbooks, changing exam systems, and comprehensive structural support. Al Zeera's (1990) proposals for a 'wholistic' Islamic paradigm for the Orientation programme at the University of Bahrain similarly requires English to be taught within an utterly reconceptualized and Islamic framework.

Such proposals, however, face difficult struggles against both those whose interests are in favour of maintaining the links between English and a notion of internationalism (thus making claims as to its neutrality and the primacy of international intelligibility) and those for whom a particularization of English in a certain direction becomes a move towards communalism (thus making claims to other rights to particularization). Furthermore, with the domination of Western teaching practices, theories and textbooks around the world, a constant rearguard battle has to be fought to maintain such a project. Malaysia is currently at a very interesting juncture in its gradual move towards Islamization and the simultaneous recent emphasis on English. The government, despite its strong nationalist and pro-Islamic stances, has been steering a delicate course between the more radical calls for Islamization from Islamic groups such as the Pan Malaysian Islamic Party (PAS) and the fears expressed by the non-Muslim sectors of the population. While the PAS has suggested that the current Islamization programme is but a disguise for the underlying secular orientation of the government, liberals, even from within the Malay community, have expressed their concern that the process is dangerously divisive. According to the Tunku, 'too much emphasis on religion will lead to misunderstanding as Malaysia is a country of mixed population and mixed religions, and would not be congenial to the happy relationship that exists among the people today' (*The Star*, 28 April 1987). At the same time, the government is constantly stressing the need for education in Malaysia to meet the needs of economic development, a process which inevitably includes education in English. Thus English gets caught up in this debate around the future of Malaysia as an Islamic state.

The process of Islamization, however, is also bringing certain changes to the English language curriculum. With the increased

Islamic content in the secondary school curriculum (*Kurikulum Bersepadu Sekolah Menengah*: KBSM), curriculum writers are not only required to ensure that there is no inappropriate material in textbooks (such as the non-Islamic celebration of birthdays), but they must also include aspects of the new Muslim-dominated moral curriculum in their work. Whether such changes will continue and have a lasting effect, and whether this ultimately may constitute an Islamic approach to English language teaching in Malaysia remains to be seen. Such changes may produce a certain Islamicization of English, but battles will always have to be fought around the use of English in wider contexts and with other communities' concerns over the changing face of English. The complex worldliness of English is tied up with questions of colonialism, neocolonialism, religion, education, knowledge and resistance. For Malays, these relationships are then bound up with their own negotiation of identity between their position within the larger Islamic community (*umma*) and their position as a linguistic and cultural group within Malaysia (Hussin Mutalib, 1990).

ENGLISH AND THE MEDIA

English, then, is closely intertwined with class, ethnic, religious and cultural issues in Malaysia. This section will focus on current roles that English plays in Malaysian life and particularly at English and the media. According to Asmah Haji Omar (1987), 'at the unofficial level, English is spoken in almost every aspect of Malaysian life, particularly in the urban areas. In private and multinational firms, it seems to be the language of the management group. English is spoken widely in the shopping centres although the variety that is used is mostly Malaysian English' (p. 164). Both Ożóg (1990) and Nik Safiah Karim (1989) confirm that English is the dominant language in business, is still quite widely used in tertiary education, is widely used on television, and 'is the language of – the officially frowned upon, yet growing – Western pop culture' (Ożóg, 1990, p. 312). Citravelu (1985) summarizes the position of English as 'needed in this country for purposes of higher education, for communication with the world intellectual community, for research, for science and technology, for the maintenance of trade and diplomatic relations' (p. i).

Domains such as tourism also require mention here, especially since Malaysia has been making special efforts to increase tourism.

Books, journals and magazines

There is a major schism between the public and private sectors, with Bahasa Malaysia used about 70 per cent of the time in government but English used predominantly in the private sector. Citravelu (1985) predicts that although increased use of Bahasa Malaysia generally should bring about more use in the public sector, the expansion of the economy is always creating new jobs and therefore more uses for English in the private sector. Thus, especially with the growth of the English-oriented computer industry, increases in the use of Bahasa Malaysia are offset by increases in the use of English in the business world. With almost all of the professional literature for business (e.g. *Far Eastern Economic Review* or the Malaysian *Investors Digest* or *Malaysian Business*), law and medicine in English, good skills in English are always going to remain important.

This difficulty can also be seen at the universities. While the gradual conversion of all state schools (except Chinese and Tamil primary schools) to Bahasa Malaysia has been successfully carried out, the problems faced in converting the university system from English to Bahasa Malaysia have been more extensive. Academic staff were predominantly non-Malay and many, especially the older ones, were far from proficient in the national language. A study conducted at the Universiti Sains Malaysia found that two-thirds of the students felt that lecturers lacked the expertise to lecture in Bahasa Malaysia (*The Sunday Star*, 6 February 1983). Lecturers, most of whom were English-educated, also faced the difficulty of finding suitable scientific terminology in Bahasa Malaysia, although extensive language planning projects have remedied this somewhat (see Asmah Haji Omar, 1979). Another problem was that of the 320,000 copies of reading material in the university library, only 10 per cent were in Bahasa Malaysia; very few audiovisual materials were in the national language and none of the 5,000 rolls of microfilm (*The Sunday Star*, ibid.). Citravelu (1985) found that many of the books available in Malaysian universities are still in English. Looking at the list of books printed by the *Dewan Bahasa dan Pustaka* (the main publisher of Malay books) in Bahasa Malaysia between 1970 and 1984, she finds, for example, only one for engineering, four for law, eight for medicine, and sixteen for economics (Citravelu, 1985, pp. 29–30). She also cites an estimate that less than 5 per cent of academic writing in Malaysia is in the national language.

Although the creation of terminology in Bahasa Malaysia has made translation more of a possibility, many specialists are unwilling to spend their time on translation, with the result that the few translations available have often been done by people with limited technical knowledge, rendering the texts inaccurate and causing students to prefer the originals in English. It is also of course the case that to keep up with modern academic work, it is imperative to read the most recent publications in English. A rough count I conducted of the almost 2,000 journals and periodicals at the Universiti Sains Malaysia (Penang) – from *A & U: Architecture and Urbanism*[7] to the *Zoological Journal of the Linnaean Society* – found only about forty (2 per cent) that used Bahasa Malaysia. Even amongst these, both languages are often used. Thus, while *The Malaysia Journal of Economic Studies* is entirely in English, the *Jurnal Ekonomi Malaysia* is about half in English and half in Bahasa Malaysia, and while the law journal *Kanun: Jurnal Undang-Undang Malaysia* is entirely in Bahasa Malaysia, *Jurnal Undang-Undang/Journal of Malaysian and Comparative Law* is largely in English. Of the other journals and periodicals, almost all are in English: The Scandinavian *Acta Chemica Scandinavia* is in English, as is the Swedish *Geografiska Annaler*, while *Chemische Berichte* (Germany) and *Economia Internazionale* (Italy) are about half in English. This is not, it should be noted, applicable only to the sciences: of the 135 education journals, for example, only two use Bahasa Malaysia.

Once again, the intentions of the government to increase the use of Bahasa Malaysia have been partially halted by the power of English in the world and its connections to academic discourse. The dominance of English in academic domains is clearly bound up with relations of academic dependence. Selvaratnam (1986) argues that despite the continued replacement of expatriate staff through the 1970s and 1980s (a process which has now led to the virtual replacement of this once dominant body), the new Malaysian academics are 'trained in and oriented towards an academic culture and belief and value system that is dominantly

Western' (p. 39). Thus many local academics continue to depend on and perpetuate 'the same Western-dominated beliefs and value system about theory, methodology, techniques and problems' (p. 39). Nevertheless, he also argues that the cultural politics of Malaysia and the state intervention in universities have created a 'distinctive national model, in spite of the peripheral role in knowledge generation and distribution' (p. 49). Selvaratnam therefore argues that while on the one hand universities in Malaysia must be seen as interdependent with the rest of society and both reflecting and producing change, on the other hand this occurs within the structural dynamics of the international academic and knowledge systems. This argument has interesting connections to my claim that English should be understood as interdependent with local circumstances but also tied to global relations.

Newspapers and TV

English plays an important part in the media. Although the circulation of the English language newspapers was third in 1983 at 813,000, compared with 1,521,000 for Chinese and 1,163,000 for Malay (and 189,000 for Tamil), the English papers play an important role by dint of their readership, which tends to be educated, urban and in better-paid jobs (Citravelu, 1985, pp. 62–8). Foreign news is almost exclusively dependent on the international news agencies, with Reuters dominating (see Chapter 2). Despite a commitment to developing Malaysian and regional news and programming sources (e.g. *New Straits Times*, 7 August 1983), English dominates other media, especially television. Asmah Haji Omar (1987) gives weekly figures (for around 1980) of forty-seven out of sixty-three hours on TV1 and twenty-three out of thirty-nine hours on TV2 in English. Citravelu's (1985) figures include the new private channel, TV3, and show about fifty-five hours in Malay compared with sixty-three hours in English. She predicts a possible move away from English and certainly away from English-language movies, in part because of the recent growth in the video trade. This trend has not been confirmed, however, with an overall growth in TV in English apparently reflecting the increased orientation towards English after 1985.

In the week 18–24 February 1991,[8] there were about 103 hours

(45 per cent) in English, eight-four hours (37 per cent) in Malay, thirty-two hours (14 per cent) in Chinese (Cantonese and Mandarin), and ten hours (4.5 per cent) in Indian languages (Tamil and Hindi). Indian programmes are limited to the news in Tamil on TV2 at 5.30 every evening, plus occasional films (Tamil or Hindi); Chinese programmes are generally limited to Cantonese serials (both TV2 and TV3 at 6.00), the news in Mandarin at 7.00 on TV2, and movies (often Cantonese from Hong Kong).[9] Malay programmes are more varied, with the majority of TV1 in Malay (though not by any means all, as was the case when Citravelu did her survey), and religious programmes, especially on Fridays, making up quite a large percentage. English programming is also mixed, though dominated by US entertainment shows. To take a few examples from the week under review: Tuesday 19 February saw the debut of *America's Funniest Home Videos*, which received a rave review two days later (*New Straits Times*, 21 February 1991). TV2 followed this by *Hardball* and *Legmen* (one-hour detective shows), news, and *Doctor, Doctor* (sit-com). TV3 showed *Sister Kate* and *The Golden Girls*, plus *English League Soccer*. TV1, after the regular showing of CNN at 7.00 (which is always interrupted for a few minutes for the evening call to prayer), showed the *Rambo* cartoon. Viewing for Wednesday 20th included *The Cosby Show* and *Growing Pains*. Regular features include a quiz show every evening at 7.30 on TV2 (*Give Us a Clue, Couch Potato, The Price is Right, Wheel of Fortune,* etc.). Saturday mornings have a standard menu of cartoons, and viewing for the weekend of 23–24 February included *Sesame Street, Police Academy, Roseanne, Star Trek: The Next Generation, Batman, Bugs Bunny,* and so on.

Prime Minister Mahathir Mohamad seems quite clear about the causes of this massive influx of Western programmes: 'The West controls the world mass media because a Western language, namely English, is understood in all parts of the world' (1986, p. 50). Husin Ali (1989) goes further and echoes the discussion of the role of Western media in Chapter 2 when he suggests that 'we are captives of United States political attitudes exported through the media, in that we hear all about the wickedness of their current enemies and the goodness of all their current friends' (p. 21). It is important, however, not to impute necessary effects of such media exposure: While people may be 'captives' in terms of there often being little other choice of opinion and viewing, they are not entirely captives in terms of the interpretations they can make of that viewing. It is indeed hard to judge the effects of this dominance of Western programming and many conversations with people revealed a complete spectrum of opinion from little or no effect to the potential destruction of Malaysian ways of life. Certain anecdotal evidence suggests some of the ways it is affecting people's everyday lives. One father, for example, suggested to me that the attitudes towards children and parents shown in *The Cosby Show* were changing his own teenage children's attitudes towards him. And in an article in *New Straits Times* (19 January 1991), a mother muses on the respective merits of 'Asian' methods of bringing up children compared with 'liberal' American approaches, as displayed in a recent episode of *Roseanne*. She determines to 'try and find the right combination of Asian and Western common sense to bring up my girls'. While we cannot assume *what* readings are made of these programmes, we can assume that readings *are* made in a complex mixture of admiration, rejection, accommodation, and so on.

One reason for the increase in English-language TV, apart from following general trends in government attitudes towards English, has been that RTM, the government broadcasting body that controls TV1 and TV2 has had to 'corporatize', i.e. become more financially accountable. This is one of those particularly interesting and complex interconnections between English and global relationships. The move to corporatize is of course connected to shifts both in the global economy and, more importantly, recent discourses on economics, discourses which, once again, are supported by and supportive of the spread of English. In the case of Malaysian television, American movies and TV programmes, and the advertising that they attract, are a far better financial proposition than locally made programmes. The advertising also tends to follow the programmes, so that Chinese and Malay programmes may attract more local commercials aimed at a specific clientele, while US programmes attract some of the larger international sponsors such as McDonalds, Kentucky Fried Chicken[10] and the Cigarette manufacturers. Since the direct advertising of cigarettes on Malaysian TV is not permitted, major sponsors are now Dunhill (not the cigarette manufacturer but the maker of elegant European products), Lucky Strike (not the cigarette company but the maker of clothes for motorbike riders), Peter Stuyvesant (not the cigarette manufacturer but the travel agent) and Benson Hedges (not the cigarette manufacturer but the maker of gold products).

Of particular interest here is not so much the issue of what is being marketed through cigarette manufacturers' advertising as what images and conjunctions between images are being produced. The banning of direct advertising had forced these advertisers to work harder on the production of a series of connected images that link their brand names to a desirable life-style. Thus they have had to go beyond the square-jawed Marlboro Man smoking on a lonely American prairie to make connections between the brand names and images of desirable life-styles through European elegance or Californian fun. This sets up connections between what is desirable, what is modern, what is elegant, what is chic, the foreign context of these desires, and the English language. Alongside the whole problematic issue of cigarette companies' massive moves to encourage smoking around the world, therefore, there is also the question of the types of images they mobilize to do so. It is the conjunction between, say, Roseanne's methods of child-rearing and English, or between Peter Stuyvesant's 'young, exciting, original' images of California and English, that work in a reciprocal reinforcement of the language and of the images. The language of the United States, of development and modernity, of excitement and youth, comes with the images of European elegance, American leisure and so on, each reinforcing the other.

Despite the frequency of English-language movies on TV – the 1991 new year season featured such films as *Red Heat* and *Rambo III* – and despite the growing video market, movie-going is still popular. The most popular movie for 1990 was *Teenage Mutant Ninja Turtles*, which (surprise, surprise) 'came smack in the middle of Turtle-mania in the country, when any child above five could say "Raphael, Michaelangelo, Leonardo, Donatello" in one breath' (*New Straits Times*, 3 January 1991). This is, no doubt, something of an exaggeration, but it does suggest once again the careful coordination of language, movies and commercial interests. I found a Chinese cake-store in Kuala Lumpur selling hand-decorated Teenage Mutant Ninja Turtle birthday cakes. The second most popular film was *Tango & Cash* (Sylvester Stallone and Kurt Russell), followed by *The Gods Must be Crazy II*, *Die Hard 2*, *Gremlins 2*, *Robocop 2*, *Dark Angel*, *Back to the Future II*, *Best of the Best*, and *Back to the Future III* (*New Straits Times*, 3 January 1991). Clearly, the American movie industry has a firm hold here, with the success of remakes perhaps suggesting a particularly adherent following.

THE DEBATES CONTINUE

The fortunes of English in Malaysia have waxed and waned and waxed again, and it never seems far from the centre of debate. Recently, there has been increased interest in and concern about English, due in part to a relaxing by Malays now that Bahasa Malaysia seems firmly in place as the national language. It also appears to follow economic trends, the renewed interest in the mid 1980s coinciding with an economic recession. Most recently, concern about falling standards has come once again to the fore, and especially since only 50.6 per cent of the students sitting the high school (SPM) exam in 1990 passed, a decline of 8 per cent compared to 1989 (*The Straits Times*, 12 March 1991). This led to the Prime Minister warning once again that 'in this modern era, knowledge of one language only is insufficient, and the English language is recognized as an international language' (*The Straits Times*, 9 March 1991). He warned that a pass in the SPM exams might have to be made compulsory (in 1991, English was a compulsory subject but a pass in the exams was not). Meanwhile, the low SPM results were the centre of another political battle between the two most likely successors to Mahathir Mohamad. Both vice-presidents of UMNO, the then Minister of Education, Anwar Ibrahim (Minister of Finance in 1991), and the former Minister of Education, Abdullah Ahmad Badawi (Foreign Minister in 1991), were battling over who to blame for the apparently declining standards in English (*The Straits Times*, 12 March 1991). In an ironic twist, could the choice of Prime Minister for Malaysia in the twenty-first century be influenced by the relative successes of these two Malay nationalists in promoting English in the school system during the 1980s?

Articles and letters about English can constantly be found in Malaysian newspapers, the principal themes being questions of levels and standards and the overall need for English. Dealing with the levels of English proficiency, a number of writers have worried whether standards are dropping, so that students will no longer be able to read texts at universities or compete in business. As others have pointed out, however, including Hyacinth Gaudart in her weekly column on English in *The Star* (3 September 1989), there are many more students now learning English than before, so an overall decline in average performance may be expected when compared with the former élitist system. Another question around standards concerns the actual nature of the language itself. Alistair King of the British Council in Kuala Lumpur bemoans 'the influence of sub-standard linguistic models on my students'. Outside his classrooms there is a 'morass of slipshod, incorrect English usage'. If standards are not maintained, he declares, 'the language will degenerate into a piginized variety – as indeed is the case among many Malaysian speakers of English' (*The Star*, 28 July 1990). This argument, which received both agreement (*The Star*, 9 August, 20 August) and disagreement (11, 25 August) is clearly a view from the old colonial centre, as it remains in the British Council Building perched on a small hill overlooking the city centre.

With respect to the more general questions about the need for English, we can make a rough division between those who stress the international and neutral nature of English and those who are more concerned about possible cultural and political implications of the spread of English. The majority seem to fall into the first category (at least over the past few years) and take up arguments quite similar to those outlined in Chapter 1: 'While Bahasa Malaysia remains our much respected national language, English should be accepted as an important functional language and not be misconstrued otherwise' (*New Straits Times*, 24 April 1990); English is merely a 'means or instrument with the best and most speedy access to learning' (*New Straits Times*, 1 February 1988); 'whether one likes it or not, one has to recognize that English had, through the long passage of time, evolved as the most popular international language ... used by many to disseminate information on important matters including advanced technology' (*New Straits Times*, 2 June 1990). The similarities between these comments and the dominant discourse of EIL, discussed in previous chapters, are intriguing. Once again they stress (popular) choice and functionalism and fail to ask how the language 'evolved' as it did, or what, for example, the implications may be of the use of English 'by many to disseminate information on important matters'.

Letters by Rustam A. Sani (*New Straits Times*, 16 April, 2 June 1990), by contrast, place the English language within the context of a ' "relationship of dependency" with English-speaking economic powers of the world' and the continued importance of the struggle to make Bahasa Malaysia an effective national language (2 June). Such a view comes somewhat closer to my arguments concerning the worldliness of English. I shall end this discussion, therefore, with a quote from his 16 April letter in which he suggests that one cannot talk of modernization and English without understanding in more complex terms the relationship between English and international relations: 'There is nothing that the English language can do for us in terms of modernising our minds if its role is conceived merely, as we do now, in terms of understanding instructions from our multinational bosses on the factory shopfloor.'

This chapter has been an attempt to come to terms with the contemporary worldliness of English in Malaysia. I have been trying to show how it is not only the power and position of English in the world that needs to be considered, not only the importance of the relationship between English as an international language and other global discourses that have to be taken into account, but also the struggles around English in its local contexts. Thus it is the complex relationships between English and dominant discourses of Malaysian politics – Malay nationalism, *bumiputra*ism, ethnic factionalism, Islamization, mass education and popular culture – that need to be considered if some sense of the worldliness of English is to be understood. Nevertheless, Rustam Sani's words also bring us back to a key issue that I do not wish to lose sight of in this discussion of the complexities of the local contexts of English: English operates globally in conjunction with capitalist forces, especially in the operations of multinational corporations. I shall close this chapter on this note, not only as an instance of English being seen in its worldliness rather than from within the discourse of EIL, but also in order to refocus attention on the worldliness of English in terms of its global reach and connections. This is an issue which will remain important for the discussion of Singapore. In the same letter, Rustam Sani also points to the effects of Singapore's use of English by suggesting it has produced 'an ambience quite similar to a Hilton Hotel lobby anywhere in the world'. It is to considerations of the worldliness of English in Singapore that I shall turn in the next chapter.

NOTES

1. My argument here is closely related to Foucault's (1980a) stress on the importance of 'local struggles' and his suggestion that the 'universal' intellectual now needs to give way to the 'specific' intellectual (1980a, p. 126), someone who uses their knowledge, competencies and

relations to the truth in the field of political struggles in order to have both local and general effects on the functioning of the apparatuses of truth (pp. 128–32).

2. The United Malays National Organization (UMNO) was formed in 1946 to focus opposition against the Malaya Union proposed by the British. Its success in renegotiating the Federation of Malaya in 1948 brought it much support and kudos among Malays. It was UMNO that led the Alliance that negotiated independence in 1957 and formed the first government, and still UMNO (now *UMNO Baru*) that dominates Malaysian politics today.

3. I should emphasize once again that my criticism here is not of the intentions of the Tunku, but rather of the effects of his class position and British education. This should not detract from his overall position in Malaysian history and the deep sorrow felt by so many at his death in 1990. The testimonies paid to him in the human rights journal, *Aliran Monthly* (**10**, no. 12) are evidence of the widespread respect which is his due.

4. As Caldwell (1977b) points out, the 'State of Emergency' declared between 1948 and 1960 to counter the threat of communist insurgencies had the effect of playing down the class basis of the struggle (by naming it as an ethnic – Chinese – issue rather than a class struggle), of establishing and perpetuating the emphasis on ethnicity as the principal division in the society, of helping the British to establish a leadership favourable to their interests, and of effecting control over the rural Chinese population.

5. This view has been questioned by a number of people, however. See especially the fierce argument between Tan Chee Beng and Kua Kia Soong in *The Star* in 1984, reprinted in Kua Kia Soong (1990).

6. There is, of course, a great deal more that could be said about this topic (see, among many examples, Mazrui, 1990).

7. Incidentally, this journal is one of the few foreign journals that is not entirely in English, being in English and Japanese.

8. I stopped a previous calculation in mid-January due to the outbreak of the 'Gulf War'. During this time, CNN was broadcast more frequently and, with broadcasting starting earlier, there were more early morning 'fillers', including English cartoons. While this is interesting in itself – CNN's coverage of the 'Gulf War' may have dramatically increased English-language broadcasting, and, we may suppose, influenced many attitudes, worldwide – this week would not have been representative. Interestingly, it has recently been decided that both CNN and the BBC World Service will be available direct by satellite in 1994. The information for this brief survey was gathered through careful reading of the TV guides and by watching TV almost

continuously during a week when I was running a high fever in a small and cheap hotel in the Chinatown area of Kuala Lumpur.

9. The Chinese population in Kuala Lumpur is majority Cantonese, although in the country as a whole, Hokkien predominate.

10. We should not overlook the significance of the spread of American fast-food restaurants. As one businessman told me, while some years ago business dinners had been long, drawn-out affairs in local restaurants, now it was not uncommon to go to McDonalds for twenty minutes. Fast-food restaurants in countries like Malaysia are not the cheap option they are in North America; rather they are a place for the young and trendy, for young people in business, and so on. Again, they represent a certain vision of modernity, a vision which so often is linked to English.

SEVEN

The worldliness of English in Singapore

Its choice of language is certainly consistent with its own notion of a
national past that does not go beyond the immediate colonial history,
and a vision of a cultural future that does not go beyond an ambience
quite similar to a Hilton Hotel lobby anywhere in the world.
(Rustam A. Sani, *New Straits Times*, 16 April 1990)

Presumably, the output of such a melting pot will be ethnically neutral,
speaking only the common language of English, celebrating the
international festival of Christmas, watching The Cosby Show and
embracing the 'global pop culture'.
(Cheng Shoong Tat, *The Sunday Times*, 3 February 1991)

We do not wish to be a pseudo-Western society. While we need to
learn and use English to master technology and enhance our
competitive edge in the international business community, we should
not let the use of English override the importance of keeping our links
to our cultural roots strong and healthy.
(Education Minister Dr Tony Tan, quoted in
The Sunday Times, 10 March 1991)

ENGLISH AS A USEFUL LANGUAGE

Walk into any large book store in Singapore and you will be
confronted by an array of material familiar to anyone from an
English-dominant country, from Enid Blyton to Barbara Cartland,
from business manuals to computer journals. It is only very
recently that a dramatic growth in Singaporean literature in
English (see Chapter 8) has brought local writing in English to the
main bookshelves from its former obscurity in a back corner under

the heading 'Local Interest', or 'Singapore and Malaysia', or 'South East Asia'. English permeates many corners of Singapore life from education to work to entertainment. It is common for visitors to Singapore to be struck less by its claims to represent 'Instant Asia' for tourists than by its similarity to a (sanitized) multicultural city in North America. Indeed, Rustam Sani suggests that it has created 'an ambience quite similar to a Hilton Hotel lobby anywhere in the world' (*New Straits Times*, 16 April 1990). And it is tempting at times to agree with Catherine Lim's (1991) contention that the new generation of Singaporeans is 'more at home with McDonalds and Madonna and Michael Jackson than with the customs of their ancestors' (p. 5).

The connections between English and various forms of culture and knowledge are still in some areas linked to Singapore's colonial history. Thus, Catherine Lim (1986) remarks that 'the attachment to British standards seems to be central to the government's policy on English language standards in Singapore' (p. 238). And yet, of course, despite the continuing strength of these links to Britain and the fairly tight controls over the media, Singapore's use of English also exposes it to the spread of American popular culture. It is not surprising, therefore, to find Singaporean life discussed in terms of American popular culture.[1] An article in *The Sunday Times* (3 February 1991), for example, discusses the appeal of the Simpsons (recently started) as a counter-balance both to the strains and pressures of success-oriented Singapore, and to the happy perfection of middle-class life portrayed in shows such as *The Cosby Show*: 'We all get tired, I suppose, of trying to live like the Cosbys, the Keatons or any of the other sit-com families to whom the very thought of a frayed sofa or a small kitchen is anathema.' Meanwhile, because of the dominance of English and the effectiveness of the pro-Mandarin campaign (a campaign aimed to discourage the use of 'dialects' in favour of Mandarin), many families are experiencing similar disruptions to those faced by many immigrant families in North America: grandparents and grandchildren, even parents and children, do not share a common language in which they can communicate more than rudimentarily.

Catherine Lim (1989) suggests that the role that English has come to play in Singapore makes it quite unique in the world, since no other former colony has gone on to officially adopt English as the working language:

While the status of English in the post-independence Third World declined or was reversed *vis à vis* the native languages, in Singapore it went on from strength to strength, until today, it is the language that enjoys the highest status and support among the nation's 2.6 million people. There are four official languages in multi-racial Singapore – English, Chinese, Malay and Tamil – but in practice, English dominates, both in the institutional and private life of the nation. It is the language of government, of administration and employment. It is the medium of instruction in all the schools and tertiary institutions. It is the only one of the four official languages whose informal use extends across all ethnic groups and socio-economic levels. Hence by any indicator – official status, social prestige, extent of use, number of speakers – English is the dominant language in Singapore.

(p. 1)

There are grounds for some circumspection here, however; quite whether English indeed enjoys such widespread 'informal use' and 'support' across both ethnic groups and socioeconomic levels is open to question; and in what ways Singapore is so different from former colonies such as Kenya, Zimbabwe, or Australia needs to be established. What is perhaps more interesting than the accuracy of these statements, however, is the tacit celebration of this widespread use of English in Singapore.

The most common rationale given for this dominance of English by Singaporeans is couched in terms of its usefulness and neutrality, in terms of Singapore's practical needs. Thus, Ser Peng Quee (1987), for example, explains that 'Singapore needs a pool of citizens who are competent in English in order to sustain its economic progress. Since English is the language of international trade, a knowledge of English among Singapore workers will thus attract not only investment from the developed industrial nations, but also enable Singapore to gain access to the scientific and technological expertise from the developed nations' (p. 2). Catherine Lim (1989), while acknowledging that there are also other social and political factors involved, nevertheless sees the primary factor as 'the unique usefulness of English to Singapore at every stage in the history of its development' (p. 2), and suggests that the 'economic usefulness of English has been and continues to be its *raison d'être* in pragmatic, achievement-oriented Singapore' (p. 3). While such pragmatic and exogenous arguments may seem to account sufficiently for the adoption of English in Singapore, they also leave a number of important questions unasked and unanswered.

First, it is important to observe that at no point does it appear to have been overt government policy to encourage the complete dominance of English. And yet, Wilson (1978) suggests that this was nevertheless a constant covert goal: 'Singapore ... appears unique in Southeast Asia, in encouraging the use of the language of its former colonial rulers, and it is tempting to suppose that, although nowhere clearly stated as a matter of policy, this has been the aim of the Government' (p. 237). Catherine Lim (1989) is less circumspect in her appraisal of government policy when she asserts that the government has in fact given 'total and uninterrupted support' (p. 3) to English. Clearly, at the very least, we must account for government policies rather than assuming some vague sense of national choice for pragmatic reasons. But, second, such political decisions are likely influenced by many other circumstances, especially, as discussed in the last chapter, class and ethnic struggles such as the sharp divide between the English- and the Chinese-educated. While it is tempting to see the use of English in Singapore as a result of Singapore's establishment as 'a "neo-colonial" beach-head in post-colonial Southeast Asia' (George, 1973, p. 178), or to conclude that 'the evidence from Singapore in fact appears to support the theory of English linguistic imperialism' (Phillipson, 1992, p. 316), when we look at the complexities of the cultural politics of Singapore, it is clear that, as with Malaysia, there are many local conditions that affected the use of English. How, for example, does one start to reconcile on the one hand the start of the vigorous pro-Mandarin campaign – a campaign aimed at promoting the use of Mandarin throughout the Chinese community – with, on the other hand, the simultaneous switch from Chinese-medium to English-medium education of Nanyang University, the symbol of linguistic and cultural pride for many Chinese Singaporeans? Finally, when looking at all the pragmatic arguments for the spread of English, we need to recognize such pragmatism as an ideological stance in itself.

On the one hand, then, it is important to see countries such as Singapore within the global capitalist system discussed in Chapter 2. Thus, it is important to recognize that many aspects of Singaporean culture are part of a global network of discursive systems, and that the connections suggested in the opening paragraph between English and Hilton Hotels or Michael Jackson are indeed very real. On the other hand, it is important not to assume a deterministic relationship of imperialism here. It is impossible to discuss the worldliness of English without looking in depth at the local cultural politics of Singapore, and particularly at the discourses of pragmatism, multiracialism and meritocratism that define many aspects of Singapore life. Thus, we need to try to account not only for why English has come to be so widely used in Singapore but also how it has come to be described in particular ways, how it is, for example, that 'the multiracial character of its people and the pragmatic language planning of the government' can be seen to account for 'Singapore's interesting language situation' (Kwan-Terry, 1993, p. 75).

THE MAKING OF SINGAPORE

Much of the success story of Singapore is well known: the rapid ascendancy of this small, scarcely industrialized island to become a major financial centre; the massive provision of government housing; the building of a modern, clean and beautiful city; and the development of a highly efficient education system. Almost as well known are some of the more negative aspects of this progress: the muzzling of trade unions in order to attract foreign investment; the defeat or removal of virtually all opposition to the government; the constant campaigns to control anything from language use to toilet-flushing; the attempts to improve the genetic make-up of the society; the strict techno-bureaucratic control of daily life; the careful picking and grooming of leaders to maintain these policies; universal male conscription and the attempt to build a 'rugged' society; and the planned reproduction of socioeconomic inequality through the rigidly meritocratic education system. Of interest to the theme of this chapter, however, are not so much the fine details of this story, but rather the relationship between English and the discourses that produced and were produced by this postcolonial history of Singapore.

The colonial legacy to Singapore left it, in the mid-1950s, a place of considerable unrest and uncertainty, with anti-colonial feeling widespread, communal violence constantly smouldering in the city, and a strong communist or socialist influence especially among the Chinese-educated and, more generally, the large poor sections of the society. Between 1950 and 1957, there had been a series of strikes, protests and riots involving particularly the militant trade union movement and the Chinese middle schools. It was clear that the anti-colonial sentiment was not merely a question of ethnic pride or nationalism but was also part of a broadly-based reaction to the socioeconomic inequalities in Singapore. Enrolment in English schools had continued to increase so that by 1954 it exceeded the enrolment in Chinese schools (Colony of Singapore, 1954). There seem to have been two main reasons for this. First, with minimal secondary education in anything but English, those who attended Chinese schools were condemned to employment requiring only elementary education. The communist takeover in China in 1949 had also made the option of sending students to China for higher education either impossible or unacceptable. Raffles College and the King Edward VII College of Medicine had combined in 1949 to form the University of Malaya, a prestigious institution giving high social, economic and political prospects to those educated in English. Second, however, it also appears to have been government policy to wean students away from the Chinese schools, which, especially since the 1949 revolution in China, had become even more politically active centres of Chinese nationalism and revolutionary fervour. Education policies in the post-war years had continued to develop a small English-speaking élite, which generally appeared to support British interests and was largely at odds with the Chinese-educated majority. The early 1950s saw considerable unrest in Chinese schools, culminating on 13 May 1954 in bloody clashes between police and students demonstrating against the national conscription laws. Large economic disparities on the island led to active trade union representation and radical left policies among students, who were also clearly influenced by events in China.

Despite government discouragement of Chinese education, and the social and economic reasons for learning English, there was still strong backing for Chinese education and resentment of the growing use of English: 'The English language was regarded by the non-English-educated as the language of the colonial masters and the values and purposes of English-medium education as foreign and anti-national' (Gopinathan, 1976, p. 71). This led to a growing split between the English- and the Chinese-educated in Singapore. While some sent their children to English schools, others, as they had done for the last hundred years in organizing their own schooling, set about organizing their own Chinese university, leading to the founding of Nanyang University in 1957.

Even trishaw- and taxi-drivers reputedly contributed to the fund by donating a day's earnings (Wilson, 1978), so testifying to the strength of feeling about the need for Chinese education and to the frustration at the spreading use of English.

Under the new 1955 government of the Labour Front – a loose coalition of English-educated intellectuals with leftist leanings – an all-party commission was formed to look into education in the colony. The *Report of the All-Party Committee* (Singapore Legislative Assembly, 1956), based on a sense of 'Singapore-centred loyalty' and a 'Malayan consciousness', recommended a system in which there would be vernacular education in the four main languages – Chinese, English, Tamil and Malay – with English as a compulsory language and Malay as an 'additional compulsory language'. These proposals were by and large adopted by the government, though the importance given to Malay was downplayed (and especially so following Singapore's departure in 1965 from the newly-formed Malaysia). Little was done, however, to institutionalize the four languages in employment, and there was virtually no provision made for either Tamil or Malay secondary education. This report was nevertheless of great significance, not merely in terms of the adoption of its proposals but also in terms of its consolidation of the definitions of 'race' and language that were to dominate Singaporean cultural politics after independence. As Puru Shotam (1987) puts it, the report 'constitutes a milestone in the social construction of language meanings in Singapore' (p. 80).

Lee Kuan Yew and the PAP

The People's Action Party (PAP) had been founded in 1954 and, under its Secretary-General, Lee Kuan Yew, was made up of largely English-educated liberal nationalists. To gain popular support, however, the PAP courted socialist groups and their popular leader, Lim Chin Siong, bringing widespread support to the PAP as a pro-communist, anti-colonialist party. Clearly, however, the existence of a socialist government in Singapore was antithetical to both British and Malayan interests (there was talk of Singapore being 'Malaya's Cuba'), as well as to the interests of the English-educated élite in Singapore itself. Once popular support for the PAP had been secured, a series of struggles for control of the party ensued, the liberal faction under Lee Kuan Yew eventually prevailing. But in 1956 and 1957, the central executive almost fell into the hands of the left-wing faction of the party. Each time, however, the ruling Labour Front (LF) party (now under Lim Yew Hock since David Marshall's resignation) suddenly ordered a 'communist purge' and imprisoned dozens of leftist leaders. As George (1973) suggests, such events point towards a degree of collusion between the PAP executive, the government and the colonial authorities. According to Sweeney (1977), the British realized that Lee Kuan Yew's right wing of the PAP was the group 'best equipped to safeguard British interests when Singapore eventually became self-governing or independent'. They then sacrificed the Labour Front and promoted Lee's faction within the PAP. Meanwhile, Lee Kuan Yew made it clear to the British that 'his revolutionary anti-colonial rhetoric was no more than a ploy which would be dropped at the appropriate time' (pp. 212-13).

In 1959 the PAP was swept to power, gaining 53.4 per cent of the vote and forty-three of the fifty-one seats. While this number indeed included a powerful group of socialist politicians, the government moves to curtail left-wing activity by restricting trade unions and student activity led them to break away in 1961 and form the *Barisan Sosialis* (Socialist Front). In the tense political atmosphere around the negotiations to merge Singapore with Malaya, a merger for which Lee Kuan Yew with his constant warnings of communist plots and communal violence was among the strongest advocates, a move to defuse 'anti-Malaysia' sentiment led to the re-arrest of the leading leftist politicians, including Lim Chin Siong, in 1963. Having joined Malaysia, after a somewhat dubious referendum, the PAP called a quick election, winning thirty-seven seats (46.9 per cent of the votes) to the Barisan Sosialis' thirteen (33.3 per cent). That the socialist party could be so successful, despite the fact that many of its leaders were in jail and that it had had virtually no time to prepare for the election, was testament to the continued strong support for left-wing policies.

During the two brief but turbulent years before its expulsion from Malaysia, and in the years following 1965 as an independent state, Singapore politics were dominated by the PAP. Opposition workers were arrested and detained without trial, the activities of the Chinese schools and universities were curtailed, anti-union legislation was passed, the jury system was abolished, the judiciary was brought under government control, and various organizations were set up to institutionalize PAP control. In 1966 all opposition members in parliament resigned, arguing that their presence served no democratic purpose and merely legitimated PAP activity. Since then, the PAP has held virtually every seat in parliament, with clean sweeps in 1968, 1972, 1976 and 1980; the loss of a by-election in 1981 and two seats in 1984 caused serious concern in the party. The PAP has become synonymous with government and parliament, effectively controlling the army, police force and judiciary through a number of measures that included a law whereby expulsion from the party also meant expulsion from parliament, High Court appointments being made by the prime minister, control over radio and television, licensing of newspapers and the withdrawal of these licences if the papers were critical of the government (the *Nanyang Siang Pau*, *Eastern Sun* and *Singapore Herald* have all been closed down), the right to imprison political opponents without trial on a two-year renewable basis (Chia Thye Poh has been in prison for over twenty-five years), the right to deprive citizens of their citizenship and the requirement of 'suitability certificates' to enter higher education.

Certain of these restrictions have since changed ('suitability certificates' were dropped in 1978, for example), and the PAP can certainly claim both that it was faced with a daunting task when it took over the leadership of the small and factionally divided island and that it has achieved remarkable success in building Singapore into a modern and thriving state. Nevertheless, the way in which the PAP gained and held power raises many questions in terms of democracy, human rights and equality. This process has, of course, attracted considerable attention over the years. Buchanan (1972), for example, argues that the PAP, which he describes as a 'right-wing party, whose ideology closely reflects the rationale of entrepôt economics and the prevailing patterns of political and economic control in a quasi-colonial situation' (p. 283), maintained power by supporting the local and foreign commercial élite and Western political interests in the region, by developing a tightly disciplined and all-pervasive party machine, by strict regimentation of society and by the political élitism of the party's leadership. George (1973) describes the process of control as 'totalitarianism without the saving grace of honesty' (p. 155), and points particularly to the dramatic changes in government policy: 'The people elected Lee in 1959 on a left-wing, democratic, anti-colonial,

Malaysia platform. Today his government supports capital against labour, denies democratic rights to the people, facilitates the continuance of a colonial logic in Southeast Asian economics and is out of Malaysia' (p. 203). According to Gook Aik Suan (1981), 'The fascist rule of the PAP in Singapore is necessitated by nothing other than the creation of "stable" political conditions to allow Western imperialist exploitation.' He goes on to suggest that Singapore has become a 'pleasant' (though sterile) place for expatriates to live because 'the lingua franca is English and the consumer tastes are all dictated by the West', and that the 'economic miracle' that receives so much praise in the West 'consists of nothing more than a pragmatic strategy of prostituting itself to the different factions of foreign capital' (p. 251). All these writers point to the deep-seated inequalities in Singapore, a topic that has been addressed more recently by Clammer (1985): 'Singapore is one of the most highly inegalitarian societies in the world: indeed the dominant ideology looks upon the idea of egalitarianism with hostility and suspicion' (p. 166)

What is of principal interest to the discussion here, however, is the multiplicity of ways in which control has been exerted in Singapore. In *Singapore: The Ultimate Island*, a book not available in Singapore, T.S. Selvan (1990) focuses on a range of means by which the PAP's dominance of Singapore has been effected: the Housing and Development Board (HDB) policies, which broke up any racial group into different areas; the highly élitist education system; the Medisave health scheme and the debates over who should have children and who should not; language policies favouring English as a supposedly neutral medium of development and Mandarin as a means to homogenize the different Chinese groups; the conscription of all male citizens over eighteen into compulsory military service; the setting up of the Central Providence Fund (CPF) to control citizens' use of their money; the consolidation of leadership by gradually passing on positions of power to carefully picked and groomed future leaders;[2] the use of the CPF to help people own their own apartments; the undermining of opposition politics; the muzzling of the free press; the encouragement of technocrat-managers and economists as politicians; the advocacy of 'consensus' rather than oppositional politics; and the stress on Asian and Confucian values.

The purpose of this critical overview of Singaporean politics is not to develop the type of Machiavellian picture of Lee Kuan Yew and the PAP that is the focus of Selvan's book, but rather to try to understand the implications for the worldliness of English of the development of such a highly controlled society. It is important here, then, that the focus moves away from a vision of power in the hands of the few, to a more Foucauldian analysis of power permeating a social and cultural order. Thus, the significant part of this analysis is the way in which Singapore has become an extremely tightly controlled society, and, to return to the central theme of this chapter, English has come to play a very particular role within that society; Singapore English is a very particular social, cultural and political construct that plays a key role in making sense of Singaporean life.

SINGAPORE ENGLISH

Before pursuing the issues raised above, however, it is important to acknowledge that the role of English in Singapore has attracted a great deal of interest, especially from linguists. There is some useful information to be gleaned from these studies, though, as I shall argue, there are also a number of limitations. As would be expected from my discussion of the discourse of EIL, especially in Chapter 4, the centrality of positivism and structuralism has led these studies to be more concerned with descriptions of the interior workings of language (features of Singapore English) than with attempts to relate language to social, cultural, political, economic, or historical issues.

Sociolinguistic profiles

A good starting point is with Kuo's (1976, 1977, 1980a) sociolin-guistic profiles of Singapore. Working largely with information from the national census and other surveys (which admittedly has the drawback that questions asked in different years may be incompatible with each other, and suffers from the unreliability of self-report data, especially in the highly political domain of language use), Kuo provides large-scale statistical analyses of language use in Singapore. The 1957 census identifies thirty-three mother-tongue groups, of which twenty were spoken by more than a thousand people. These include 433,718 Hokkien speakers (30 per cent of the population), 246,478 (17 per cent) Teochow, 217,640 (15.1 per cent) Cantonese, 74,498 (5.2 per cent) Hainanese, 66,597 (4.6 per cent) Hakka, and five other Chinese language groups; 166,931 (11.5 per cent) Malay, plus two other Malayo-Polynesian groups; 75,617 (5.2 per cent) Tamil, 20,063 (1.4 per cent) Malayalam, plus four other Indian languages of Indo-European origin spoken by less than 1 per cent of the population; and English with 26,599 (1.8 per cent) speakers (Kuo, 1980a, p. 41). Using Fishman's (1971) definitions of major and minor languages, Kuo (1976) argues that Singapore has five major languages (Malay, Mandarin, Tamil, English and Hokkien) and three minor languages (Teochow, Cantonese and Hainanese). Of the many points of interest here, it is worth dwelling on three salient issues. First, there is clearly great diversity within the supposed four 'races' of Singapore, each being divided into a number of smaller language groups. Second, the four official languages – Mandarin, Tamil, Malay and English – were the mother tongues of only 18.6 per cent of the population. Third, the two principal contenders for the position of national language, English and Mandarin (Malay is officially the national language), were spoken by only 1.9 per cent of the population (1.8 per cent English and 0.1 per cent Mandarin) as a mother tongue in 1957. It also worth observing that since Hokkien was said to be understood by 97 per cent of the Chinese, and 77.9 per cent of the total population (Kuo, 1980a), it was clearly an important lingua franca, at least in the Chinese community.

Kuo (1980a) estimates that in 1980 not more than 2 or 3 per cent of the population were native speakers of Mandarin. And yet, according to a recent survey (*The Sunday Times*, 18 November 1990), the languages most frequently spoken at home by parents of primary school children were, for Chinese, 67.9 per cent Mandarin, 26.2 per cent English, and only 5.6 per cent 'dialects'. Kwan-Terry's (1989) study of language use among Chinese school children and their parents found that although about three-quarters of the parents in the survey used a Chinese language with their spouse at home (p. 27), with only a very small proportion using English, language use to children varied greatly, with many parents using more Mandarin or English, depending on economic and educational background. A comparison of 'predominant household language' between 1980 and 1990 (Kwan-Terry, 1993) shows increases in English (from 11.6 per cent to 20.3 per cent) and Mandarin (10.2 per cent to 26.3 per cent) and a decrease in 'Chinese dialects' (from 59.5 per cent to 36.7 per cent). Such figures clearly reflect changing patterns of language use in Singapore as parents prepare their children for the school system by using Mandarin and English. Equally interesting, however, the disparities between different surveys point to the need to treat such figures with circumspection, since self-report data, especially on topics around language and education in Singapore, may often reflect people's understanding of government policies rather than actual language use (see Bloom, 1986; Le Page, 1984). Such surveys, especially those that are officially published in *The Straits Times*, may construct rather than reflect the realities of language use.

Looking more specifically at the use of English in Singapore, Tay (1979) describes six principal domains of use: (1) As an official language (and despite its supposed equality with the other official languages, predominantly *the* official language); (2) The language of education; (3) The working language of both private and public sectors; (4) The lingua franca for both *intra-* and *inter*-ethnic communication; (5) The expression of national identity; (6) The international language. At least one domain that she does not include is religion, in which, as Clammer (1980) has shown, English is strongly linked to the increasingly prestigious and popular (and middle-/upper-class) Christianity, while other languages are associated with more 'traditional' forms of religion. While the use of English in these domains seems fairly uncontentious (though we might ask what happened to Hokkien as a lingua franca), as I shall discuss at greater length later, the fifth domain – English as the language of national identity – is a complex and problematic issue.

Describing Singapore English

Much of the rest of the work on English in Singapore (for example Crewe, 1977a; Foley, 1988; Platt and Weber, 1980) is concerned primarily with linguistic and sociolinguistic descriptions of Singapore English and questions of standardization. Some writers, such as Elliott (1980) or Crewe (1977b), who argues that Singapore English is a 'non-native dialect of English', have been more concerned with showing the 'errors' of Singaporean English when compared with standard British English. Most, however, have argued that Singapore English (SE) should be recognized as a variety in its own right, and that the task therefore is to describe and standardize it. As I said in Chapter 1, this is the dominant focus of the discourse of EIL. A key work here is Platt and Weber's (1980) model of English in Singapore as a lectal continuum, a view which has influenced many other writers (e.g. Catherine Lim, 1986; Tay, 1979; Thumboo, 1988). There are some interesting observations and figures in Platt and Weber: they found, for example, that the hundred Singaporeans in their study reported very high use of English to children (average 93.5 per cent), compared with use to mothers (average 9.4 per cent), and that, relative to other languages, English was used by 16.8 per cent of the sample in self–father conversations, 6.9 per cent in self–mother conversations, in 31.3 per cent of self-spouse, 35 per cent of self-sibling, and 46.4 per cent of self–children conversations. Like the figures given above, these also suggest a society undergoing major language shifts. But, as with much of the linguistic work that aims to describe local varieties of English, there are a number of problems here. Most importantly, by focusing only on those who 'used English in at least one domain or sub-domain' (p. 119), by excluding the non-English-medium educated because their English is 'not quite like the typical SE' (p. 109), and by presenting a static and hierarchical view of society through their use of 'lects' (acrolect, mesolect, basilect; which Bloom (1986, p. 420) refers to as the 'invidious continua' of mainstream linguistics), they tend once again to reproduce hierarchical views of society and ignore the complexities of linguistic, social and ethnic groupings.

Tay and Gupta (1983) have gone the furthest towards describing Standard Singapore English (SSE), though there have been constant calls to further this work (e.g. Gopinathan and Saravan, 1985; and see Gupta, 1989). Catherine Lim (1986) has also dealt at length with SSE and focuses particularly on the notion of 'linguistic insecurity' as it is manifested among English language teachers in their repudiation of Singapore English. She argues for the need to oppose the constant appeal to exogenous models of English and to codify and legitimate Singapore English, a process which, she feels, will serve a crucial function in 'promising the release of *linguistic energies'* (p. 322). Nevertheless, she too runs into problems when, having argued against the use of British English as a model and argued for the codification of SSE for use in Singapore education as a means to overcome the 'linguistic insecurity' of teachers, she then argues that 'since standard British English happens to be a standard internationally understood' (p. 328) and one that Singapore has followed, it should be used as a model for writing in schools. This choice, on *'pragmatic rather than ideological grounds'* (p. 328; emphasis in original), would differ from the model for spoken English, which would be based on local varieties. Not only does this reproduce the dubious distinction between pragmatism and ideology (a distinction which is itself a product of the discourse of pragmatism, to which I shall return), but it also appears to come dangerously close to suggesting one form of English for one group (who will not go on to higher education) and another form for another (who will).

What such questions of language variety and linguistic (in)security start to point towards is another crucial issue, language and identity. To what extent have Singaporeans come to identify with English, to what extent is it felt that it can express Singaporean identities, and to what extent can it be a unifying national language? Chiew (1980) argues that national identity is associated with bilingualism – one of the two languages being, of course, English – since those educated in bilingual streams scored higher on her measures of 'national identity'. Despite the problems with this positivistic classification of national identity, this does suggest an important role for English in a notion of being Singaporean. Llamzon (1977) suggests that English indeed fills both pragmatic and symbolic concerns as a national language. Thus, while Wilson (1978) suggests that historically the English-educated were a small, isolated group cut off from the other ethnic groups on the island, the current ubiquity of English suggests that its use may now be a key definition of Singaporean identity. To pursue such questions, however, we need more complex understandings of language, culture, discourse and identity than those offered by applied linguistics, and we need to be wary of how surveys may create as much as reflect what they hope to find.

The problem here is that the large amount of work on English in Singapore has tended to deal with English as a mainly neutral and useful medium, a view that can be seen as constituted both by the discourse of EIL (see Chapter 4) and by the similar attempts by the government to construct English as a neutral medium of communication. As Clammer (1985) points out, the social sciences in Singapore tend to be concerned with structuralist and positivist questions; they are more interested in methodology than in framing issues within a cultural or political context. Such connections are not of course coincidental, and it is interesting to observe here how Singapore's attempts to 'depoliticize' language are supported by the depoliticizing discourse of EIL. Once again, here is a good example of the interconnectedness of English and the discourse of EIL. The dominant use of English in Singapore is surely linked to the empiricist, quantitative and positivistic orientation of Singaporean social sciences; meanwhile, the use of English is also supported by these same features in the discourse of EIL which allows academics to avoid any questions around the cultural politics of English in Singapore.

We need to take seriously views such as Pendley's (1983) that

> Close associations exist between the social and political goals of the political leadership, the nature of the dominant ideology, and the language and communications policy pursued by Singapore's political leadership. Both ideology and language policy ... [are] attempts by the political leadership to alter the communicative structure of society, to increase its control over the channels and media, and to a lesser extent the content of communication, and to influence the consciousness of individuals in ways which are consistent with the dominant goals of social transformation.
>
> (p. 57)

In terms of language and identity, Bloom (1986) points to what he sees as the 'crux of the problem', namely that 'on the one hand English is this marvellous instrument of nationbuilding, the language of the "true" Singaporean; on the other hand it is a language learned strictly for the purpose of getting rich, divorced from the traditional values of Singapore's component peoples, the language of ... the religion of "moneytheism" ' (p. 402). This brings us back to the concept of worldliness. Rather than making assumptions about 'official' or 'major' languages, rather than handing out questionnaires asking which of several categories people associate with being Singaporean, it is important always to consider that to engage in the act of speaking English in Singapore (or anywhere else) is to speak in a complex social, cultural and political context: it is to be engaged in a social practice. We cannot usefully proceed with a discussion of English in Singapore without attempting to understand much more about the cultural politics of Singapore. We cannot ask questions about language and identity without knowing more about how language and identity are being constructed at particular historical, cultural and political conjunctures.

PRAGMATISM, MULTIRACIALISM AND MERITOCRATISM

Benjamin (1976) suggests that the most significant legacy of British colonial rule may have been not so much the institutionalization of the English language but the institutionalization of the notion of race. The division of Singaporean society into four 'races' – Chinese, Malay, Indian (Tamil) and Eurasian – has become a central means by which Singaporean life is defined. Singapore's 'multiracial' ideology insists that each person must belong to one of these races – indeed, it is marked on each Singaporean's identity card – and that with this racial identity come both a culture and a language, irreducible essences inherited from the father. Thus, in a typically gendered and racialist twist, one's 'mother tongue' is defined by one's father's 'race', so that Baba Chinese, for example, who speak Malay, must nevertheless study their 'mother tongue', Mandarin, at school (see Clammer, 1985), or the daughter of a single Hokkien-speaking mother, formerly married to a Hindi-speaking man, must study her 'mother tongue', Tamil. Benjamin (1976) argues that there are a number of consequences of this multiracialism: race becomes the principal division of society, there is a high degree of racial stereotyping and there is a strong tendency towards defining boundaries and maintaining conformity, leading in turn to a tendency towards dichotomizing (East/ West, 'hippy'/'rugged', Chinese-educated/English-educated, etc.) and to a stress on cleanliness (anti-litter, anti-hippy, short hair, toilet-flushing, etc.).

Following similar arguments to Benjamin's, Clammer (1985) likewise starts with the centrality of multiracialism to Singapore life and then goes on to suggest other forms of classification that are tied up with it: 'the act of demarcating, the importance of boundaries and the significance of ideas of pollution are all widespread in Singapore society' (pp. 24–5). He argues that the 'Singapore ideology' is

> to a great extent bound up with *classifying* things, people, events, attitudes and relationships, and that this pervasive classificatory activity is closely bound up with strong feelings for the necessity of *order*: tidyness, the fear of 'social pollution', and that this ideology is expressed symbolically through conservative dress, short hair, anti-litter campaigns, the language policy, urban renewal (the intolerance of villages and other 'untidy' zones in the city) and the self-image of the 'rugged society'.
>
> (p. 165)

Taking a slightly different approach, I think this salience of classification is a product of the construction of a powerful discursive field. The putting into discourse of certain knowledges is always an issue of classification, of what gets left out (subjugated knowledges), of what gets put in, and of how discourse produces knowledge. Just as Foucault (1979) shows the techniques of classification and tabulation were crucial in the regulation and production of 'docile bodies' in eighteenth-century Europe, so I want to argue here that classification is an effect of the establishment of a powerful discursive field in the development of Singapore as a highly disciplinary society. Rather than multi-racialism being a result of an a priori tendency towards classification, this classification is a product of the putting into discourse of a notion of racial difference. The construction of a discursive field around pragmatic concerns and social and racial difference made of Singapore a highly classified society.

The discourses of Singapore

In pursuing these ideas further, Clammer's (1985) analysis is useful in that he points to one other important issue in his discussion of Singapore ideology, namely 'the exaltation of the philosophy of pragmatism', which, he suggests, 'needs to be seen in the context of the anti-ideological stance and technocratic politics, of positivism in the social sciences and of the commodity fetishism of the materialistic consumer society' (p. 168). Exploring this notion in much greater depth, Chua

Beng-Huat (1983) draws attention to a problem with a great deal of the discussion around Singapore politics, namely that it is couched within a liberal conception of politics and ideology, and thus tends to see politics as the open, observable process of public negotiation between competing points of view (the different ideologies of the different parties). This liberal conception of politics, he suggests, too often leads to the 'depoliticization thesis' (p. 32) in Singapore. Thus, Catherine Lim (1989), for example, describes as a 'political masterstroke' the government's achievement when it '*depoliticised* English' (p. 4), or can suggest a choice of British English on 'pragmatic rather than ideological grounds' (1986, p. 328). One particular danger of accepting this depoliticization thesis, Chua Beng-Huat suggests, is 'the possible theoretical slippage into an acceptance of the PAP's governing strategies as "pragmatic", as non-ideologically informed strategies' (p. 33). The government's success in actively propagating a very particular notion of the 'practical' and in 'convincing even academics and intellectuals to accept this conception of "practical" is indicative of its ideological success and not of the end of ideology nor the end of politics' (p. 33).

Gopinathan (1980) takes issue with the claims that English has been depoliticized, since 'cultural and political issues are interwoven with language policies' (p. 177). Concerned primarily with language education, he observes that the politics of language has obscured many of the important pedagogical issues around bilingualism. Thus, 'the idealization of language continues to persist, causing the formulation of problems and policies to be very often a matter of politics rather than pedagogy. The professional's role is seen as primarily one of implementation' (p. 179). This has led to the problem, for example, that 'there has been no precise formulation of the objectives of the bilingual policy beyond stating that it would help interethnic communication and provide cultural ballast' (p. 185). It is interesting to observe, furthermore, that the whole structure of educational bilingualism supports the East/West culture/technology divides by using English for instruction in science, mathematics and other technological or scientific subjects, and the mother tongues for civics, humanities, and the like.

In 'reopening ideological discussion' in Singapore, Chua Beng-Huat (1983) therefore sees the ideology of pragmatism as central. This he describes as 'an ideology that embodies multi-lingualism and its attendant multi-culturalism as the central cultural elements. This, together with a vigorous economic development orientation that emphasizes science and technology and centralized rational public administration as the fundamental basis for industrialization within a capitalist system, financed largely by multi-national capital' (p. 30). The first aspect of this pragmatic ideology was the two-pronged strategy to encourage investment from foreign capital and to curb the power of the trade unions. From this orientation flowed a view of education as human capital development and an education system based on a fierce concept of meritocracy, then a population policy which favoured the supposedly genetically more endowed, a language policy which adopted English as the language of pragmatic choice with mother tongues as a cultural counterbalance, and policies which enforced a tough regulation of social discipline. The logic of pragmatism comes to define everything in terms of economic–technical rationality, rendering antithetical all arguments based on moral or ethical grounds. Thus all decisions are defined, initiated, defended or evaluated in terms of economic gain, so that questions raised about the geneticist population policy, the competitiveness of the school system or the dominance of the PAP are dismissed by appeal to pragmatic concerns. It is tempting in some ways to see this orientation towards pragmatism as a result of Singapore's position within the global economy and thence a result of an exogenous incursion of rational/technological thought into Singaporean life. As Chua Beng-Huat (personal communication) has pointed out, however, it is more important to understand Singaporean agency in this process and thus to see the development of a culture of capitalism and pragmatism not so much as an external imposition on Singapore but rather as a local development. Neither should English be seen as either a cause or an effect of this process but rather as an integral part.

Following Foucault (1980a), I prefer to operate with a concept of discourse rather than ideology since it avoids the reduction of language and culture to a secondary position (see Chapter 2), escapes the trap of 'false consciousness' and allows for a sense of the productive and counter-discursive as well as the constraining (see Pennycook, in press). Thus, we are able to investigate, as Chua Beng-Huat has done more recently, the 'cultural construction and national identity of Singapore' through a ' "genealogy" of the discursive objects called "Singapore" and "Singaporeans" ' (Chua

Beng-Huat and Kuo, 1990, p. 2). It is then possible to see how being Singaporean is a particular discursive construction constantly mediated by the use of English. This suggests that the social, economic and cultural policies of the PAP and the practices that they put into place established a broad discursive field characterized by pragmatism, multiracialism and, for want of a better word, meritocratism. Together these discourses have very particular effects on Singaporean life, both in their ways of classifying and organizing knowledge about Singapore and being Singaporean and with respect to their disciplining and organizing of society.

On the one hand this discursive field has disciplining effects: it defines the criteria by which judgements of what is good, bad, right, wrong and so on can be made within pragmatic, techno-rational, economic dimensions; it defines the principal ways of understanding difference in Singaporean society according to racial difference; and it posits a natural distribution of power and wealth according to inherent ability. On the other hand, this discursive field is also productive, that is to say it produces a symbolic order, a narrative of Singaporean life. These discourses interweave, not only in terms of their classificatory systems but also in terms of how people understand their lives as Singaporeans: to live in Singapore is to find one's life constructed around a narrative of pragmatic rationality, racial difference and social hierarchy. Thus these discourses both limit and produce ways of thinking and making sense of life in Singapore in terms of pragmatic and techno-rational decisions for economic development, in terms of identity and difference being defined principally by belonging to a certain race with its attendant language and culture, and in terms of a highly competitive social order and education system with room at the top for only the very special few. Each of these will have particular implications for the construction of Singapore English.

Multiracialism and pragmatism

Not only does the discourse of multiracialism tend to make race the primary category of identity and difference in Singapore, but it is also tied to a view of multiculturalism which, rather than emphasizing and seeking to explore an understanding of cultural difference, instead tends to relegate culture to the domain of the personal and to superficial areas of behaviour. Ethnic culture is thus 'relegated to the realm of private and voluntaristic, individual or collective practices that are most pronounced in the form of ethnic cultural festivals' (Chua Beng-Huat and Kuo, 1990, p. 8). Heterogeneity, as Puru Shotam (1987) points out, has always been seen as a problem. Thus, while overtly making appeal to a support for multicultural difference, the discourse of multiracialism is far more linked to a denial of cultural difference.[3] Multiracialism in Singapore, then, has always been more closely tied to a question of homogeneity than to heterogeneity and has constantly been used to promote standardization rather than diversity in the population. Chua Beng-Huat and Kuo (1990) argue that 'the promotion of a disciplined workforce was ... given precedence over the promotion of ethnic culture from the very outset of independence, and remains so today' (p. 7).

These discourses of multiracialism and pragmatism can be seen in the way Housing and Development Board (HDB) policies have constantly been in favour of mixing people of all ethnic groups together and preventing ethnic groupings. Thus, as old villages and towns with their different ethnic groupings were cleared to make way for the new apartment blocks, people were unable to indicate more than a general preference for where they wished to live, while quota systems regarding the ethnic make up of estates, and later individual blocks of flats, were quietly imposed. While this has not necessarily increased ethnic mixing, it has removed the possibility of politics based on ethnicity. The response to difference and diversity, then, has been to inscribe them within the discourse of multiracialism and, in conjunction with a discourse of pragmatism, to emphasize standardization and homogeneity. Thus, faced with the possibilities of ethnic politics, it has been possible to appeal to the rational need for 'better' housing, economic development and racial harmony, and so to redistribute the population in government-built flats. A similar issue emerges around the different Chinese communities, where, faced with linguistic diversity and clan loyalties, it has been possible to appeal to notions of racial commonality, common Chinese heritage, and once again, the need for cooperation and economic development, and thus to emphasize Mandarin at the expense of Chinese 'dialects'. The discourse of multiracialism not only has the effect of classifying people by race but also produces a narrative whereby cultural identity is valorized in the private but not the public domain, thus rendering cultural difference a 'problem' within the context of Singapore. By appealing to pragmatic solutions to this problem, it has been possible to deflate cultural identity as a political force.

Meritocratism and pragmatism

The disciplining, classifying and standardizing effects of the concordance between the discourses of pragmatism and merito-cratism can be seen in the much-discussed views on hereditary capacities. After the passing of legislation to legalize abortion and sterilization, Lee Kuan Yew gave a speech in which he argued that intelligence was genetically based and determined by socioeconomic level, children of professionals and executives having higher IQs than those of manual workers (*The Mirror*, 5 January 1970). The problem, he argued, was that the former were having smaller families and the latter larger families, so that unless steps were taken, 'the quality of the population would deteriorate'. With this in mind, and the new laws in place, he was thus able to encourage family planning, arguing that it was essential to 'take the first tentative steps towards correcting a trend which can leave our society with a large number of the physically, intellectually and culturally anaemic'. These arguments led in turn to the infamous 'graduate mother' policies in the 1980s, whereby women who had graduated from university were given priority in enlisting their children into primary schools of their choice, and women of lower educational achievements were given a cash grant of S$10,000 to dissuade them from having more than two children. The Social Development Unit (SDU) was also set up by the government to match couples of similar educational backgrounds. Clearly the discourses of pragmatism and meritocratism (and particularly its eugenic and social Darwinistic elements) were combining to construct a series of policies that maintained and justified a highly inegalitarian and prejudicial system.[4] That these views seem to be still commonly held in Singapore can be seen in an article in *The Straits Times* (28 November 1990), which discusses a 1990 University of Minnesota study on hereditary intelligence. The article pours scorn on 'egalitarian doctrinaires' and 'social engineers with schemes to equalize IQs', and suggests that 'the people who hold the most intellectually demanding and the most prestigious and high paying jobs have a status with a certain amount of "legitimacy" ', namely their genetic superiority. To believe that 'differences in intelligence were basically environmental', the article suggests, is 'to be categorised with flat-earth views about our planet'.

In this section I have been arguing that rather than some Machiavellian story of Lee Kuan Yew's and the PAP's governance of Singapore, or a view only of a tight ideological system set up by the ruling party, it is through the many social policies and practices that a broad discursive field came into being. Through the emphasis on economic development, the 'rugged society', and rational planning, and the privileging of questions of technical and bureaucratic efficiency over questions of public politics, class, race, gender, ethics or morality, a powerful discourse of pragmatism emerged. The stress on the racial make-up of Singapore has led to a discourse of multiracialism, which stresses an equation between race, language and culture, and suggests that conflict between the races is inevitable unless firm control is maintained. Finally, the discourse of meritocratism allows for a highly meritocratic education system and the need for firm government by a chosen few.[5] This broad field of power/knowledge relationships plays a major role in the regulation and production of social life in Singapore, classifying life in very particular ways and favouring rigorous control of the physical and social body as a necessary curtailment of social, sexual, physical, cultural, economic or political activity. Most importantly for this chapter, this type of understanding helps to question and go beyond the acceptance of the pragmatic, multiracial or meritocratic explanations of the position of English that have so dominated discussion of English in Singapore.

PRAGMATIC, MULTIRACIAL AND MERITOCRATIC ENGLISH

In the discursive construction of Singaporean life, English is the neutral language of global communication, of business and technology, the pragmatic choice for the people of Singapore. It is also, as the neutral language of internationalism and as a language identified with no particular ethnic group in Singapore, the language of choice for interethnic and non-communal communication. Finally, as the language of industry and commerce, the language of law and government and the language of education, it is the language of social and economic prestige, the language that all parents want their children to be fluent in so that they too can enjoy the new-found prosperity of the nation. In looking at the 'narration of the nation', at the cultural and discursive construction of Singaporean identity, it is important to acknowledge, too, that while Singaporean social life may be a very closely woven and sticky web, there are also inevitable ambivalences and contradictions here. Bhaba (1990) stresses the importance in exploring 'the Janus-faced ambivalence of language itself in the construction of the Janus-faced discourse of the nation' (p. 3). The exploration of English and the discursive construction of Singaporean identity in this section, therefore, will include an understanding of the necessary ambivalence of such constructions. This is similar to Dissanayake's (1990) view that national identity is a 'polyvalent discourse where materiality, history, ideology and symbology interact in diverse and complex ways' (p. 130). Furthermore, as Puru Shotam (1987) demonstrates, it is important to understand that while the élite do indeed have the power to institutionalize some of their definitions and meanings of language, it is also in the everyday negotiation of meanings of language and culture that people's own meanings are forged. This section will focus on how English figures in the complex intersections of constructions of personal and national identity in Singapore, and how being Singaporean is a discursive construction mediated constantly through English. The discourses of Singapore produce an understanding of life that is constantly articulated in English.

English, neutrality and deculturalization

Most apparent in many of the pronouncements on English is the connection between the language and science and technology, and its role as a neutral medium of communication between the different races of Singapore. English, Lee Kuan Yew explains, 'gives us access to the science and technology of the West' and provides a 'neutral medium' for all different races (*The Mirror*, 20 November 1972). Elsewhere, he urges the learning of English as a neutral and pragmatic language: 'For all of us, let us press on with English. It is our common working language. It cuts across all racial and linguistic groups. It provides a neutral medium, giving no one any advantage in the competition for knowledge and jobs' (*The Mirror*, 19 June 1978). The primary consideration for education is to enable children to gain the skills necessary for them to help Singapore participate in the world economy. Thus, the foremost requirements are vocational training and a knowledge of English, which is 'the language of the investing industrialists, whether Americans, Japanese, Germans, Swiss, French, or British' (*The Mirror*, 17 April 1972). Children 'must understand how to work the machines in the factory, how to receive and give instructions' (ibid.). This, then, is a classic articulation of the pragmatic function of English: it is a neutral medium for the gaining of important knowledge, a neutral medium for inter-racial communication, and an essential language for participation in the global economy (and for giving and taking instructions).

At this point, however, a different element is added, namely the problem of 'deculturalization'. As Lee Kuan Yew explained in his National Day Rally speech in 1978:

> A person who gets deculturalised – and I nearly was, so I know the danger – loses his self-confidence. He suffers from a sense of deprivation. For optimum performance, a man must know himself and the world. He must know where he stands. I may speak the English language better than the Chinese language because I learnt English early in life. But I will never be an Englishman in a thousand generations and I have not got the Western value system inside; mine is an Eastern value system. Nevertheless I use Western concepts, Western words because I understand them. But I also have a different system in my mind.
>
> (*The Mirror*, 14 September 1978)

This is a complex passage that needs some unravelling. Deculturalization, it would seem, could mean two things: either by learning the neutral, decultured, pragmatic language of English, at the expense of one's mother tongue, one could end up with no culture, a disembodied, deculturalized boat adrift on the sea of pragmatism; or, by learning English at the expense of one's mother tongue, one could end up with a different culture, namely the culture associated with the language. The pragmatic approach to English would suggest that it is the first meaning which is meant, since in this view English is a neutral medium. Yet Lee Kuan Yew's words seem to suggest that the dangers are not so much of having no culture but rather of becoming 'an Englishman' or absorbing 'the Western value system'. So clearly English is not merely a neutral medium but is closely tied either to a national/ cultural identity (English-ness) or to a more general cultural– epistemological order (Western values). This is where a certain tension emerges between the pragmatic view of English as a neutral language and the discourse of multiracialism, which assumes a close connection among race, 'mother tongue', culture and identity.

Of significance, too, in Lee Kuan Yew's remarks, is the argument that to avoid the threat of deculturalization/Westernization, one needs to stress the maintenance of an 'Eastern value system' and that by having both systems in one's mind, one can maintain a functional divide between the practical use of English and the more personal and cultural investment in one's mother tongue. As Lee Kuan Yew suggests:

> Our special circumstances lead us rationally to accept the fact that English is the working language of our society. However, we all want our culture, values and philosophy of life to remain dominant over those of America, Britain, or other parts of the English-speaking world. This requires that we know enough of our own mother tongues to appreciate our traditions and approach to life.
>
> (*The Mirror*, 19 June 1978)

On the one hand, then, English is a neutral, pragmatic language, essential for Singapore's development, but on the other it is a language tied to forms of Western culture and knowledge which threaten Asian cultural identities. It is important, therefore, to maintain competence in a mother tongue as a form of 'cultural ballast'. Another dimension to this argument enters the picture when we look at what are taken to be Western values. As Dr Tay Eng Soong, Minister of State (Education) suggested in a speech at the National University of Singapore in 1982, English 'becomes the vehicle through which the mass media and TV purvey values from abroad, mainly from the US and the UK' (*The Straits Times*, 13

December 1982). These values include such undesirable qualities as 'hippyism, a libertine pre-occupation with self-gratification, the cult of living for today and for myself and to hell with others'. The implications of this view go beyond simply the need for first language maintenance, for now 'censorship can and must be imposed to keep out such values'. Furthermore, since 'it has been observed that those who are most easily influenced by fads and fashions such as sporting long, greasy hair or wearing soiled jeans are those with low educational achievement and poor cultural and home background', there is the need for moral education: 'schools have and can play an enormous role in encouraging and inculcating good habits, for example, punctuality, cleanliness, truthfulness, teamwork through, for example, team games and the uniformed groups, habits of physical fitness, sense of responsibility, etc.' (ibid.). English has now become in this view not merely the bearer of cultural values that threaten local values by dint of their difference, but the bearer of Western decadence, to guard against which it will be necessary to set up educational programmes designed to teach correct moral values, especially to those of 'low educational achievement and poor cultural and home background'. Thus, while on the one hand English is said to be the neutral language of business and technology, on the other hand it is portrayed as the bearer of undesirable Western values to which working-class Singaporeans ('with low educational achievement and poor cultural and home background') are particularly vulnerable.

So English in this context is no longer the neutral medium of interracial communication and modern knowledge, nor is it only the medium of a different cultural order; rather, it is closely connected to an immoral and decadent way of life from which Singaporeans, and especially working-class Singaporeans, will have to be protected. This will be done by greater attention to the mother tongues, which are argued to be the bearers of traditional Asian values. Tay Eng Soong elsewhere warns that 'if nothing is done in schools to properly teach a second language – the mother tongue – to a reasonably high standard for general communication, the home language could readily degenerate into a local patois'. Home languages ('dialects') are 'generally of a low level' and if strict control is not applied 'we run a real risk of becoming "Caribbeanized" in both language and culture within one or two generations from now' (*The Straits Times*, 3 December 1982). This doubly-prejudiced analogy (it operates both as slur on working-class Singaporeans and on the peoples and cultures of the Caribbean) has also been used by Lee Kuan Yew, who warns Singaporeans to preserve their cultures in order to avoid becoming 'an even more enfeebled deculturalised Caribbean calypso-type society' (*The Mirror*, 20 November 1972).

Measures to combat English

Here, then, the argument takes another step forward, this time suggesting that the reinforcement of mother tongues does not, of course, mean support for home languages, since this could lead to a degeneration into 'patois' and a 'deculturalized Caribbean' society. The word 'deculturalized' at this point seems to suggest not only the dangers of becoming too highly influenced by a culture which is not 'one's own' but also the general mixing and cross-fertilization of cultures and thus their lack of 'purity'. This position then leads to an argument for increased support for the racial 'mother tongue', namely Mandarin (and Tamil for Indians, and Malay for Malays). The discourses of meritocratism, pragmatism and multiracialism combine here to support a policy of language standardization, aimed predominantly at working Chinese people.

This, then, was the pro-Mandarin campaign. Begun in 1979, it has been a vigorous campaign through the media and posters to encourage the Chinese population to 'Use Mandarin, not Dialects'. While ostensibly a result of the Goh Report's (*Report on the Ministry of Education*, 1978) criticisms of the high drop-out rates and low levels of bilingualism in the schools, it must clearly be seen as yet another means of effecting social control. Thus, while it is easy to pick apart the educational rationales for the pro-Mandarin campaign (see, e.g. Newman, 1986), it is more important to try to understand the underlying social, cultural and political rationales. First, it is worth observing that the campaign has been aimed predominantly at working people – workers and the workplace in 1982, hawker centres and market places in 1983, parents and children in 1984, transport workers in 1985, eating establishments in 1986, and so on. Second, it clearly served government interests by establishing better means of communication for the heavily government-influenced public media: 'It is thus an attempt to rationalize the communication of ideological messages throughout the social system' (Pendley, 1983, p. 56). But lastly, it is connected to a whole attempt to create a more rigid moral order in Singapore. Thus, Pendley suggests that 'Mandarin is seen as a vehicle of historico-cultural identification among the Chinese ethnic hierarchy, a form of identity and consciousness which negates identification on other bases, such as social class, status, income, or occupation and which embraces a value system which allows social difference to be accepted, that is, the legitimating function of ethno-historical ideology' (p. 56).

Thus the reaction to the supposed threat of Western decadence through English was the implementation of a language policy that endeavoured to wipe out the use of the different Chinese languages in favour of Mandarin, and the connecting of this to a Chinese cultural identity that emphasized Confucian values. Chua Beng-Huat (1990) has suggested that 'Confucianism' is a new aspect of Orientalism (see Chapters 2 and 3) which has emerged from Western intellectuals' attempts to account for the economic successes of the South East Asian newly industrialized nations, and has been taken up by many South East Asians, especially by Singapore politicians, for their own purposes. This discourse, which defines people as hard-working, pragmatic, self-disciplined, and oriented towards education, the family and collectivism, 'requires for its own rationality the ever unchanging character of a quiescent subject, rationalizing his/her subjugation as loyalty and suppressing any impulse to protest in the interest of social harmony' (p. 12). As Singaporean politicians reacted to what they came to define as 'excessive individualism', an obsession with the self and with material possessions which was linked to the widespread use of English, they looked to this Confucian/Mandarin connection to regain a firmer sense of social, cultural and moral control. Thus, as Chua Beng-Huat remarks, 'the issue of individualism and cultural identity became ideologically linked' (p. 16). Just as the dominant conservative discourses of the United States and the UK in the 1980s were stressing 'family values', even 'Victorian values', so the Singaporean leadership took up the discourse of Confucianism as a guiding set of conservative principles that stressed loyalty, conformity and 'family values'.

English, then, has been caught in a complex web of cultural politics based on an East–West divide. A great deal has in fact been written in Singapore about the spurious divide between the East and the West (see, for example, Ho Wing Meng, 1989), on the claims that there can be neutral technological transfer, on the problems with equating culture with tradition (see Chew, 1976), and on the supposed values ascribed to Asia and the West. Pendley (1983) comments that 'this functional division entails a change in the very content of cultural and ethnic identity in the direction of a stylized ritualized concept and practice of culture confined for the most part to traditional forms and practices carried out in private or primary group settings or, if publicly, within traditional and legally defined patterns. Culture is seen as being divorced from politics' (p. 52). It is within these ambivalent divides that some of the dilemmas over English emerge. How can one deal with a language that is both a neutral medium for development and the bearer of foreign and undesirable values? How can one develop an attachment towards a national language (which English unofficially undoubtedly is) which is linked only to economic success? 'The equation of English and wealth on the one hand, and the role of English in national identity on the other, is very disturbing to some people' (Bloom, 1986, p. 403). Catherine Lim (1989) suggests that Singapore now 'perceives English as largely responsible for having created tremendous obstacles to the development of a national identity. The use of English has brought into being a whole generation of Singaporeans who are more at home with western-oriented lifestyles and value-systems than with the traditions of their parents and grandparents' (p. 6). Similarly, Selvan (1990) argues that 'paradoxically, the blessing of English language which has brought the different races together will turn out to be Lee's biggest nightmare' (p. 36). This, he suggests is because English has brought with it "undesirable" Western influences, including an 'enchantment with Western political ideas, that Lee worries will undermine the very prosperity of the country in the long run. Catch 22' (p. 303).

English and inequality

Another result of the tension between a depoliticized English and an emphasis on mother tongues has been the drawing of attention away from the position English plays in a highly inequitable and meritocratic society. Thus, on the one hand, Chua Beng-Huat and Kuo (1990) draw attention to the 'strategic effect of pushing ethnic cultural sentiments out of the frontline of politics, while maintaining an appearance of being accorded its rightful significance in society' (p. 8). On the other hand, Pendley (1983) suggests that the divide between English for practical use and mother tongues for cultural identity can be seen as 'a means to both conceal and legitimate the socio-economic dominance of English over the various Asian languages by relegating the Asian mother tongues, with the possible exception of Mandarin ... to the domain of culture and family life' (pp. 51–2). Similarly, Puru Shotam (1987) discusses the astute political move 'to retain the powerful social and economic dominance of English, simply by relegating it to the back seat in the discussions on the mother tongue' (p. 84).

English functions not only within the discourse of pragmatism (English is a neutral language necessary for economic growth) and the discourse of multiracialism (English is a neutral Singaporean language that bridges the 'problem' of ethnicity), but it is also operates within the discourse of meritocratism. Kuo (1985) discusses, but does not explore in much depth, the observation that 'competence in English is associated with social mobility and socioeconomic status' (p. 342). Using the large-scale survey data for Singapore, he notes that knowledge of English correlates most clearly with difference of income level, with only 35 per cent of the lowest income bracket in 1975 claiming to understand English, as opposed to 77.5 per cent of the top income bracket (other languages were more evenly spread over income groups). Kwan-Terry (1993) supplies figures that show that 66.1 per cent of the highest income group in 1980 were literate in English only, while only 2 per cent were literate in Chinese only. It is important to understand how the education system functions to promote English as the most important language and to (re)produce socioeconomic inequality. The system is one marked by examinations and streaming, with students at the end of Primary 3 (aged from nine to ten) being examined and streamed into 'normal bilingual', 'extended bilingual' and 'monolingual' streams (the top few are put into a special 'gifted' programme). The crucial criterion for the stream that will probably decide your future career path is English.

In her study of home languages, use of tutors and educational success, Kwan-Terry (1991) shows the close relationship between income and educational level and between the educational level of the father and the demand for extra language lessons. With streaming occurring so early, and English being such a crucial element in this process, children who come from a family background where English is extensively used have an immense advantage over others. Thus, 60.5 per cent of the students in the 'gifted' stream at primary level came from backgrounds where the parents used English, whereas only 2.3 per cent came from backgrounds where Chinese 'dialects' were used. In the monolingual stream, the opposite was true, with English-background children not represented and 60.6 per cent from 'dialect' backgrounds. Kwan-Terry also found that more than half of the students in Singapore's primary schools resort to extracurricular language lessons, predominantly with personal tutors. The largest demand is for English, especially among middle-income parents; lower-income parents invested less in extra lessons (for obvious financial reasons) while upper-income parents used their financial resources to pay for lessons in the second language/mother tongue (since it was often not used at home, having been replaced by English). She shows that children from English-speaking homes where the father has a university education have a far greater chance of success (in a system that offers success only to a limited few) since their language background and their economic resources help them to cope with the linguistic demands of the school system. The meritocratic education system, moreover, further cements social stratification by making it almost impossible for students from lower socioeconomic classes to move from the conditions into which they are born. Kwan-Terry (1991) concludes that while a great deal of money and effort is put into trying to make up for the disadvantages caused by children's language backgrounds, the social and educational system presents little real prospect for change.

The presence and power of English can be felt throughout the society, from the difficulties faced by, for example, taxi drivers, who have to pass a test of English for their licence, to the resentment felt by those who have been educated in the Chinese stream and now find themselves at the bottom of the employment ladder. Or, as Puru Shotam (1987) points out, English ability is a criterion by which Indian men may choose their wives, since such ability should imply greater learning potential or a prerequisite for acceptance in the middle or upper classes: 'The close association between English, career prospects, and socioeconomic ability must also be seen in the sexist dimension underlying life in the Singaporean Indian realm' (p. 166). In fact, levels of English ability are indelibly bound up with socioeconomic levels, a point which leads Gopinathan (1980) to comment that 'the politicization of language was an inevitable consequence when access to political and economic power was founded on language ability' (p. 194).

The functional divide between English for science and technology and mother tongues for cultural maintenance militates against any easy adoption of English as a national or supraethnic language, since it also implies the adoption of pragmatism and rational purposive thought as a national ideology. The other side of this divide, the identification of race with an essentialized notion of culture which is then relegated to the private and personal domains, also renders problematic the concept of 'diversity' as it is constructed within the 'unity in diversity' slogan. Furthermore, the identification of English with social and economic privilege – what Pendley (1983) calls Singapore's 'linguatocracy' (p. 50) – once again makes it a language for some to adopt and cling to but a language for others to reject or resent. The identification of language with one race and one culture, while in some ways freeing English into some role outside ethnic politics, on the other hand renders it always a stranger in the Singaporean definitions of identity, and also ties it to external models and standards.

CONCLUSION

constantly re evaluated

The worldliness of English in Singapore is, like any other worldliness, complex. It is constituted and reconstituted through the discourses of pragmatism, multiracialism and meritocratism, caught in some critical ambivalences amid the cultural politics of Singapore. It is both the language of modernity and the language of decadence, the 'first language' (i.e. the medium of education) but not the 'mother tongue' (the racially assigned language), a neutral medium of communication yet the bearer of Western values, the language of equality and yet the distributor of inequality, the language of Singaporean identity and yet the mother tongue of few. What the future holds is unclear. The anti-Mandarin and therefore pro-English sentiment of the early years, a reaction to the feared connections between Mandarin and communism, has shifted among the leadership to a growing concern with the implications of the widespread use of English. The Indian and Malay communities have been expressing concern over the vehemence of some of the pro-Mandarin campaigns, especially the 1990 campaign with its slogan 'If you are Chinese, make a statement – in Mandarin', since these campaigns often seem to deal with the Chinese as if they were the sole inhabitants of the country, and, by emphasizing Mandarin with such force, appear to undermine the position of English. The English-dominant élite are also getting nervous about what they see as an excessive drive to spread Mandarin,[6] and indeed it is claimed that one cause of emigration to English-speaking countries has been the recent stress on Mandarin (see, for example, Kwan-Terry, 1993). The erosion of the position of English seems on the face of it unlikely, given its power in the world and its institutionalization and connections to the élite in Singapore. But with the 'planning mentality' (Kuo, 1985, p. 338) of Singapore,[7] anything may be possible.

This chapter, then, has attempted to show how the widespread adoption of English is in some ways linked to a Singaporean capitalist culture that is tied to the outside world, but in many others is bound up with the local cultural politics of Singapore. Just as in the previous chapter it became clear that the position of English in Malaysia was intimately tied up with the struggles between Chinese and Malay middle classes and battles within the Malay community for different visions of the country, so in this chapter I have tried to show how a battle between the English- and Chinese-educated and the development of a highly regulated society also had major implications for English. The dominant discourses of pragmatism (English for science and technology), multiracialism (English as a bridge across races) and meritocratism (English as the crucial gatekeeper to social and economic prestige) constructed a complex and ambivalent discursive field around English. Singaporean identity is a discursive construct constantly mediated through English, while English is also a particular construction constantly mediated through the discourses of Singapore.

The worldliness of English in Singapore and Malaysia – or indeed anywhere, for these chapters have I hope served as examples rather than particular cases – has particular implications for English language teachers. Clearly, to believe that one's job is 'just to teach the language' could only make sense from within the discourse of EIL. From the point of view that I have outlined here, to teach English, or to be involved in the education of English teachers, invokes a range of complex cultural and political issues. As an English teacher in Malaysia, one is confronted by the position of English relative to the cultural politics of Malay ascendancy, *Bumiputra*ism, Islamization, the Chinese hold on the economy, different models of development, differential distribution of power and wealth by class and ethnicity, Malaysia's position within a shifting global economy, Islamic opposition to secular knowledge and Western culture, and so on. To teach in Singapore is to be caught up in the connections between English and pragmatism, multiracialism and meritocratism, ambivalences around its benefits and its harms, around an East–West divide, its position as a *de facto* national language, its connections to wealth and privilege, and so on. Clearly, one can never 'just teach the language'. Some of the pedagogical implications of the worldliness of English will be pursued more explicitly in Chapter 9. Before doing so, however, it is important to explore one further aspect of this worldliness of English, namely how using English does not imply a deterministic imposition of cultural and discursive frameworks; rather, English can be used and appropriated in different ways. Chapter 8, therefore, looks first of all at the concept of 'writing back', at how postcolonial and anticolonial struggles have emerged in English. Following that, however, through my discussion of English-language writing in Singapore and Malaysia, I shall show how the conditions of possibility for such 'writing back' are constrained and produced by the different cultural politics of Singapore and Malaysia.

NOTES

1. An analysis of a typical week's television viewing (13–19 December 1990) showed a large amount of American content, including *Roseanne*, *Teenage Mutant Ninja Turtles* (the shops were flooded with Turtle items that Christmas), *The Cosby Show*, professional wrestling and movies such as *Lethal Weapon*. Saturday morning started with *Bugs Bunny* at 9.00 a.m., followed by *Sesame Street*, another two-and-a-half hours of

cartoons, and then Debbie Boone's *Hug-A-Long Songs* at midday. I sometimes wonder what the effects may be some day of an entire generation of children around the globe having been brought up on Saturday morning cartoons.

2. Selvan discusses at length the possibility of Lee Kuan Yew becoming the next president (now that that position has been changed to more than the ceremonial position it was previously) and the careful grooming of his son, Lee Hsien Loong, currently a Deputy Prime Minister, but clearly a strong candidate for Prime Minister in the future. Such an analysis, however, tends to focus too much on individual despotism rather than the broader field of social control that has been put into play.

3. This applies particularly to the public domain. As Puru Shotam (1987) has shown, the discourse of multiracialism is certainly not all-determining with respect to people's understandings of their private cultural identities.

4. Lee Kuan Yew has also made pronouncements on racial differences, suggesting that East Asian people (Chinese, Japanese) are hard-working and industrious, while the South East Asians (Malays, Filipinos, etc.) tend to be lazy (see *The Mirror*, 21 October 1968; *Eastern Sun*, 23 December 1968).

5. Pragmatism and meritocratism can also be seen in the way the PAP has constantly chosen and nurtured a political élite, epitomized perhaps by the quiet handing over of the prime ministership by Lee Kuan Yew to Goh Chok Tong in November 1990. Goh Chok Tong, educated like Lee Kuan Yew at Raffles Institute, had been 'talent-spotted' in 1976 and then groomed for the party leadership. Nearly all of the top politicians have followed a similar path; in fact, of the eleven 'new generation' of leaders for the 1980s (*The Mirror*, 1 January 1982), five went to Raffles Institute, one to Victoria College and two to St Joseph's Institute, while all but one had degrees from universities in England, Australia or the United States. Such a process, which amounts virtually to selective breeding, has been likened to Plato's view of the necessity for a eugenically bred and nurtured ruling class (see Selvan, 1990, p. 53). Indeed Stella Kon's play *Trial* (see next chapter) draws this parallel specifically.

6. According to the *Far Eastern Economic Review* (24 January 1991), there are rumours afoot that the government is seriously hoping to emphasize Mandarin at the expense of English.

7. Goh Chok Tong recently announced that he hoped to make Singaporeans a more fun-loving people; see, for example, *New Straits Times*, 8 January 1991.

EIGHT

Writing back: the appropriation of English

African literature can only be written in the African languages of the peasantry and working class, the major alliance of classes in each of our nationalities and the agency for the coming revolutionary break with neo-colonialism.

(Ngũgĩ, 1985, p. 125)

Those of us who have inherited the English language may not be in a position to appreciate the value of the inheritance. Or we may go on resenting it because it came as part of a package deal which included many other items of doubtful value and the positive atrocity of racial arrogance and prejudice which may yet set the world on fire. But let us not in rejecting the evil throw out the good with it.

(Achebe, 1975, p. 219)

Depart:
You knew when to come,
Surely know when to go.
Do not ignore, dismiss,
Pretending we are foolish;
Harbour contempt in eloquence.
We know your language.

(From *May 1954*, Edwin Thumboo, 1979, p. 15)

While my discussion of the worldliness of English in Singapore and Malaysia – by focusing on local as much as global contexts of English – has helped avoid the problems of the deterministic assumption that the imposition of English has necessary effects, the danger remains that these specific contexts of cultural, political, class and ethnic relations appear nevertheless deterministic. This chapter, therefore, raises questions of human agency, and resistance, of how English can be appropriated for different ends. Clearly, such questions will have great significance for any pedagogy that seeks to deal critically with English (see Chapter 9). Specifically, this chapter deals with postcolonial writing in English, or what has been termed 'writing back'. There are some limitations in dealing with 'literature', particularly because it is generally a minority occupation relative to other more popular forms of cultural production such as film or cricket (see Chapter 2). Nevertheless, as long as such limitations are kept in mind, it provides a rich domain of exploration because of the centrality of language to literature and because of the extended debate and discussion that it has engendered. The first part of the chapter looks generally at postcolonial writing and what it means to appropriate English. Thus, given what Achebe (1975, p. 220) has described as 'the importance of the world language which history has forced down our throats', I want to ask what the possibilities are for taking that language and reusing it, for reshaping realities through that language. The second part of the chapter looks more specifically at the conditions of possibility for such writing by discussing the worldliness of English-language writing in Singapore and Malaysia.

POSTCOLONIAL ENGLISH

As the discussion of the worldliness of English in the two previous chapters showed, the specific contexts in which English (or, of course, any language) is involved are complex and quite possibly contradictory. In a collection of articles on the political sociology of English in Africa, Mazrui (1975a) maps out the diverse relationships between the spread of English and religious, political and academic concerns. On the one hand, he argues that learning English will almost certainly lead to a degree of 'Westernization', since 'language is the most important point of entry into the habits of thought of a people. It embodies within itself cumulative associations derived from the total experience of its people' (p. 48). Yet, on the other hand, he also points out how English helped the formation of the pan-African movement and African nationalism: 'the English language was an important causal factor in the growth of African national consciousness' (p. 48).

As English spread into Africa through trade, missionary work and education, it developed close ties with religion, intellectual work and politics. As the definition of what it meant to be 'educated' came to be seen increasingly in terms of Western education, and, therefore, in terms of ability in English (or other European languages), speaking English and being an intellectual came to be almost synonymous: 'in the initial stages of the Western impact an African in British Africa was regarded as "an intellectual" if he had acquired some fluency in the English language' (p. 90). Indeed, the word 'scholar' came to refer to all those who were articulate in English. As opposition to colonial rule became more clearly articulated, however, it was, by and large, these very intellectuals, those who could speak the colonizers' language, those who could communicate to the wider community across and beyond the newly-created nations, who came to articulate anticolonial sentiments. The European languages became the languages of unity and political expression in many nations. As Achebe (1975) says with respect to English in Nigeria, 'if it failed to give them a song, it at least gave them a tongue, for sighing' (p. 218).

Colonialist education already bore the seeds of joint oppositional action by providing a common education and language. Thumboo (1988) describes a conference on Commonwealth Literature in the early 1960s, where

> the Indians, West Indians, Pacific Islanders, Singaporeans, Malaysians, Maltese, Africans and Sri Lankans (Ceylonese then) discovered that they had learnt the same nursery rhymes, studied virtually the same selection of poems, the same plays and novels; read the same grammars, the same language series (Ballard's Junior and Senior *Fundamental English*), consulted the same collection of model essays; debated the same topics; had the same selection of History, Geography and Hygiene texts; had gone through the same rituals on Empire Day – come sunshine or rain – and, in many instances, knew 'God Save the Queen' better than their recently adopted National Anthems.
>
> (p. 131)

But the effects of such an education were never complete, the discourses of colonialism never completely determining, and so out of such communities of similarly-educated writers have grown alternative communities of opposition.

When we start to investigate the uses of English in colonial and postcolonial societies, then, it becomes important to acknowledge its importance not only as the language of imperialism but also as one of the key languages of resistance. English and the European languages were indeed the languages of the oppressors, the languages of cultural penetration, the languages of political and economic manipulation, threatening local languages, cultures and knowledges, and changing for ever certain ways of life. But they were also the languages of political opposition and of founding new ways of enunciating the struggle for independence. As Mazrui (1975a) puts it, 'among the functions of the English language in the Commonwealth must indeed be included a function which is unifying. What are often overlooked are some of the *anti-Commonwealth* tendencies which are also part of the English language' (p. 191). Similarly, in her study of the struggles over language and voice in Puerto Rico, Walsh (1991) argues that 'while colonialism has exercised the power of language to suppress cultural (and national) unity, language, as a dynamic and dialectic force, has also stimulated antagonism and opposition' (p. 4).

The crucial issue here, then, is that in looking at the spread of English and various forms of culture and knowledge, we cannot assume any necessary cultural or linguistic imperialism. Both Milton Obote and Julius Nyerere, for example, were passionate readers of Milton and Shakespeare respectively. Thus, while we may criticize and deconstruct the canon of English literature for its class, race and gender ideologies and exclusions, for the cultural and political interests of both its construction (see Chapters 3 and 4) and its subsequent readings, we cannot ascribe to it deterministic meanings and effects. One more example provided by Mazrui (1975a) illustrates this most clearly. In many ways, it is hard not to see many of Kipling's poems as little other than symbolic of Euro-American imperialism. Indeed, it has been common for critics from George Orwell to the present day to see Kipling's poetry as nothing but an apologia for Anglo-Saxon imperialism ('The White Man's Burden' was written on the eve of the US colonization of the Philippines). And yet, on the eve of an election in Nairobi, the Kenyan politician Tom Mboya stood in front of a huge crowd and recited Kipling's poem '*If*'. In Kipling's depiction of the unflappable British colonial bureaucrat, Mboya and his audience also saw qualities to be admired: 'If you can keep your head when all about you / Are losing theirs and blaming it on you'. The poet of Anglo-Saxon imperialism had become the poet to inspire African leadership. As Mazrui puts it, 'the cultural penetration of the English language was manifesting its comprehensiveness. That was in part a form of colonization of the African mind. But when Rudyard Kipling is being called upon to serve the purposes of the Africans themselves, the phenomenon we are witnessing may also amount to a decolonizing of Rudyard Kipling' (p. 209).

This starts to raise some crucial questions. If Obote and Nyerere could draw inspiration from Milton and Shakespeare, if Kipling could be read at a political rally in Kenya, it is perhaps tempting to suggest that there is indeed nothing at all to be concerned about in cultural and linguistic expansion, that all texts, languages and cultural forms are open to any interpretations. Such optimism is as unsupportable, however, as a position of complete deterministic pessimism. The key question is, under what conditions are there possibilities of making alternative readings, readings that go against the grain of the cultural and discursive frames in which language is lodged? This is, of course, a question of cultural politics, a question of how we can struggle to create alternatives in the face of the linguistic, cultural and discursive limitations on those possibilities. In this light, Spivak's (1987) pessimism concerning the double articulation of silencing faced by Third World women may be quite justified. Nevertheless, I want to look here at how, to use Salman Rushdie's phrase, the empire writes back to the centre (see Ashcroft, Griffiths and Tiffin, 1989).

RE-PRESENTING POSTCOLONIAL WORLDS

European or African languages?

Both Achebe (1975) and Ngũgĩ (1985, 1986), in their explorations of the language of African literature, refer back to the 1962 gathering of writers in Makerere, under the title 'A Conference of African Writers of English Expression'. It seems that, in all the discussion around what did and what did not constitute African literature, the key issue of which language was to be used was never addressed. Ngũgĩ takes this omission to signify the unquestioning acceptance with which English (and other European languages) was taken to be the language of literature in Africa. Where the question was asked 'how best to make the borrowed tongues carry the weight of our African experience' (1985, p. 112), approval was still sought from the centre to confirm that, after the necessary 'literary gymnastics', 'the result would be accepted as good English' (p. 113). While acknowledging the achievements of Achebe, Soyinka, and others, Ngũgĩ feels that their work 'belongs to an Afro-European literary tradition which is likely to last for as long as Africa is under the rule of European capital in a neo-colonial set-up' (p. 125). He himself, after over twenty years' writing in English, has returned to his first language, Gikuyu, for literary expression. For a literature to be subversive, to awaken revolutionary potential in African workers and peasants and to oppose neocolonial exploitation and the dominance of the colonial languages and cultures, it must be a literature in the languages of the people. 'African literature', Ngũgĩ (1985, p. 125) suggests, 'can only be written in the African languages of the peasantry and working class, the major alliance of classes in each of our nationalities and the agency for the coming revolutionary break with neo-colonialism'.

For Achebe (1975), however, there is a different option: 'I have been given this language and I intend to use it' (p. 223). While acknowledging the importance of writing in African languages, Achebe sees these, at least in the context of Nigeria, as 'ethnic literatures', as distinct from the 'national literature' written in English. Since national and African unity has been dependent on the use of European languages, he feels that despite the obvious difficulties and problems in their continued use, they should not be rejected. Thus, although it may still be necessary to continue to resent the forced use of English 'because it came as part of a package deal which included many other items of doubtful value and the positive atrocity of racial arrogance and prejudice which may yet set the world on fire ... let us not in rejecting the evil throw out the good with it' (p. 219). In African writing in English he sees 'a new voice coming out of Africa, speaking of African experience in a world-wide language' (pp. 221–2).

On the one hand, then, there is the position exemplified by Audre Lorde's (1984) statement that 'the master's tools will never dismantle the master's house' (p. 110), suggesting that struggle against the neocolonial centres cannot be carried out in the language of those centres. On the other, there is the belief that English can indeed be used against itself. Ngũgĩ argues that the only way to break the neocolonial stranglehold is to develop a subversive literature in the languages of peasants and workers. To write in the European languages, he feels, is to be part of the African petty bourgeoisie, to be part of an Afro-European literary tradition, to be 'a pretender to the throne of the mainstream of African literature' (p. 122), to remain tied to the centre for ultimate approval, and to avoid the real possibilities of fighting neocolonial oppression by writing for working people. By contrast, Achebe believes that the English language can be used and changed to express African experience, and to write in local languages is to remain confined by local, 'ethnic' concerns. Clearly, there is an important divide here, a divide based both on politics and views of language, but also possibly a divide that is reconcilable. Ngũgĩ's insistence on writing in Gikuyu is a significant political action, and his criticisms of the 'African petty bourgeoisie' need to be borne in mind, but he is perhaps too ready with his dismissal of the possibilities of writing back in English. While it is indeed important to write politically in the local languages of the people, it is also important, perhaps imperative, to engage with the English language. Language is not merely a *means* to engage in struggle but it is also a principal *site* of struggle, and thus to take up a cultural political project must require a battle over the meanings of English.

Making new English

This still leaves us, however, with the difficult question of whether the colonial languages can be brought to bear and express the experiences of the colonized, or whether to write in these languages is forever to be bound to a language that expresses reality differently. Is it possible, the Indian writer Raja Rao asked in the introduction to *Kanthapura* (1938, p. vii), to 'convey in a language that is not one's own the spirit that is one's own'. Achebe (1975, p. 223) quotes James Baldwin:

My quarrel with English language has been that the language reflected none of my experience. But now I began to see the matter in quite another way ... Perhaps the language was not my own because I had never attempted to use it, had only learned to imitate it. If this were so, then it might be made to bear the burden of my experience if I could find the stamina to challenge it, and me to such a test.

Achebe himself concludes that 'the English language will be able to carry the weight of my African experience. But it will have to be a new English, still in full communion with its ancestral home but altered to suit its new African surroundings' (p. 223).

It is essential that we have a clear idea of what is implied by such an idea of 'a new English'. As the discussion of the discourse of EIL (Chapters 1 and 4) suggested, where this notion of 'new Englishes' has been taken up, it has generally been done so in terms of variation in the linguistic system of English. Thus the issue has been one of describing lexical, grammatical or phonological divergences from the central standards of the language. My development of a notion of worldliness, by contrast, has focused on the location of language within its diverse contexts and on the meanings that can be expressed in the language. To return for a moment to the discussion of the meanings of Kipling, Milton or Shakespeare in the context of African politics: it is more significant to look at the possibilities of alternative meanings – whether these alternatives are expressed in a different linguistic form or not – than to assume that different linguistic forms give rise to alternative expression.

Clearly, then, a key issue here is how meaning is understood. From a structuralist point of view, meanings are a series of relationships within a linguistic system and thus for transformational–generative linguists, saying new things in a language is as easy as generating new sentences from an internal language machine. A representationalist view of language (see Chapter 4), by contrast, posits a real world that exists prior to language and which is represented by language. Saying something new, in this view, is a question of finding new words to represent new realities. As Steiner (1975) points out, however, this view, which is so commonly used to explain the diversity of human languages, does not allow for a sense that humans use language to represent the world as they wish to: it ignores the possibility that 'language is the main instrument of man's refusal to accept the world as it is' (pp. 217–18). If Steiner's view still seems to posit a world that is being 'mis-represented' rather than represented – Steiner talks of 'the world as it is' as if reality and experience can exist prior to and outside language – it does allow for a sense of human agency and creativity in cultural and linguistic construction.

What is at stake here, then, is a different understanding of language and reality. Rather than adopting a view of meaning as residing in a system or a pregiven reality, the concept of worldliness, by contrast, takes meanings as produced in social and personal activity, language being as much constitutive as reflective of social reality. Writing back, therefore, *produces* realities as well as reflects them. The production of such meanings, however, is always an issue of cultural politics, of struggles over meanings as they are located within language and discourse. Thus, as mentioned before, language is as much a *site* as it is a *means* for struggle. Weedon (1987) suggests that 'once language is understood in terms of competing discourses, competing ways of giving meaning to the world, which imply differences in the organization of social power, then language becomes an important site of political struggle' (p. 24). This is not, of course, to say that changes of syntax, lexicon, phonology and so on are not important, but rather to argue that we need to highlight meaning above structure and to see meaning as struggled over within a larger question of cultural politics rather than as a representation of reality or a shift within a system. Such a view, as Ashcroft, Griffiths and Tiffin (1989) suggest, distances itself 'from the universalist view of the function of language as representation, and from a culturally essentialist stance which might reject the use of english because of its assumed inauthenticity in the "non-English" place' (p. 42).

Abrogation, diremption, appropriation, redemption

Ashcroft, Griffiths and Tiffin (1989) suggest two crucial strategies in the process of 'writing back': *abrogation*, a denial and refusal of the colonial and metropolitan categories, its standard of normative or 'correct' usage, its claim to fixed meanings inscribed in words; and *appropriation*, whereby the language is seized and re-placed in a specific cultural location. Essentially, 'Post-colonial writing abrogates the privileged centrality of "English" by using language to signify difference while employing a sameness which allows it to be understood' (1989, p. 51). It is by creating new meanings, by opposing the centre's claim to control over the meanings and forms of the language that this process starts: 'by inscribing meaning, writing releases it to a dense proliferation of possibilities, and the myth of centrality embodied in the concept of a "standard language" is forever overturned. It is at this moment that English becomes *english*'[1] (p. 87).

Useful concepts though these are, they still seem to leave the inscribing of these new meanings as a process internal to the language, as a question of opposing only the ways in which English itself is constructed and used. One of the key debates in postcolonial representation has focused on how to seek not so much new ways of saying things but rather new things to say. The problem here is that in searching for a new Black, African, Asian or other identity, there is the danger of replicating the same dichotomies and dualisms put into place by colonialism. Thus Soyinka (1976) criticizes the *Negritude* movement that arose from the work of Aimé Césaire and Leopold Senghor for reproducing European stereotypes by emphasizing their supposed opposites, and thus emotional, integrative and musical aspects of Black cultures: 'Negritude stayed within a pre-set system of Eurocentric intellectual analysis both of man and society and tried to re-define the African and his society in those externalised terms' (p. 136). Hountondji (1983) and Mudimbe (1988) point to similar difficulties in attempts to define African philosophy. Mudimbe argues that 'Western interpreters as well as African analysts have been using categories and conceptual systems which depend on a Western epistemological order' (p. x). Similarly, Hountondji suggests that much of this search must be seen as part of a colonialist discourse that preserves imperialist domination both by predicating a universalist Africa and by locating philosophy in the unconscious shared essence of a primitive collective, as 'little more than an ethnophilosophy, the imaginary search for an immutable, collective philosophy, common to all Africans, although in an unconscious form' (p. 38). The African intellectual is then faced with the problem that 'dialogue with the West can only encourage "folklorism", a sort of collective cultural exhibitionism which compels the "Third World" intellectual to "defend and illustrate" the peculiarities of his tradition for the benefit of a Western public' (p. 67). For Hountondji, African philosophy should not be sought in some essentialized version of African thought, 'in some mysterious corner of our supposedly immutable soul, a collective and unconscious world-view which it is incumbent on us to study and revive' but rather in writing by Africans which they describe as philosophical, 'in that very discourse through which we have been doggedly attempting to define ourselves' (p. 33).

There are, then, difficult questions concerning the construction of Africa and the Orient within discourses of the West (itself the counterpart of those discursive constructions), and thus the vexed issues of what counts as African culture or philosophy, and how, crucially, one can avoid 'folklorism', 'collective cultural exhibitionism' and the need to 'defend and illustrate the peculiarities of [one's] tradition for the benefit of a Western public'. The key point here is that in looking for new ways of representing a postcolonial world, there are dangers of reproducing the same colonial divisions that have defined 'civilized' and 'primitive', 'scientific' and 'non-scientific', 'religion' and 'superstition', 'modern' and 'traditional', and so on. As these writers suggest, however, by avoiding culturally essentialist positions that operate ultimately with the same divisions, and by working instead to challenge these categories and to think the world differently, there is far greater potential for cultural renewal. Linking this idea back to the question of English, the idea of appropriating English needs to be related to the question of how possible meanings can be expressed in the language within the wider social, cultural and political contexts of its use. Thus, just as Ngũgĩ (1985) argues that it is not ultimately sufficient for African literature merely to be written in African languages, since it must also 'carry the content of our people's anti-imperialist struggles to liberate their productive forces from foreign control' (p. 127), so an appropriation of the language must include a struggle beyond the language itself to engage with broader battles around culture, knowledge and inequality. Put another way, the issue is not so much one of structural variety, of describing and validating new varieties of English, but rather of the cultural politics of using the language.

In an attempt elsewhere (Pennycook, 1990a) to describe the broader process both of opposing central categories of culture and knowledge and of resurrecting alternative forms, I used the (somewhat awkward) terms 'diremption' and 'redemption', diremption being the challenge to (splitting asunder of) the hegemonizing character of prevailing Western discursive practices, and redemption being the emancipation of subjugated knowledges and identities that have been submerged beneath or marginalized by these predominant discursive practices. While this is admittedly rather a crude formation using equally infelicitous terminology, it is nevertheless important to see writing back as necessarily including both abrogative and diremptive action and both appropriative and redemptive action. Abrogation/diremption can be seen as a process of challenging both central language practices and central discourses, while appropriation/redemption becomes the use of language to represent local contexts in conjunction with insurgent knowledges and cultural forms. This view links both Achebe's call to use the language 'which history has forced down our throats' and Ngũgĩ's insistence that African literature must 'carry the content of our people's anti-imperialist struggles'. In some ways this is akin to what has been termed 'resistance literature' (see Harlow, 1987), but such a project should not be located only within the formal political domain. My argument, therefore, is that writing back does not have to be necessarily identifiable as in the service of a fight for 'political freedom' (as with, say, writing in support of the Palestinian struggle), but rather that writing back by necessity must take up cultural battles and counter-discursive positions, and thus is involved in a broader question of cultural politics.

This position, then, suggests that while it is of course essential to support local languages and mother-tongue education, and while these languages are also an essential location for anticolonial struggle, it is equally crucial to see the importance of English both as a means and a site of struggle. Just as certain readings of texts can only be made within certain cultural and discursive contexts, however, so the possibilities for writing back only occur under certain conditions. Thus, while writing back may be a goal of postcolonial literature, it has to be stressed that there is no easy route to such writing, no way in which it can simply be achieved through a certain writing approach. On the contrary, writing back must be seen in the context of the worldliness of English, and thus as emerging from 'a multiplicity of political, social, institutional, technical and theoretical *conditions of possibility*' (Gordon, 1980, p. 243). Thus the conditions of possibility for writing back can only be discussed in their local specificities. It is to the different conditions of possibility for writing in Singapore and Malaysia that the next section turns.

WORLDLY TEXTS IN A WORLDLY LANGUAGE

The point in looking at 'literature' is not to examine it as literature *per se*, to evaluate the style, to discuss themes, to look at plot and character; nor is it to conduct a linguistic analysis and examine the type of language used, the particularities of Singapore or Malaysian English.[2] Rather, it is closer to Fernando's (1986) view that 'all literary works, however private, or lyrical or public, are anchored intricately in a live context of culture, history, and environment, and it should be the critic's task to trace this relationship' (p. 116). This section, therefore, attempts to deal with the worldliness of the writers, texts, critics and readers in relation to the worldliness of English. Dissanayake (1990) suggests that, caught between the contradictory tensions of modernization and national identity, writers in English are perhaps destined to produce 'multiple and fragmented expressions of self' (p. 130). In looking at writing in Singapore and Malaysia, then, at writing within the complex discursive and cultural political contexts described in Chapters 6 and 7, it is important to understand how writing in English gets constructed from within these discourses and also intersects with other questions of gender, ethnicity, class, modernization, self and national identity.

Despite the limitations of dealing with literature, it has the advantage of sometimes illuminating an issue far more vividly than any other domain of language use. One good example of this can be found in a telling passage from Han Suyin's (1956) novel . . . *And the Rain my Drink*, which draws on her own experiences as a doctor in Malaya, and describes more powerfully than any other writing the chasm between the English-educated and those educated in other languages:

> Among the doctors few can speak to all the patients, for in Malaya a university education, by its very insistence upon excellence in English, hampers a doctor from acquiring the vernacular languages of this country.

> And thus at night, when the patients confide in the darkness and in their own tongue what they have withheld from physician and nurse, I begin to understand the terror, the confusion, the essential need to prevaricate of those who are always at someone else's mercy, because they cannot communicate with those who decide their fate, except through an interpreter.

In the process, how many deviations, changes, siftings, warpings, and twistings; how many opportunities for blackmail and corruption, before, transformed, sometimes unrecognizable, the stories of the poor who do not speak English reach their rulers, who are hand-picked, among their own peoples, on the basis of their knowledge of English.

(p. 31)

The inward turn from Engmalchin to aestheticism

Writing in English in Singapore and Malaysia can be said to have started to emerge in the late 1940s with the publication of the Singapore literary magazine, *Cauldron*. This early poetry, as Koh Tai Ann (1981) points out, was largely derivative of the classical English tradition, and thus while some contained regional references, they tended in form and style to follow closely the works to be found in the English canon. Soon, however, with the growth of national consciousness as the region moved towards independence in the postwar years, more emphasis was put on reflecting more closely the local cultural and linguistic situation. Wang Gungwu's 1950 collection of poems, *Pulse*, the first English-language publication in Singapore and Malaya (aside from journals), was a conscious effort to explore a Malayan identity. In 1950, the word 'Engmalchin' was coined and a number of writers started trying to write in this concoction of English, Malay and Chinese.

While this somewhat awkwardly artificial attempt to reflect the multilingual context soon floundered, it should not be so quickly dismissed as it has at times been, for it was nevertheless a symbol of the profound struggle poets were undergoing to find a way of writing within the context of a developing sense of national identity. The early writing of Wang Gungwu, Ee Tiang Hong, Lloyd Fernando and others reflected these attempts to develop a form of 'Malayan English', an English suited to the local environment. Such attempts also met with some fierce opposition to this sacrilegious use of English, since, as Brewster (1989) puts it, 'to use language in a way other than that sanctioned by the English canon offended the neo-colonial sensibility' (p. 6). While there was certainly a degree of naivety in experiments such as 'Engmalchin' and limitations to such projects as the listing of local flora and fauna for use in poetry, and while it is certainly also true that these early poets were by and large but a small group writing for each other, this early period nevertheless indicates some of the questions that arise in trying to express 'a post-colonial consciousness in the language of colonialism' (Brewster, 1989, p. 15). The problem was to find ways to 'situate themselves as the subject of the language rather than adopting linguistic and literary frames of reference which cast them and their experiences as deviations from the "norm". In this process the language is reconstructed and the self reinvented' (ibid.).

These early struggles seem to have lost way, however, as the struggles for national, ethnic and personal identity were increasingly defined by the official discourses of post-independence nations. Writing in English took a new direction, more towards a symbolist orientation. By exploring the inner self, by writing with passion from some inner landscape of Malayan consciousness, it was argued, a new, truer form of Malayan identity would emerge. This shift marked a reorientation in the early writing in English away from the more socially and politically committed hopes of forging a new Malayan identity towards a more aesthetic and psychologistic orientation. Brewster (1989) comments that this belief that they could produce change through writing on the intensity of their inner feelings and experiences was 'a product of bourgeois liberal humanist idealism and itself a remnant of colonialism' (p. 29). This, then, was the inward turn from Engmalchin to aestheticism, a shift which in some ways characterizes the later differences between Malaysian and Singaporean writing.

Since these early beginnings, a small but growing literature has developed in Singapore, including a fairly extensive collection of poetry by writers such as Goh Poh Seng, Lee Tzu Pheng, Chandran Nair, Edwin Thumboo, May Wong, Arthur Yap, Robert Yeo, and others (see, e.g. Thumboo, 1976); a small collection of novels, including works by Goh Poh Seng, Catherine Lim, Christine Lim, and Tan Kok-Seng; a small number of plays by writers such as Goh Poh Seng, Stella Kon and Robert Yeo; and a more extensive body of short stories by Catherine Lim, Chandran Nair, Arthur Yap, and others (see, e.g. Yeo, 1978). As we shall see later, Singapore writing in English has recently undergone a significant change, with writing moving from the more 'literary'-oriented to achieve a new popular form in the stories and novels of young writers such as Philip Jeyaretnam, Claire Tham, Adrian Tan and Simon Tay. Meanwhile, in Malaysia, with the very different role that English has come to play, the future of writing in English seems uncertain. Nevertheless, there is a small but rich collection of works in the poetry of Ee Tiang Hong, Mohd. Haji Sellah and Shirley Lim, plays by Kee Thuan Chye and others, the significant novels by Lloyd Fernando, Lee Kok Liang and K.S. Maniam, and the short stories of Lee Kok Liang, Shirley Lim, Lim Beng Hap and others (e.g. Fernando, 1968).

DECENTRED VOICES: WRITING IN MALAYSIA

The discussion of English and the cultural politics of Malaysia in Chapter 6 immediately suggests some difficulties for the English-language writer in Malaysia, difficulties of a rather different nature from those faced by writers in Singapore. With the struggle for Malay ascendancy and the dominance of Malay linguistic, cultural, religious and political symbols as representative of a claimed Malaysian national identity, clearly the writer in English is in a position far less central to the cultural and political life of the country. Part of the struggle to promote a Malay identity has been through the construction of a Malay literary tradition.[3] This process Ee Tiang Hong (1988) has referred to as an 'official canonization of Malaysian literature, amounting to the writing of a national literary history' (p. 15). Tham Seong Chee (1981a) argues that literature in Bahasa Malaysia has been used to 'actively promote a political viewpoint, motivated by the desire either to remove existing beliefs or to destroy them' (p. 217). Literature in Bahasa Malaysia has been supported by Malay leaders in order to 'bolster the development of a common political culture' (ibid.). Thus, the 'political élite has influenced Malay literary response, culminating in the dominance of the Malay politico-bureaucratic élite in the realm of ideas, beliefs, and ideology' (1981b, pp. 278–9).

There are, then, some parallels between the establishment of a Singaporean canon in English and of a Malaysian canon in Bahasa Malaysia. In the context of these struggles for the assertion of Malay and its literary tradition, to write in other languages – Chinese, Tamil, English – may be seen as merely 'sectional' at best, and communal or even subversive at worst. Harrex (1981) argues

that 'given Malaysia's policy regarding language and literature –
with Malay declared the national language and literature, and the
other languages relegated to "sectional" literatures – and given as
well the intricate relationship between cultural self-expression and
the politics of nationalism, the very act of writing in whatever
language is spoken in Malaysia is in a rather special sense a
political activity' (p. 317). Choice of language, then, is always a
political choice. To write in a language other than English in
Singapore is to place oneself on the Singaporean margins[4] and to
run the risk of being accused of 'ethnocentricity' or even
subversion. To write in a language other than Bahasa Malaysia in
Malaysia can bring similar accusations, although the special status
of English both in Malaysia and in the world bring different
implications from writing in, say, Chinese. But to write in English
in Malaysia today is to write increasingly from the margins.

Speaking as a Malaysian woman writing in English, Shirley Lim
(1990) points to the double marginalization of her position. Women
writers are marginalized first by gender within patriarchal societies
that have no function for women beyond the 'nurturer'. The works
of women writers everywhere 'display like scars the deleterious
effects of multiplying marginalizations' (p. 176). Second, as a
woman writer in English, she is marginalized by her choice of
language within a society that equates national identity with
national language policy, denying English a role in the cultural
expression of identity. 'In order to write in this doubly colonial
world', she argues, 'the self must be in exile' (p. 180). She has
written eloquently of her problematic connections to English in her
poem '*Lament*':

> I have been faithful
> To you my language,
> Language of my dreams,
> My sex, my laughter, my curses.
> How often have I
> Stumbled, catching you
> Short when you should be
> Free, snagging on curves,
> Till fools have called me
> Fool. How often have you
> Betrayed me, faithless!
> Disowned me – a woman
> You could never marry,

Whom you have tired
Of long ago. . . .

(Shirley Lim, 1985, pp. 60–1: extract)

For both Shirley Lim and Ee Tiang Hong, the legacy of colonial education and English is something of an ambiguous one. Shirley Lim (1986) points to the dangers of assuming too simple or deterministic an effect of colonial education; where she once wished to dismiss Wordsworth, who 'made us look for daffodils, so we never saw the *bunga raya* (hibiscus) growing everywhere in Malaysia' (p. 128), she later came to acknowledge the importance of the formative influence of Wordsworth's romantic subject on her own poetic subjectivity. Ee Tiang Hong (1988) makes a similar point when he suggests that learning to sing 'Britons never, never, never shall be slaves' did not necessarily lead him to feel that others – namely he and his friends as colonial subjects – would or had become slaves, but rather encouraged him to take up the struggle of never becoming enslaved. These comments echo to some degree my discussion earlier in this chapter of the taking up of Rudyard Kipling, Milton or Shakespeare to inform an anti-colonial politics. Nevertheless, Shirley Lim (1990) points to many of the problems that came with this colonial education. While, for example, she received the benefits of 'the splendid weight of the English language and its poetry', she was also burdened 'with their image, assumptions, values, history and ideology, not to mention their prosodic forms, rhymes, silly poses, cheap sentimentality, Cliff Richards's songs, tinned crackers, boiled sweets, and Cadbury chocolates, all the colonial trivia of Malaysian daily life which adds up to a crackpot culture' (p. 188). And even when freed from the burden of colonialism, she points out, she is still not free, 'for colonial education has shaped both the spirit of independence and the language of independence' (p. 188).

By looking at these implications of colonial education, the forces in the world that still bring the colonial spirit to life, and the complex marginalizations of a Malaysian woman writing in English, Shirley Lim (1990) shows the complexities, contradictions and struggles she faces. Colonialism gave her an education in which 'the essential processes of identity formation are ironically the very processes stripping the individual of Asian tradition and communal affiliation' (p. 188) In this educational process, therefore, 'in "marrying" the English language, the engendering of self occurs as the consciousness of alienation from a native culture. Subjectivity is articulated in a foreign or second tongue' (p. 189). Given this conflictual process of education and identity formation, it is no wonder, she suggests, that for a woman writer 'terms such as deracination, alienation and anomie ring in her ear like identity markers' (p. 189). In order to write from such a space, it is essential, she argues, to recognize the social, cultural, political and historical locations of self, to recognize a 'material self', which is to 'begin to write politically, with a sense of history and larger forces at work outside the subject' (p. 188). This material self, she insists, 'rejects universality as the lesson of the master's tools, and insists on political realism as the space for self-creation' (p. 189).

Meanwhile, creative writing in English seems to be in decline, as fewer people gain sufficient proficiency in the language to write and there seem to be fewer discursive positions available for creative writing. Its finest period was probably between ten and fifteen years ago, with the publication of three novels: Lloyd Fernando's *Scorpion Orchid* (1976), Lee Kok Liang's *Flowers in the Sky* (1981), and K.S. Maniam's *The Return* (1981). *Scorpion Orchid*, which Shirley Lim (1988) describes as a 'deeply political novel' (p. 147), is an exploration of the divisions and tearing apart at independence of a friendship between four young men of Chinese, Eurasian, Indian and Malay origin. The breaking up of their friendship parallels the loss of faith in a just and equal multicultural society amid the riots that accompanied independence. *Flowers in the Sky* revolves around an encounter between a wealthy Indian doctor and his patient, a buddhist monk, a story of religious roots and practices, and relations to community. *The Return*, along with its rich description of alienation and conflict through an English education, is the story of a struggle for social and economic independence, a quest for identity mediated between the caste system (and its rejection), an English education, the history of the family and its links to South India, the relationship to religion, and the finding of a place to live and work on the pluralistic Malaysian soil. All three texts, in a rich and complex way, deal with questions of ethnicity, education, language, religion, independence, pluralism, community and identity. All three writers could be said to have made English their own. There is perhaps a note of sadness here that Malaysian literature in English may have had its day but this must also be seen as an inevitable product of the Malaysian struggles over the worldlinesss of English.[5]

Alternative spaces

What Shirley Lim is pointing to in her discussion of writing is that to understand questions of language and identity it is essential to go far beyond the pregiven categories of ethnic or national identity and to view our identities as multiply constructed within relations of language, gender, culture, politics and power. English in Malaysia has moved from the eye at the centre of colonial power to a position, for creative writers, on the margins. Writing in English may both reflect marginality (how today does one come to choose this language to write in?) and reproduce marginality (by writing in English, one positions oneself as possibly subversive, or sectional, or marginal). But such marginality is also linked to more marginal politics. Ee Tiang Hong has also acknowledged the very political nature of writing in English in Malaysia. While he had earlier (1971) argued for the artist's concern with art for its own sake and with universal issues, towards the end of his life he was convinced of the importance of politically committed writing. The first poem, 'Statement', in his last collection, *Tranquerah* (1985), is something of a manifesto:

> Let it never be said
> by our own children
> that on the night we had
> to stand and be counted
> we sat at our tables,
> scrabbling.
>
> (Ee Tiang Hong, 1985, p. 1: extract)

Ee Tiang Hong's shift from his early arguments in favour of the aesthetic, apolitical and universal stance of the artist, to his later works demanding political action, reflected the shifting domains of use for English. As he said in his poem 'Statement', he would prefer the 'explicit and to the point' over the 'poetical', that one 'stand and be counted' rather than sitting and 'scrabbling'. If the future of English as a language of literary expression in Malaysia is probably on the way out, it nevertheless remains the language in which much critical work on legal, political and economic matters is published: the language of Kua Kia Soong's (e.g. 1990) critical work on Chinese schools and national culture, of Lim Kit Siang's (e.g. 1986) political speeches, of accounts of the 1987 arrests (Kua Kia Soong, 1989; Zulkifli Ahmad, 1990), of the human rights journal, *Aliran Monthly* (which, until the beginning of 1991, was allowed to publish only in English), and of the writings of the Aliran president, Chandra Muzaffar (e.g. Muzaffar, 1989). There have also been occasional plays, such as Kee Thuan Chye's *1984 Here and Now* of a highly political nature, and the recent collection of Fan Yew Tong's (1990) overtly political poetry:

> Our national culture is made up
> of sterling qualities of
> unquestioning obedience
> and lapdog obsequiousness. . .
> (From *Our National Culture*, Fan Yew Tong, 1990,
> p. 32: extract)

The conditions of possibility that produced the Malaysian literary voices of the last thirty years have changed as English has moved to the margins of Malaysian literary life. But, as discussed in Chapter 6, English is still widely used in other domains, and if anything, seems to be gaining strength as a language of political criticism, a role which is doubtless helped by the wider contexts of English use outside Malaysia. This brief discussion of writing in Malaysia has shown that the possibilities of using language are always constrained and produced by local cultural politics.

CENTRED VOICES: WRITING IN SINGAPORE

Back in 1954, a young Edwin Thumboo, blooded in the riots that were sweeping Singapore, wrote one of his most powerful poems, 'May 1954':

Depart white man.

Your minions riot among
Our young in Penang Road
Their officers, un-Britannic,
Full of service, look
Angry and short of breath.

You whored on milk and honey.
Tried our spirit, spent our muscle,
Extracted from our earth;
Gave yourselves superior ways
At our expense, in our midst.

Depart:
You knew when to come;
Surely know when to go.
Do not ignore, dismiss,
Pretending we are foolish;
Harbour contempt in eloquence.
We know your language.
My father felt his master's voice,
Obeyed but hid his grievous, wounded self.
I have learnt:
There is an Asian tide
That sings much power
Into my dreaming side:
My father's anger turns my cause.

Gently, with ceremony;
We may still be friends,
Even love you . . . from a distance.

(Thumboo, 1979, pp. 14–15: extract)

We know your language. And here it is being turned against the colonizer, used as the medium for an anticolonial battle cry. It is interesting to observe that Lee Kuan Yew's political speeches of the time were also redolent with such anti-British sentiment. Indeed, the parallel with Lee Kuan Yew is not a casual one, for the change by Lee Kuan Yew and the PAP from a socialist-based, anticolonialist party to a party that gradually gained and maintained immense control in Singapore, is paralleled by the change among English-language writers from a group of young poets exclaiming their anticolonialist feelings and experimenting with ways of expressing a new national and independent identity to a group at the centre of the institutionalizing forces of English. The seeds of change are perhaps there in the final, forgiving stanza above: 'We may still be friends, / Even love you . . . from a distance'.

The point here, then, is not to reproduce some standard linear history of the development of Singaporean literature but rather to show the worldliness of writers, texts, critics and readers. As Shirley Lim (1989b) explains, 'local English-language writing closely reflects the sociopolitical and material reality of the local English-language world and, instead of falling in with any neat categories of periodization or theoretical progressive development, exhibits this reflective relationship in its pattern of false starts and fallings away' (p. 33). By dint of their indelible connections to English, and the shift of English from the language of the colonial masters to the language of Singaporean power, Thumboo and other writers have moved with the language to the new centres of power. Thus, Thumboo, now Professor of English Language and Literature and Dean of the Faculty of Arts and Social Sciences at the National University of Singapore, editor of many volumes of Singaporean writing, Singapore's 'poet laureate' as Shirley Lim (1989a) has called him, now has a very different relationship to English and the centre of power, both because his own facility with the language has brought him to a position of influence and because the English language in Singapore has changed its relationship to the cultural politics of Singapore. In the introduction to an important collection of Malaysian and Singaporean poetry, Thumboo speaks of the legacy of the English language:

> The English language remains one of the less ambiguous legacies of British imperialism. Objections to its retention in ex-colonies invariably subside when the practical benefits are calculated, the lack of any real alternative finally realised. It provides ready access to the world at large and offers, in multi-cultural societies especially, a vital bridge between various linguistic groups.
>
> (1976, p. vii)

In his 'intertextual' reading of Thumboo's work, Birch (1986) argues that 'a writer like Edwin Thumboo inevitably has a vested interest in his English-educated roots' (p. 164). Birch suggests that Thumboo's dilemma, in which he is torn between a sense of identity in an Asian past and a heritage derived from an English education, gradually resolves itself in favour of the latter. The 'vested interests' of a professor of English literature, of a writer in

English, outweigh earlier renunciations. To avoid the dangers of this argument resting merely on the notion of the 'interests' of an individual, however, it is important to see this resolution within the broader context of the reciprocal relationship between the growing institutionalization of writers in English and the growing institutionalization of the English language in Singapore. Thus the issue is not merely the 'interests' of these writers as individuals but the whole relationship between the worldliness of these writers and the worldliness of the English language in Singapore. It is now the language of the Singaporean powerful, embedded within the central discourses in the metropolitan institutions, controlled and regulated by the central academic institutions. It is indeed interesting to observe that Thumboo has even written a poem in praise of the Regional English Language Centre (RELC).[6] The poem ends: 'So here our languages have a home; / Here we are brother's keeper' (quoted in Birch, 1986, p. 169). Commenting on this suggestion that at RELC 'the languages are kept in good order, stored away for safe keeping, and controlled by the people who have an interested dialectic in controlling them', Birch concludes that 'control, then has simply passed from the hands of one privileged group to another' (1986, p. 170). Thus, the writers and the language take root in the central institutions in the country, controlled and controlling.

For English-language writers, and for the language they write in, there has therefore been a reciprocal process of institutionalization which has greatly affected the conditions of possibility for writing in English. Shirley Lim (1989a) argues that most writers in English adopt an 'aesthetical ideology' (p. 524). In contrast to writers in Indonesia or the Philippines, for example, who feel that writing must involve political commitment, in Singapore 'the English-language writer . . . seems to hold hard to his special status as an artist. By appealing to the Western liberal tradition of the artistic domain, he appeals to features of objectivity, creative freedom, and the absolute nature of literary standards which effectively separate, protect and insulate the writer from external social forces and pressures' (p. 524). This 'aesthetical stance' is also tied up with the institutionalization of the writers. Thus, Shirley Lim (1989a) goes on to suggest that

The Singapore writer seeks autonomy and freedom of artistic concerns from state-dictated aims. Yet, because he is almost always university-educated and working in the Civil Service or in government-controlled institutions (as a teacher, professor, journalist, doctor, administrator, and so on), he belongs to the small, English-educated élite whose interests are inextricably bound up with governmental, bureaucratic aims and whose independence of action and thought consequently is constrained.

(pp. 540–1)

Shirley Lim is arguing, then, that writers and writing can never be dissociated from the economic, cultural and political forces that surround them, and that the Singaporean writers' 'aesthetical stance' tends to 'constrict, to exclude any reflection or representation of political and institutional concern and activity' (p. 527). With writers and literary critics forming a small and closely-knit group (indeed, they are often in fact one and the same), literary criticism tends also to reflect this position. Koh Tai Ann (1989) points to this when she argues that the reasons for the elevation of poetry over prose in Singapore, and of some poets to canonical status, are 'less in the quality of the works as such, and more in the criteria by which it is being judged, and by whom, with what kind of social and institutional support or interest' (p. 275). Shirley Lim (1989b) also draws attention to the problems that arise when the writers and critics form such a closely connected group, and are furthermore bound to exogenous models of literary criticism: 'There is an inherent contradiction between the particular history of social and political formation of the Singaporean ethos and identity, and so of Singapore literature, and the positivistic progressive mentality of literary criticism as it is being practised on Singapore literature' (p. 32).

It is also interesting to observe here the connections between this exogenous model of literary criticism and the English language. There is a parallel here between, on the one hand, the dominance of positivism in Singaporean social sciences (see Clammer, 1985) and the arguments that legitimate the widespread use of English and, on the other hand, the dominance of the 'aesthetical stance' in Singaporean literary criticism, which, like the structuralist and positivistic stances of the social sciences, denies the cultural and political contexts and implications of texts, and the institutionalization of English and its writers. Furthermore, in denying political or social involvement, in refusing to deal with the political in their work, writers in fact reflect state ideology remarkably closely, especially the discourse of pragmatism. Thus to write in Singapore, to write amid the discourses of pragmatism, multiracialism and meritocratism, it is hard not to reflect the discursive framework that constitutes Singapore life and identity; insurgent literary practices have been few and far between. Meanwhile, literary criticism, caught up in the same relationships, tends to construct a version of Singaporean literature that reflects more the interests of the critics and their uses of positivistic approaches to criticism than what is of interest and value in Singaporean writing. This has led Brewster (1989) to conclude that 'Singapore writing and the teaching of literature ... is heavily influenced by neo-colonial attitudes' (p. 36). Similarly, Shirley Lim (1989a) argues that 'English-language writing has never freed itself from the over-whelming effects of British colonialism' (p. 526).

Literature and liberation

From their similar beginnings at the University of Malaya (then in Singapore), Edwin Thumboo and Ee Tiang Hong have gone their different ways, the one a voice from the centre, the other, until his death in 1990, a voice increasingly from the margins (he had been living 'in exile' in Australia for many years). This is closely connected to the way the language they write in, English, has been differently constructed in Singapore and Malaysia, on the one hand denied its political nature as it has moved increasingly towards the centre of Singaporean life, on the other a medium for political struggle as it has moved increasingly towards the margins of Malaysian life. To illustrate this further, it is worth making a brief comparison of their views on literature and liberation (from a collection of essays on literature and liberation in South East Asia). For Thumboo (1988), liberation requires changes through education, the 'refurbishing of folkways and sociocultural patterns' (p. 125), changes which 'cannot be achieved without organization' (p. 124). 'Orderly opportunities for individual growth', he argues, 'are best ensured through the impartial and sustained energies of government applied to the creation and distribution of these opportunities' (p. 124). For Thumboo, then, liberation is a process of individual development brought about by government-controlled, structured opportunities through education. Important in this process is literature written in English, since this is the language of education and the common language of Singaporeans. He predicts that more Singaporeans will write in English and 'while regretting the extent this will have on the growth of literature in other languages', he applauds the continued expansion since writing in English is 'the most multiethnic in reach', unlike writing in Bahasa Malaysia, Chinese or Tamil, 'whose gravity is still ethnocentric' (p. 145). Thumboo's model of liberation, then, is a highly normative one, concentrating on the development of the individual through government-controlled education. Literature in English plays a functional role in supporting the growth of English and halting the 'ethnocentrism' of literature in other languages, or, as he has put it elsewhere (1990), helping in the 'conversion of the tribes'.

For Ee Tiang Hong (1988) by contrast, liberation 'begins with a questioning of the assumption that any given reality is there for good, absolutely' (p. 21). The reality that has to be challenged, he suggests, 'is the network of ideological state apparatuses that have perpetuated the monopoly of one particular ideology by maintaining a state of endemic conflict between the dominant ideology and the dominated ideology' (p. 22). This he describes as the 'Malay hegemony in every major sphere of life', the 'mindless submission to the dangerous and divisive dogmas of Nation, Race and Language' (p. 18). For Ee Tiang Hong, then, the writer must take up a political struggle: 'The door to open debate and the politics of consensus having been shut, the way seems to be open for writers in English to take the role of the adversary, to liberate themselves from the new colonialism, whose metropolis is no longer eight thousand miles away but at their very doorstep' (p. 20). The writer, therefore, must be involved in the struggle to oppose injustices, to 'debunk the myths of race (or ethnicity) wherever the myths have been surreptitiously woven into the texts that constitute the official curriculum and the literary canon, finally passing as knowledge and wisdom' (p. 24). The writer's relationship to education, then, is as someone who can help challenge and interrogate the central ideologies of the curriculum.

Ee Tiang Hong's version of literature and liberation is one in which the margins challenge the centre, in which the writer takes up a struggle to oppose the pernicious ideologies of the state. For Thumboo, the writer helps the spread of these ideologies by helping the margins to be incorporated into the centre ('the conversion of the tribes'). Both agree on the importance of accepting local norms of the language – Singaporean and Malaysian English – but again their views differ fundamentally on the object of such an acceptance. For Thumboo (1988), local language should be used 'to include an appropriate language in order to sustain the impression of reflecting reality' (p. 143). The use of Singaporean English, then, is to reflect local conditions, a view which bears the normative implications of a representationalist view of language. For Ee Tiang Hong (1988), by contrast, the issue is not so much one of *reflecting* reality but of *changing* reality, of getting away from one's position 'as a subservient colonial to the metropolitan master' (pp. 23–4), and of taking up the political project of 'extending the range of human happiness' (p. 24) by opposing dominant ideologies in Malaysia and extending the means for articulating an alternative view of the world.

The Singaporean writer in English faces a number of difficult problems posed by the particular construction that English has become within the cultural politics of Singapore. While the dominance of English and its widespread institutional support have made the choice of writing in the language of the former colonizers much less salient than it is elsewhere, the functional divide between English and the 'mother tongues' and the divide between 'Western' and 'Asian' values, apparently place the writer in a difficult position. If English is the language only of the technological, scientific and commercial domains, a 'deculturalized' or 'deculturalizing' language, while the mother tongues are the bearers of 'cultural values', is there indeed any position from which the English-language writer can express any sort of cultural identity? Or again, how can one express some notion of cultural–ethnic identity, if identity is defined in terms of 'race' and English is but a neutral bridge language between the races? 'The very act of writing', Shirley Lim (1989a) suggests, 'must already be associated with "otherness", "alienation", and "Westernization"' (p. 531).

Yet we need to be cautious here and to avoid necessarily imputing such feelings of alienation or Westernization. Despite its links to outside norms and models, English is in many ways a very Singaporean language, embedded in the web of Singaporean life. What is of importance here is that in looking at how the conditions of possibility for writing in Singapore restrict and produce particular forms of writing, it would be a mistake to allow this to be a closed, deterministic argument and thus to see the critical ambivalences around English, the elements of social control and the discursive construction of Singaporean identity as offering no alternative. If, as suggested earlier in this chapter, identity is understood as a multiple space forged between the often contradictory claims of modernization, cultural and national identity, language policy, meritocratism, pragmatism and multi-racialism, we can start to see that there may indeed be gaps and possibilities between the all-embracing discursive framework of Singapore.

FROM AESTHETICISM TO YUPPYISM: THE NEW WRITING IN SINGAPORE

While Malaysian writing (at least as far as 'literature' is concerned) has been pushed to the margins, the increasingly widespread use of English in Singapore has produced new conditions of possibility for writing. English is always/already worldly, is always bound up with the cultural politics of Singapore, but this is never a static position either in terms of the worldliness of the language, the discourses that are available, or the subjectivities of the writers. Although there has been a reciprocal institutionalization of English and English-language writers that has brought them into the central institutions of Singapore, there have also emerged other conditions of possibility for writing, with the emergence of a new English-speaking middle and upper-middle class.

Although this new literature burst on the scene rather unexpec-tedly towards the end of the 1980s, it is worth pointing to what seem to be its precursors. This is writing that started to bridge the gap between the 'aesthetical stance' of the makers of the Singapore canon and popular writing. Shirley Lim (1989a) goes as far as to describe it as a counter-tradition by dint of its use of Singaporean English, emphasis on local traditions and social and political criticisms. Two notable plays (both of which had a great deal of difficulty getting produced) are Stella Kon's fascinating *Trial*, in which she draws powerful and critical parallels between Plato's Republic and Singapore, and Robert Yeo's *One Year Back Home*. Yeo argued strongly that 'What the play is saying implicitly, to the audience and to Singaporeans who listen to people like me, is speak up, be bold about what you have to say and don't be afraid that, just because you speak out, the government is going to come down hard on you' (*The Straits Times*, 20 November 1980). Not surprisingly, few theatre groups were prepared to stage the play. Max Le Blond, who did agree to produce Yeo's play, has strongly criticized Singapore theatre, arguing that 'more than any other cultural form on this island, our English language theatre remains shackled by a colonial consciousness and a colonial view of reality' (1986, p. 115).

Two other writers are worthy of brief mention here: Catherine Lim and Christine Lim. Christine Lim is interesting in that, although less popular, her recent work suggests both some of the possibilities and the limitations of writing in Singapore. After struggling with the tensions between materialism and idealism in her earlier *Rice Bowl* (1984), Christine Lim points in a new direction in *Gift from the Gods* (1990), in which she explores the lives, struggles and origins in Malaysia of three generations of women. In the gendered focus of the book – the stories of these women and their struggle to escape definitions of worth according to their ability to bear sons ('the gift from the gods') – and in the search for histories and memories of Singapore in Malaysia, there appear to be interesting possibilities for writing. And yet, the third generation of these women, Yenti, now living in Singapore, seems also to present the dilemma here, for in this 'act of remembrance' there is also 'a severance of the ties that bound me to what I was' (p. 213), a cry of warning that Singapore's choice of language may indeed leave it adrift from the cultures, histories and memories that surround it. Thus, in the possibilities for cultural renewal that emerge from this book, through a new writing of women's memories and cultural histories, there also emerge the limitations and difficulties of dealing with a past from which one is so alienated. Memory may act as more of an act of 'severance' than as a reconstituting of the past, for the dominance of English may have severed the possibility of making those connections.

Catherine Lim is important because she has straddled the divide between the popular and the canonical, being the first writer to achieve both large sales of her books and critical acclaim. She it was who started to move Singaporean English-language books from an obscure corner in the bookstores to a place in the best-seller section. Dealing by and large with pastiches of different aspects of contemporary Singapore life, she has managed to tell stories of Singaporeans in a language that is accessible to the expanding English book-reading public. Her books reflect both the language of Singaporeans (at least in dialogue) and some of the concerns of Singaporeans. Her short story, *Monster* (1978), and her novel *The Serpent's Tooth* (1982), for example, highlight the neglect of and disrespect towards the older generation Chinese by the new English-speaking materialist middle class. In *The Serpent's Tooth* a key metaphor for this destruction of the old cultural order in favour of the new pragmatic and élitist one can be found in the proposal to build the new government élite school (where the central character's son hopes to go) on top of the old Chinese graveyard (where her mother-in-law believes she will be buried). Catherine Lim's work is, therefore, a precursor to the new literature both in terms of bridging the gap between the 'aesthetical stance' of the old order and the possibilities of a more popular stance, and in terms of a warning that the more traditional beliefs and practices of older Singaporeans are about to be swept aside by the more materialist and pragmatic concerns of a new generation. Ultimately, however, all these writers seem to have found difficulty in writing against the dominant discourses of Singapore. In spite of his bold statements some years before, Robert Yeo appeared to signal a retreat with the publication of his light and unpleasantly sexist novel, *The Adventures of Holden Heng* (1986). Morse (1991) is probably right when she suggests that, in the end, despite their critical elements, novels such as *The Serpent's Tooth*, Christine Lim's *Rice Bowl* and Stella Kon's *The Scholar and the Dragon* (1986), 'exactly meet the expectations of the governmental agenda ... discuss the same kind of issues raised by the newspapers and magazines of the area, the educational establishments, and no doubt the papers of government policy-makers' (p. 142).

'Beem' literature

With a new generation of English-dominant Singaporeans emerging, however, there are new conditions of possibility for writing. Reading the sudden new spate of writing from Singapore, I was struck by a powerful image. Back in 1972, Goh Poh Seng wrote what Koh Tai Ann (1984) calls the first serious novel in English in

Singapore, *If We Dream too Long*. It is the story of Kuang Meng, a ruminative and vacillatory young Singaporean caught between his dreams and the drabness of everyday life, between his vague ideals for a better life and his daily life in a dull job and his parents' government flat, between the opportunism of one old school friend, who is marrying into money, the escape of another old friend, who is leaving for England, and the pragmatism of his neighbour, who is busy making the best of his life as it is. After his father suffers a stroke, the novel leaves Kuang Meng forced to support his parents and thus to continue his job and accept the 'realities' of Singapore life. I have a vision here of a generation of Kuang Mengs accepting their lot, subjugating their dreams to a pragmatic acceptance of daily life in Singapore. And what has now emerged, twenty years later, is the fruit of that submersion, a new Singaporean, wealthy from the labour of their parents. There is a new generation emerging from the blocks of government flats, an educated youth concerned with money and material goods and enjoying themselves, a generation fluent in English and starting to read and write literature that suits their own interests and concerns, but a generation wondering where the dreams have gone and how to name them. This feeling is perhaps summed up by a brief passage from a story in Simon Tay's (1991) recent collection, *Stand Alone*: 'It was all set: a good job, a good wife who could raise a nice family, maintain a nice flat, a good future free of both disasters and good aspirations which would be frustrated. But lacking something, although Sam realised he could not find words for what he wanted and what he dreamt' (p. 75).

It is into the newly opened space of the popular that the new writing has moved with a flood of novels and short stories, including Philip Jeyaratnam's *First Loves* (1987) and *Raffles Place Ragtime* (1988), Adrian Tan's *The Teenage Textbook* (1988) and its sequel *The Teenage Workbook* (1989), Claire Tham's *Fascist Rock. Stories of Rebellion* (1990), and Simon Tay's *Stand Alone* (1991). These books are written for and by the new Singaporean young, or, as is often said, the 'Singaporean yuppy'; they deal with issues of teenage or young adult love, with fashion and rebellion, and, especially in *Raffles Place Ragtime* and *Stand Alone*, with the world of the newly affluent Singaporean young, a world of lawyers and business people, of the National University of Singapore- or the overseas-educated, of Rolex watches, Calvin Klein, and owning a 'Beem' (a BMW). This sudden emergence of a new voice in

Singapore, an articulation of the concerns of a new, wealthy, pleasure-seeking, yet slightly alienated youth, has, it would seem, somewhat rocked the closely-guarded literary scene.

This new writing has emerged from the conditions of possibility for writing that have been produced by the shifting position of English in Singapore. It is a writing that reflects the connections between materialism and English, the construction of identity through the discourses of pragmatism, multiracialism and merito-cratism, and a shifting syncretic culture that is a blend of local and Western icons. Along with the fascination with material wealth, there are also many expressions of a youthful alienation: 'She needed once and for all to escape. . . . She felt suffocated . . . with this crowd of people in a rush, a rush for degrees, jobs, careers, spouses, houses, children' (Jeyaratnam's *Raffles Place Ragtime*, 1988, p. 123); 'In all that frenzy the heart of Singapore had been neglected' (Jeyaratnam's *First Loves*, 1987, p. 155); or the passage from Simon Tay's (1991) *Stand Alone* quoted above. Koh Tai Ann (1991) views this with some alarm, speaking of the 'disturbing feature . . . of a pervasive sense of an alienation which expresses itself through a refusal to subscribe to precisely those images and sentiments of national identity the earlier generation had struggled so hard to create' (p. 11). But while in some senses she may be right, what is missing here is an understanding that this writing is exactly a product of what the earlier generations created. These writers, all young, all well-educated (Claire Tham, for example, studied law at Oxford, Jeyaratnam law at Cambridge), seem dissatisfied with, but simultaneously caught up in, the world of Singapore materialism. But that is the central difficulty in the emergence of this new writing. As with the quotation earlier from Simon Tay's *Stand Alone*, in which Sam *'could not find words for what he wanted and what he dreamt'*, the new writers are seeking to find a new space that both acknowledges the new materiality and pragmatism of Singapore as part of their new cultural heritage, but simultaneously points to the limitations of the possibilities for their living and writing. Without a clearer politics and broader range of (counter-)discursive positions, this writing will continue to reflect these cultural ambivalences produced by the conditions of possibility for writing in Singapore.

Why, Catherine Lim has asked in frustration (personal com-munication), can Singaporeans not write like Achebe or Ngũgĩ? The answer seems to lie in the conditions of possibility for writing and the nature of attempts to produce a position counter to the central categories of writing and meaning. If 'Beem' is a new word in Singapore English, it is also an appropriation of English in a very particular direction. The issue is not so much that new words are coined but that they serve a certain politics. It is not enough to try to reflect local conditions or to scatter local terms and phrases into one's writing. Rather, it is impossible to develop a counter-tradition without taking up what I called an abrogative/diremptive and appropriative/redemptive project, a stance in one's writing that challenges both central linguistic controls and central discursive formations. This centre is increasingly situated in Singapore itself rather than outside, and so, to constitute a Singaporean writing back, writing must attempt to redefine the discursive constructions of Singaporean life and identity and the central norms of language if new conditions of possibility for writing are to emerge. A 'Beem' reproduces rather than challenges those central norms.

FROM WRITING BACK TO TEACHING BACK

The central theme in this chapter has been to point to the indissoluble links between the worldliness of English and the social, cultural and political location of writers, texts and readers. This produces and constrains the conditions of possibility for writing and reading, and indeed for all language use in Singapore and Malaysia, for my use of literature in English has been to show one connected aspect of language use rather than demonstrating a special case. Lest this all sound somewhat deterministic, I should reiterate that the issue is the *conditions of possibility*, the production of and constraints on language use in different contexts. Singapore, where English has become the language of a highly competitive and élitist education system, the language of government and business, the language used in virtually all significant domains of power, writers in English and the language they use have become embedded in the central institutions which play an important role in the maintenance of the discursive framework within which much of Singaporean life is defined. For the English-language writer in Malaysia, by contrast, the language, although remaining in wide use in the private, professional and commercial domains, has been pushed to the margins as a medium for cultural or personal expression. From that position, however, it has become a language of opposition, a language through which some of the central discursive frameworks of Malaysian life can be challenged.

Other conditions of possibility obtain for other domains of language use, but language is always produced and constrained within a domain of cultural politics. This has particular significance for pedagogical issues since it suggests that to use language, one's possible meanings are always produced, constrained and struggled over within a particular set of cultural and discursive as well as linguistic options. To teach English within the discourse of EIL is to maintain a faith in the possibility of 'just teaching the language', and a belief in the existence of firmly established shared meanings which need to be taught in order for one's students to be able to communicate with a global community. To teach from a point of view of the worldliness of English is to understand that possible meanings occur within the cultural politics of the local context as well as within a more global context. The discussion of writing in this chapter has not been an idle excursion into literary criticism, therefore, but rather an attempt to illustrate how language use is never independent of cultural politics. As will become clear in the next chapter, furthermore, there are important parallels to be drawn between a notion of 'writing back' and a notion of 'teaching back'.

NOTES

1. Ashcroft, Griffiths and Tiffin maintain a distinction between English and english: 'We need to distinguish between what is proposed as a standard code, English (the language of the erstwhile imperial centre), and the linguistic code, english, which has been transformed and subverted into several distinctive varieties throughout the world' (p. 8).
2. It is important to acknowledge some of the limitations on this study. First, it only deals with literature *in English*, and therefore excludes literature in other languages in Singapore and Malaysia, which, in the latter case, is by far the majority (see, for example, Banks, 1987). Second, literature must be seen as only one very particular domain of language use and cultural production and not, as is often the case, a central domain of cultural production. Finally, although 'literature' has been fairly loosely defined, a number of writers who might have been

discussed have been excluded: the English-educated Straits Chinese at the turn of the century (see Clammer, 1981); colonial officers such as Hugh Clifford, George Maxwell and, later, Anthony Burgess; and temporary visitors to the region such as Joseph Conrad, Somerset Maugham and Han Suyin.

3. To talk of 'construction' is not of course to deny the existence of a rich heritage of writing in Malay, but rather to suggest a process of 'inventing tradition' (see the discussion of the invention of tradition in Britain in the nineteenth century in Chapter 4) in order to give historical legitimacy to a present order.

4. Though it should be noted that to write in Chinese, Tamil or Malay may link one with the literatures of China, Taiwan and Hong Kong, India, or Indonesia and Malaysia.

5. These three novels may mark the end of creative writing in English in Malaysia. Lloyd Fernando has given up his professorship at the University of Malaya and is now practising law. Lee Kok Liang has retired and, despite his statements that he intends to continue writing, it is unclear whether he will indeed produce much more. Ee Tiang Hong was living in Australia until his death in 1990. Shirley Lim is living and working in the United States and apparently feeling increasingly distanced from Malaysia: 'I am losing / Ability to make myself at home' (*Visiting Malacca*, 1980). Of these writers, only K.S. Maniam is still living and writing in Malaysia.

6. Now called only the Regional Language Centre, apparently as a result of French and German involvement in the centre. This dropping of the word 'English', however, may have had more to do with the process of making less salient the central role of the institute, which continues to be the dissemination of English in South East Asia.

NINE

Towards a critical pedagogy for teaching English as a worldly language

> The fight against dependency is made possible by empowering the next generation to use the weapon that created it – the English language.
>
> (Zahra Al Zeera, 1990, p. 360)

> The project of possibility requires an education rooted in a view of human freedom as the understanding of necessity and the transformation of necessity.
>
> (Simon, 1987, p. 375)

> ... when we talk of 'mastery' of the Standard language, we must be conscious of the terrible irony of the word, that the English language itself was the language of the master, the carrier of his arrogance and brutality. Yet, as teachers, we seek to grasp the same language and give it a new content, to de-colonise its words, to demistify its meaning ...
>
> (Searle, 1983, p. 68)

The discussion of the worldliness of English in previous chapters suggested that it is impossible to separate English from its many contexts and thus that a key tenet of the discourse of EIL – that it is possible to 'just teach the language' – is equally untenable. In this chapter I intend to pursue this further by suggesting that not only is the notion of 'just the language' an impossibility but so is the notion of 'just teaching'. To teach is to be caught up in an array of questions concerning curriculum (whose knowledges and cultures are given credence?), educational systems (to what extent does an educational system reproduce social and cultural inequalities?) and classroom practices (what understandings of language, culture, education, authority, knowledge or communication do we assume in our teaching?). This chapter will explore ways of developing critical pedagogies to confront the worldliness of English.

The discussion of 'writing back' in the previous chapter, of appropriating English for divergent purposes, suggested a useful parallel between writing back and 'teaching back', of developing critical pedagogies to enable our students to write, read, speak, listen back. Ngũgĩ (1985) argued that not only must African literature be in African languages, it must also take up a stance critical of neocolonial oppression. Similarly, Ee Tiang Hong (1988) argued that Malaysian writers in English must now 'take the role of the adversary, to liberate themselves from the new colonialism' (p. 20). There is an important connection here between this view of politically committed writing and a politically committed critical pedagogy. Just as to 'write back' is more than an issue of sprinkling new lexis and grammar around, and necessarily involved a broader and more committed abrogative/diremptive and appropriative/redemptive project, so a critical pedagogy of English needs to embrace a position oppositional to the central language norms *and* to the central discursive constructs.

An important theme in the last chapter was also the way in which the discursive frameworks and cultural politics of Singapore and Malaysia constrained and produced the conditions of possibility for using English. A key concept to be added to this notion of conditions of possibility is the idea of *voice*, since it allows for a way of addressing the conjunction between subjectivities, language practices and discourses. For Giroux (1988), voice refers to 'the means at our disposal – the discourses available to use – to make ourselves understood and listened to and to define ourselves as active participants in the world' (p. 199). As bell hooks (1988) points out, there are two particular dangers to be avoided in the use of a notion of voice: first, it is important not to see voice simply as non-silence, but rather to understand it in terms of what is said (and perhaps not said), in terms of using language 'as revolutionary gesture' (p. 12). Second, it is important not to assume that there is some form of 'true' voice, as either the expression of a 'true' self or of a pure cultural essence. Rather, as Walsh (1991) suggests, voice can be understood as the place where the past, collective memories, experiences, subjectivities and meanings intersect. It is a site of struggle where the subjectivity of the language-user confronts the conditions of possibility formulated between language and discourse.

It is worth pointing out here that although most of the contexts of English use discussed so far have been in what is often termed an 'EFL' context as opposed to an 'ESL' context, many of the points in this chapter may apply equally to both contexts. Indeed, the distinction itself remains problematic (see Phillipson, 1992) and is clearly blurred both in countries such as Singapore, Hong Kong or India, where English may be a second language to some and a foreign language to others, and – a point that often gets overlooked – in the supposedly 'English-speaking countries', where access to and use of English can be very limited for some people. Many of the issues around the spread of English between countries can also be applied to questions of the spread of English within countries, leading Mukherjee (1986) to describe ESL in Britain as 'an imported new Empire'. As Auerbach (1993), Crawford (1989), Cummins (1989), Ovando (1990), Walsh (1991) and many others have pointed out, the battle over bilingual education in North America has always been a battle for different political visions of difference and diversity.

CRITICAL PEDAGOGIES

As a broad and loosely linked area of educational theory and practice, critical pedagogy can be described as education grounded in a desire for social change (see, for example, Giroux, 1988; McLaren, 1989; Simon, 1992; Weiler, 1988). Viewing schools not as sites where a neutral body of curricular knowledge is passed on to students with various levels of success, critical pedagogy takes schools as cultural and political arenas where different cultural, ideological and social forms are constantly in struggle. The question then becomes how to construct a theory and practice of education that can, on the one hand, account for why some 'disadvantaged' students fail to 'succeed' in school and, on the other, develop ways of teaching that offer greater possibilities to people of colour, ethnic minorities, working-class students, women, gays and lesbians, and others, not only in order that they might have a better chance of 'success' in the ways traditionally defined by education but also in order that these definitions of success, both within schools and beyond, can be changed. Broadly speaking, then, critical pedagogy aims to change both schooling and society, to the mutual benefit of both.

Recently, Giroux (1991) has suggested nine principal features of critical pedagogy. First, he discusses the ways in which education produces not only knowledge but also political subjects. This focus is linked to Giroux's particular stress on the possible role for education in transforming American political life and opening up a public sphere for radical democracy. More generally, whatever visions of democracy we may hold, most critical educators would probably agree that education plays an important role in the construction of student subjectivities and that in order to change society, we need a vision of how students, as future adult citizens, might act in different social, cultural and political ways. Second, ethics needs to be understood as central to education, suggesting that the issues we face as teachers and students are not just questions of knowledge and truth but also of good and bad, of the need to struggle against inequality and injustice. Third, we need to understand difference both in terms of how student and teacher identities are formed and how differences between groups are maintained. This emphasis on difference, furthermore, seeks not only to understand and validate differences (according to class, race, ethnicity, gender, sexual orientation and so on) but also to move towards their partial transformation in terms of making the boundaries between them less opaque.

Fourth, Giroux points to the importance of opposing the notion of curriculum knowledge as a sacred text in favour of an understanding of how different types of culture and knowledge are given precedence in schools. The crucial issue here is to turn classrooms into places where the accepted canons of knowledge can be challenged and questioned, their construction seen not as a process of discovering universal and inevitable truths but rather as a very particular process of knowledge formation and truth claims. Fifth, critical pedagogy should seek not only to critique forms of knowledge but also to work towards the creation of new forms. By opposing knowledge as it is canonized in school subjects and academic disciplines, by making the everyday and the particular (student culture and knowledge) part of a school curriculum, and by developing forms of critique and counter-memory, it may be possible to encourage the emergence of alternative forms of culture and knowledge. Sixth, any concept of reason that makes particular claims on truth, particularly the universalist claims of Enlighten-ment Reason, needs to be reformulated. This means, among other things, rejecting claims to objectivity in favour of more partial and particular versions of knowledge, truth and reason.

Seventh, a critical pedagogy must include not only a language of critique but also a vision of a better world for which it is worth struggling. Such a vision involves a certain degree of utopianism, a belief in alternative possibilities, a way of moving beyond the despair into which a critical and ethical view of the world can often lead us. Eighth, teachers need to see themselves as, in Giroux's phrase, 'transformative intellectuals'. This view of teaching aims to oppose the way teachers are today often positioned as classroom technicians employed to pass on a body of knowledge, and in its place offers a version of teaching that removes the theory–practice divide and stresses the significance of working towards social transformation. Finally, critical pedagogy works with a notion of 'voice' that emphasizes the political nature of the subject and searches for ways in which students can come to voice that are not so much celebrations of individual narration as they are critical explorations of how we are speaking subjects.

Such an approach to education raises many issues for those of us engaged in teaching English to speakers of other languages. First, and most generally, it brings to the fore basic questions about education, social inequality and change. One of the problems with applied linguistics, as I have argued at greater length elsewhere (Pennycook, 1990c; and see also Chapter 4), has been its divorce from educational theory and the tendency to deal with language learning as a predominantly psycholinguistic phenomenon isolated from its social, cultural and educational contexts. It is essential that as language teachers we have not only ways of thinking about language and language learning but also ways of thinking about education and inequality. Second, as teachers, we need to ask ourselves what sort of vision of society we are teaching towards. Are we merely attempting to fulfil predefined curricular goals or do we have an ethical understanding of how education is related to broader social and cultural relations and that therefore there is a need to teach towards a different version of the curriculum and a different vision of society? Third, do we understand the syllabus of English as a canonical truth to be handed on to our students or is it something to be negotiated, challenged and appropriated? Finally, do we see English language teaching as connected to the construction of social difference and the struggle for voice?

While such a view of education has important implications for teaching, it also presents a number of problems. There is the danger, for example, that critical pedagogy has now become reified and institutionalized. Ellsworth (1989) has specifically addressed this problem in her accusation that it is founded on 'repressive myths'. She argues that it is too abstract and utopian, is based on rationalist assumptions, and is too little grounded in classroom realities. If critical pedagogy is to be useful, it must avoid dogmatic or abstract prescriptions. Simon (1992) has also suggested that 'critical pedagogy is in danger of terminal ossification' (p. xvi). The problem, he suggests, has been in the attempts to define and establish critical pedagogy as a domain of academic work, with all the problems of 'disciplining' such a process entails (see Chapter 4). This has resulted in a 'deleterious attempt to reify its assumptions, commitments and practices', an attempt epitomized in the tendency to 'locate critical pedagogy as encrusted in the work of Paulo Freire' or 'to define a set of "founding fathers" for critical pedagogy as if an authentic version could somehow be found in a patriarchical vanishing point' (p. xvi). Following Simon, I am using the term critical pedagogy (or pedagogies) here not as some prescriptive set of practices but rather as a heuristic around which those of us who share certain pedagogical and political visions can group. Chapters discussing teaching practices nevertheless still run the danger of prescriptivism.[1] When we write from within the powerful structures of institutionalized educational discourse, it is virtually impossible to avoid speaking with/as authority. Of course, this may lead to anything from complete acceptance (unlikely) to complete rejection (more likely) of my ideas, but I know too, as a teacher, that sections on teaching practice often appear frustratingly out of touch with how I understand my own classroom 'realities'. The ideas offered in this chapter, then, are done so in an attempt to lay out some general concerns in developing critical pedagogies of English.

Who do you think you are ...?

A further difficulty in discussing critical practice emerges from challenges to one's right to engage in pedagogies that appear disruptive to the status quo, a problem that applies to all critical educators but becomes particularly salient when one works, as I do, as a 'Western' language teacher in 'foreign' contexts. 'Just who do you think you are', the question is asked by other (usually

Western) teachers, 'pushing your political views down these students' throats?' Once again, it is a criticism worth listening to. It is equally important, however, to appreciate some of the misconceptions about a critical pedagogy embodied in such a challenge. First, since I would argue that all education is political, that all schools are sites of cultural politics, then it cannot be claimed that more traditional or standard forms of education are neutral while the critical approach that I am advocating here is 'political'. A central contrast in this book has been between the apolitical version of language that is so firmly ensconsed in the discourse of EIL, and the notion of worldliness with its cultural and political associations. Neither the version of language produced by the discourse of EIL, nor the discourse of EIL itself can be accepted as neutral, for both language and discourse always imply a politics. No knowledge, no language and no pedagogy is ever neutral or apolitical. To teach critically, therefore, is to acknowledge the political nature of all education; it is not to take up some 'political' stance that stands in contradistinction to a 'neutral' position.

Second, it is worth recalling Achebe's (1975) comment concerning 'the importance of the world language which history has forced down our throats' (p. 220). If there are many problems with a view that the world has simply chosen English, then it is important to understand that for many people, such as Achebe, English is a language that has been forced upon them. If people are still either themselves interested in studying English or are obliged to do so by an education system, an approach to teaching which takes into account both the history of the imposition of the language and the current conditions and implications of its expansion surely has far more to offer its learners than a teaching approach that claims that learning English is a natural, neutral and beneficial process. Thus while some people might want to raise questions about the morality of taking a political stance on language, I would argue that the only ethical position is to do so. The discourse of EIL presents an easily amenable position that considers English to be the universally chosen neutral language of global communication. To teach ethically our teaching practices and philosophies need to oppose such a view.

Third, to assume that a critical approach necessarily implies a dogmatic preaching of a political standpoint is not only to fail to appreciate the political nature of all education, but it is also to make unwarranted assumptions about both the political and the pedagogical in critical pedagogy. Since I have argued that all education, culture and knowledge is political, this is not a liberal humanist version of politics as governmental and policy-making processes that are argued over by people from different political parties. Rather, I am arguing for an understanding of politics as infused into everyday life as we struggle to make meanings for ourselves and others. Thus, a critical pedagogy does not advocate the teaching of a fixed body of political thought but aims to help students to deal with their struggles to make sense of their lives, to find ways of changing how lives are lived within inequitable social structures, to transform the possibilities of our lives and the ways we understand those possibilities.

Finally, with respect to the specific position from which I commonly teach, namely as 'a foreigner', it is worth raising some questions about how one is being constituted here. When, for example, I walked into ESL classrooms in Canada, where I was also officially a 'foreigner', there was clearly little important difference between myself and many non-foreign teachers of Anglo-American origin. When a 'Canadian' teacher walks into a 'Canadian' classroom to teach English to 'Canadian' students, much of what he or she does is sanctioned by the authority of these nationalist labels, yet the cultural and political background of both students and teacher remain quite undefined in this formulation. My point here is that we need to understand relations between students and teachers in ways other than according to the official discourses of nationalism. It is worth considering that as teachers of English as a second or foreign language, we *native speakers* are all, in a sense, foreigners before our classes. Thus a framework that bifurcates foreigner and non-foreigner by dint of status accorded by visa requirements or immigration documents is not a good criterion by which to judge one's right to take up a particular pedagogical project. Two of the problems with seeing one's status as primarily that of a foreigner are first that this ignores other possibilities of connection; it is to understand oneself as constituted within the discourses of national and cultural identity, thus overlooking a range of other possible linkages such as gender or class or age. Second, it ignores one's position within the discourses that support one's position abroad, usually constituting the foreigner as knowledgeable 'expert'. In many ways it is this status that needs to be problematized and deconstructed, a process that would indeed be part of the critical pedagogy that I am trying to delineate here.

The critical educator

To teach critically implies a particular understanding not only of education in general but also of the critical educator. A key problem with the way in which teachers are constructed by the discourse of EIL is that they (we) are seen as classroom technicians (cf. Giroux, 1988; Apple, 1986), using the latest and most scientific methods to convey the much sought-after neutral medium of communication: English. With the gradual consolidation of applied linguistics, furthermore, there has been a constant move towards educational expertise being defined as in the hands of the predominantly male Western applied linguistic academy, rather than in the hands of the largely female teaching practitioners, many of whom work on both the domestic and the international periphery (see Pennycook, 1989a). In order to pursue critical pedagogies of English, then, we need a reconceptualization of the role of teachers and applied linguists that does away with the theory–practice divide and views teachers/applied linguists as politically engaged critical educators.

Giroux's (e.g. 1988, and see above) formulation of teachers as 'transformative intellectuals' is useful here. A transformative intellectual Giroux defines as 'one who exercises forms of intellectual and pedagogical practice that attempt to insert teaching and learning directly into the political sphere by arguing that schooling represents both a struggle for meaning and a struggle over power relations' (p. 174); and 'one whose intellectual practices are necessarily grounded in forms of moral and ethical discourse exhibiting a preferential concern for the suffering and struggles of the disadvantaged and oppressed' (pp. 174–5). This view of the teacher, then, foregrounds the importance of political engagement and transformative goals, and stresses the role of teacher as intellectual rather than technician. Elsewhere, Giroux (1988) refers to transformative intellectuals as 'bearers of "dangerous memory"', intellectuals who keep alive the memory of human suffering along with the forms of knowledge and struggles in which such suffering was shaped and contested' (p. 99). The notion of 'dangerous memory' is taken from Welch's (1985) feminist liberation theology that seeks to use such dangerous memories of marginality, oppression and suffering to educate towards a more just and hopeful vision of society. The notion of dangerous memory has interesting connections to the idea of worldliness, for, if nothing else, the notion of the worldliness of English constitutes a means of bringing dangerous memories of English to bear on one's pedagogy. We need to be cautious here, however, lest this version of the transformative intellectual appears to be too advocative of teacher-generated agendas. As critical educators, we need to recognize the specific location of our work and to ensure that we are not merely bringers of dangerous memories but producers of and listeners to our students' memories.

Two other significant formulations of critical educators are Simon's (1992) 'cultural workers' and Foucault's (1980a) 'specific intellectual'. Simon argues that classrooms are sites of cultural politics and that teachers can usefully be viewed as cultural workers. This allows for an understanding of how educators are linked to other people engaged in sites of cultural production other than the classroom and suggests ways in which teachers can make connections with people in other domains who are committed to similar transformative projects. Foucault's formulation of the ' "specific intellectual" as opposed to the "universal" intellectual' (1980a, p. 126) makes it similarly possible to 'develop lateral connections across different forms of knowledge and from one focus of politicization to another' (p. 127). The specific intellectual on the one hand relinquishes claims to universality, objectivity, or a theoretical stance as distinct from practice, and on the other hand engages in 'local struggles' around representation, culture and the apparatuses of truth. This view of the specific intellectual is significant since it links to that side of the worldliness of English that is necessarily local and specific to that context. Both concepts enable critical educators to see ourselves not as isolated individuals but as people engaged with a community of other cultural and political workers in similarly critical and transformative projects. Thus, we can see ourselves as engaged on the one hand with local and global specificities around the worldliness of English and, on the other hand, with struggles around culture, language and knowledge that are being confronted by other people in different domains. Connections can be made between, for example, educators and writers, artists, environmental activists, people involved in alternative development programmes, human rights activists, or members of different groups engaged in struggles over gender or ethnic inequalities. This is where the critical educator as specific intellectual needs to understand the cultural politics of her or his educational context, trying to understand, for example, issues of gender, religion, ethnicity and economic and political power in the contexts in which we work.

Finally, one further dimension of the critical educator is as 'listening intellect'. One problem suggested above is that critical educators may be seen as coercive, as pontificating critical pedagogues. This is not merely a question of how we are viewed, however; it is also an essential critique which should always be borne in mind in order to enhance self-reflexivity and attentiveness to the cultures, knowledges, languages and voices of others. This I think is encapsulated in Rajni Kothari's call for

> a *listening* intellect instead of the usual pontificating one with which the intellectual merely hands out both specific solutions and larger visions. Such an intellect has a pluralist conception of intellectual tasks instead of a monolithic, universalizing and unifying model that applies everywhere (if it doesn't work somewhere, the fault is of the people, or of tradition, or of politics). Intellectuals identify with the victims of history, are involved in the political process (not riding above it) and are moved by passion and commitment (instead of cold 'scientific' analysis without a sense of *personal* involvement).
>
> (1987, p. 290)

It is this notion of listening that we as critical English language educators, indeed all critical educators, need to raise to a position of prominence: listening to our students, listening to other teachers, listening to other cultural and political workers; listening. For a critical pedagogy of English in the world to emerge, there must be much more listening between educators, much more profound sharing of pedagogical insights between teachers from different backgrounds and much more thinking about how we can listen to our students.

Kramsch's (1993) summary of 'the main features of a critical language pedagogy' (p. 244) includes similar features: 'awareness of global context', which stresses the need to acknowledge the complexities of the meanings students are trying to produce with limited language skills, and which is akin to Schenke's (1991a; b) arguments for understanding how students come to class 'already knowing'; 'local knowledge' of our students, since 'our major task is not, as some teachers believe, to find ever better ways of "making students talk", but to understand in ever more sensitive ways why they talk the way they do, and why they remain silent' (p. 245); and 'ability to listen', since a great deal of teacher education has focused either on teachers' modelling language or listening for linguistic forms, rather than listening 'to silences and to their students' implicit assumptions and beliefs' or to their own assuptions and beliefs (p. 245). Putting these different conceptions of critical educators together, a role emerges for a critical educator of English who is personally and politically committed, who understands him- or herself as a specific rather than a universal intellectual, who is engaged with both the local context and the global domain, who works not in isolation but with other cultural and political workers, and who listens while always acknowledging the difficulties and partialities of those listenings.

DISCOURSE, LANGUAGE AND SUBJECTIVITY

In other discussions of the implications of teaching English around the world, the predominant focus has been on questions of standards and intelligibility. Thus Quirk (1985), for example, praises the BBC World Service of London, All India Radio of Delhi, *The Straits Times* of Singapore, and the *Japan Times* of Tokyo for their 'use of a form of English that is both understood and respected in every corner of the globe where any knowledge of any variety of English exists' and their adherence to 'forms of English familiarly produced by only a minority of English speakers in any of the four countries concerned' (p. 6). Kachru (1985), by contrast, proposes the setting up of an international institute for research on varieties of English, pointing out that this is not a proposal for the codification of English but rather for 'initiating collaborative efforts between the native and non-native users of English for monitoring, as it were, the direction of change in English, the uses and usage, and the scope of the spread and its implications for intelligibility and communication' (p. 27). Strevens (1980) has taken up the more immediate pedagogical question of 'When is a localized form of English a suitable model for teaching purposes?' (p. 84). He concludes that different native-speaker models are more appropriate in EFL areas (where English is not widely used), and local models are more appropriate in ESL areas (where English is more widely used). Furthermore, models should be relative to levels of educational achievement (the higher the educational level, the more widely intelligible the model should be) and that 'the native speaker of English must accept that English is no longer his possession alone' (p. 90).

These are not, of course, trivial concerns, for they have major implications for teacher education, textbook-writing, curriculum design and classroom teaching. Nevertheless, since my focus has been on the meanings that can be expressed in English rather than the forms through which those meanings may be realized, questions around language models are not central to the discussion here. More critical analyses of the global spread of English have been less common and so too have been suggestions about pedagogical implications. One suggestion has come from Rogers (1982), who argues that since so few children will be able to benefit from the false hopes and promises proferred by an English education, we should consider teaching less English: 'Is it ethical to go on teaching English to so many children, and so encourage them to believe that it will automatically entitle them to a better job, an office job, a manager's job with a big car, a house and two sets of clothes, a "better" life?' (p. 145). Given the large numbers of students learning English 'for no obvious reason', the low quality of much of that education and the false hopes that it holds out for its students, he suggests we should reconsider the point of this education and indeed attempt to reduce the amount of English taught.

While Rogers' point is well taken – there are indeed questions to be asked about the quantity, quality and false hopes of English educations – his solution, as responses to his article (Abbott, 1984; Prodromou, 1988) suggest, is problematic. First, from an educational viewpoint, it is problematic to identify English as the language of wealth and prestige (however inequitable access to it may be and however frequent the false promises of advancement may be) and then to suggest giving less students access to it. As Prodromou (1988) points out, Rogers' proposal is, ironically, 'an élitist solution' to the problems of language and élitism (p. 73). Thus, even if we had the power to change how much English gets taught, removing English from syllabuses around the world remains an unsatisfactory solution. Secondly, of course, the reduction of English teaching is not something over which most of us have much control. While we can seek to oppose the spread of English in various ways, the issue is perhaps more one of how we can find ways of dealing with English by establishing critical pedagogies of English.

Phillipson (1992), meanwhile, seems reluctant to draw pedagogical implications from his analysis of 'English linguistic imperialism'. He ends his book wth the question 'Can ELT contribute constructively to greater linguistic and social equality, and if so, how could a critical ELT be committed, theoretically and practically, to combating linguicism?' (p. 319). The key focus here is encapsulated in the phrase 'anti-linguicist strategies' (1988, p. 353), in developing means to oppose 'linguicism'. This highlights first-language maintenance while seeking a greatly diminished role for English. Phillipson's point of intervention differs from mine, however; for while he is concerned primarily with language planning and thus ways of protecting 'linguistic human rights', my focus is on cultural politics and pedagogy, and thus ways of changing how people are represented and can represent themselves in English (more a question of 'cultural rights' rather than just 'linguistic rights'). While Phillipson's concerns are important, therefore, they still seem to leave us with the question of what to do pedagogically with English, a question that is of more direct concern to language teachers than issues of language planning. Thus, in attempting to 'avoid the destruction that English has wrought on other languages and cultures in its march to the position it now occupies in the world' (Ngũgĩ, 1993, p. 39), we need not only strong support for first languages, bilingual education, and so on, but also pedagogical strategies to deal with English. It is worth quoting at some length Searle's call for such a pedagogy:

> Let us be clear that the English language has been a monumental force and institution of oppression and rabid exploitation throughout 400 years of imperialist history. It attacked the black person who spoke it with its racist images and imperialist message, it battered the worker who toiled as its words expressed the parameters of his misery and the subjection of entire peoples in all the continents of the world. It was made to scorn the languages it sought to replace, and told the colonised peoples that mimicry of its primacy among languages was a necessary

badge of their social mobility as well as their continued humiliation and subjection. Thus, when we talk of 'mastery' of the Standard language, we must be conscious of the terrible irony of the word, that the English language itself was the language of the master, the carrier of his arrogance and brutality. Yet, as teachers, we seek to grasp that same language and give it a new content, to de-colonise its words, to de-mystify its meaning, and as workers taking over our own factory and giving our machines new lives, making it a vehicle for liberation, consciousness and love, to rip out its class assumptions, its racism and appalling degradation of women, to make it truly *common*, to recreate it as a weapon for the freedom and understanding of our people.

(p. 68)

Teaching back

A number of critical approaches to language education have touched on some of these challenges. In the context of developing curriculum guidelines for adult ESL learners in Australia, Candlin (1989) shows how a curriculum was developed around the relationships among certain *issues* (for instance, questions of race, gender, class, rights), the particular *institutions* in which such issues are salient for the students (family, school, work, etc.), different text types or *expressions* (e.g. stories, cartoons, descriptions, poems), and discoursal orders or *functions* (persuasion, dominance, solidarity, and so on). Methodologically, this curriculum then operates through a sequence of *investigating* (what problems does a particular text pose?); *thinking* (what information needs to be explored?); *codifying* (in what ways is this personally relevant?); *dialoguing* (what resources are needed to explain the text?); *critiquing* (what are the underlying issues?); and *acting* (what out-of-classroom action should be taken?). Overall, such an approach, Candlin suggests, helps in 'the relativising, personalising and problematising of experience, the enhancing of skills of intercultural understanding, in particular seeking social and cultural explanations for language use, and the extending of knowledge and awareness gained in the classroom setting to address learners' personal life issues in the wider social context of intercultural behaviour outside the institution' (p. 22).

Other attempts to develop critical pedagogies of English have been based on a more Freirean (e.g. 1970) approach to pedagogy. Graman (1988), for example, argues that second language education needs 'an approach that addresses the existential, political, and axiological questions touching the lives of both students and teachers' (p. 441). In order to 'develop the critical consciousness and linguistic ability needed to function not as servants but as active decisionmakers' he suggests an approach to education that fosters 'authentic dialogue about reality so that the immediate need to confront real problems and resolve them can be met' (p. 441). Similarly, Auerbach (1986) has criticized competency-based ESL education for transmitting a fixed canon of supposedly necessary functional competencies without ever encouraging a questioning of those competencies. She has also drawn on the Freirean notion of a problem-posing curriculum to increase critical consciousness of issues around student lives (Auerbach and Wallerstein, 1987). While there are a number of limitations with Freirean-based pedagogies (see Weiler, 1991), Freire needs to be acknowledged as the inspiration for a great deal of current critical pedagogy, and such approaches certainly come close to the type of practice I am interested in here.[2]

From a slightly different perspective, Catherine Walsh (1991) argues that

> Given the hegemonic, racist, sexist, and anti-bilingual circumstance of US schooling ... there is a need to develop specific pedagogies that recognize and interrogate Puerto Rican students' past and present realities, to include the experiences, perceptions, and voices that have traditionally been shut out, and to encourage movement toward critical bilingualism – the ability to not just speak two languages, but to be conscious of the sociocultural, political, and ideological contexts in which the languages (and therefore the speakers) are positioned and function, and of the multiple meanings that are fostered in each.
>
> (p. 127)

Walsh's key term here is *voice*, a concept which I think helps us move further forward in developing critical pedagogies for English. The notion of voice is used not in the sense of an individual phenomenon in isolation, a question of merely using language, or enunciating a 'true self' or a cultural essence, but rather to refer to a contested space of language use as social practice, as English-users struggle to negotiate meanings between subjectivities, language and discourse. If we understand language teaching in terms of helping people to both find and create voices in a new language, this notion of voice and the conditions of possibility that produce and regulate it will have considerable significance for a critical pedagogy of English. This type of critical practice, therefore, does not in the least advocate a transmission model of education, some form of teaching that seeks to preach a certain political point of view. Such an approach would be pedagogically poor and politically naive. The notion of voice, by contrast, suggests a pedagogy that starts with the concerns of the students, not in some vapid, humanist 'student-centred' approach that requires students to express their 'inner feelings', but rather through an exploration of students' histories and cultural locations, of the limitations and possibilities presented by languages and discourses. The issue in teaching critically, then, is one of working with students to come to terms with the continuing struggles over language, knowledge and culture, over what is constituted as knowledge, and how one is represented and can come to represent oneself in the world. Voice is not just a non-silence, a mouthing of words, or a mastery of lexis, pronunciation or syntax; it is a place of struggle in the space between language, discourse and subjectivity. So a critical practice in English language teaching must start with ways of critically exploring students' cultures, knowledges and histories in ways that are both challenging and at the same time affirming and supportive.

In broad terms, then, one might say that a critical pedagogy of English in the world is an attempt to enable students to write (speak, read, listen) back. The notion of voice, therefore, is not one that implies *any* language use, the empty babble of the communicative language class, but rather must be tied to a vision of the creation and transformation of possibilities (cf. Simon, 1987). These voices that we are seeking to help students to find and create are *insurgent* voices, voices that speak in opposition to the local and global discourses that limit and produce the possibilities that frame our students' lives. The tripartate construction of voice (language, dicourse and subjectivity) suggests three important domains for action here: the discursive, the linguistic and the subjective. Discursive action addresses the discursive construction of reality, how our lives are made and regulated within different discourses, and particularly how certain discourses intersect with English. Linguistic action looks at the language itself, at its norms and standards and at the possibilities for change. Subjective action considers the subjectivities of the students, their histories, memories, lives, cultural locations. Although these distinctions are somewhat contrived since language, discourse and subjectivity cannot in fact be practically separated, they do seem to help in thinking through how to develop critical pedagogies of English.

Discursive Intervention

Dealing first with the disursive domain, the concept of worldliness would seem to be a far more useful position from which to start teaching English in the world than is a view of English as a neutral medium for communication. It implies an understanding of how English is implicated in a range of social, cultural, economic and political relations, how it may be linked, for example, to a colonial history, to the inequitable distribution of resources within a country, to the invasion of North American popular culture, to struggles for economic and political ascendancy, to a split between public and private sectors of an economy, or to a schooling system which as a result promotes inappropriate forms of culture and knowledge. Such relationships need to be understood both with respect to their location within global economic, communication, educational and other systems, and in their local specificities.

This notion of worldliness connects the linguistic and discursive domains in a way that presents a first step forward in a critical pedagogy of English. This domain might be called *discursive intervention*, an attempt to make central to English teaching the connections between the language and significant discourses. Many of us who teach English as a second language and who wish to make our teaching more relevant, interesting and critical have taken up various 'social issues' in our classes, thus dealing with issues such as abortion, euthanasia, the environment, the crime rate and so on. One problem with this, however, is that such issues often remain tangential both to students' lives and to the position of English. This also suggests a misplaced priority: making the selection of 'serious issues' primary, rather than emphasizing the need to deal seriously with all issues.[3] The worldliness of English, by contrast, presents part of the curricular focus. It is precisely to the worldliness of English that a curriculum of critical English pedagogy can turn in the first instance. Thus, it is the connections between English and popular culture, development, capitalism, dependency, and so on that can make up part of the 'content' of a critical pedagogy of English.

One key domain which immediately presents itself here is the relationship between English and popular culture. While studies of popular culture have focused on diverse cultural forms from T-shirts to motorcycle gangs, from dancing to Australian beaches, a key focus has remained on the visual media (see Gurevitch et al., 1982; Giroux and Simon, 1989). One of the outcomes of this focus, has been the questioning not just of the canon of English literature but also the canonization of written texts. Once English studies starts to be concerned with a broad concept of cultural criticism, and once it is acknowledged that students are often far more invested in popular music, film and video than in various textual forms, then visual popular media suggest themselves as a central curricular focus. This is surely also true for many ESL/EFL students, whose primary involvement with English may come through film, television, video and music. An important focus of a critical pedagogy for English, then, might well be on the images and content of films, advertisements, news programmes, rock videos and so on. This area of discursive intervention, therefore, would look to examine critically the relationships between English and popular culture.

Another particular form of this discursive intervention that I took up a few years ago involved the connections between English and Christianity (see Chapters 3 and 6), which became of particular concern to me while teaching in China because of the increasing numbers of Christian missionaries who were there as thinly disguised English language teachers. In a course on 'British and American Culture', a course that had always previously consisted of lectures on the political and education systems, festivals and holidays of the United States and UK, I decided to add a section on American fundamentalism to the curriculum. In the context of the period of the 'Open Door Policy', when China was being flooded with English language teaching and a plethora of images of and contacts with the seductive 'West', countries such as the United States, despite official suggestions that China should only take very carefully what was appropriate from the West, were being cast in a very favourable light. Thus, many young Chinese were becoming interested and fascinated by what the glamorous and modern Western world[4] had to offer, amongst which was, of course, Christianity. I felt, therefore, that it was important to make available to my students alternative readings of the United States that drew links between fundamentalism and right-wing politics and showed how the vast expansion of English language learning was being used by those who sought only to 'convert' their students and preach their right-wing politics. The object here was to give my students ways of thinking about connections between the language they were so busily engaged in learning and other cultural and political complexes around modernity, Christianity, the Open Door Policy, anti-abortion campaigns ('The Right to Life'), Chinese population problems and family policies, freedom of speech, and so on.

Another example comes from my current situation in Hong Kong. My students sometimes seem hemmed in by criticisms: they are told that their English isn't good enough ('standards have declined'), but neither is their Chinese; they are caught between two cultures, East and West, Chinese and British; their cultural horizons rarely extend beyond local pop music and low-quality films. They are, in the words of Lord and T'sou (1985, p. 18; quoted with approval by Phillipson, 1992), 'cultural eunuchs': 'with insufficient command or literacy in either English or Chinese, the individual becomes only a social animal functioning in a verbal and cultural vacuum'. So deeply ingrained have such criticisms become that my students have told me this themselves: their English and Chinese are poor and they have no culture. For me, an immediate task in my teaching was to work with my students to explore how such definitions of their cultural and linguistic lives had been put into place, how and why the discourse of declining standards has developed, how 'East' and 'West' are particular constructs and need not represent a subtractive vacuum but rather a range of possibilities, how the growth of Cantonese popular culture in the 1970s was part of a larger movement to oppose colonial rule and expand Cantonese identity. Then we needed to explore English-language popular culture to see how different and multiple readings of this emerged, to find ways to understand connections between English and local and global forms of culture and to oppose the detrimental definitions with which these students are having to cope. What sort of a notion of culture is it that allows for a concept like 'cultural eunuchs'?

As some students wrote recently (in a group project):

As English plays an important role in Hong Kong, those who have good command of English are always regarded as élite group and skilled professionals, while those who have poor English standard are regarded as inferior and belonging to working class. Thus, social discrimination is likely to occur. We think that the academic performance may not reliably reflect working ability and working performance and we should not only adore foreign language and neglect our own language.

The struggle for Cantonese language and culture and for political rights has necessarily involved a struggle against English, yet at the same time it has also had to include an acknowledgement that English has become an intrinsic part of Hong Kong's economic success. English is a massive social divider in Hong Kong, demarcating social and economic prestige. Writing about the medium of education in Hong Kong, another group of students suggested that 'The result of using English as the medium of instruction is that too much emphasis is put on a good command of English, without attaching appropriate importance to critical thinking.' It is to an exploration of these very worldlinesses of English that a critical ELT curriculum can turn. These, then, are curricular decisions based on an understanding of the worldliness of English, an attempt to make a discursive intervention between English and some related discourses. Other questions around international relations, education, global capitalism, modernity, fundamentalism, colonialism, development or popular culture suggest themselves here.

Linguistic action

If a central aspect of the abrogative/diremptive and appropria- tive/redemptive process is the attempt to locate a critical pedagogy of English relative to the central discursive formations with which English is bound up, such a pedagogy also requires a position relative to the central norms of language use. There are two principal aspects to this: first, the need to ensure that students have access to those standard forms of the language that are of significance within the context in which one teaches; and, second, that students are encouraged to use English in their own way, to appropriate English for their own ends. This relationship between the need to give students access to those forms of language, culture and knowledge that are privileged within a society and the need to help students to develop their own forms of language, culture and knowledge often in opposition to the central norms is a key question for critical pedagogy. As critical educators, we are faced by something of a dilemma between student, curriculum and institutional requirements on the one hand and our own visions of critical pedagogy on the other. As Simon (1987) points out, however, an important issue in critical pedagogy is not merely helping students to 'make it' but also trying to change the possibilities for the students both in terms of how they understand their lives and in terms of the possibilities with which they are presented. 'The project of possibility' Simon (1987, p. 375) suggests, 'requires an education rooted in a view of human freedom as the understanding of necessity and the transformation of necessity'.

Searle (1983) argues that it is fundamentally important that, given the power and history of English, students be helped to *master Standard English* rather than achieve functional competence in the language or mastery of non-standard forms. Only then, he suggests, will they have the means to combat English. His point is well taken, though it does not explore sufficiently the difficulties of defining standard English. In order to take up Roger Simon's challenge to both understand and to change necessity, it is important, first, to have a good understanding of the relative importance of different standards of English (local, national and international) and to teach forms of English judiciously in accordance with that understanding; second, to teach standard forms critically, so that students are aware of how such forms have developed and how they are linked to central norms of linguistic and cultural appropriacy; and third, to ensure that students have access to those forms of the language that are of particular significance in significant discourses. Rather than assuming some monolithic version of the standard language, therefore, we can acknowledge, on the one hand, multiple standards, and on the other, the particular importance of certain language forms because of their relationship to certain discourses.

If giving students access to forms of standard Englishes is important, so too is the need to allow them the space to experiment and play with English. This, as the poet John Agard makes clear in 'Listen Mr Oxford Don', is a significant site of struggle:

... I ent have no gun
I ent have no knife
but mugging de Queen's English
is the story of my life

I dont need no axe
to split/up yu syntax
I dont need no hammer
to mash/up yu grammar

Dem accuse me of assault
on the Oxford dictionary/
imagine a concise peaceful man like me/
dem want me to serve time
for inciting ryme to riot
but I tekking it quiet
down here in Clapham Common

I'm not a violent man Mr Oxford don
I only armed wit mih human breath
but human breath
is a dangerous weapon ...

(Cited in Andersen, 1988, p. 235)

Thus, we need to encourage what MacCabe (1988) calls, in a positive sense, 'broken English', where 'breaking' is an attempt to dislodge the central language norms and to recreate other possibilities. While on the one hand, therefore, I need to help students meet the criteria for 'success' as they are defined within particular institutional contexts, as a critical educator I need also to try to change how students understand their possibilities and I need to work towards changing those possibilities. I am not, therefore, advocating a *laissez-faire* approach to language forms that encourages students to do as they like, as if English language classrooms existed in some social, cultural and political vacuum. Rather I am suggesting that first, we need to make sure that students have access to those standard forms of the language linked to social and economic prestige; second, we need a good understanding of the status and possibilities presented by different standards; third, we need to focus on those parts of language that are significant in particular discourses; fourth, students need to be aware that those forms represent only one set of particular possibilities; and finally, students also need to be encouraged to find ways of using the language that they feel are expressive of their own needs and desires, to make their own readings of texts, to write, speak and listen in forms of the language that emerge as they strive to find representations of themselves and others that make sense to them, so that they can start to claim and negotiate a voice in English.

Exploring subjectivity

In many ways, the most difficult of the three interlinked domains is that of student subjectivity, for we have to consider very carefully here questions of knowability and accessibility of subjectivities – especially when teachers are not from the same cultural and linguistic backgrounds as their students – both from the point of view of linguistic and cultural differences and from the point of view of pedagogical practice. Once we make student subjectivity a focus of our critical pedagogy and make claims to understanding and investigating students' cultural positions, histories and lived experiences, we need to tread carefully. Much of North American critical pedagogy seems to assume that education can best be done through discussion, a form of negotiation and open exchange of views in the public domain of the classroom. This is problematic in terms of making simplistic assumptions about pedagogy, in terms of ignoring cultural difference (despite the frequent emphasis on 'difference'), and in terms of the pragmatic constraints under which many teachers work. With respect to the first issue, Simon (1992) has pointed out that 'the concept of a dialogic pedagogy is perhaps one of the most confused and misdeveloped ideas in the literature on critical teaching. At a simplistic level it has been taken as a process within which a student "voice" is "taken seriously" and in this respect is counterposed to a transmission pedagogy' (p. 96). Clearly, any useful critical pedagogy for English must go beyond such simplistic beliefs in "dialogue".

All this becomes much more complex, furthermore, when viewed from a perspective of cultural difference, either in terms of teacher–student differences[5] or in terms of the belief that *all* classes can work this way. Welch (1991) has suggested that genuine conversation with other cultural traditions leads to a fundamental challenge to views such as those espoused by Habermas (e.g. 1984), in which it is suggested there are universal concepts of reason through which true communication can be achieved. Rather, she suggests, 'if other cultures are to be included, assessment of the criteria of successful conversation and of the norms for that conversation must be joined' (p. 94). One problem with critical pedagogy that Ellsworth (1989) points to is its belief in the 'knowability' of things. Thus we need to repond to her challenge: 'What diversity do we silence in the name of "liberatory" pedagogy?' (p. 299). On the one hand we need to ask to what extent we are able to listen to and understand our students in order to take up their concerns and positions; on the other hand we need to ask to what extent our pedagogy is meaningful in particular contexts so that in its very practice it does not become a new form of cultural imposition. There often appears to be an overconfidence in the ability of critical educators to hear, understand and deal with student subjectivities and voice. I do not want to suggest starting only with a notion of difference and incommensurability, but neither do I want to speak with such assurance about 'border crossing' (see e.g. Giroux, 1991) or 'similarities within difference' (see Kanpol, 1990; Pennycook, 1991).

Finally, it is important to understand that classrooms in many parts of the world are not generally sites where discussion as understood in this North American sense can occur. Classes are often large and classrooms are places where the word of the teacher carries a great deal of importance. Typically, furthermore, students often do not come to class with an interest in finding about each other but come already knowing each other. My students in China, for example, ate together, lived together in the same dormitory rooms, studied together in the same classes, and spent their spare time together. There can be very close relationships between students, very interesting discussions between students, close relationships between students and teachers and extensive discussions between students and teachers, but the classroom is not generally where these happen. To develop critical pedagogies for ELT, therefore, we need to learn very carefully how education happens in the different contexts of our teaching, and to question assumptions about dialogue, classroom roles, teacher–student relationships and so on.

As critical educators, then, we need to learn to hear our students, to be 'listening intellectuals', for if a critical pedagogy of English is concerned with helping students find, develop and create voices in

English, a teacher needs to know both how to understand those voices and how to make those voices pedagogically accessible. 'What is *not* needed', Roger Simon (1992) argues, 'is the pretensions of empathy, the claim to share an understanding of the positions and feelings of others, but rather the recognition of the impossibility of such claims and hence the requirement that we listen and try to hear what is being said' (p. 72). As teachers we also need to consider very carefully the partiality of our own listenings; as Arleen Schenke (1991b) suggests in her discussion of autobiography and memory work in ESL: 'Because autobiographical work in teaching is a practice in "breaking the silence" of personal and social histories, and because these histories, in ESL teaching in particular, are traversed by legacies of colonialism, it matters fundamentally who speaks and who listens, under what conditions of possibility, and along the lines of which political and pedagogical agendas' (p. 48). As critical educators we need a great deal of flexibility in our teaching and we need to do a great deal of listening and learning if our pedagogy is to be successful.

Elsa Auerbach's (e.g. 1993) emphasis on participatory action research, first language literacy and bilingual education is one way in which students' lives and lived experiences can come to play a major role in language education. Another way forward is through what Arleen Schenke (1991b) has called a 'genealogical practice in memory work' (p. 47), a practice that can start to attend to the discursive formation of student (and teacher) subjectivity and memory. It is in the difficult process of attending not only to the autobiographies *per se* of students (the experiences, stories and histories they relate) but also to 'the voice, the autobiographical "I" through which such experiences are narrated and heard . . . that we touch upon the discursive formations of subjectivity and memory, and that we can work towards a more historicized and engaged practice of feminist/ESL teaching' (1991b, p. 48). Out of such emergent voices one can start to construct a critical pedagogy that deals increasingly with student subjectivities and local understandings of how people's lives are constructed and constricted through different discourses and lived experiences. The notion of voice, understood as the coming to language amid different discourses and subject positions, can present useful strategies for a critical practice. Voice, as Giroux (1988), hooks (1988), Schenke (1991b) and Walsh (1991) all stress, implies a sense of agency. It implies ways of making ourselves understood, defining ourselves as active participants in the world, becoming agents in the process of making history, coming to terms with the complex relations that inform consciousness and position people relative to others, moving from silence to speaking as a revolutionary or oppositional gesture, reading, writing, speaking, listening against the grain. If we can construct pedagogies that take up the discursive domains particularly related to English and to the students, that explore linguistically how students can come to make meanings for themselves, that seek to start with student subjectivities, there is a possibility that we can effectively help students to find and negotiate voices in English.

INSURGENT KNOWLEDGES, THE CLASSROOM AND THE WORLD

In this final section I want to step back from the classroom once again and speculate on some possible outcomes of such a critical pedagogy in a larger context. Specifically, I want to raise two key points: first, if the global spread of English has cultural and political implications for those who learn and use it, it also has implications for those that have instigated the spread. Or, to put it another way, if part of this critical project is to decolonize English, there may also be the need to decolonize the colonizers' minds. Second, if English can indeed be appropriated and used for diverse ends, it may, by dint of its widespread use, offer interesting possibilities for the spread of alternative forms of culture and knowledge and for new forms of communal action.

Crusoe's savage mind

Phillipson (1992) starts his chapter on what he calls the colonial linguistic inheritance with the following quote from *Robinson Crusoe*: 'I was greatly delighted with my new companion, and made it my businesss to teach him everything that was proper to make him useful, handy, and helpful; but especially to make him speak, and understand me when I spake, and he was the aptest schollar that ever was' (Defoe, 1719/1965, p. 213;[6] quoted in Phillipson, 1992, p. 109). Phillipson suggests that this is one of the first published instances of English language teaching and that it is worth considering Politi's (1985) remark that Robinson Crusoe is the unacknowledged father of the British Council. He goes on to point out that when simplified readers were first produced by a British publisher to further the expansion of English, the first title published was *Robinson Crusoe* (Longman New Method Series, 1926). Phillipson's main point here is that Crusoe's relationship with Friday reflects the 'racial structure of western society at the heyday of slavery' (p. 109). Such a relationship, Phillipson argues, is a crucial element in the early process of 'English linguistic imperialism'. For Phillipson, then, Crusoe's assumption of mastery over Friday and his immediate start on the project of teaching Friday English (rather than, for example, learning Friday's language), are iconic moments in the long history of the global spread of English. Phillipson is indubitably right in many ways, and it is worth asking ourselves today to what extent we are teaching in Crusoe's footsteps.

Nevertheless, I wish to follow a slightly different tack here. As with Karl Marx's and Adam Smith's interests in Crusoe as the epitome of Western economic rationalism and self-sufficiency, Phillipson sees Crusoe as the epitome of imperialist mastery, a key figure in the European attempt to gain political and economic mastery over vast areas of the world. Brantlinger (1990), on the other hand, focuses on Crusoe as the epitome of the 'irrational' mastery over and construction of the Other. For Brantlinger, the crucial moment in this story is the discovery in the sand of the footprint. As he points out, from that moment on, Crusoe is plagued by wild imaginings of 'savages': Crusoe is a man 'perfectly confused and out of myself' (Defoe, 1719/1910, p. 143); '... nor is it possible to describe how many various shapes affrighted imagination represented things to me in, how many wild ideas were found every moment in my fancy, and what strange unaccountable whimsies came into my thoughts by the way' (p. 143). From this moment on, his cave is renamed his castle, and he lives in perpetual fear of the arrival of the cannibals, a fear that grows ever greater as his wild imaginings increase: 'The further I was from the occasion of my fright, the greater my apprehensions were' (pp. 143–4).

As Brantlinger says, 'What Crusoe cannot master – or get to call him "master" – he sees only as savagery and desert island' (p. 2). This is not, of course, new to Defoe, for the long tradition of creating these often cannibalistic, always primitive and savage Others can be traced in European imagination from Columbus and Caliban to Kipling and Conrad (see Tatlow, 1992; Ngũgĩ, 1993). The lesson Brantlinger draws from this is that while Defoe's intended moral lesson was presumably one of mastery and self-mastery, 'it seems just as possible to see in Crusoe's mastery – of the island, of the cannibals, of Friday, of fate – a kind of madness, the antithesis of self-mastery' (p. 3). Crusoe, he suggests, never learns the main lesson that is offered by cultural studies, namely that 'in order to understand ourselves, the discourses of "the Other" – of all the others – is that which we most urgently need to hear' (p. 3). This, then, is the other side of the colonial coin, not the Anglicist imposition of English for economic and political gain, but the Orientalist construction of the inarticulate Other. Part of this critical pedagogical project must aim, then, in hearing the 'discourses of the Other', to challenge that long legacy of colonial and neocolonial Othering that has always been the flip side of English language teaching. The point here is that if on the one hand we need to understand how, as language teachers we walk in Crusoe's footsteps, we need, on the other hand, to consider how that footprint in the sand, the threatening mark of the colonized Other, has left a long cultural imprint in the malleable tissues of our minds.

Decolonizing the colonizers' minds

This, then, raises the challenge of the possible decolonization of the colonizers, and not merely in some narrow sense of colonialism but rather in the sense of the whole past and present process of cultural imposition. For Ngũgĩ (1986), decolonizing the minds of the colonized can only be done in isolation from the language of the colonizers, a process of rejecting the language, culture and epistemologies of the colonizers in favour of a return to African languages, literary forms, cultures and epistemologies. For Nandy (1983), however, this process involves a decolonizing of both the colonized *and* the colonizers' minds. He argues that we must understand the 'degradation of the colonizer', that the colonizer should not be seen as a 'conspiratorial dedicated oppressor' but rather as a 'self-destructive co-victim with a reified life style and parochial culture' caught in the hinges of history (p. xv). What becomes important in this view, then, is the need to decolonize the colonizers' minds in the process of opposing and dismantling structures of inequality.[7]

As Fanon (1967) amongst others has pointed out, it was European middle-class culture that came to dominate colonialism. Nandy argues that we need to understand how colonialism brought particular modes of oppression in the colonizers' culture to the fore; thus, various traits of racism, of imputing superiority to Western culture, of the domination of women by men, of the disciplinary culture of European childhood were emphasized and reinforced during colonialism. Just as in Chapter 3 I discussed the effects of colonialist and imperialist ideology on attitudes to language in Victorian England, so the continued spread of English and the continued dominance of the discourse of EIL have had broad effects on our lives more generally. As Nandy (1983) describes part of this process, colonialism 'de-emphasized specula- tion, intellection and *caritas* as feminine, and justified a limited cultural role for women – and femininity – by holding that the softer side of the human nature was irrelevant to the public sphere. It openly sanctified – in the name of such values as competition, achievement, control and productivity – new forms of institu- tionalized social Darwinism' (p. 32). While Nandy's somewhat essentialized view of 'femininity' is slightly problematic, the general point is worth reiterating: the culture of colonialism not only had devastating effects on the colonized but also affected the colonizers by constructing a narrower set of discursive options. A similar point has been made about patriarchy: the issue is not merely one of women redefining ways of knowing and being, but also of men looking at how the construction of masculinity is an oppressive site in terms of the limited possibilities it offers us for thought and action. This argument has great significance for the issues I am discussing here, for it suggests that the formation of counter-discursive positions in English has implications not merely for the re-presentation of the post-colonized self but also for the re- presentation of the post-colonizing self. Linked both discursively and linguistically, colonized and colonizers, post-colonized and post-colonizers, are constantly affecting each other through our discourses and counter-discourses, and English in many ways holds out the greatest hope for a possible decolonizing of the colonizers' minds. If we need absolutely to deal critically with the worldliness of English, we also need to acknowledge the possibilities that might emerge from this process. Writing back offers, therefore, not only possibilities for the former colonized but also for the former colonizers, as new meanings, new counter-discourses come into play in our shared language.

Common counter-articulations

I have made the notion of voice central to my discussion here, as we try to enable students to come to ways of expressing, changing, negotiating voices in English. In this process of exploring histories and relationships to discourses, of how subjectivities have been formed in relationship to English, students engage in what amounts to a form of genealogical practice (Schenke, 1991b), an attempt to insurrect both those knowledges subsumed within the dominant discourses and those knowledges that have been discarded as unworthy and inferior. This is a crucial aspect of the appropriative/redemptive project as students come to voice insurgent knowledges, memories and cultures that emerge as the dominant discourses are brought into question. Such a project has significance not merely for students, however, but for much wider communities. English offers an expanded community of users. If insurgent knowledges can emerge through English, they may have an effect far broader than if they had been voiced in other languages; insurgent knowledges emerging from a particular context now have the possibility of achieving international reach. Such a process is not unproblematic, however, since new knowledges and cultural forms may get not only dispersed but also diffused: they may lose their insurgency. 'Is it not perhaps the case that these fragments of genealogies are no sooner brought to light, that the particular elements of the knowledge one seeks to disinter are no sooner accredited and put into circulation, than they run the risk of re-codification, re-colonisation?' (Foucault, 1980a, p. 86). Like Foucault, my only response to this danger is to continue to struggle and continue to hope, for I believe that the spread of English, if dealt with critically, may offer chances for cultural renewal and exchange around the world.

English offers a community of speakers through which oppositional projects can be taken up. Said (1990) speaks of the
possibilities presented by some of the new social and political
movements around the world, such as new and insurgent
democracy or ecology movements, but laments that few of these
movements 'have the capacity and freedom to generalise beyond
their own regionally local circumstances' (pp. 10–11). But English
does offer some possibilities in enabling what Said calls a 'common
counter-articulation' (p. 11). To articulate critical moments in
English can open up possibilities of joint struggles. If English is the
major language through which the forces of neocolonial exploitation operate, it is also the language through which 'common
counter-articulations' can perhaps most effectively be made. I want
to conclude, then, on a certain note of optimism here and suggest a
role for the English language classroom in the world that makes it
not the poor cousin to other classes that it so often seems to be, but
rather a key site in global cultural production. Counter-discourses
formulated through English and the articulation of insurgent
knowledges and cultural practices in English offer alternative
possibilities to the colonizers and post-colonizers, challenging and
changing the cultures and discourses that dominate the world. In
some senses, then, the English language classroom, along with
other sites of cultural production and political opposition, could
become a key site for the renewal of both local and global forms of
culture and knowledge. I shall close this book here on this
optimistic note, in the hope that critical English language
educators may be able to use the concept of worldliness I have
been developing here and engage in a critical, transformative and
listening critical pedagogy through English.

NOTES

1. I have discussed this issue of prescriptivism elsewhere (Pennycook,
   1989a).
2. Freirean-based approaches often run the danger of setting out 'goals of
   liberation and social and political transformation as universal claims'
   (Weiler, 1991, p. 469) and operate with a problematic view that
   'consciousness' about the 'truth' and 'reality' can be achieved and can
   be liberating. I do not intend these reservations, however, to detract

from the broader orientation of work such as Elsa Auerbach's (e.g. 1993).

3. In talking of dealing seriously with all issues, I do not mean to suggest that critical pedagogy should be some dour project lacking in humour. Rather, we need to learn from the lesson that cultural studies has taught us by dealing with diverse aspects of cultural life, but always critically and often humorously.

4. I think it is worth pointing out once again that notions such as the 'Western world' always need to be treated with circumspection. Part of the influence of Christianity and its connections to a modern and English-language life-style in fact derives from Hong Kong.

5. These remarks apply particularly to ESL classes and to EFL classes where the teacher is a 'non-native teacher' (see Chapter 5 for a discussion of this term). Clearly, the question of cultural difference between teachers and students is not one that the majority of teachers around the world necessarily face.

6. I have here given the date, page numbers and wording of the edition used by Phillipson. The version of Crusoe from which I have been working is cited here as 1719/1910 and has a slightly different text. The page number for the above quote is p. 195 in my version.

7. There is of course a danger here that colonizers be seen as innocent co-victims of some historical process of colonization. The point here, however, is that the process of colonization constructed both colonized and colonizers in particular ways. For further discussion, see Bhaba (1983) and JanMohamed (1985).

References

Abbott, G, 1984, 'Should we start digging new holes?', *ELT Journal* **38** (2): 98–102.

Achebe, C, 1975, 'English and the African writer' in A Mazrui, *The political sociology of the English language*, pp. 216–23, The Hague/Paris: Mouton (Appendix B).

Alatas, Syed Hussein, 1971, *Thomas Stamford Raffles, 1781–1826: schemer or reformer?*, Sydney: Angus & Robertson.

Alatas, Syed Hussein, 1977, *The myth of the lazy native*, London: Frank Cass.

Alexandre, P, 1972, *Languages and language in Black Africa*, Evanston: Northwestern University Press (translated by FA Leavy).

Ali Fatimah, 1987, 'The Malaysian educational system and Islamic educational ideals', *Muslim Education Quarterly* **4** (2): 73–84.

Altbach, PG, 1981, 'The university as center and periphery', *Teachers' College Record* **82** (4): 601–22.

Al Zeera, Z, 1990, *Evaluation of the orientation program at the University of Bahrain: a sociocultural perspective*, unpublished doctoral dissertation, University of Toronto (OISE).

American and Canadian Committees on Modern Languages, 1928, *Modern Language Instruction in Canada*, Toronto: University of Toronto Press.

Andaya, BW, Andaya, LY, 1982, *A history of Malaysia*, London: Macmillan.

Andersen, R, 1988, *The power and the word: language, power and change*, London: Paladin.

Appadurai, A, 1990, 'Disjuncture and difference in the global cultural economy', *Public Culture* **2** (2): 1–24.

Apple, M, 1986, *Teachers and texts: a political economy of class and gender relations in education*, New York: Routledge & Kegan Paul.

Archer, M, 1990, 'Theory, culture and post-industrial society' in Featherstone, M (ed.), *Global culture: nationalism, globalization and modernity*, London: Sage, pp. 97–119.

Arnove, RF (ed.), 1982a, *Philanthropy and cultural imperialism: the foundations at home and abroad*, Boston: GK Hall & Co.

Arnove, RF, 1982b, Introduction in Arnove, RF (ed.), *Philanthropy and cultural imperialism: the foundations at home and abroad*, Boston: GK Hall & Co, pp. 1–23.

Ashcroft, B, Griffiths, G, Tiffin, H, 1989, *The empire writes back: theory and practice in post-colonial literatures*, London & New York: Routledge.

Ashraf, Syed Ali, 1987, 'Education and values: Islamic *vis-à-vis* the secularist approaches', *Muslim Education Quarterly* **4** (2): 4–16.

Ashworth, M, 1979, *The forces which shaped them*, Vancouver: New Star Books.

Asmah Haji Omar, 1979, *Language planning for unity and efficiency*, Kuala Lumpur: Penerbit Universiti Malaya.

Asmah Haji Omar, 1982, *Language and society in Malaysia*, Kuala Lumpur: Dewan Bahasa dan Pustaka.

Asmah Haji Omar, 1987, *Malay in its sociocultural context*, Kuala Lumpur: Dewan Bahasa dan Pustaka.

Asmah Haji Omar, 1990, *Attitudes in the learning of English among Malaysian students: a case study*, paper presented at the National Seminar on the Teaching of English as a Second Language, 22–24 January 1990, Genting Highlands, Malaysia.

Auerbach, E, 1986 'Competency-based ESL: one step forward or two steps back?', *TESOL Quarterly* **20**: 411–12.

Auerbach, E, 1993, 'Re-examining English Only in the ESL classroom', *TESOL Quarterly* **27** (1): 9–32.

Auerbach, E, Wallerstein, N, 1987, *English for action*, New York: Addison Wesley.

Bakhtin, M, 1981, *The dialogic imagination: four essays*, Austin Texas: University of Texas Press (translated by Caryl Emerson and Michael Holquist, edited by Michael Holquist).

Bamgbose, A, 1982, 'Standard Nigerian English: issues of identification' in Kachru, BJ (ed.), *The other tongue: English across cultures*, Urbana: University of Illinois Press, pp. 99–111.

Bamforth, D, 1993, 'Teaching as marketing', *ELT Management*, 11 February, pp. 2–4.

Banks, DJ, 1987, *From class to culture: social conscience in Malay novels since independence*, Yale University: South East Asian Studies.

Baran, PA, 1957, *The political economy of growth*, New York: Monthly Review Press.

Batsleer, J, Davies, T, O'Rourke, R, Weedon, C, 1985, *Rewriting English: cultural politics of gender and class*, London: Methuen.

Baynes, K, Bohman, J, McCarthy, T (eds), 1986, *After philosophy: end or transformation?*, Cambridge, Mass: MIT Press.

Behr, E, 1978, '*Anyone here been raped and speaks English? A foreign correspondent's life behind the lines*, Sevenoaks: Hodder & Stoughton.

Benjamin, G, 1976, 'The cultural logic of Singapore's "multiracialism" ' in Riaz Hassan (ed.), *Singapore: society in transition*, Kuala Lumpur: Oxford University Press.

Beretta, A, Davies, A, 1985, 'Evaluation of the Bangalore Project', *ELT Journal* **39** (2): 121–7.

Beretta, A, 1990, 'Implementation of the Bangalore Project', *Applied Linguistics* **11** (4): 321–37.

Berlin, J, 1988, 'Rhetoric and ideology in the writing class', *College English* **50** (5): 477–94.

Berman, EH, 1982, 'The foundations' role in American foreign policy: the case of Africa post 1945' in Arnove, RF (ed.), *Philanthropy and cultural imperialism: the foundations at home and abroad*, Boston: GK Hall & Co, pp. 203–32.

Bhaba, Homi K, 1983, 'The Other question . . .', *Screen* **24** (6): 18–36.

Bhaba, Homi K, 1990, Introduction, 'Narrating the nation' in Bhaba, HK (ed.), *Nation and narration*, London: Routledge.

Birch, D, 1986, 'Cunning beneath the verbs: demythologising Singapore English poetry' in Hyland, P (ed.), *Discharging the canon: cross-cultural readings in literature*, Singapore: Singapore University Press, pp. 147–90.

Black, M, Coward, R, 1990, 'Linguistic, social and sexual relations: a review of Dale Spender's *Man Made Language*' in Cameron, D (ed.), *The feminist critique of language: a reader*, London: Routledge.

Blasius, M, 1984, 'The discourse of world order' in Walker, RBJ (ed.), *Culture, ideology and world order*, Boulder, Colorado: Westview Press.

Bloom, A, 1987, *The closing of the America mind: how higher education has failed democracy and impoverished the souls of today's students*, New York: Simon & Schuster.

Bloom, D, 1986, 'The English Language and Singapore: a critical survey' in Kapur, BK (ed.), *Singapore studies: critical surveys of the humanities and social sciences*, Singapore: Singapore University Press, pp. 337–458.

Bodine, A, 1975, 'Androcentrism in prescriptive grammar: singular "they", sex-indefinite "he" and "he or she" ', *Language in Society* **4** (2): 129–46.

Bokamba, EG, 1982, 'The Africanization of English' in Kachru, BJ (ed.), *The other tongue: English across cultures*, Urbana: University of Illinois Press, pp. 77–98.

Bokamba, EG, 1991, 'The pronoun system in Nigerian Pidgin: a preliminary study' in Cheshire, J (ed.), *English around the world: Sociolinguistic perspectives*, Cambridge: Cambridge University Press, pp. 509–17.

Bourdieu, P, 1973, 'Cultural reproduction and social reproduction' in Brown, R (ed.), *Knowledge, education and cultural change*, London: Tavistock.

Bourne, J, 1988, ' "Natural acquisition" and a "masked pedagogy" ', *Applied Linguistics* **9** (1): 83–99.

Bowles, S, Gintis, H, 1976, *Schooling in capitalist America: educational reform and the contradictions of economic life*, New York: Basic Books.

Boyd-Barrett, JO, 1982, 'Cultural dependency and the mass media', in Gurevitch, M, Bennett, T, Curran, J, Woollacott, J (eds), *Culture, society and the media*, London and New York: Methuen.

Bradley, D, 1991, '/ae/ and /a:/ in Australian English' in Cheshire, J (ed.), *English around the world: sociolinguistic perspectives*, Cambridge: Cambridge University Press, pp. 227–34.

Brantlinger, P, 1985, 'Victorians and Africans: the genealogy of the myth of the dark continent', *Critical Inquiry*, 12 August, pp. 166–203.

Brantlinger, P, 1990 *Crusoe's footprints: cultural studies in Britain and America*, New York: Routledge.

Brewster, A, 1989, *Towards a semiotic of post-colonial discourse: university writing in Singapore and Malaysia 1949–1965*, Singapore: Heinemann Asia for Centre for Advanced Studies, NUS.

British Council 1959–60, *Annual Report*, London: The British Council.

British Council 1960–61, *Annual Report*, London: The British Council.

British Council 1968–69, *Annual Report*, London: The British Council.

British Council 1974–75, *Annual Report*, London: The British Council.

British Council 1986–87, *Annual Report*, London: The British Council.

British Council 1990, *The British Council Corporate Plane 1991/1992 to 1993/1994*, London: The British Council.

Brown, ER, 1982, 'Rockefeller medicine in China: professionalism and imperialism' in Arnove, RF (ed.), *Philanthropy and cultural imperialism: the foundations at home and abroad*, Boston: G K Hall & Co., pp. 123–46.

Brown, G, 1990, 'Cultural values: the interpretation of discourse', *ELT Journal* **44** (1): 11–17.

Brumfit, CJ, 1984, 'The Bangalore procedural syllabus', *ELT Journal* **38** (4): 233–41.

Brumfit, C, 1985, 'Creativity and constraint in the language classroom' in Quirk, R, Widdowson, HG (eds), *English in the world: teaching and learning the language and literatures*, Cambridge: Cambridge University Press, pp. 148–57.

Buchanan, I, 1972, *Singapore in Southeast Asia: an economic and political appraisal*, London: G Bell & Sons.

Burney, S, 1988, *The exotic and the restless: representation of the 'Other' in colonialist discourse*, paper presented at ISISSS '88, University of British Columbia.

Caldwell, M, 1977a, 'The British "Forward Movement" 1874–1914' in Amin, M, Caldwell, M (eds), *Malaya: the making of a neo-colony*, Nottingham: Spokesman Books, pp. 13–37.

Caldwell, M, 1977b, 'From "Emergency" to "Independence" 1948–57'. In Amin, M, Caldwell, M (eds), *Malaya: The making of a neo-colony*, Nottingham: Spokesman Books, pp. 216–65.

Candlin, CN, 1981, 'Form, function and strategy in communicative curriculum design' in Candlin, CN (ed./trans.), *The communicative teaching of English*, Harlow: Longman, pp. 24–44.

Candlin, CN, 1984, 'Syllabus design as a critical process', *Language Learning and Communication* **3** (2): 129–45.

Candlin, CN, 1989, 'Language, culture and curriculum' in Candlin, CN, McNamara, TF (eds), *Language learning and curriculum*, Sydney: NCELTR, pp. 1–24.

Carnoy, M, 1974, *Education as cultural imperialism*, New York: David McKay.

Carr, EH, 1946, *The twenty years' crisis 1919–1939*, 2nd edn, London: Macmillan.

Casewit, SD, 1985, 'Teaching English as a foreign language in Muslim countries', *Muslim Education Quarterly* **2** (2): 4–24.

Chai Hon-Chan, 1964, *The development of British Malaya 1896–1909*, Kuala Lumpur: Oxford University Press.

Chai Hon-Chan, 1971, *Planning education for a plural society*, Paris: UNESCO.

Cheeseman, HR, 1931, 'Compulsory education', *Education in Malaya*, Kuala Lumpur: Government Press, 1948, collected articles.

Chelliah, DD, 1947, *A history of the educational policy of the Straits Settlements with recommendations for a new system based on the vernaculars*, Kuala Lumpur: The Government Press.

Cheshire, J (ed.), 1991, *English around the world: sociolinguistic perspectives*, Cambridge: Cambridge University Press.

Chew, Shirley, 1976, 'The language of survival' in Hassan, R (ed.), *Singapore, society in transition*, Kuala Lumpur: Oxford University Press, pp. 149–54.

Chiew Seen-Kong, 1980, 'Bilingualism and national identity: a Singapore case study' in Afendras, E, Kuo, ECY (eds), *Language and society in Singapore*, Singapore: University of Singapore Press, pp. 233–53.

Chua Beng-Huat, 1983, 'Re-opening ideological discussion in Singapore: a new theoretical direction', *Southeast Asian Journal of Social Science* **11** (2): 31–45.

Chua Beng-Huat, 1985, 'Pragmatism of the People's Action Party Government of Singapore: a critical assessment', *Southeast Asian Journal of Social Science* **13** (2): 29–46.

Chua Beng-Huat, 1990, *Confucianization in modernizing Singapore*, paper presented at 'Beyond the Culture?' The Social Sciences and the Problem of Cross Cultural Comparison', Evangelical Academy at Loccum West Germany, 22–25 October 1990.

Chua Beng-Huat, Kuo, ECY, 1990, *The making of a new nation: cultural construction and national identity in Singapore*, paper presented at the Cultural Policy and National Identity Workshop East-West Center, Honolulu, Hawaii, June 1990.

Citravelu, Nesamalar, 1985, *The status and role of English in Malaysia*, research report, United States Information Agency.

Clammer, J, 1980, 'Religion and language in Singapore', in Afendras, E, Kuo, ECY (eds), *Language and society in Singapore*, Singapore: Singapore University Press, pp. 87–115.

Clammer, J, 1981, 'Straits Chinese literature: a minority literature as a vehicle of identity' in Tham Seong Chee (ed.), *Essays on literature and society in Southeast Asia: political and sociological perspectives*, Singapore: Singapore University Press, pp. 287–302.

Clammer, J, 1985, *Singapore: ideology, society, culture*, Singapore: Chopmen Publishers.

Clifford, H, 1898, *Studies in brown humanity*, London: Grant Richards.

Clifford, H, 1927, *In court and kampong*, London: The Richards Press.

Clifford, J, 1988, *The predicament of culture: twentieth century ethnography, literature and art*, Cambridge, Mass: Harvard University Press.

Clive, J, 1973, *Macaulay: the shaping of the historian*, New York: Knopf.

Cohn, B, 1983, 'Representing authority in Victorian England' in Hobsbawm, E, Ranger, T (eds), *The invention of tradition*, Cambridge: Cambridge University Press.

Colony of Singapore 1954, *Department of Education Annual Reports*, Singapore: Government Printing Office.

Conrad, AW, Fishman, JA, 1977, 'English as a world language: the evidence' in Fishman, JA, Cooper, RL, Conrad, AW (eds), *The spread of English: the sociology of English as an additional language*, Rowley, Mass: Newbury House, pp. 3–76.

Cooke, D, 1988, 'Ties that constrict: English as a Trojan horse' in Cumming, A, Gagne, A, Dawson, J (eds), *Awarenesses: proceedings of the 1987 TESL Ontario Conference*, Toronto: TESL Ontario, pp. 56–62.

Coombs, D, 1988, *Spreading the word: the library work of the British Council*, London and New York: Mansell Publishing.

Corder, SP, 1973, *Introducing applied linguistics*, Harmondsworth: Penguin.

Corrigan, P, 1987, 'In/forming schooling' in Livingstone, DW (ed.), *Critical pedagogy and cultural power*, Toronto: Garamond Press.

Crawford, J, 1989, *Bilingual education: history, politics, theory and practice*, Trenton, NJ: Crane Publishing.

Crewe, W (ed.), 1977a, *The English Language in Singapore*, Singapore: Eastern Universities Press.

Crewe, W, 1977b, 'Singapore English as a non-native dialect' in Crewe, W (ed.), *The English language in Singapore*, Singapore: Eastern Universities Press, pp. 96–119.

Crowley, T, 1989, *The politics of discourse: the standard language question in British cultural debates*, London: Macmillan.

Crystal, D, 1987, *The Cambridge Encyclopedia of Language*, Cambridge: Cambridge University Press.

Crystal, D, 1988, *The English language*, Harmondsworth: Penguin.

Cummins, J, 1989, *Empowering minority students*, Sacramento, CA: California Association for Bilingual Education.

Day, R, 1980, 'ESL: a factor in linguistic genocide?' in Fisher, JC, Clarke,

MA, Schachter, J (eds), *On TESOL '80, Building Bridges: research and practice in teaching English as a second language*, Washington, DC: TESOL.

Day, R, 1985, 'The ultimate inequality: linguistic genocide' in Wolfson, N, Manes, J (eds), *Language of inequality*, Berlin: Mouton, pp. 163–81.

Deckert, G, 1992, 'A pedagogical response to learned plagiarism among tertiary-level ESL students', *Occasional Papers in Applied Language Studies*, Hong Kong Baptist College, November 1992, pp. 49–56.

Defoe, D, 1719/1910, *The life and adventures of Robinson Crusoe*, Oxford: Clarendon.

de Lauretis, T. (ed.), 1986, *Feminist studies/critical studies*, Bloomington: Indiana University Press.

de Quincey, T, 1862, *Recollections of the lakes and the lake poets*, de Quincey's Works, Vol. II, Edinburgh: Adam & Charles Black.

Derrida, J, 1974, *Of grammatology*, Baltimore: Johns Hopkins University Press.

Derrida, J, 1978, *Writing and difference*, Chicago: University of Chicago Press.

de Terra, D, 1983, 'The linguagenesis of society: the implementation of the national language plan in West Malaysia' in Bain, B (ed.), *The sociogenesis of language and human conduct*, New York: Plenum Press.

Dissanayake, Wimal, 1990, 'Self, modernization and national identity: contextualizing English creative writings in Asia and the Pacific', *World Englishes* **9** (2): 125–36.

Donaldson, F, 1984, *The British Council: the first fifty years*, London: Jonathan Cape.

Dreyfus, HL, Rabinow, P, 1982, *Michel Foucault: beyond structuralism and hermeneutics*, Chicago: University of Chicago Press.

DuBois, M, 1991, 'The governance of the Third World: a Foucauldian perspective on power relations in development', *Alternatives* **16** (1): 1–30.

Edwards, D, Mercer, N, 1987, *Common knowledge: the development of understanding in the classroom*, London: Routledge.

Ee Tiang Hong, 1971, 'The poet and his role', *Focus* **5**: 120–31.

Ee Tiang Hong, 1976, *Myths for a wilderness*, Singapore: Hienemann Education Books.

Ee Tiang Hong, 1985, *Tranquerah*, Singapore: Department of English Language and Literature, NUS.

Ee Tiang Hong, 1988, 'Literature and liberation: the price of freedom' in Thumboo, E (ed.), *Literature and liberation: five essays from Southeast Asia*, Manila: Solidaridad Publishing House, pp. 11–41.

Elliott, AB, 1980, *A study of the frequency and classification of errors in the English used by science and mathematics graduates having Chinese as their first language*, Singapore: RELC.

Ellis, D, 1990, *Cross-cultural relevance in EFL materials production with special reference to Muslim culture*, paper presented at AILA '90.

Ellsworth, E, 1989, 'Why doesn't this feel empowering? Working through the repressive myths of critical pedagogy', *Harvard Educational Review* **59** (3): 297–324.

Escobar, A, 1985, 'Discourse and power in development: Michel Foucault and the relevance of his work to the third world', *Alternatives* **10**: 377–400.

Esling, J, 1991, 'Sociophonetic variation in Vancouver' in Cheshire, J (ed.), *English around the world: sociolinguistic variation*, Cambridge: Cambridge University Press, pp. 123–33.

Fairclough, N, 1989, *Language and power*, London: Longman.

Fan Yew Teng, 1990, *The song of the Merbok*, Kuala Lumpur: Egret Books.

Fanon, F, 1967, *Black skin, white masks*, New York: Grove Press.

Federated Malay States, various years, *Reports on the Federated Malay States*, London: HMSO (also contains reports for individual states, e.g. *Perak Annual Report*).

Federation of Malaya, 1951a, *Report of the Committee on Malay Education*, Kuala Lumpur: Government Printing Office, the 'Barnes Report'.

Federation of Malaya, 1951b, *Chinese schools and the education of the Chinese Malayans. The report of a mission invited by the Federation Government to study the problem of the education of Chinese in Malaya*, Kuala Lumpur: Government Press/HT Ross, the 'Fenn–Wu Report'.

Federation of Malaya, 1956, *Report of the Education Committee*, Kuala Lumpur: Government Press, the 'Razak Report'.

Fernando, L. (ed.), 1968, *Twenty-two Malaysian stories*, Singapore: Heinemann Education Books.

Fernando, L, 1976, *Scorpion orchid*, Singapore: Heinemann Education Books.

Fernando, L, 1986, *Cultures in conflict: essays on literature and the English language in South East Asia*, Singapore: Graham Brash.

Fishman, JA, 1971, 'National languages and languages of wider communication in the developing nations' in Fishman, JA (ed.), *Language in sociocultural change*, Stanford, CA: Stanford University Press, pp. 191–223.

Fishman, JA, 1977a, 'The spread of English as a new perspective for the study of "language maintenance and language shift" ' in Fishman, JA, Cooper, RL, Conrad, AW (eds), *The spread of English*, Rowley, Mass: Newbury House, pp. 108–35.

Fishman, JA, 1977b, 'Knowing, using and liking English as an additional language' in Fishman, JA, Cooper, RW, Conrad AW (eds), *The spread of English*, Rowley, Mass: Newbury House, pp. 302–26.

Fishman, JA, 1982a, 'Sociology of English as an additional language' in Kachru, BJ (ed.), *The other tongue: English across cultures*, Urbana: University of Illinois Press, pp. 15–22.

Fishman, JA, 1982b, 'Whorfianism of the third kind: ethnolinguistic diversity as a worldwide societal asset', *Language in Society* **11**: 1–14.

Fishman, JA, Cooper, RW, Conrad, AW (eds), 1977, *The spread of English*, Rowley, Mass: Newbury House.

Fishman, JA, Cooper, RL, Rosenbaum, Y, 1977, 'English around the world' in Fishman, JA, Cooper, RW, Conrad, AW (eds), *The spread of English*, Rowley, Mass: Newbury House, pp. 77–107.

Flaitz, J, 1988, *The ideology of English: French perceptions of English as a world language*, Berlin/New York/Amsterdam: Mouton de Gruyter.

Foley, D, 1984, 'Colonialism and schooling in the Philippines 1898–1970' in Altbach, PG, Kelly, GP (eds), *Education and the colonial experience*, New Brunswick: Transaction Books, 2nd revd edn, pp. 33–54.

Foley, J (ed.), 1988, *New Englishes: the case of Singapore*, Singapore: Singapore University Press.

Foucault, M, 1970, *The order of things: an archeology of the human sciences*, New York: Vintage Books.

Foucault, M, 1972, 'The discourse on language' in M Foucault, *The archeology of knowledge*, New York: Tavistock Publications.

Foucault, M, 1979, *Discipline and punish: the birth of the prison*, New York: Vintage Books.

Foucault, M, 1980a, *Power/knowledge: selected interviews and other writings 1972–1977*, New York: Pantheon Books (edited by Colin Gordon).

Foucault, M, 1980b, *The history of sexuality, Volume 1: An introduction*, New York: Vintage Books (trans. R Hurley).

Foucault, M, 1984, 'What is an author?' in Rabinow, P (ed.), *The Foucault reader*, New York: Pantheon Books.

Frank, AG, 1966, 'The development of underdevelopment', *Monthly Review*, 17–30 September.

Freire, P, 1970, *Pedagogy of the oppressed*, New York: Seabury Press.

Frith, S, 1983, 'The pleasures of the hearth' in *Formations of Pleasure*, London: Routledge & Kegan Paul, pp. 101–23.

Fu, GS, 1987, 'The Hong Kong bilingual' in Lord, R, Cheng, HNL (eds), *Language education in Hong Kong*, Hong Kong: The Chinese University Press, pp. 27–50.

Gallagher, M, 1985, 'Women and NWICO' in Lee, P (ed.), *Communication for all: new world information and communication order*, Maryknoll, NY: Orbis, pp. 33–56.

Galtung, J, 1971, 'A structural theory of imperialism', *Journal of Peace Research* **8** (2): 81–117.

Galtung, J, 1980, *The true worlds: a transnational perspective*, New York: Free Press.

Galtung, J, 1985, 'Social communication and global problems' in Lee, P (ed.), *Communication for all: new world information and communication order*, Maryknoll, NY: Orbis, pp. 1–16.

Gendzier, I, 1985, *Managing political change: social scientists and the Third World*, Boulder, Colorado: Westview Press.

George, J, Rev., 1867, *The mission of Great Britain to the world, or some of the lessons which she is now teaching*, Toronto: Dudley & Burns.

George, TJS, 1973, *Lee Kuan Yew's Singapore*, London: Andre Deutsch.

Gibbons, A, 1985, *Information, ideology and communication: the new nations' perspectives on an intellectual revolution*, Lanham, MD: University Press of America.

Gibbons, J, 1990, 'Applied linguistics in court', *Applied Linguistics* **11** (3): 229–37.

Giroux, HA, 1983, *Theory and resistance in education: a pedagogy for the opposition*, South Hadley, MA: Bergin & Garvey.

Giroux, HA, 1988, *Schooling and the struggle for public life: critical pedagogy in the modern age*, Minneapolis: University of Minnesota Press.

Giroux, H, 1991, 'Modernism, postmodernism and feminism: rethinking the boundaries of educational discourse' in Giroux, H (ed.), *Postmodernism, feminism and cultural politics: redrawing educational boundaries*, New York: SUNY Press, pp. 1–59.

Giroux, H, Simon, R and contributors, 1989, *Popular culture, schooling and everyday life*, Toronto: OISE Press.

Goh Poh Seng, 1972, *If we dream too long*, Singapore: Island Press.

Gook Aik Suan, 1981, 'Singapore: a third world fascist state', *Journal of Contemporary Asia* **11** (2): 244–54.

Gopinathan, S, 1976, 'Towards a national educational system' in Hassan, R (ed.), *Singapore: society in transition*, Kuala Lumpur: Oxford University Press, pp. 67–83.

Gopinathan, S, 1980, 'Language policy in education' in Afendras, E, Kuo, ECY (eds), *Language and society in Singapore*, Singapore: Singapore University Press, pp. 175–202.

Gopinathan, S, Saravanan, V, 1985, 'Varieties of English and educational linguistics', *Singapore Journal of Education* **7**: 64–71.

Gordon, C, 1980, Afterword in Gordon, C (ed.), *Power/knowledge: selected interviews and other writings 1972–1977 by Michel Foucault*, New York: Pantheon Books, pp. 229–59.

Government of Singapore, 1965, *Singapore year book*, Singapore: Government Printing Office.

Government of Malaysia, 1975, *Third Malaysia plan 1976–1980*, Kualu Lumpur: National Printing Department.

Government of Malaysia, 1980, *Fourth Malaysia plan 1981–1985*, Kuala Lumpur: National Printing Department.

Government of Malaysia, 1985, *Fifth Malaysia plan 1986–1990*, Kuala Lumpur: National Printing Department.

Graman, T, 1988, 'Education for humanization: applying Paulo Freire's pedagogy to learning a second language', *Harvard Educational Review* **58** (4): 433–48.

Grant, L, 1993, 'Where have all the raped Bosnian women gone?', *The Globe and Mail*, Saturday 14 August 1993, p. D1.

Greenwood, J, 1985, 'Bangalore revisited: a reluctant complaint', London: George Bell & Sons.

Guest, E, 1838/1882, *A history of English rhythms*. London: George Bell and Sons.

Gupta, Anthea Fraser, 1989, 'Singapore colloquial English and standard English', *Singapore Journal of Education* **10** (2): 33–9.

Gurevitch, M, Bennett, T, Curran, J, Woollacott, J (eds), 1982, *Culture, society and the media*, London and New York: Methuen.

Habermas, J, 1972, *Knowledge and human interests*, London: Heinemann.

Habermas, J, 1984, *The theory of communicative action*, Boston: Beacon Press.

Hall, DGE, 1964, *A history of Southeast Asia*, London: Macmillan.

Han Suyin, 1956, . . . *And the rain my drink*, Harmondsworth: Penguin.

Harlow, B, 1987, *Resistance literature*, New York: Methuen.

Harrex, SC, 1981, 'Social changes and fictional dynamics: an approach to some Indian and Malaysian English-language writers' in Wang Gungwu, Guerrero, M, Man, P (eds), *Society and the writer: essays on literature in modern Asia*, Canberra: Australian National University, pp. 295–319.

Harris, R, 1980, *The language-makers*, Ithaca, NY: Cornell University Press.

Harris, R, 1981, *The language myth*, London: Duckworth.

Harris, R, 1987, *The language machine*, London: Duckworth.

Harris, R, 1988, 'Murray, Moore and the myth' in Harris, R (ed.), *Linguistic thought in England, 1914–1945*, London: Duckworth, pp. 1–26.

Harris, R, 1991, 'English versus Islam: the Asian voice of Salman Rushdie' in Chan, M, Harris, R (eds), *Asian voices in English*, Hong Kong: Hong Kong University Press, pp. 87–96.

Hindmarsh, RX, 1978, 'English as an international language', *ELT Documents: English as an international language* **102:** 40–43.

Hing Ai Yun, 1984, 'Capitalist development, class and race' in Husin Ali, S (ed.), *Ethnicity, class and development: Malaysia*, Kuala Lumpur: Persatuan Sains Sosial Malaysia, pp. 296–328.

Hirsch, JD Jr, 1987, *Cultural literacy: what every American needs to know*, Boston: Houghton Mifflin.

Ho Seng Ong, 1952, *Education for unity in Malaya*, Penang: Malayan Teachers' Union, 1949, Ed D Dissertation, University of Denver.

Ho Wing Meng, 1989, 'Value premises underlying the transformation of Singapore' in Kernial Singh Sandhu, Wheatley, P (eds), *Management of success: the moulding of modern Singapore*, Singapore: Institute of Southeast Asian Studies, pp. 671–91.

Hobsbawm, E, 1983, Introduction, 'Inventing traditions' in Hobsbawm, E, Ranger, T (eds), *The invention of tradition*, Cambridge: Cambridge University Press.

Holsti, KJ, 1985, *The dividing discipline*, Boston: Allen & Unwin.

hooks, bell, 1988, *Talking back: thinking feminist, thinking black*, Toronto: Between the Lines.

Hountondji, P, 1983, *African philosophy: myth and reality*, Bloomington: Indiana University Press.

Howatt, APR, 1984a, *A history of English language teaching*, Oxford: Oxford University Press.

Howatt, APR, 1984b, 'Language teaching traditions: 1884 revisited', *ELT Journal* **38** (4): 279–82.

Husin Ali, S, 1984, 'Social relations: the ethnic and class factors' in Husin, Ali S (ed.), *Ethnicity, class and development: Malaysia*, Kuala Lumpur: Persatuan Sains Sosial Malaysia, pp. 13–31.

Husin Ali, S, 1989, 'Direct from America into our living-rooms', *Aliran Monthly* **9** (9): 20–1.

Hussin Mutalib, 1990, *Islam and ethnicity in Malay politics*, Singapore: Oxford University Press.

Hymes, D, 1983, 'Report from an underdeveloped country. Toward linguistic competence in the United States' in Bain, B (ed.), *The sociogenesis of language and human conduct*, New York and London: Plenum Press.

Illich, I, 1981a, *Shadow work*, Boston: M Boyars.

Illich, I, 1981b, 'Taught mother language and vernacular tongue', Introduction in Pattanayak, DP (ed.), *Multilingualism and mother-tongue education*, Delhi: Oxford University Press, pp. 1–39.

Inkeles, A, Smith, DH, 1974, *Becoming modern*, London: Heinemann Education Books.

Ishak Shari, Jomo, KS, 1984, 'The new economic policy and "national unity" ' in Husin Ali, S (ed.), *Ethnicity, class and development*, Kuala Lumpur: Persatuan Sains Sosial Malaysia, pp. 329–55.

Iyer, P, 1988, *Video night in Kathmandu and other reports from the not-so-far East*, New York: Random House Vintage Departures.

James, CLR, 1963, *Beyond a boundary*, New York: Pantheon Books.

JanMohamed, AR, 1985, 'The economy of manichean allegory: the function of racial difference in colonialist literature', *Critical Inquiry* **12** (Autumn): 59–82.

Jernudd, B, 1981, 'Planning language treatment: linguistics for the third world', *Language in Society* **10** (1): 43–52.

Jespersen, O, 1922/1969, *Language: its nature, development and origin*, London: George Allen & Unwin.

Jespersen, O, 1938/1968, *Growth and structure of the English language*, Toronto: Collier-Macmillan.

Jeyaratnam, P, 1987, *First loves*, Singapore: Times Books International.

Jeyaratnam, P, 1988, *Raffles place ragtime*, Singapore: Times Books International.

Jochnowitz, G, 1986, 'Teaching at a provincial Chinese university', *American Scholar* **55** (4): 521–7.

Joseph, GG, Reddy, V, Searle-Chatterjee, M, 1990, 'Eurocentrism in the social sciences', *Race and Class* **31** (4): 1–26.

Judd, EL, 1983, 'TESOL as a political act: a moral question' in Handscombe, J, Orem, RA, Taylor, BP (eds), *ON TESOL '83*, Washington, DC: TESOL, pp. 265–73.

Kachru, BJ, 1982a, Introduction, 'The other side of English' in Kachru, BJ (ed.), *The other tongue: English across cultures*, Urbana: University of Illinois Press.

Kachru, BJ, 1982b, 'Models for non-native Englishes' in Kachru, BJ (ed.), *The other tongue: English across cultures*, Urbana: University of Illinois Press, pp. 31–57.

Kachru, BJ, 1985, 'Standards, codification and sociolinguistic realism: the English language in the outer circle' in Quirk, R, Widdowson, HG (eds), *English in the world*, Cambridge: Cambridge University Press.

Kachru, BJ, 1986, *The alchemy of English: the spread, functions and models of non-native Englishes*, Oxford: Pergamon Press.

Kachru, BJ, 1990, 'World Englishes and applied linguistics', *World Englishes* **9** (1): 3–20.

Kachru, BJ, Quirk, R, 1981, Introduction in Smith, LE (ed.), *English for cross-cultural communication*, London: Macmillan.

Kallen, J, 1991, 'Sociolinguistic variation and methodology: *after* as a Dublin variable' in Cheshire, J (ed.), *English around the world: sociolinguistic perspectives*, Cambridge: Cambridge University Press, pp. 61–74.

Kamal Hassan M, 1987, 'Education and community development', *Jurnal Pendidikan Islam*, December 1987, 1–18.

Kanpol, B, 1990, 'Political applied linguistics and postmodernism: towards an engagement of similarity within difference. A reply to Pennycook', *Issues in Applied Linguistics* **1** (2): 238–50.

Kanyoro, Musimbi RA, 1991, 'The politics of the English language in Kenya and Tanzania' in Cheshire, J (ed.), *English around the world: sociolinguistic perspectives*, Cambridge: Cambridge University Press, pp. 391–401.

Kearney, R, 1988, *The wake of imagination*, Minneapolis: University of Minnesota Press.

Kee Than Chye, 1987, *1984 here and now*, Petaling Jaya: K Das Ink.

Kelly, LG, 1969, *25 centuries of language teaching*, Rowley, Mass: Newbury House.

Koh Tai Ann, 1981, 'Singapore writing in English: the literary tradition and cultural identity' in Tham Seong Chee (ed.), *Essays on literature and society in Southeast Asia: political and sociological perspectives*, Singapore: Singapore University Press, pp. 160–86.

Koh Tai Ann, 1984, 'Intertextual selves: fiction-makers in two "Singapore" novels' in Nicholson, CE, Chatterjee, R (eds), *Tropic crucible: self and theory in language and literature*, Singapore: Singapore University Press, pp. 163–92.

Koh Tai Ann, 1986, 'The empire's orphans: stayers and quitters in *A bend in the river* and *Scorpion orchid*' in Hyland, P (ed.), *Discharging the canon: cross-cultural readings in literature*, Singapore: Singapore University Press, pp. 38–53.

Koh Tai Ann, 1989, 'Self, family and the state: social mythology in the Singapore novel in English', *Journal of Southeast Asian Studies* **20** (2): 273–87.

Koh Tai Ann, 1990, 'Telling stories, expressing values: the Singapore novel in English', *Tenggara* **25:** 96–109.

Koh Tai Ann, 1991, '*Making the self at home: the writing in English from Peninsular Malaya/Malaysia and Singapore*, paper presented at the International Conference on Migration, 7–9 February 1991, NUS/RELC.

Kon, S, 1986, *The scholar and the dragon*. Singapore: Federal Publications.

Kopf, D, 1984, 'Orientalism and the Indian educated élite' in Altbach, PG, Kelly, GP (eds), *Education and the colonial experience*, New Brunswick: Transaction Books, 2nd revd edn, pp. 117–36.

Kothari, R, 1981, 'Cultural roots of another development', *Development: seeds of change* **3/4:** 80–2.

Kothari, R, 1987, 'On humane governance', *Alternatives* **12:** 277–90.

Kramsch, C, 1993, *Context and culture in language teaching*, Oxford: Oxford University Press.

Krashen, SD, Terrell, TD, 1983, *The natural approach: language acquisition in the classroom*, Oxford: Pergamon Press.

Kua Kia Soong, 1985, *The Chinese schools of Malaysia: a protean saga*, Kuala Lumpur: United Chinese School Committees Association of Malaysia.

Kua Kia Soong, 1986, *Of myths and mystification*, Kuala Lumpur: Annual Magazine Arcade.

Kua Kia Soong (ed.), 1987a, *Defining Malaysian culture*, Petaling Jaya: K Das Ink.

Kua Kia Soong (ed.), 1987b, *Polarisation in Malaysia: the root causes*, Kuala Lumpur: K Das Ink for Malaysian Chinese Research and Resource Centre.

Kua Kia Soong, 1989, *445 days behind the wire: an account of the Oct 87 ISA detentions*, Kuala Lumpur: Resource and Research Centre, Selangor Chinese Assembly Hall.

Kua Kia Soong (ed.), 1990, *Malaysian cultural policy and democracy*, Kuala Lumpur: Resource and Research Centre, Selangor Chinese Assembly Hall.

Kuo, Eddie CY, 1976, 'A sociolinguistic profile' in Riaz, Hassan (ed.), *Singapore: society in transition*, Kuala Lumpur: Oxford University Press.

Kuo, Eddie CY, 1977, 'The status of English in Singapore: a sociolinguistic analysis' in Crewe, W (ed.), *The English languages in Singapore*, Singapore: Eastern Universities Press, pp. 10–33.

Kuo, Eddie CY, 1980a, 'The sociolinguistic situation in Singapore: unity in diversity' in Afendras, E, Kuo, ECY (eds), *Language and society in Singapore*, Singapore: Singapore University Press, pp. 39–62.

Kuo, Eddie CY, 1980b, 'Multilingualism and mass media communications in Singapore' in Afendras, E, Kuo, ECY (eds), *Language and society in Singapore*, Singapore: Singapore University Press, pp. 116–36.

Kuo, Eddie CY, 1985, 'Language and social mobility in Singapore' in Wolfson, N, Manes, J (eds), *Language of inequality*, Berlin: Mouton, pp. 337–54.

Kuo, Eddie CY, Chen, PSJ, 1983, *Communication policy and planning in Singapore*, London: Kegan Paul International.

Kwan-Terry, Anna, 1989, 'Education and the pattern of language use among ethnic Chinese school children in Singapore', *International Journal of the Sociology of Language* 80: 5–31.

Kwan-Terry, Anna, 1991, 'The economics of language in Singapore: students' use of extracurricular language lessons', *Journal of Asian Pacific Communication* 2 (1): 69–89.

Kwan-Terry, Anna, 1993, 'Cross-currents in teaching English in Singapore', *World Englishes* 12 (1): 75–84.

Laitin, D, 1977, *Politics, language and thought: the Somali experience*, Chicago: University of Chicago Press.

Le Blond, M, 1986, 'Drama in Singapore: towards an English language theatre' in Hyland, P (ed.), *Discharging the canon: cross-cultural readings in literature*, Singapore: Singapore University Press, pp. 112–25.

Lee Kam Hing, 1981, 'Malaysia: new state and old elites' in Jeffrey, R (ed.), *Asia – the winning of independence*, London: Macmillan, pp. 213–57.

Lee Kok Liang, 1981, *Flowers in the sky*, Kuala Lumpur: Heinemann Asia.

Le Page, RB, 1984, 'Retrospect and prognosis in Malaysia and Singapore', *International Journal of the Sociology of Language* 45: 113–26.

Le Page, R, 1985, 'Language standardization problems of Malaysia set in context', *Southeast Asian Journal of Social Science* 13 (1): 29–39.

Le Page, R, Tabouret-Keller, A, 1985, *Acts of identity*, London: Cambridge University Press.

Lerner, D, 1958, *The passing of traditional society*, New York: Free Press.

Lim Kit Siang, 1986, *Malaysia: crisis of identity*, Petaling Jaya: Democratic Action Party.

Lim, Catherine, 1982, *The serpent's tooth*, Singapore: Times Books International.

Lim, Catherine, 1986, *English in Singapore: a study of its status and solidarity and the attitudes to its use*, unpublished doctoral dissertation, National University of Singapore, Singapore.

Lim, Catherine, 1989, *The role of English in the development of a national identity in a multilingual setting: the Singapore dilemma*, paper presented at the International Conference on 'Language Learning: Theory into Practice', 17–19 July 1989, Kuala Lumpur.

Lim, Catherine, 1991, *'English for technology – Yes! English for culture – No!' A writer's views on a continuing Southeast Asian dilemma*, paper presented at the International Conference on 'Language Education: Development and Interaction', Ho Chi Minh City, 30 March – 1 April, 1991.

Lim Suchen, Christine, 1984, *Rice Bowl*, Singapore: Graham Brash.

Lim Suchen, Christine, 1990, *Gift from the gods*, Singapore: Graham Brash.

Lim, Shirley, 1980, *Crossing the peninsula and other poems*, Singapore: Heinemann Education Books.

Lim, Shirley, 1985, *No man's grove*, Singapore: Department of English Language and Literature.

Lim, Shirley, 1986, 'Reading Wordsworth on the equatorial line' in Hyland, P (ed.), *Discharging the canon: cross-cultural readings in literature*, Singapore: Singapore University Press, pp. 126–32.

Lim, Shirley, 1988, 'Voices from the hinterland: plurality and identity in the national literatures in English from Malaysia and Singapore', *World Literature Written in English* **28** (1): 145–53.

Lim, Shirley, 1989a, 'The English-language writer in Singapore' in Kernial Singh Sandhu, Wheatley, P (eds), *Management of success: the moulding of modern Singapore*, Singapore: Institute of Southeast Asian Studies, pp. 523–51.

Lim Geok-Lin, Shirley, 1989b, 'Finding a native voice – Singaporean literature in English', *The Journal of Commonwealth Literature* **24** (1): 30–48.

Lim Geok-Lin, Shirley, 1990, 'Semiotics, experience and the material self: an inquiry into the subject of the contemporary Asian woman writer', *World Englishes* **9** (2): 175–91.

Llamzon, TA, 1977, 'Emerging patterns in the English language situation in Singapore today' in Crewe, W (ed.), *The English language in Singapore*, Singapore: Eastern Universities Press, pp. 34–45.

Loh Fook Seng, P, 1970, 'The nineteenth-century British approach to Malay education', *Jurnal Pendidekan* **1** (1): 105–15.

Loh Fook Seng, P, 1975, *Seeds of separatism: educational policy in Malaya 1874–1940*, Kuala Lumpur: Oxford University Press.

Loh Kok Wah, 1984, 'The socio-economic basis of ethnic consciousness: the Chinese in the 1970s' in Husin Ali, S (ed.), *Ethnicity, class and development: Malaysia*, Kuala Lumpur: Persatuan Sains Sosial Malaysia, pp. 93–112.

Lord, R, T'sou, BK, 1985, *The language bomb*, Hong Kong: Longman.

Lorde, A, 1984, *Sister/outsider*, Trumansburg, NY: The Crossing Press.

Loveday, L, 1982, *The sociolinguistics of learning and using a non-native language*. Oxford: Pergamon Press.

Lubega, S, 1988, 'English as an international language: the concept and misconceptions', *Journal of English as a Second Language* **1**: 54–64, Nigeria.

Luk Hung-Kay, B, 1991, 'Chinese culture in the Hong Kong curriculum: heritage and colonialism', *Comparative Education Review* **35** (4): 650–68.

Luke, A, McHoul, A, Mey, JL, 1990, 'On the limits of language planning: class, state and power' in Baldauf, RB Jr, Luke, A (eds), *Language planning and education in Australasia and the South Pacific*, Clevedon: Multilingual Matters, pp. 25–44.

Lyons, J, 1981, *Language and linguistics*, Cambridge: Cambridge University Press.

Macaulay, TB, 1835/1972, 'Minute on Indian Education' in Clive, J, Pinney, T (eds), *Thomas Babington Macaulay. Selected writings*, Chicago: University of Chicago Press.

MacCabe, C (ed.), 1985, *Futures for English*, Manchester: Manchester University Press.

Mahathir bin Mohamad, 1970, *The Malay dilemma*, Kuala Lumpur: Federal Publications.

Mahathir bin Mohamad, 1986, *The challenge*, Petaling Jaya: Pelandak Publications.

Maher, J, 1986, 'The development of English as an international language of medicine', *Applied Linguistics* **7** (2): 206–18.

Malshe, M, 1989, 'The communicative approach and ESL pedagogy in India: some theoretical and practical implications', *Journal of English and Foreign Languages* **4** (December): 39–51, CIEFL Hyderabad.

Maniam, KS, 1981, *The return*, Kuala Lumpur: Heinemann Asia.

Marckwardt, AH, 1967, 'Teaching English as a foreign language: a survey of the past decade', *The Linguistic Reporter*, Supplement 19, pp. 1–8.

Mariam Zamani Bt Md Ismail, 1983, *Sociocultural factors that affect Malaysian students' attitudes towards English*, unpublished master's thesis National University of Singapore.

Marshall, DF, 1986, 'The question of an official language: language rights and the English Language Amendment', *International Journal of the Sociology of Language* **60**: 7–75.

Martin, E, 1987, *The woman in the body*, Boston: Beacon Press.

Masemann, VL, 1986, 'Critical ethnography in the study of comparative education' in Altbach, PG, Kelly, GP (eds), *New approaches to comparative education*, Chicago: University of Chicago Press, pp. 11–25.

Maxwell, G, 1927/1983, 'Some problems of education and public health in Malaya' in Kratoska, PH (ed.), *Honourable intentions: talks on the British Empire in South-East Asia delivered at the Royal Colonial Institute 1874–1928*, Singapore: Oxford University Press.

Mayhew, A, 1926, *The education of India*, London: Faber & Gwyer.

Maznah, M, Saravanamuttu, J, 1990, 'The case for integration' in Kua Kia Soong (ed.), *Malaysian cultural policy and democracy*, Kuala Lumpur: Resource and Research Centre, Selangor Chinese Assembly Hall, pp. 99–108.

Mazrui, A, 1975a, *The political sociology of the English language*, The Hague/ Paris: Mouton.

Mazrui, A, 1975b, 'The African university as a multinational corporation: problems of penetration and dependency', *Harvard Education Review* **45**: 191–210.

Mazrui, A, 1986, 'From the Semites to the Anglo-Saxons: culture and civilization in changing communication', *Alternatives* **11** (1): 3–43.

Mazrui, A, 1990, 'The Satanic Verses or a satanic novel? Moral dilemmas of the Rushdie Affair', *Alternatives* **15** (1): 97–121.

McCallen, B, 1989, *English: a world commodity. The international market for training in English as a foreign language*, London: The Economist Intelligence Unit.

McCrum, R, Cran, W, MacNeil, R, 1986, *The story of English*, New York: Elizabeth Sifton Books/Viking.

McLaren, P, 1989, *Life in schools: an introduction to critical pedagogy in the foundations of education*, New York: Longman.

Mead, R, 1988, *Malaysia's national language policy and the legal system*, New Haven, Conn: Yale University South East Asia Studies.

Mey, J, 1985, *Whose language? A study in linguistic pragmatics*, Amsterdam: John Benjamins.

Meyer, WH, 1988, *Transnational media and Third World development: the structure and impact of imperialism*, New York: Greenwood Press.

Ministry of Education, 23 March, 1956, *Report of the Official Committee on the Teaching of English Overseas*, London: Ministry of Education.

Ministry of Education, 1979, Report on the Ministry of Education 1978. Singapore: Ministry of Education (The 'Goh Report').

Mohd. Nor Wan Daud, Wan, 1989, *The concept of knowledge in Islam and its implications for education in a developing country*, London: Mansell.

Morgan, B, 1987, 'Three dreams of language *or* No longer immured in the Bastille of the humanist word', *College English* **49** (4): 449–58.

Morgenthau, HJ, 1952, 'Another "great debate": the national interest of the US', *The American Political Science Review* **46** (4): 971–8, reprinted in Smith, M, Little R, Shackleton, M (eds), 1981, *Perspectives on world politics*, London: Croom Helm/The Open University Press, pp. 47–53. Page numbers in text refer to this edition.

Morgenthau, H, 1973, *Politics among nations*, New York: Alfred A Knopf.

Morse, R, 1991, 'A case of (mis)taken identity: politics and aesthetics in some recent Singaporean novels' in Chan, M, Harris, R (eds), *Asian voices in English*, Hong Kong: Hong Kong University Press, pp. 131–45.

Moskowitz, G, 1978, *Caring and sharing in the foreign language class*, Rowley, Mass: Newbury House.

Mowlana, H, 1986, *Global information and world communication*, New York and London: Longman.

Mudimbe, VY, 1988, *The invention of Africa: gnosis, philosophy and the order of knowledge*, Bloomington: Indiana University Press.

Mukherjee, T, 1986, 'ESL: an imported new empire?', *Journal of Moral Education* **15** (1): 43–9.

Murray, DM, 1982, 'The great walls of China', *Today's Education* **71**: 55–8.

Muzaffar, Chandra, 1984, 'Has the communal situation worsened over the last decade? Some preliminary thoughts' in Husin Ali, S (ed.), *Ethnicity, class and development: Malaysia*, Kuala Lumpur: Persatuan Sains Sosial Malaysia, pp. 356–82.

Muzaffar, Chandra, 1989, *Challenges and choices in Malaysian politics and society*, Penang: Aliran.

Nagle, JS, 1928, *Educational needs of the Straits Settlements and Federated Malay States*, unpublished doctoral dissertation, Johns Hopkins University.

Nandy, A, 1983, *The intimate enemy: loss and recovery of self under colonialism*, Delhi: Oxford University Press.

Nandy, A, 1989, *The Tao of cricket: on games of destiny and the destiny of games*, New Delhi: Penguin.

Nayar, PB, 1989, *From Krasher to Ashen: ethnocentrism and universality in TESOL*, paper presented at TESOL '89, San Antonio, Texas.

Naysmith, J, 1987, 'English as imperialism?', *Language Issues* **1** (2): 3–5.

Ndebele, NS, 1987, 'The English language and social change in South Africa', *The English Academy Review* **4**: 1–16.

Nelson, C, 1982, 'Intelligibility and non-native varieties of English' in Kachru, BJ (ed.), *The other tongue: English across cultures*, Urbana: University of Illinois Press, pp. 58–73.

Newman, J, 1986, 'Singapore's Speak Mandarin Campaign: the educational argument', *Southeast Asian Journal of Social Science*, **14** (2): 52–67.

Newmeyer, FJ, 1986, *The politics of linguistics*, Chicago: University of Chicago Press

New Straits Times, Kuala Lumpur.

Ngũgĩ wa Thiong'o, 1985, 'The language of African literature', *New Left Review* **150** (March/April): 109–27.

Ngũgĩ wa Thiong'o, 1986, *Decolonising the mind: the politics of language in African literature*, London: James Currey.

Ngũgĩ wa Thiong'o, 1993, *Moving the centre: the struggle for cultural freedoms*, London: James Currey.

Nicholson, L (ed.), 1990, *Feminism/postmodernism*, New York and London: Routledge.

Nik Safiah Karim, 1989, *The controlling domains of Bahasa Malaysia: the story of language planning in Malaysia*, paper presented at the Third Tun Razak Conference, Ohio University, Athens, Ohio, 1–2 April 1989.

Niranjana, Tejaswini, 1992, *Siting translation: history, post-structuralism and the colonial context*, Berkeley: University of California Press.

Ogden, CK, 1968, *Basic English: International Second Language*, New York: Harcourt Brace & World Inc. A revised and expanded version of *The system of Basic English*, prepared by EC Graham.

Osman-Rani, H. (1990) Economic development and ethnic integration: the Malaysian experience. *Sojourn* **5** (1): 1–34.

Ovando, CJ, 1990, 'Politics and pedagogy: the case of bilingual education', *Harvard Education Review* **60** (3): 341–56.

Ożóg, ACK, 1989, 'English for Islamic purposes – a pleas for cross-cultural consideration' in Bickley, V (ed.), *Language teaching and learning styles within and across cultures*, Hong Kong: Institute of Language in Education.

Ożóg, CK, 1990, 'The English language in Malaysia and its relationship with the National Language' in Baldauf, RJ Jr, Luke, A (eds), *Language planning and education in Australasia and the South Pacific*, Clevedon: Multilingual Matters, pp. 305–18.

Palmer, HE, 1917/1968, *The scientific study and teaching of languages*, London: Oxford University Press.

Pattanayak, DP, 1969, *Aspects of applied linguistics*, London: Asia Publishing House.

Pattanayak, D, 1986, Foreward in Annamalai, E, Jernudd, B, Rubin, J (eds), *Language planning: proceedings of an institute*, Mysore and Honolulu: Central Institute of Indian Languages and East West Center.

Pêcheux, M, 1982, *Language, semantics and ideology: stating the obvious* (translated by Harbans Nagpal), London: Macmillan.

Peirce, BN, 1989, 'Toward a pedagogy of possibility in the teaching of English internationally', *TESOL Quarterly* **23** (3): 401–20.

Peirce, BN, 1990, 'The author responds', *TESOL Quarterly* **24** (1): 105–12.

Pendley, C, 1983, 'Language policy and social transformation in contemporary Singapore', *Southeast Asian Journal of Social Science* **11** (2): 46–58.

Pennycook, A, 1989a, 'The concept of Method, interested knowledge and the politics of language teaching', *TESOL Quarterly* **23** (4): 589–618.

Pennycook, A, 1989b, 'English as an international language and the insurrection of subjugated knowledges', paper presented at the Fifth International Conference of the Institute of Language in Education, Hong Kong, 13 December 1989: 'LULTAC '89', published in Bickely, V (ed.), *Language use, language teaching and the curriculum*, Hong Kong: Institute of Language in Education.

Pennycook, A, 1989c, ' "The Chinese they" Creating and reflecting the discourse on China', paper presented at the First OISE Graduate Student Conference, OISE, 16 May 1989.

Pennycook, A, 1990a, 'The diremptive/redemptive project: postmodern reflections on culture and knowledge in international academic relations', *Alternatives* **15** (1): 53–81.

Pennycook, A, 1990b, 'Towards a critical applied linguistics for the 1990s', *Issued in Applied Linguistics* **1** (1): 9–29.

Pennycook, A, 1990c, 'Critical pedagogy and second language education', *System* **18** (3): 303–14.

Pennycook, A, 1991, 'A reply to Kanpol', *Issues in Applied Linguistics* **2** (2): 305–12.

Pennycook, A, in press, 'Incommensurable discourses', *Applied Linguistics* **15**.

Phillipson, R, 1986, 'English rules: a study of language pedagogy and imperialism' in Phillipson, R, Skutnabb-Kangas, T (eds), *Linguicism rules in education*, Roskilde University Centre, Denmark, pp. 124–343.

Phillipson, R, 1988, 'Linguicism: structures and ideologies in linguistic imperialism' in Cummins, J, Skutnabb-Kangas, T (eds), *Minority education: from shame to struggle*, Avon: Multilingual Matters.

Phillipson, R, 1991, 'Some items on the hidden agenda of second/foreign language acquisition' in Phillipson, R, Kellerman, E, Selinker, L, Sharwood-Smith, M, Swain, M (eds), *Foreign/second language pedagogy research*, Clevedon: Multilingual Matters, pp. 38–51.

Phillipson, R, 1992, *Linguistic imperialism*, Oxford: Oxford Univesity Press.

Piepho, H.-E., 1981, 'Establishing objectives in the teaching of English' in Candlin, CN (ed./trans.), *The communicative teaching of English*, Harlow: Longman, pp. 8–23.

Platt, J, Weber, H, 1980, *English in Singapore and Malaysia: Status, Features, Functions*, Kuala Lumpur: Oxford University Press.

Platt, J, Weber, H, Ho, ML, 1984, *The new Englishes*, London: Routledge & Kegan Paul.

Politi, J, 1985, Commentary in Quirk, R, Widdowson, HG (eds), *English in the world: teaching and learning the language and literatures*, Cambridge: Cambridge University Press.

Popkewitz, TS, 1984, *Paradigm and ideology in educational research*, Basingstoke: Falmer Press.

Porter, E, 1987, 'Foreign involvement in China's colleges and universities: a historical perspective', *International Journal of Intercultural Relations* **11** (4): 369–85.

Prabhu, NS, 1987, *Second language pedagogy*, Oxford: Oxford University Press.

Prabhu, NS, 1990, 'Comments on Alan Beretta's paper: "Implementation of the Bangalore Project" ', *Applied Linguistics* **11** (4): 338–40.

Preston, PW, 1986, *Making sense of development*, London and New York: Routledge & Kegan Paul.

Pride, JB, 1979, 'Communicative needs in the use and learning of English' in Richards, JC (ed.), *RELC Occasional Papers, No. 8, New Varieties of English: issues and approaches*, Singapore: SEAMEO RELC, pp. 33–72.

Prodromou, L, 1988, 'English as cultural action', *ELT Journal* **42** (2): 73–83.

Puru Shotam, Nirmala, 1987, *The social negotiation of language in the Singaporean everyday life world*, unpublished doctoral dissertation, National University of Singapore, Singapore.

Quirk, R, 1981, 'International communication and the concept of nuclear English' in Smith, LE (ed.), *English for cross-cultural communication*, London: Macmillan.

Quirk, R, 1985, 'The English language in a global context' in Quirk, R, Widdowson, HG (eds), *English in the world*, Cambridge: Cambridge University Press.

Quirk, R, 1988, 'The question of standards in the international use of English' in Lowenberg, PH (ed.), *Language spread and language policy: issues, implications and case studies*, Georgetown University Round Table on Language and Linguistics, Washington, DC: Georgetown University Press.

Raffles, Lady SH (ed.), 1835, *Memoir of the life and public services of Sir Thomas Stamford Raffles*, London: J Murray.

Rahim, A, 1993, 'The political economy of English education in Muslim Bengal: 1871–1912', *Comparative Education Review* **36** (3): 309–21.

Rahim, SA, 1986, 'Language as power apparatus: observations on English and cultural policy in nineteenth-century India', *World Englishes* **5** (2/3): 231–39.

Raimes, A, 1990, 'The TOEFL Test of Written English: causes for concern', *TESOL Quarterly* **24** (3): 427–42.

Rajah, MT, 1990, 'Socio-political changes and their implications for second language learning: the case of Malaysia' in Harrison, B (ed.), *Culture and the Language Classroom ELT Documents* **132**: 108–16.

Rampton, MBH, 1990, 'Displacing the "native speaker": expertise, affiliation and inheritance', *ELT Journal* **44** (2): 97–101.

Ranger, T, 1983, 'The invention of tradition in colonial Africa' in Hobsbawm, E, Ranger, T (eds), *The invention of tradition*, Cambridge: Cambridge University Press.

Rao, Raja, 1938, *Kanthapura*, London: George Allen & Unwin.

Report of the Education Review Committee, 1960, Kuala Lumpur: Government Printers (The 'Rahman Report').

Richard, N, 1987, 'Postmodernism and periphery', *Third Text* **23**: 5–12.

Richards, IA, 1943, *Basic English and its uses*, London: Kegan Paul.

Richards, JC, 1982, 'Singapore English: rhetorical and communicative styles' in Kachru, BJ (ed.), *The other tongue: English across cultures*, Urbana: University of Illinois Press, pp. 154–67.

Robins, RH, 1979, *A short history of linguistics*, New York: Longman, 2nd edn.

Robinson, I, 1975, *The new grammarians' funeral: a critique of Noam Chomsky's linguistics*, Cambridge: Cambridge University Press.

Rogers, J, 1982, 'The world for sick proper', *ELT Journal* **36** (3): 144–51.

Rostow, WW, 1960, *The stages of economic growth: a non-communist manifesto*, Cambridge: Cambridge University Press.

Rust, VD, 1991, 'Postmodernism and its comparative education implications', *Comparative Education Review* **25** (4): 610–26.

Said, E, 1978, *Orientalism*, New York: Random House.

Said, E, 1983, *The world, the text and the critic*, Cambridge, Mass: Harvard University Press.

Said, E, 1990, 'Figures, configurations, transfigurations', *Race and Class* **32** (1): 1–16.

Sampson, GP, 1984, 'Exporting language teaching methods from Canada to China', *TESL Canada Journal* **1** (1): 19–31.

Savage, VR, 1984, *Western impressions of nature and landscape in Southeast Asia*, Singapore: Singapore University Press.

Schenke, A, 1991a, 'Speaking the autobiographical "I" in poststructuralist practice: a pedagogy of voice and memory work', unpublished master's thesis, University of Toronto/OISE, Toronto.

Schenke, A, 1991b, 'The "will to reciprocity" and the work of memory: fictioning speaking out of silence in ESL and feminist pedagogy', *Resources for Feminist Research* **20** (3/4): 47–55.

Schiller, HI, 1985, 'Strengths and weaknesses of the new international information empire' in Lee, P (ed.), *Communication for all: new world information and communication order*, Maryknoll, NY: Orbis, pp. 17–32.

Schramm, W, 1964, *Mass media and national development*, Stanford, CA: Stanford University Press.

Schultz, TW, 1980, Nobel lecture, 'The economics of being poor', *American Economic Review* **8** (4): 639–52.

Searle, C, 1983, 'A common language', *Race and Class* **25** (2): 65–74.

Searle, C, 1990, 'Race before wicket: cricket, Empire and the White Rose', *Race and Class* **31** (3): 31–48.

Searle, C, 1993, 'Cricket and the mirror of racism', *Race and Class* **34** (3): 45–54.

Selvan, TS, 1990, *Singapore: the ultimate island (Lee Kuan Yew's untold story)*, Clifton Hill, Victoria, Aus: Freeway Books.

Selvaratnam, V, 1986, 'Dependency, change and continuity in a western university model: the Malaysian case', *Southeast Asian Journal of Social Science* **14** (2): 29–51.

Ser Peng Quee, Larry, 1987, *Sociocultural factors and attitudes of Chinese Singaporeans towards English and Mandarin*, unpublished master's thesis, National University of Singapore, Singapore.

Shafi, Mohammad, 1983, 'Teaching of English as a foreign language: the Islamic approach', *Muslim Education Quarterly* **1** (1): 33–41.

Shaharuddin Maaruf, 1988, *Malay ideas on development: from feudal lord to capitalist*, Singapore: Times Books International.

Shapiro, MJ, 1989, 'A political approach to language purism' in Jernudd, BH, Shapiro, MJ (eds), *The politics of language purism*, Berlin: Mouton de Gruyter.

Shaw, GB, 1950, 'The problem of a common language', *Atlantic Monthly* **186** (October: 4): 61–2.

Shaw, GB, 1983, Preface to *Pygmalion*, Harmondsworth: Penguin.

Shuy, RW, 1974, 'The medical interview: problem in communication', *Primary Care* **3**: 365–86.

Sibayan, BP, 1990, 'Insights from language planning based on the Philippine experience' in Bickley, V (ed.), *Language use, language teaching and the curriculum*, Hong Kong: Institute of Language in Education, pp. 54–72.

Siddiqui, Haroon, 1992, 'The new Silk Road to Central Asia', *The Toronto Star*, 24 April, p. A25.

Silva, ET, Slaughter, SA, 1984, *Serving power: the making of the academic social science expert*, Westport, CT: Greenwood Press.

Simon, R, 1987, 'Empowerment as a pedagogy of possibility', *Language Arts* **64**: 370–82.

Simon, RI, 1992, *Teaching against the grain: essays towards a pedagogy of possibility*, Boston: Bergin & Garvey.

Singapore Legislative Assembly, 1956, *Report of the All-Party Committee of the Singapore Legislative Assembly on Chinese Education*, Singapore: Government Printing Office.

Skutnabb-Kangas, T, Phillipson, R, 1989, *Wanted! Lingustic human rights, Rolig Papir 44*, Roskilde Universitetscenter.

Smith, A, 1980, *The geopolitics of information: how Western culture dominates the world*, New York: Oxford University Press.

Smith, DA, 1962, 'The Madras "Snowball": an attempt to retrain 27,000 teachers of English to beginners', *English Language Teaching* **17** (1): 3–9.

Smith, O, 1984, *The politics of language 1791–1819*, Oxford: Clarendon Press.

So, DWC, 1987, 'Searching for a bilingual exit' in Lord, R, Cheng, HNL (eds), *Language education in Hong Kong*, Hong Kong: Chinese University Press, pp. 249–68.

Soyinka, W, 1976, *Myth, literature and the African world*, Cambridge: Cambridge University Press.

Spivak, GC, 1987, *In other worlds: essays in cultural politics*, London: Methuen.

Steiner, G, 1975, *After Babel*, Oxford: Oxford University Press.

Steiner, G, 1984, *George Steiner: a reader*, Harmondsworth: Penguin.

Stevenson, RL, 1988, *Communication, development and the Third World*, New York and London: Longman.

Stewart, S, 1986, 'Shouts on the street: Bakhtin's anti-linguistics' in Morson, GS (ed.), *Bakhtin: essays and dialogues on his work*, Chicago: University of Chicago Press, pp. 41–57.

Straits Settlements, various years, *Straits Settlements Annual Departmental Reports*, Singapore: Government Printing Office. Contains annual education report.

Straits Settlements, 1870, *Report of the Select Committee of the Legislative Council to enquire into the state of education in the colony*, Singapore: Government Printing Office. Reprinted in Wong Hoy Kee and Gwee Yee Hean, 1980.

Strevens, P, 1980, *Teaching English as an international language: from practice to principle*, Oxford: Pergamon Press.

Sutherland, J, 1989, 'Nice words and bad language', *Times Literary Supplement* **4522**, 1–7 December, p. 1332.

Sweeney, G, 1977, 'Singapore 1945–57' in Mohamed Amin, Caldwell, M (eds), *Malaya: the making of a neo-colony*, Nottingham: Spokesman Books, pp. 199–215.

Swettenham, Frank, 1907/1955, *British Malaya*, London: Allen & Unwin.

Swettenhan, FA, 1896/1983, 'British rule in Malaya' in Kratoska, PH (ed.), *Honourable intentions: talks on the British Empire in South-East Asia delivered at the Royal Colonial Institute 1874–1928*, Singapore: Oxford University Press.

Tan Chee Beng, 1984, 'Acculturation, assimilation and integration: the case of the Chinese' in Husin Ali, S (ed.), *Ethnicity, class and development: Malaysia*, Kuala Lumpur: Persatuan Sains Sosial Malaysia, pp. 189–211.

Tan, Adrian, 1988, *The teenage textbook*, Singapore: Hotspot Books.

Tan, Adrian, 1989, *The teenage workbook*, Singapore: Hotspot Books.

Tatlow, A, 1992, *'Those savages – that's us': textual anthropology*, inaugural lecture from the chair of Comparative Literature, University of Hong Kong, 22 October 1992.

Tay, Mary WJ, 1979, 'The uses, users and features of English in Singapore' in Richards, JC (ed.), *RELC Occasional Papers No. 8: New varieties of English: issues and approaches*, Singapore: SEAMEO RELC, pp. 91–111.

Tay, Mary WJ, Gupta, A Fraser, 1983, 'Towards a description of standard Singapore English' in Noss, R (ed.), *RELC Anthology Series #11: Varieties of English in Southeast Asia*, Singapore: RELC.

Tay, S, 1991, *Stand Alone*, Singapore: Landmark Books.

Tham Seong Chee, 1981a, 'The politics of literary development in Malaysia' in Tham Seong Chee (ed.), *Essays on literature and society in Southeast Asia: political and sociological perspectives*, Singapore: Singapore University Press, pp. 216–52.

Tham Seong Chee, 1981b, 'Literary response and the social process: an analysis of the cultural and political beliefs among Malay writers' in Tham Seong Chee (ed.), *Essays on literature and society in Southeast Asia: political and sociological perspectives*, Singapore: Singapore University Press, pp. 253–86.

Tham, Claire, 1990, *Fascist rock stories of rebellion*, Singapore: Times Books International.

Thumboo, E (ed.), 1976, *The second tongue: an anthology of poetry from Malaysia and Singapore*, Singapore: Heinemann Educational Books.

Thumboo, E, 1979, *Ulysses by the Merlion*, Singapore: Heinemann Educational Books.

Thumboo, E, 1988, 'Literature and liberation: history, language, paradigms, lacunae' in Thumboo, E (ed.), *Literature and liberation: five essays from Southeast Asia*, Manila: Solidaridad Publishing House, pp. 123–53.

Thumboo, E, 1990, 'Conversion of the tribes: societal antecedents and the growth of Singaporean poetry', *World Englishes* **9** (2): 155–73.

Ting, YR, 1987, 'Foreign language teaching in China: problems and perspectives', *Canadian and International Education* **16** (1): 48–61.

Titone, R, 1968, *Teaching foreign languages: an historical sketch*, Washington, DC: Georgetown University Press.

Toh Kin Woon, 1984, 'Education as a vehicle for reducing economic inequality' in Husin Ali, S (ed.), *Ethnicity, class and development: Malaysia*, Kuala Lumpur: Persatuan Sains Sosial Malaysia, pp. 224–64.

Tollefson, JW, 1986, 'Language planning and the radical left in the Philippines: the New People's Army and its antecedents', *Language Problems and Language Planning* **10** (2): 177–89.

Tollefson, JW, 1988, 'Covert policy in the United States refugee program in Southeast Asia', *Language Problems and Language Planning* **12** (1): 30–42.

Tollefson, J, 1989, *Alien winds: the re-education of America's Indochinese refugees*, New York: Praeger.

Tollefson, J, 1991, *Planning language, planning inequality: language policy in the community*, Harlow: Longman.

Tomlinson, B, 1986, 'Using poetry with mixed ability language classes', *ELT Journal* **40** (1): 34–41.

Tongue, RK, 1974, *The English of Singapore and Malaysia*, Singapore: Eastern Universities Press.

Traber, M, 1985, Foreword in Lee, P (ed.), *Communication for all: new world information and communication order*, Maryknoll, NY: Orbis Books, pp. ix–xiii.

Treichler, PA, Frankel, RM, Kramarae, C, Zoppi, K, Beckman, HB, 1984, 'Problems and *Prob*lems: power relationships in a medical encounter' in Kramarae, C, Schulz, M, O'Barr, WM (eds), *Language and power*, Beverley Hills: Sage Publications, pp. 62–88.

Trench, RC, 1881, *English past and present*, London: Macmillan.

Underwood, R, 1989, 'English and Chamorro on Guam', *World Englishes* **8** (1): 73–82.

Urwin, C, 1984, 'Power relations and the emergence of language' in Henriques, J, Holloway, W, Urwin, C, Venn, C, Walkerdine, V (eds), *Changing the subject: psychology, social regulation and subjectivity*, London: Methuen, pp. 264–322.

Viswanathan, Gauri, 1989, *Masks of conquest: literary study and British rule in India*, New York: Columbia University Press.

Vološinov, VN, 1973, *Marxism and the philosophy of language*, Cambridge, Mass: Harvard University Press. Originally published in 1929.

Walker, RBJ, 1984, 'World politics and Western reason: universalism, pluralism, hegemony' in Walker, RBJ (ed.), *Culture, ideology and world order*, Boulder, Colorado: Westview Press.

Walkerdine, V, 1984, 'Developmental psychology and the child-centred pedagogy: the insertion of Piaget into early education' in Henriques, J, Holloway, W, Urwin, C, Venn, C, Walkerdine, V (eds), *Changing the subject: psychology, social regulation and subjectivity*, London: Methuen, pp. 153–202.

Wallerstein, I, 1990, 'Culture as the ideological battleground of the modern world-system' in Featherstone, M (ed.), *Global culture: nationalism, globalization and modernity*, London: Sage, pp. 31–55.

Walsh, C, 1991, *Pedagogy and the struggle for voice: issues of language, power and schooling for Puerto Ricans*, Toronto: OISE Press.

Watson, JKP, 1983, 'Cultural pluralism, nation-building and educational policies in Peninsular Malaysia' in Kennedy, C (ed.), *Language planning and language education*, London: George Allen & Unwin, pp. 132–50.

Weedon, C, 1987, *Feminist practice and poststructuralist theory*, Oxford: Basil Blackwell.

Weiler, K, 1988, *Women teaching for change: gender, class and power*, South Hadley, MA: Bergin & Garvey.

Weiler, K, 1991, 'Freire and a feminist pedagogy of difference', *Harvard Educational Review* **61** (4): 449–74.

Welch, S, 1985, *Communities of resistance and solidarity: a feminist theology of liberation*, Maryknoll, NY: Orbis Books.

Welch, S, 1991, 'An ethic of solidarity and difference' in Giroux, H (ed.), *Postmodernism, feminism and cultural politics: redrawing educational boundaries*, New York: SUNY Press, pp. 83–99.

West, M, 1934, 'English as a world language', *American Speech* IX (3): 163–74.

White, AJS, 1965, *The British Council: the first 25 years 1935–1959*, London: British Council.

White, R, 1987, 'Managing innovation', *ELT Journal* **41** (3): 211–18.

White, R, Martin, M, Stimson, M, Hodge, R, 1991, *Management in English language teaching*, Cambridge: Cambridge University Press.

Widdowson, HG, 1968, 'The teaching of English through science' in Dakin, J, Tiffen, B, Widdowson, HG (eds), *Language in education: the problem in Commonwealth Africa and the Indo-Pakistan sub-continent*, London: Oxford University Press, pp. 115–75.

Widdowson, P (ed.), 1982, *Re-reading English*, London: Methuen.

Williams, R, 1976, *Keywords: a vocabulary of culture and society*, London: Fontana.

Wilson, HE, 1978, *Social engineering in Singapore: educational policies and social change 1819–1972*, Singapore: Singapore University Press.

Wodak-Engel, R, 1984, 'Determination of guilt: discourse in the courtroom' in Kramarae, C, Schulz, M, O'Barr, WM (eds), *Language and power*, Beverley Hills: Sage Publications, pp. 88–100.

Wong Hoy Kee, F, Ee Tiang Hong, 1971, *Education in Malaysia*, Kuala Lumpur: Heinemann Educational Books Asia.

Wong Hoy Kee, F, Gwee Yee Hean (eds), 1980, *Official reports on education: Straits Settlements and the Federated Malay States 1870–1939*, Singapore: Pan Pacific.

Wong, IFH, 1981, 'English in Malaysia' in Smith, LE (ed.), *English for cross-cultural communication*, London: Macmillan.

Worsley, P, 1985, *The three worlds: culture and world development*, London: Weidenfeld & Nicolson.

Wu, JY, 1983, '*Quchang buduan* – a Chinese view of foreign participation in teaching English in China', *Language Learning and Communication* **2**: 111–16.

Wuthnow, R, Hunter, J, Bergesen, A, Kurzweil, E, 1984, *Cultural analysis*, London: Routledge & Kegan Paul.

Yeo, R (ed.), 1978, *Singapore Short Stories*, Vols I and II Singapore: Heinemann Education Books.

Yeo, R, 1986, *The adventures of Holden Heng*, Singapore: Times Books International.

Yorio, C, 1986, 'Consumerism in second language teaching and learning', *Canadian Modern Language Review* **42** (3): 668–87.

Yu, VWS, Atkinson, PA, 1988, 'An investigation of the language difficulties experienced by Hong Kong secondary school students in English-medium schools: 1, The problems', *Journal of Multilingual and Multicultural Development* **9** (3): 267–84.

Zainudin Salleh, M, Zulkifly Osman, 1982, 'The economic structure' in Fisk, EK, Osman-Rani, H (eds), *The political economy of Malaysia*, Kuala Lumpur: Oxford University Press.

Zakaria Haji Ahmad, 1982, 'The political structure' in Fisk, EK, Osman-Rani, H (eds), *The political economy of Malaysia*, Kuala Lumpur: Oxford University Press, pp. 88–103.

Zakaria Haji Ahmad, 1987, Introduction, 'History, structure and process in Malaysian government and politics' in Zakaria Haji Ahmad (ed.), *Government and politics of Malaysia*, Singapore: Oxford University Press.

Zuengler, JE, 1982, 'Kenyan English', in Kachru, BJ (ed.), *The other tongue: English across cultures*, Urbana: University of Illinois Press, pp. 112–24.

Zuengler, J, 1985, 'English, Swahili or other languages? The relationship or educational development goals to language of instruction in Kenya and Tanzania' in Wolfson, N, Manes, J (eds), *Language of inequality*, Berlin: Mouton, pp. 241–54.

Zulkifli Ahmad, 1990, *Escape from tyranny in Malaysia*, Petaling Jaya: Penerbitan Dinamik.

Index

357